Russian Culture

MARGARET MEAD: Researching Western Contemporary Cultures

Published in association with The Institute for Intercultural Studies

General Editor: William Beeman, Brown University

RUSSIAN CULTURE

Berghahn Books

NEW YORK · OXFORD

The People of Great Russia: First published
in the Norton Library 1962
Soviet Attitudes Toward Authority: First published by
William Morrow & Company, Inc., New York, 1955

Published in 2001 by

Berghahn Books
www.berghahnbooks.com

Library of Congress Cataloging-in-Publication Data

Russian culture / Margaret Mead, Geoffrey Gorer, John Rickman.
  p. cm. -- (Margaret Mead--the study of contemporary western cultures ; v. 3)
  The people of Great Russia, by Geoffrey Gorer and John Rickman, was first published
in London, by Cresset Press, in 1949; Soviet attitudes toward authority, by Margaret
Mead, was first published in New York, by McGraw-Hill, in 1951.
  Contents: Russian camera obscura : ten sketches of Russian peasant life, 1916-1918 /
by John Rickman -- The people of Great Russia / by Geoffrey Gorer and John Rickman
-- Soviet attitudes toward authority / [Margaret Mead].
  ISBN 1-57181-230-X -- ISBN 1-57181-234-2 (alk. paper)
  1. National characteristics, Russian. 2. Soviet Union--Civilization. 3.
Russians--Psychology. 4. Communism--Soviet Union. 5. Authority--Psychological
aspects. 6. Soviet Union--Social conditions. 7. Peasantry--Russia--Social life and
customs. I. Rickman, John, 1891-1951. II. Gorer, Geoffrey, 1905- People of Great
Russia. III. Mead, Margaret, 1901-1978. Soviet attitudes toward authority. IV. Series.

DK268.3 .R87 2000
947--dc21   00-046786

British Library Cataloguing in Publication Data

A catalogue record for this book is available from the British Library.

Printed in the United States on acid-free paper.

CONTENTS

Soviet Attitudes Toward Authority

Margaret Mead

PENETRATING VIEWS OF RUSSIAN CULTURE
Introduction: Russian Culture in the 20th Century

*T*his edition of works of Margaret Mead, Geoffrey Gorer and John Rickman, unites under a single cover three quite different opuses. Different indeed, because the texts by Gorer, Rickman and Mead are written in quite variant tone and style. All of these classic texts are of undoubted historical interest, and they have strong relevance for our understanding of Russian culture and society today. It is a pleasure to have them made available for a new generation of readers. As a group of studies they have the additional value of presenting pictures of Russia during three different historical periods. In this way a careful reader can see not only common characteristics of Russian life through the years, but also the evolution of Russian cultural and social institutions. The works also build on each other. Rickman's work influenced Gorer and Gorer's research in turn influenced Mead. In this way, there is a satisfying completeness to the whole collection. They are compelling to read together, quite aside from any evaluation of their scientific or scholarly value.

In this essay, I hope to provide an assessment of the practical and scholarly theoretical value of these works today. Since half a century has elapsed since their first publication, posing such a question might seem to make little sense. Too much may seem to have changed since these works were written, both in our understanding of ethnosocial and ethnopsychological characteristics of the Russian people, and in the very circumstances and conditions of life in Russia in the post-Communist era.

However, this is true only at first glance. To be sure, these three works all begin with limited factual data, which some might characterize as insufficiently reliable. The analyses contain some errors, although the data discussed by the three authors may be read and re-read today with utmost interest. Paradoxically, however, the conclusions here strike a highly resonant chord; one cannot fail to agree with many of them. Indeed many retain the ring of truth even today.

Therefore any evaluation of these texts must be divided into two or rather three aspects: an assessment of the basic data, of the analysis, and of the conclusions. The three assessments will vary in intensity among the three works.

Rickman's Sketches of Russian Peasant Life

Sketches of Russian Peasant Life (1916-1918) by John Rickman is not a scholarly study (and was never meant to be one). For me, it is an excellent example of *belles lettres*, truly artistic sketches of something incredibly remote and alien to any modern Russian reader. The Russia described here is not merely different from the Russia of today: it is so alien as to represent another planet. This, combined with the author's wit and talent, makes it absorbing and fascinating to read. Rickman's sketches also show us the enormous development, both purely technological and psycho-cultural, seen in the Russian village in 80 years—just one life span! It also shows that, despite all the whining lamentations today about the catastrophic poverty and degradation of the Russian countryside, the current situation compared to the picture of 1916, is like the difference between heaven and earth.

The question nobody can answer is this: What would a Russian village be like, for better or worse, if there had been no October Revolution—no 70 years of the so-called socialism, with all its disasters and achievements. I note by comparison that the modern Mexican or Turkish village, though of course quite unlike its prototype of 1916, differs less than the Russian peasant village today differs from the one described by Rickman. In any case, these sketches by themselves make an extremely rewarding reading.

Gorer's People of Great Russia

Geoffrey Gorer wrote his text only 30, not 80 years after Rickman. By his observation, the general pattern of living had not yet changed by that time. To some extent, this is true. I have not studied even superficially the stages of evolution of any Great Russian village. However, I have carried out interviews, together with a rather detailed questionnaire and, for more recent dates, done an observational study of more than 60 Armenian villages for the period 1910-1980. From this research, I conclude that the stages of evolution in Great Russia were more or less similar.

According to my findings, the most drastic changes in the Soviet countryside occurred in the 1950s and 1960s, when Nikita Khrushchev liberated Soviet peasants from their secondary collective-farm serfdom by issuing them domestic passports. This enabled them to leave their villages and look for jobs in cities. Khrushchev's action had a profound feedback effect on life in the countryside. However, the changes of this period were probably more in the sphere of material culture, i.e. domestic architecture and general patterns of living, while important psychological and behavioral changes came earlier, in the 1930s. Some of these changes, which were not emphasized by Gorer, were clearly negative, rising from collectivization (organization of collective farms), followed by the expulsion, exile and even extermination of hundreds of thousands of relatively well to do, industrious farmers. These dislocations were accompanied by ubiquitous shortages of food and even famine in certain regions. Nevertheless, other developments were positive, stemming from the broad-scale establishment of new institutions and offices for education and health service. Gorer does mention these facts (chapter 2, end of paragraph 2), but only in a few lines, and he obviously underestimates their significance.

On the other hand, Gorer overstates the case when he writes in Chapter 1 of his study, that most of the members of the former upper classes, the greater and lesser nobility and the merchants seem to have been either killed or exiled in 1917 and the years following. All classes, nobility and peasants, merchants and workers alike were more or less equally affected in the bloody toll of October revolution, civil war, and Stalinist purges of the 1930 s and 1940 s. But it certainly was not a total extermination.

In my own childhood in Tbilisi (Tiflis), in the 1930 s, nearly all of the friends and colleagues of my parents (doctors, teachers, low rank employees) were descendants either of the families of middle ranking gentry (like my Russian mother) or of relatively low ranking, moderately wealthy merchants (like my Armenian father). The choice at the time of the Revolution, either to be killed or to flee to Europe and America, pertained generally only to families of highest nobility or the richest merchants. In fact, there are many descendants of the families of nobility, and of middle-rank and petty gentry among my colleagues in Moscow today, though they did not publicize the fact prior to the breakup of the Soviet Union. Indeed, many still do not discuss their ancestry.

The people my family associated with were, as a group, never explicitly anti-Communist. Some of them were even Communist party members. Nevertheless, their behavioral patterns, and to some extent even their basic values, differed considerably from those of the peasants. Without a doubt, their social attitudes influenced considerably those peasant descendants who moved upward in the enormous upheaval of vertical mobility that characterized the Soviet society from 1920 to 1960. On a smaller scale, their influence continues even today.

Gorer emphasizes that many of the characteristics that he considers typical for peasants, do not apply to the members of the former upper castes (nor, it would seem, to many members of the intelligentsia), possibly because they were chiefly brought up by governesses and tutors belonging to different cultures and with different standards (Chapter 2, Paragraph 8). It is true that even in the nineteenth century a foreign tutor was a luxury that very few could afford. There were definitely none after 1917. However, other channels, Western literature foremost among them, provided a flow of different standards to the educated strata of society. Let us remember that, while Eugene Onegin was taught by monsieur L'Abbé, a wretched Frenchman, his female antipode, Tatiana Larina, had to be content with a Russian peasant Nyanya and a pile of French books. Still, her letter to Onegin was written in French. Indeed, French, German, and English books, in original or in translations, constituted no less than half of the total reading of the intelligentsia, not only prior to 1917, but also in the 1920s, 1930s and, to a lesser degree, later as well. For these reasons, any upward mobility was (and largely remains today) connected with a certain degree of inevitable and nearly automatic Westernization. Additionally, it is important to note that among all factions of the upper strata of Soviet society, the Communist Party functionaries and leaders were, as a rule, the least educated, and consequently, the least westernized, and the most peasant-like. This is clearly exemplified by such colorful figures as Nikita Khrushchev, Leonid Brezhnev, Konstantin Chernenko, and recently Alexander Lukashenko, Boris Yeltsin and others.

The hypothesis that the swaddling of infants affected Russian culture is central to Gorer's approach, but I will not discuss its validity. What is instrumental, after all, is not the swaddling itself, but the feeling of constraint caused by swaddling and the emotion of suppressed rage resulting from a temporary inability to get rid of this constraint. Constraint, not swaddling, is the key word, and constraint can be caused by many factors, not only by swaddling, and not only in infancy, but at any age. Suffice it to read the last lines of the last essay by Rickman: "... hearing of the fall of the Czar, nearly everyone rejoiced at the release from constraint."

The release and rejoicing turned out to be rather short-lived. A new constraint was to follow, that of Communist dictatorship, lasting until the very end of the 1980s, and ending with a new release in the demise of the Soviet Union in the 1990s. Now, in 2001, we witness constant and persistent attempts by President Putin and his KGB classmates to swaddle the Russian people once more, but nobody knows, how efficiently or for how long.

Therefore it seems plausible, that many of Gorer's assumptions and observations are quite correct, since the ultimate result of swaddling is constraint. There is no doubt that constraint is a feeling regularly experienced by practically every Russian, both in childhood and adulthood, and not only as the result of swaddling.

Gorer limits his discourse to ethnic Great Russians. There probably are considerable ethnopsychological differences, between Great Russians and Ukrainians, let alone Georgians, Armenians etc., supposedly caused, inter alia, by a different character and duration of serfdom in these nations. Physical constraint in infancy is probably greater in Georgia and Armenia. Babies in those regions are not only swaddled but also tightly tied to the bottom of a specific cradle (Georg. aquani, Arm. ororots). Although this is a custom that has been often and severely criticized by local medical experts, it still by and large remains in usage among rural populations in Georgia, Armenia and Azerbaijan. Nevertheless, the specific psychological features that are, according to Gorer, allegedly predetermined by swaddling constraint in infancy, seem to be less pronounced among Georgians and Armenians, than among Russians. Perhaps the compensatory mechanisms mitigating social and political constraint in those societies were better evolved and more efficient than in Russia proper.

I was rather surprised not to find in Gorer's text a clear discussion of the problem of shame and guilt. By the time his book was published, the notion of two cultural typologies, one of shame and one of guilt, had already been well developed in anthropology. By the way, it was exactly Margaret Mead who greatly contributed to the dichotomy of these cultural notions in the course of realization of the project on "Cooperation and Competition". Instead, Gorer talks of guilt as only one of the devices that human societies have developed for controlling their members (Chapter 2, Paragraph, 5). Among other similar devices, he lists fear, shame, and pride. While there are clear-cut cultures of shame and cultures of guilt, one never hears about a culture of pride. This is quite understandable, because this would be only an inverse definition of the culture of shame. Similarly, an inverse definition of the culture of guilt would be a culture of righteousness, a term into which Western cultures would fit only too well. As concerns a culture of fear, this might be a viable notion, especially fit for the Stalinist Russia of 1936-1953. In fact, it is an appropriate characterization for a society in crisis, often quite prolonged, and not in homeostasis. Gorer considers a very unusual aspect of Russian character, the superimposition of control through inducing external shame on a more archaic sense of diffuse guilt. I can hardly understand what Gorer means here, but his resulting statement rings true: Great Russians manifest considerable interest in large ethical problems, but are apparently little occupied with moral rules of conduct.

As I mentioned above, I myself was raised in two parallel cultures, Armenian and Russian. Armenian culture, like all those of the Caucasus, Near East and practically of all Asia, is a culture of shame par excellence. I always thought that Russian culture with all its giants of self-flagellation, like Tolstoy, Chekhov and Dostoyevsky, emphasized confession, which is just another form of the European culture of guilt. Gorer justifiably identifies this as the Russian pouring out of the soul. However, this practice is perhaps not carried to the incredible extremes seen in its modern Anglo-Saxon manifestation, exemplified by current American politically correct sentiments for racial, sexual and other minorities.

Nevertheless, in the last decade something has definitely changed, though I do not know what exactly: either the very psychology of Russians, or my perception of it. In any case, the famous harbinger of perestroika, Tengiz Abuladze's brilliant film *Repentance* was the first and the last attempt to atone for every possible transgression. It should be noted that this film was, after all, Georgian, not Russian, but Russians have been profoundly affected by this film, and cited it innumerable times, especially the phrase: no road is worth a penny, unless it leads to the Shrine. The obstacles on the road to the Shrine were numerous, depending on the speaker. Many agents were accused of erecting these obstacles, among them the IMF, CIA, NATO, the West in general, Jews in particular, Freemasons, democrats, intellectuals, oligarchs, and so on. However, none of the Russians ever said: and we are guilty, too. Everybody considered himself or herself to be immaculate, while the rest of the world was seen to be full of squalor.

This inability to recognize one's own guilt seems to be rather a new phenomenon in Russia and indicates a decisive shift towards a typical culture where shame predominates. This new culture stands somewhere in between the stubborn and arrogant denial of any guilt by Turks in the Armenian genocide early in the twentieth century, and Japan s shyly elusive unwillingness to talk about guilt in World War II atrocities.

One can only try to guess what may be the reason for this shift. One cause may be the loss by the Great Russian Big Brother exercising unquestioned authority over all younger brothers, in the other Soviet Republics. Alternatively, it may indicate the role played by the growing impact of non-Slav actors among leaders in the post-communist social scene: including artists and authors, businessmen and managers, philosophers and politicians. It may also reflect, apart from the above factors, the spontaneously growing occidentophobia, or anti-Westernism, among expanding circles of Russian and Byelorussia societies. This is in sharp contrast to the increasingly pro-Western orientations of the Ukraine, the republics of the Caucasus and the Baltic states. It may be something else, who knows! It is only obvious that this something began long before the beginning of the current massive and many-faceted humiliation of Russians by the West. It certainly began years before the NATO intervention in Kosovo, though this action added considerably to the recent process of Russia becoming increasingly eastern, and less and less western. However, Kosovo was only the final stroke in a long chain of all the possible and impossible things the West carried out in the 1990s, to maximally alienate Russia from itself. These actions had the result that slavophilic trends in Russia became more dominant over the Westernist trends in 2000 than at any other time in the twentieth century. They exceeded the excesses of the 1980s, or even the 1950s, following the communist authorities' launch of their massive propaganda campaign against cosmopolitanism in 1949.

Altogether Gorer lists eight basic negative emotions instrumental in the shaping of the Russian attitude to the world, though he admits the list to be far from exhaustive. These eight emotions are soviest (conscience), vina (guilt), grekh (sin), styd (shame), stradanie (suffering), skuka (boredom), toska (melancholy), and pozor (humiliation). Some of my translations of these terms differ from Gorer's, and I would argue with some of his explanations. However, truly valid translations and comments would require a highly elaborate lexicological exegesis for these semantic fields. Most of these words do not fully coincide in Russian and English. Nevertheless, the mere fact that the words are different does not mean that people in the different societies do not share the spectrum of emotions suggested by them.

In his introduction to the 1961 edition of his study, Gorer writes that the central ideas of his opus are contained in Chapter 5, Conclusions, and in the ten political maxims contained therein. He also admits that these maxims are not necessarily to be deduced from swaddling hypotheses or other documentation he utilized in the previous chapters; they could be derived from other sources.

Gorer writes in Chapter 5: the mass of the population is oppressed by diffuse feelings of guilt and hostility. Remember, that he wrote this in the 1940s and 1950s. Hostility certainly was present in Russia at that time. Some feeling of guilt was probably also present, mostly caused by perceptions of inadequately, or insufficiently performed duty. In the 50 years since that time the feeling of guilt seems to have completely evaporated, along with any remains of the notion of duty. Hostility, on the other hand, has increased tremendously. The rest is probably correct and remains more or less unchanged, so that, irrespective of primeval sources and the analysis of data, Gorer's basic conclusions deserve attention even today.

Concerning his Ten Commandments, that is, the ten political maxims, I find them highly valuable. Were I the president or prime minister of some truly great and honorable country, like Thomas More's Utopia, Hermann Hesse's Castalia, or Jonathan Swift's Brobdingnag, I certainly would use them as the main principles for dealing with Russia, both in the 1950s and today. Moreover, these maxims are so good indeed, that I probably would stick to them firmly in dealing with any great power in general, whether China or the United States of America.

Margaret Mead and *Soviet Attitudes Towards Authority*

Now let us consider the final opus published in this volume, *Soviet Attitudes Towards Authority* by Margaret Mead. I have profound respect for this matriarch of American cultural anthropology, and her accurate study. However, I also find it remarkable that at the time of its publication her study was paralleled by another important work, George Orwell's coded portrait of the Soviet Union, *1984*, which had already appeared in print. The novel *1984* suggests many of the same things that Mead's work does, but in a more condensed and artistic way. Anybody who has read *1984* could read Mead's work as a commentary and collection of factual sources for Orwell's novel.

In this capacity, Mead's book is exceptionally valuable. Indeed, some highly talented authors may succeed in rendering political events artistically, not only immediately after the facts, but sometimes long before the facts. So, for example, Lewis Carroll's *Hunting of the Snark*, though written much more than a century ago, can be read as a surprisingly precise and detailed description of Russian history from the ascension of Gorbachev until the abdication by Yeltsin. However, a key is required before we can equate the Bellman with Gorbachev, the Baker with Yeltsin, and the Barrister's dream with endless debates in the State Duma. Perhaps in considering Orwell and Mead together, my additional comments from the viewpoint of an inside observer of Soviet society will promote a better understanding of both.

My remarks below are certainly not meant to diminish in any way the validity and correctness of Mead's basic postulates. Derived from all available written sources, her analysis is completely reliable. However, they should be augmented by additional data from the immediate post-World War II period, which have not yet been adequately published, and which, unfortunately, may never be written. Hoover's Archives for Peace, War and Revolution and Mead and Benedict's research effort, Columbia University Research in Contemporary Cultures (RCC), made tremendous advances in gathering memories about the events of 1917-1921 and some later years. But no effort of a similar magnitude has been launched to collect memories of people who lived from 1930 to 1950.

To begin with, Mead's work seems, in retrospect, to be misnamed. To match the contents more closely, the book's title might well have been *The Attitudes of Soviet Authorities Towards the Masses*. Indeed, Mead had plenty of reliable materials to ascertain the attitudes of the Soviet leadership. For obvious reasons in the 1950s she could not know with equal precision how the masses responded to these attitudes.

Many Russians, coming for the first time to the USA for a more or less continuous duration of stay, are often quite shocked by the naïveté with which Americans seem to accept a semi-official mythology about their own national history (themes such as the Wisdom of the Founding Fathers, the Greatness of American Democracy, Equal Opportunity for All, the virtues of former presidents, and so on). Perhaps many Americans would not classify these notions as myth or propaganda at all, but most Russian observers of American life, based on their own experience think of them in this way. Americans may be far less naive than they appear to superficial outside observers. Still, the gap between these national mythologies and their seeming acceptance at face value was and is certainly narrower in America than it was in Russia in the 1930s through the 1950s.

Perhaps the number of True Believers of communist ideology was larger in the 1920s than in later years. However, after the Stalinist purges of the 1930s and 1940s the contrast between slogans and reality was too sharp to go unnoticed by the majority of the population. I am aware of two main categories of Red True Believers, i.e. ardent supporters and official propagators of the communist ideology. The first group consisted of young people in their late teens, mostly freshmen and sophomore university students, recruited into the leading strata of ubiquitous cells of the Komsomol (Young Communist s League). Although some stayed with the Communist Party into adult life, these young men and women often became the most determined dissidents, overt or covert, by the time they had to write their MA theses.

The second group comprised numerous petty instructors in district party committees and innumerable lecturers and teachers of Marxist-Leninist theory and the History of the Communist Party. Mostly from the poorest peasant families, certainly not well read, only modestly educated and sparingly gifted with brains by Mother Nature, these people stuck to the official dogma instinctively, since it was the only available means for them to make a decent living. The core of today's demonstrators seen on the First of May and Seventh of November, brandishing red flags and portraits of Stalin, draws chiefly from these two categories of people. The remainder of the population constituted a broad spectrum of political belief. This ranged from a pinkish-red group, who believed most of the slogans of official government propaganda, with just a few secret exceptions and reservations; to a lily-white group of those who rejected communism completely, but never said so in public.

As for the top party functionaries, officers of the police and secret services, almost all those who had any real ideology vanished in purges and trials of 1930s. By the end of World War II, in the mid-1940s, most people in the Soviet elite took to heart only a very limited ideology or perhaps none at all. They were ready to support any slogan pronounced by the supreme power, especially if complicity would increase their chances to move one step further toward the top levels of power. Margaret Mead correctly views this readiness to shift position when any prescribed belief can be easily replaced with another as being typical of Soviet Russia. However, this tendency predates the Soviet system, and may reflect cultural patterns that transcend those we see as specifically Russian.

Similar shifts could be easily observed when Paul succeeded Catherine the Great on the throne, Alexander succeeded Paul, and Nicholas succeeded Alexander, all in less than 30 years, between 1796 and 1825. By stark contrast, no repression or threat of execution could break the stoicism of Old Believers in the seventeenth and eighteenth centuries, or of SR (socialist-revolutionaries) in Czarist and Soviet prisons. In fact, extreme prowess in adapting to changing conditions and heroic stoicism in defending one's homeostasis are probably two sides of a single coin of Russian character. We see this today when about ninety percent of the politicians in the Party of Power, all bureaucrats, all successful managers of private businesses, are the same former important Communist Party functionaries, or Komsomol leaders, or ex-KGB officers. We find them today quite sincerely denouncing communist dogmas and advocating the market economy.

An important difference between the texts by Gorer and Mead is that Gorer speaks only of Great Russians, without reference to any other nationality of the former Russian Empire. Mead, on the other hand, writes about Soviet people in general. But did such an entity ever exist? What do a Byelorussia and a Tajik share in common? Or a Don Cossack and a Saha-Yakut?

The question is decidedly difficult, and must be considered dynamically over time. When Brezhnev announced the creation of a new historical community, the Soviet people, or when communist "ethnopolitologists" wrote about the formation in the Federal Republic of Germany and the German Democratic Republic of two distinct German nations, many dissident critics considered these notions to be laughable nonsense. But they cannot laugh too hard. It is sobering to realize that although it is only a decade ago that the Soviet Union ceased to exist, that Germany was divided—still, the split between Ossies and Wessies in Germany is evident, while Kazakhs, Tajiks, Chechens, and Abkhazians speak with nostalgia about good old Soviet times. Derogatory nicknames like Homo Sovieticus or the colloquial Sovok continue to exist, obviously reflecting some objective reality, a certain set of commonly shared features, even when these features are viewed only as negative ones.

At the other end of the spectrum we have the overwhelming majority of people in the titular Baltic nations (Letts, Lithuanians, Estonians), who never considered themselves as part of the Soviet community, believing themselves to be suffering from a temporary, albeit prolonged, Soviet occupation. At the same time, a handful of overtly or covertly dissident-minded metropolitan intelligentsia (including myself and a rather narrow circle of like-minded friends) discussed in our Moscow kitchens the scenarios and timings of the inevitable collapse of the USSR.

However the rank and file Soviet citizens in Kiev, Kazan, Baku, Novosibirsk and elsewhere perceived something very different. They did not dream of this collapse, and in no way anticipated it. To them, as to the majority of outside observers, it seemed that the USSR would continue to exist for an indefinite time.

This shared (though illusory) feeling of a common destiny produced some of the common features among Soviet people detailed by Mead. Another factor that led to a common shared pattern of attitudes was the universal understanding that any commercial private initiative was, if not completely impossible, then at least very risky. The safest and surest way to vertical social mobility, to an improve-

ment of one's material wealth and social status, was through education and, preferably, through a membership in the Communist Party.
These circumstances could not fail to create a certain set of shared values and orientations. Still, the differences also prevailed.

I never had an opportunity to observe from within any of the
Muslim societies of the Soviet Union, like Azeris, Tatars, or Uzbeks. As
far as the period from the 1930s to 1950s is concerned, I can speak
only of Russians, Georgians, and Armenians, all of whom belong to
very similar Orthodox Christian faiths. The differences between these
Christian ethnic communities seen as a group and those of the former
Soviet Muslim nations are probably more marked than among these
three communities compared with each other. However, even the differences among these three Orthodox communities were very significant. Referring to the above-mentioned red-white spectrum, I would
identify people in Georgia as mostly concentrated in the whitish,
non-Communist part of spectrum. Russians and especially Armenians
(who constituted the majority of the working class in Transcaucasia)
displayed more pinkish overtones, but not too noticeably. Georgians,
mostly peasants and intelligentsia recruited from the former gentry,
were probably ninety percent white, though an exceptional ability at
successful mimicry in support of the Communist Party line was
regarded more often with admiration, rather than contempt. A totally
red person in Georgia, that is, a sincerely devoted believer in the official communist ideology, was usually regarded by most people as a
fool. When in 1950, at the age of 18, I first went to Moscow to study
at Moscow University, I was definitely shocked by the fact that so
many rank and file Russians, including intelligentsia, seemed to be
rather red. Based on my youthful experience in the Caucasus, it was
surprising to see that they indeed felt some filial piety and sympathy
for Stalin, and that they were accepting a good deal of communist
propaganda at face value.

Accordingly, when at the Twentieth Party Congress Nikita Khrushchev in his famous secret speech (February 24-25, 1956) exposed
Stalin and the cult of his personality, many Russians felt disoriented
and embarrassed. The shift of loyalty demanded of them at that
moment was too enormous to execute easily. For people with a Trans-
caucasian background, Khrushchev's speech was by no means a revelation. But many Georgians reacted in a rather peculiar way. Consider
the peasants in Kardanakhi, the native village of my grandfather, and
in many other villages from whom I had learnt the truth about the
GULAGs already in the early 1940s. These people never referred to
Stalin in other terms than as the moustached one, or more explicitly,
that moustached beast (es ulvashiani mkhetsi) even in a circle of

trusted people. Now, they promptly displayed portraits of Stalin on the windshields of their tractors and lorries. In Tbilisi, spontaneous rallies of protest were held on the third anniversary of Stalin's death, and police and Russian troops killed scores of people in the ensuing riots. This was a surprising diametrical shift. However, while among Russians, it was a shift from one sort of conformity to another conformity, in Georgia the shift was from one non-conformist behavior to another kind of non-conformist behavior.

Thus, while attitudes of the authorities towards the masses were more or less the same throughout the USSR, the attitudes of masses towards authorities were rather different in different parts of the country. Even if one limits the scope of analysis to Great Russians only, significant differences among such groups as Don and Kuban Cossacks, Siberian Old Believers, St. Petersburg s working class, Pomor fishermen of Archangel, peasants of the black-soil belt of Central Russia, and other groups of the Great Russian population were still apparent.

Mead's Legacy for Russian Anthropology

It is necessary to mention, that the works of Margaret Mead in general had a profound effect on the development of Russian cultural anthropology. Her works on the anthropology of childhood were reviewed, publicized and highly evaluated by M. O. Kosven in the magazine *Sovetskaya Etnografia* in 1946-47. Since that time Russian scholars regularly consulted them. True, with the deterioration of Soviet-American political relations in late 1940s and early 1950s it became more or less *de rigueur* to charge American anthropology with the sins of cultural imperialism and racism. However, in the case of Mead this criticism was rather indirect. It was reduced mainly to a denunciation of the validity of the swaddling hypothesis and other hygienic habits learned in childhood in explaining the development of a "basic personality." Mead's approaches were even labeled "psycho-racist."

The gradual liberalization of ideological control over anthropological studies in the 1980s resulted in an ever-growing interest in Mead's heritage among Russian scholars, which was also evidenced by publishing in 1988 of selected works by Mead in a Russian translation. This book under a title *Kultura i mir detstva* (*The Culture and World of Childhood*) was published with a press run of 30.000 copies, and other publications followed.

Many of the concerns that I formulated above remained outside the scope of Rickman, Gorer and Mead's considerations. However, the value of these texts to an interested reader at the turn of the twenty-first century remains high. This is especially true considering the many upheavals of the present. In this time of transition, we tend to forget many details of our not too remote past, which have served as prerequisites for the present. It is likely that these texts are even more interesting and valuable for Russian and other non-Anglo-Saxon readers, than for British and American scholars. After all, as an old proverb goes, when Peter talks about Paul, we may not learn too much about Paul, but we certainly learn a lot about Peter.

However, to elaborate in more detail what these studies show about Americans or the British would require me to write much more than an introduction to these enlightening studies. Nevertheless, we should never forget that, according to the testimony of her friends, the main question that Mead carried from her original work in Samoa to the research that occupied the rest of her life was not "How we can understand others" but rather "How we can understand ourselves."

Given the paucity of material on Russian culture written by non-Soviet citizens, this collection of essential monographs is certainly welcome. We anticipate that in years to come, anthropologists and other social scientists from many parts of the world will come to know Russia and the peoples of the former Soviet Union in ways that were impossible in the past. It is my greatest hope that this exchange of understanding will be mutual. This is very much in the spirit of Margaret Mead who believed above all that exchange of ideas among cultures lead to progress for all of humanity.

SERGEI ARUTIUNOV,
Russian Academy of Sciences
Moscow, November 2000.

THE PEOPLE
OF
GREAT RUSSIA

A Psychological Study

by
Geoffrey Gorer
and
John Rickman

To the Living Memory
of
RUTH FULTON BENEDICT
1877-1948

INTRODUCTION

'The Russian nation is a new and wonderful phenomenon in the history of mankind. The character of the people differs to such a degree from that of the other Europeans that their neighbours find it impossible to diagnose them."

F. DOSTOIEVSKY

1

*T*his book represents a portion of a co-operative attempt to understand the people of Great Russia; to isolate and analyse the principal motives which can be discerned as informing and underlying their typical behaviour, whether this behaviour be that of large groups as described by historians and economists, or of fictional characters which have been described by Great Russian novelists, poets and playwrights and accepted by their compatriots as true or probable. Concurrently it is an attempt to explore the means by which these motives are elicited and maintained in the majority of the new members who are added to the society by birth, so that the society maintains its identity and consistency through time.

This last statement entails certain assumptions which are, in the strictest logic, unprovable but which seem at least to me highly probable. It assumes that the term 'society' implies more than a group of people inhabiting a more or less closely defined portion of the earth's surface and speaking one or more identified languages; it assumes that there are more than geographic and linguistic connections between the people who inhabited England (or Great Russia, or anywhere else) one or two centuries ago, and those who inhabit the same places today.

These connections (it is assumed) are maintained by the fact that all the members of a society share aspects of a culture, in the anthropological sense of the word: that is to say, shared patterns of learned behaviour by means of which their fundamental biological drives are transformed into social needs and gratified through the appropriate institutions, which also define the permitted and the forbidden.

'Natural' man is a figment of the philosopher's imagination. Never and nowhere has man passed infancy without the constraints and guidance of social rules. This is true even of the technically most primitive groups we know about, living on the margin of subsistence. To take a simple example, no society anywhere satisfies the hunger of its members according attention only to the individual physiological rhythms and the raw material available. All societies choose some foods and reject others (as unclean, disgusting, ritually impure, unfit for men, &c., &c.); the selected foods are (with slight exceptions) never eaten when found, but are brought to appropriate places, prepared in prescribed manner, and eaten at relatively fixed periods of the day, usually in groups who are socially formally related to one another. If by chance an individual were to eat food that his society defines as unclean or disgusting, it is likely to be followed by profound physiological disturbances, even though the neighbours across the frontier eat such food daily with impunity.

The question why any given society accepts or rejects any given food is almost always unanswerable; and it is usually unprofitable to ask such questions of origin. It can be easily observed that the people of Great Britain (or the United States) treat goat's milk as disgusting, whereas the people of Spain and Italy drink it regularly; that mussels are generally eaten on the east coast of the Atlantic and clams on the west, though both types of shell-fish occur on both coasts; that on one side of the English Channel only one type of wild fungus is normally eaten, whereas on the other more than a score are looked for and enjoyed; and so on, almost endlessly. Although historical reasons, religious beliefs or the like rationalizations may be adduced for given examples, there are far more which are passed over as self-evident. As far as I know, no European society has evolved social explanations why dogs are not eaten; in Asia, where some societies do eat dogs, those who do not have (many of them) laws or myths justifying and enjoining abstention from such available food.

What is absolutely certain is that such selections of diet and modifications of the physiological need are not biologically determined. Anybody who has had to look after a crawling or toddling child can bear witness that human infants are not born with instincts that enable them to distinguish the edible from the inedible, and reject the latter, much less distinguish between the approved and disapproved edible foods. The child has to learn which foods it may eat; to an extent which surprises many people, it also has to *learn* which foods to enjoy.

In England or the United States we are so accustomed to children preferring sweet foods, and being rewarded with puddings, ice-cream, and candies, that we tend to think of a childish preference for sweet things as 'natural'. This is, of course, not so; sugar has only been available in sufficient quantities in the Occident for such a taste to be generally developed in the last century or so; and even where sugar is plentiful, it does not follow that children prefer sweetened foods. Belgian mothers have told me that they have more difficulty in getting their children to eat the desserts than any other part of the meal; Greek mothers do not understand that children should be expected to like one part of a meal more than another. In French North Africa one can see toddlers happily chewing on raw red peppers which would bring tears to the eyes of an unaccustomed European adult. It is possible to note in any instance how and when dietetic preferences and avoidances are inculcated, and when they are so firmly established that children no longer question them but regard them as 'human nature', and would be disgusted by food other than that to which they have been habituated.[1]

Once these preferences have been established, the search for their gratification may have the most far reaching economic, political, and military consequences. The European conquest of much of Asia, with its concomitant wars and rivalries, had, as one of its chief motives, control of the spice trade; and spices were important and profitable because the European upper classes and the peoples of the Near East found unappetizing the monotonous diet which satisfied the greater number of the inhabitants of the temperate regions.

The social patterning of food preferences and avoidances does not of course deny the existence of individual preferences and avoidances within the range offered by a given society at a given time, nor even some individual shading between the accepted and rejected. A few English people learn to enjoy eating snails, and a few refuse to eat roast beef; but the English diet can be described and calculated with sufficient precision to guide the activities of large groups of people who may never have seen an Englishman eating, and who may have quite different preferences and avoidances themselves.

The transformation of physiological hunger into cultural appetite is a particularly concrete and easily verifiable illustration of the way in which all human physiological and emotional needs are patterned

1. See National Research Council Bulletins, 108 and 111, Washington, D.C.

and modified by culture. It is, of course, much easier to demonstrate how hunger is patterned, restricted, and gratified, than to demonstrate how love or hate is patterned, restricted, and gratified, for the latter can only be shown indirectly and by inference through the prolonged observation of many variables.

All societies wish for 'freedom from want'-hunger -and thirst-but each society has its idiosyncratic preferences as to the means by which its want should be alleviated; though it is true that some liberal but insular authoritarian people think they should be made to alleviate their want in the way which is 'best' for them-a quart of milk a day, for example. In the same way all societies wish for 'freedom from fear', that is to say, protection from internal and external dangers and oppressive interference; but in concrete instances this appears to have as many cultural variations as does the alleviation of want. Each society, and by this I mean the members of each society, seems to differ in what it considers the optimum of internal authority, and the demands it makes and the expectations it has from the institutions of political authority and the people who are in the positions of power. Each society too seems to interpret in an idiosyncratic way the behaviour of foreign countries and to ascribe different roles to them. Many international misunderstandings would appear to arise from the fact that each society tends to interpret the behaviour of its neighbours as though they were actuated by the same needs and motives as the interpreter would be if he acted in the same way; and this assumption would appear to be often unjustified. There seems to be no inherent reason why these political expectations and demands should not be studied and analysed in the same way as, say, economic demands.

2

Whenever a society is studied from the point of view of analysing the predominant motives of its members, it has been possible to demonstrate—or, perhaps more exactly, to suggest with great plausibility-the means by which the newborn infants are transformed into adult members of their society, with-in the great majority of cases-the wishes, the beliefs, and the habits common to members of that society. Giving the word its fullest extension, the human infant is transformed into a member of a specific society by education; but education, as here used, means much more than formal instruction; it means all the habits which are inculcated, whether consciously or not, and whether verbalized or not, from birth onwards.

Intricate and elaborate experiments with animals have confirmed the hypotheses advanced by Freud (among others) of the preponderating importance of early learning.[2] Learning probably never stops, but the increment of new learning, the rate of growth in the strength of new habits, steadily decreases with repetition. It is for this reason that the experiences of early life have such an (apparently) disproportionate effect on later development.

In the life of the individual the development of specific motives through appropriate education precedes the manifestation of these motives in adult behaviour; but this should not be interpreted to mean that, for the society as a whole, these techniques of education are the *cause* of the adult behaviour, far less to imply that the transformation of specific items of education would result in a quick or automatic transformation of adult behaviour. Individuals have a childhood, but society does not. It is possible to describe with a certain degree of accuracy the devices which a particular society employs to educate the young so that they can replace the adults; but this does not imply that there are not alternative devices to produce the same ends. We still know very little of the effects of consciously imposed social control.

In description it is almost inevitable that only one aspect of this education can be discussed at a time, but this is purely a device of exposition. It should never be forgotten that the different experiences described in sequence are often undergone simultaneously, or nearly so, by the individual; and as a consequence it is not the individual items, but the pattern and sequence of these items, which constitute the idiosyncratic education which characterizes a given society. As far as we know, there are no items of behaviour or experience which are unique to one society; as far as we know, the pattern and sequence of items, in their entirety, are all unique to specific societies.

3

This book is not founded on my own experience and observation. I made two short Intourist visits to the U.S.S.R. in 1932 and 1936; but these are not good auspices for detailed research, even if--as was not the case—I had been scientifically equipped to take advantage of what I was able to see. My Russian was--and remains rudimentary, enough to puzzle through a simple text with the aid of a dictionary.

2. In technical mathematical language, learning tends to follow a 'growth curve'.

I have attempted to interpret and analyse the experience and observation of others.

In 1947 the late Professor Ruth Benedict, of Columbia University, organized the Columbia University Research Project on Contemporary Cultures, and invited me to participate in it. The project was organized to use immigrants, refugees, and those temporarily resident in the U.S.A., as informants on countries that were not immediately accessible to field work, with France as a control. The work of the project has since been described and illustrated in *The Study of Culture at a Distance*, edited by Margaret Mead and Rhoda Métraux (Berghahn Books, 2000), which should be consulted for fuller details. I was invited to be the convener of the Russian group.

I was lucky in having a number of able collaborators in this work.[3] Nearly all of them had considerable training and knowledge in anthropology, psychology, and the other social sciences; many of them had long experience with Russia, and some of them had been born and reared in that country. We would meet at regular intervals to discuss the new material we had collected and to outline and clarify hypotheses deriving from this material, and to determine where confirmatory evidence might be found.

When I left England I had no clearly formulated ideas nor any knowledge of nor material on the Russians, save the recollections of my two short trips, vague memories of many Russian books and plays, and such knowledge of recent Russian history as is common to most well-informed Englishmen of my generation.[4] So as to avoid arriving completely empty-handed, as well as empty-minded, I had the (I still think) brilliant idea of asking my friend John Rickman if I might take with me copies of the articles which he had contributed in 1938 to the *Lancet,* under the pseudonym of 'Vratch", concerning his experiences as a country doctor with the Friends' Relief in South Russia between 1916 and 1918.

Since these articles, together with other material never printed before, constitute the first part of this book, it would be unsuitable for me to expatiate here on their many qualities. It may be of interest,

---

3.   They included Dr. Sula Benet, Dr. Margaret Mead, Dr. B. Schaffner, Dr. I. Telberg, Miss R. Zoglin, Dr. N. Leites, and Dr. M. Wolfenstein. Mrs. N. Hoyt, Mr. and Mrs. N. Calas, Miss M. Markovitz, and Mrs. S. Viton also gave help.

4.   I did leave with one prejudice, which it may be interesting to record. I disagreed strongly with those people who claimed that the Russians were not Europeans; I thought they were echoing Dr. Goebbels's propaganda line.

5.   For those who are interested in the techniques of research, I have attempted to outline in Appendix I the means by which some of the major hypotheses in this study were arrived at.

however, to describe the way in which these were used as a basis for discussion and a starting-point for research.[5]

The incident called here 'The Apology'—the story of the drunken peasant who tried to assault Dr. Rickman, and subsequently brought a formal apology witnessed by the village elders--was typed out and handed to the members of the group without any indication of its origin.

The first reaction of the Russian members of the group was that they felt there was something 'wrong' about the story. It took some discussion to elicit precisions as to what was 'wrong'; it wasn't the behaviour of the peasants, perhaps it was the doctor not acting according to his status, not acting as a superior and learned man should act when confronted with his inferiors. I then explained that the doctor was a foreigner, an Englishman; and with this explanation the incident became, for the Russian members, completely under-standable. One of the Russians said: 'I ought to have known that it was a foreigner; no Russian would kick a man who was standing up.'[6] It then developed that it was felt to be completely un-Russian to kick a standing man: you can knock a man over with your fist and then, if you are still angry, kick him when he is lying on the ground; but to kick a standing man is, for Russians, unthinkable. Subsequent interviewing showed that this feeling is very generally held; I could neither elicit explanations for it, nor was I able to fit it into any con-structs I subsequently made. Consequently this note joins a number of other observations of behaviour and attitudes which seem to be specifically Russian but which find no place in a study as short and concentrated as this.

With this difficulty out of the way, we then discussed the specif-ically Russian behaviour described: the assumption by the elders of moral responsibility (? guilt) for the action of one of their co-villagers in which they had not participated in any way and of which they were not aware till after the occurrence; the insistence on the sincer-ity of the drunkard's repentance, and the manner of evoking and test-ing it; the formality of the apology, and how the doctor responded to it, and how a Russian would probably have responded. Discussion quickly developed a first list of unpleasant emotional states recog-nized by Russians and identified by different words, and an outline of the type of behaviour which would free one of the unpleasant feel-

6. In the text, the drunkard was not kicked, but pushed into a snow-drift by a push from the narrator's foot in his belly. This misinterpretation is, however, indicative in itself, and Great Russians do not seem to make much distinction between a kick and a push with the foot or leg.

ings. This preliminary list gave a series of points to be explored in future interviews.

One of the Russians described the behaviour of the peasant as 'un-guilting' himself, a concept which could only very roughly be translated into conventional English. It was felt that this behaviour could be considered 'typically' Russian, and it was decided that it would be useful to collect and analyse other examples of 'unguilting'. One member of the group undertook to analyse and excerpt the major novels of Dostoievsky and other Russian writers to discover other examples (there are, of course, a great many); another undertook to reanalyse the accounts of the purge trials Of 1936 and after from the same point of view. Another relevant point to be investigated was the attitude of the Greek Orthodox Church towards guilt, confession and absolution; informants were to be interviewed on the subject, an attempt was to be made to interview one or more Orthodox priests, books on ritual were to be consulted. Another member of the group recalled a tale by Leskov which gave a very vivid description of the 'un-guilting' of a merchant, and undertook to translate it for us. The result of this series of investigations is subsumed later in this book.

It would of course, at least in theory, have been possible to undertake all these researches without the stimulus of 'Vratch's' experience; but it seems at any rate, to me-unlikely that we should have developed such a battery of relevant and co-ordinated work under other circumstances.

4

This summary account of one session of our group indicates the types of evidence from which the conclusions are drawn. They can be divided into interviews on the one hand, and documentary evidence on the other. There were no groups or colonies of Great Russians in the United States suitable for participant observation. The groups described as Russians in the census turned out to be chiefly Carpatho-Ukrainians (apart from the Jews of Russian origin, who were studied by another group in the project).

I did a considerable amount of the interviewing myself; but I was limited in my informants to the extent that I could only interview Russians who spoke English, French or German adequately. Interviews with interpreters were not successful. With a single exception, all my Russian informants were born members of the Orthodox Church and had lived at least till their adolescence in Great Russia. Many of my informants had reached adolescence before 1917, and had therefore grown up under the Imperial regime; the younger informants who had grown up under the Soviets were, however, of exceptional calibre.

Besides Russians, I interviewed a considerable number of non-Russians who had had good opportunities of observing Russian behaviour in recent years. These informants included journalists, government officials and their wives, businessmen, UNRAA officials, people who had lived in Eastern Germany during the Russian conquest and occupation, UNO officials, people who had studied Russian prisoners of war (forcibly enrolled in the German army or Todt organization), and the like. It was possible to have certain questions asked of a number of Russian 'displaced persons'. I regret that discretion makes it impossible to identify any of my informants by name, and to thank them publicly for their great assistance. In all, I have had access to between 300 and 400 interviews. About ten per cent of these were with technically qualified informants, who could give precise knowledge on some aspects of the lives of very many Russians. Many of these latter were interviewed several times. I have also had the benefit of John Rickman's detailed knowledge.

With two exceptions, the use of documentary evidence was not systematic; when subjects arose from the analysis of interviews and discussion on which further evidence was considered desirable, recourse was had to the excerpting and analysis of what seemed the most suitable books. Books on certain subjects which previous anthropological experience suggested would be illuminating, such as the organization of the village commune (mir) and folk-tales, were read with care. The two subjects on which the use of documentary material was systematic were the number and composition of the intelligentsia, and current and recent Soviet practices in child-rearing and education. Mrs. N. Hoyt undertook a very thorough study of the history of the intelligentsia, using all the available sources, ranging from the Russian census to memoirs, to assemble the available data about this most influential segment of Russian society;[7] and Dr. Margaret Mead supervised the analysis of all the recent and available brochures and textbooks on childrearing and pedagogy, including the analysis of several hundred photographs of children in creches and state nurseries, courteously made available by the Soviet Photo Service in New York.

Because of the unsystematic use of documentary evidence I am not including a list of the books consulted from which no direct quotation is made.

This study is confined exclusively to the people of Great Russia, inhabiting that area of Russia corresponding to the Soviet Great Russian Republic and having Russian as their mother-tongue. At the time

---

7.　This material is not used to any extent in the present study.

of the last Soviet census they represented about half the population of the U.S.S.R. In modern states the cultural and political boundaries frequently do not coincide; the multi-national character of the U.S.S.R. recognizes this fact explicitly.

Although on occasion to avoid clumsiness I have used the word 'Russian' without the prefix 'Great', no statement hereafter should be taken as applying to any group other than the Great Russians. I have not made myself--nor, as far as I know, has anyone else--studies comparable to this one on the peoples neighbouring the Great Russians. It may, however, be of interest to state my present (very tentative) hypotheses about the relation of these neighbouring societies to the Great Russians, founded on spot interviewing and reading. For the peoples to the north-west and south-west, the White Russians and Ukrainians, it appears that there is no dramatic change, no 'cultural frontier', as it were, but a gradual modification of customs and attitudes which in turn merge into those of the Baltic states and Poland respectively. In contrast with this, there seems to be a sharply delimited 'cultural frontier' to the south and south-east, the Cossacks and the various peoples of the Caucasus, a contrast marked by differences of language, of social organization, and in some cases of religion.

This study is concerned exclusively with the Great Russians, and only with a single aspect of that very complex subject, their psychology, the shared motives and views of the world which appear to be predominant among them, and which cannot be reduced to the simple biological needs for food, shelter, warmth, and so on. The fact that I do not discuss, except incidentally, such subjects a-, their history, their economics, their contemporary social and political organization and the like should not be interpreted to mean that I do not consider these subjects to be of the greatest importance for a complete picture. I do not discuss them because I do not feel myself competent to discuss them; I lack the knowledge and special training which would enable me to contribute constructively to the discussion of these aspects of human society; I cannot do more than accept the statements of recognized experts, and repeat them when they are essential to my argument. It is my hope that studies of national character, such as the one which follows, may illuminate some of the problems developed by history, economics, and political science, and suggest new subjects of research and different techniques of gathering and interpreting their data to the practitioners of these sciences and arts.

5

I have made this study with the greatest objectivity of which I am capable, but it is almost impossible to-day for a person to be without some personal bias concerning Soviet Russia. After some hesitation-for it exposes me as having followed fairly closely the intellectual trends then fashionable--I have decided that it is fair to my readers to outline in summary detail the vagaries of my biases on this subject.

I do not think I had any very definite attitudes towards Russia before my first visit there in 1932. 1 returned from this visit enthusiastic for the country and the regime Nobody I think can come into personal contact with the ordinary unofficial Russians without being deeply attracted by their warmth, their sincerity, their apparent lack of anxiety, and their enthusiasm. This was the period of mass unemployment, confusion, and despair in England and Germany (which was on our way to the U.S.S.R.); despite the evidence of very great poverty nearly everywhere in the U.S.S.R., the general enthusiasm and confidence in the future were almost intoxicating. At that period no bars were placed on the contact between foreigners and Russians, or at least, none that one could notice; provided some sort of common language could be found, Russian friendliness and hospitality were given free rein.

Between this visit and my return in 1936 my enthusiasm and partisanship increased. The spirited defence of Dimitrov at the Reichstag fire trial, the firm Soviet opposition to fascism and national-socialism as compared with our half-hearted flirtations with these monstrous tyrannies, Litvinov's unequivocal behaviour at the League of Nations contrasted sharply with the brutality and misery of the means test and hunger marches at home, and our dishonourable foreign policy. In a book which I wrote in 1935 (a good part of which was occupied with making fun of our local communists) I described myself as a 'pink' and 'a fellow-traveller'. We were political innocents in those days, and such terms were then little more than expressions of sympathy.

The material improvement in Leningrad and Moscow between 1932 and 1936 was striking; but although our visit was before the big purge trials and the subsequent xenophobia, the atmosphere seemed to me much less exhilarating. The contrasts between rich and poor, between over-privileged and under-privileged, were far more marked than they had been earlier; communist party members had been released from their earlier quasi-Franciscan vows of poverty; the food provided in the different-class canteens and restaurants varied as much in quantity and quality as in any parallel capitalist organizations.

My enthusiasm rose again with the positive Russian action in the Spanish civil war, as contrasted with our own equivocation; but it was severely deflated by George Orwell's account of his experiences in Catalonia, and by the reading of Andre Gide's *Retour de l'* U.R.S.S. and Franz Borkenau's *Third International*. I subsided into a non-political emotional indifference, from which I was shocked by the Molotov-Ribbentrop agreement. While not more 'immoral' than the Munich agreement, it destroyed completely the Soviet claims to ethical superiority.

Although most thankful for the valiant fighting qualities of the Russian army, I did not wholly share the general enthusiasm for our gallant ally, for my war-work forced my attention on their very dubious behaviour, first in Iran and subsequently in South-East Europe. By the end of the war, I considered that communism was a tyranny nearly as evil as national-socialism; I made in my own mind an explicit distinction between communists and Russians.

The final change, to date, in my bias concerning the Soviet Union occurred during the investigations on which this study is based. It seemed to me that what I had formerly described as communist could more properly be described as Russian; the continuities between Czarist and Soviet Russia appeared most striking; the contrasts, where they existed, between pre- and postrevolutionary Russia seemed like the contrasts between mirror images, or algebraical statements in which only the sign has been altered. I re-read some of Lenin as a document on Russian character; a re-reading of earlier visitors to Muscovy, especially perhaps the Marquis de Custine, seemed to confirm this belief.

This then is my bias to-day. I consider that Russia, or rather the Russian government, is an expanding proselytizing force with a system of values and methods of imposing them which shock and revolt me, and which stand in opposition to the values and methods which we honour in theory, however much we may betray them in practice. As such, Russia and its government are a potential danger to our values and our security; but this potential danger will only become actual if our weakness, our inconsistency or our mismanagement of our own affairs make us appear an inevitable prey. I think war is more likely to come through mistakes and misunderstandings than through evil intent on either side. In an attempt to lessen the occasions for unnecessary misunderstandings and misinterpretations, I am publishing this preliminary study of Russian psychology, though I am well aware of its many deficiencies and tentative character. The field is a new one; and 1 hope that this first foray will be followed by stronger forces, that this sketch-map will be amended and completed by an army of cartographers. It is an attempt to remove the sign 'terra incognita' from an important area of our political maps.

GEOFFREY GORER

Somerset,
January 1949

INTRODUCTION—1961

*T*his book was the forerunner of a series of studies of the people of Soviet Russia employing anthropological and psychological concepts (rather than political, milltary, or economic data as a technique for increasing our understanding of the implicit values and assumptions which underlie the overt behaviour of the peoples of the U.S.S.R. and their leaders. Among the books produced by my colleagues in the Russian group of Columbia University's Research in Contemporary Cultures and its successor, mention must be made of Margaret Mead's *Soviet Attitudes toward Authority* (McGraw-Hill, 1951) Nathan Leites' *The Operational Code of the Politburo* (McGraw-Hill, 1951; Nathan Leites' and Elsa Bernaut's *Ritual of Liquidation* (Free Press, 1954); H. S. Dinerstein's *Communism and the Russian Peasant* (Free Press, 1955); L. Haim son's *The Russian Marxist and the Origin of Bolshevism* (Harvard University Press, 1955); the relevant sections of *The Study of Culture at a Distance*, edited by Margaret Mead and Rhoda Métraux (University of Chicago Press, 1953). This last item contains a very full bibliography of relevant studies published up to that date. Sections of *Childhood in Contemporary Cultures*, edited by Margaret Mead and Martha Wolfenstein (University of Chicago Press, 1955) deal specifically with contemporary child-training ideals in the U.S.S.R.

Nearly contemporary with the R.C.C. studies sponsored by Columbia University and the Rand studies sponsored by the American Museum of Natural History was the Harvard Project on the Soviet Social System, under the direction of the late Professor Clyde Kluckhohn. A great number of specialized publications have come out of this project; they are mostly subsumed in *How the Soviet System Works* by Bauer, Inkeles and Kluckhohn (Harvard University Press, 1956) ; and *The Soviet Citizen* by Alex Inkeles and others (Harvard University Press, 1959). It was under the auspices of the Harvard University Research Center that Dr. H. V. Dicks intensively interviewed a considerable number of Soviet defectors and refugees in Germany (reported in his *Observations on Contemporary Russian Behaviour*, Human Relations Vol. V, No. 2, 1952), arriving at very similar conclusions to those outlined in this book.

Besides these studies which were influenced by anthropological and psychological concepts, there is a continuous stream of books on the U.S.S.R. of every level of accuracy and scholarship from the most refined to the most journalistic, a stream so great that it is almost a full-time occupation to keep abreast of the literature. When I finished this book in 1949 1 expressed the wish that 'this first foray will be followed by stronger forces, that this sketch-map will be amended and completed by an army of cartographers.' On one level, at least, this wish has been granted; but, as in the tradition of fairy stories, the granting of the wish has not altogether produced the effects wished for. There are now available infinitely more facts and judgments about the people and institutions of the U.S.S.R than there were in 1948; but it is, to say the least, questionable whether the attitudes of informed people and political leaders in the Western world towards the U.S.S.R. are more rational than they were when this book was written. And the development of rational attitudes-knowledge instead of prejudice, understanding instead of fear, humanism instead of diabolism (if the proper implication of these terms be allowed)-has been the major object of nearly all the books which have been written about the peoples and institutions of the U.S.S.R. It was quite explicitly my aim, and that of my esteemed collaborator, the late John Rickman, in publishing this book.

2

It would be disingenuous of me not to acknowledge that this book attained a certain notoriety, far beyond its readership, because of its introduction of the swaddling hypotheses and because of the widespread imputation that I affirmed that swaddling was 'the cause' of the Great Russian character, with the further implication that changing this item of infant care would by itself modify the character of Great Russians. On the factual level this is simply untrue; it is explicitly rejected in several portions of the text (pp. 8, 128-9, 198). But the fact that this rumour has had so wide a diffusion is itself of interest; and it seems worth devoting a little space to considering the possible reasons for this.

In a brilliant paper in the *American Anthropologist* (Vol. 56, NO- 3, 1954), entitled 'The Swaddling Hypothesis: Its Reception,' Margaret Mead outlined with great clarity some of the reasons for the naive confusion between studies (such as this) which try to discover how a newborn infant becomes a fully participating member of his own culture and society and historical studies of the origins of a society and its component institutions. She gives the example of language. It is perfectly possible to study in great detail how an inf ant learns to speak its own language, be it French or Russian or Thai, without implying any theory about the origin of the language learned, or the origin of languages in general. A description of the process by which individuals learn is not a history of the origins of what- is learned. She also deals in some detail with the political motives which led some groups to attack and misrepresent these hypotheses with extraordinary persistence.

In the light of experience, however, I recognize that I am somewhat to blame for the confusion. Not that I think the facts are wrong: indeed, further information has confirmed nearly all the material about the treatment of infants[1] and young children which I adduced. Where I made a mistake was the order in which I presented the data: if I had presented the data on adults before the chapters on children, portraying adult characteristics before I dealt with the antecedent early learning, I think there might have been less cause, or at least less excuse, for confusion. The reader may, if be will, make the experiment of reading Chapters III and IV of the section, *The Psychology of Great Russians*, before he reads Chapters I and 11. With this simple transposition, at least one cause of confusion might have been avoided.

To my disappointment, there have not been, as far as I know, any consistent psychological or psychoanalytic studies of the hypotheses advanced in this book; we have no further information to confirm or deny the effects on future development of restriction of hand-mouth

---

1. One of the most striking of these confirmations was an account given by the daughter of the Indian Ambassador to the U.S.S.R. of her delivery in a Moscow hospital, and the way she was taught to treat her baby by the nurses and pediatricians there. From her account we learn-a fact not reported earlier -that very young babies cry to have the swaddling replaced. (The Birth of a Baby-Moscow Style, by Parvathi Thampi. New York Times Magazine, May 20, 1956, page 19 ff.)

exploration, of grasping, or of movements of the limbs, and so on, in the first months of life. The swaddling hypotheses are still hypotheses.

3

Although from the theoretical point of view the swaddling hypotheses are the most novel features, with implications for psychodynamics and social anthropology, this book was not written with the intention of giving them prominence. From my point of view, the nub of the book, the section by which it stands or falls, is Chapter V, *Conclusions*, and above all the ten political maxims on pp. 191-94- The rest of the book, as far as my contribution is concerned (I think John Rickman's *Russian Camera Obscura* has permanent literary value and is worthy of comparison with the sketches of Turgeniev), can and should be read as documenting the ways in which and the evidence through which I derived these maxims. But the maxims themselves are not dependent on their derivation. They can be tested against Soviet behaviour today, or at any time in the immediate past, as it has been reported in all the different media of communication; and I make bold to claim that, by such tests, the maxims stand up to the history of recent years quite adequately, and can still, I think, give guidance to international relations with the U.S.S.R. and help in achieving a tolerable and durable *modus vivendi* between the West and the Soviets which will avoid the unimaginable disaster of a thermonuclear war.

I think, however, that some of these maxims are too condensed; and it may be useful to elaborate one or two of them, in particular the implication of the term *strength* in maxims (v) and (x). These read:

> (v) The analogy of the dike describes the only type of political behaviour which will contain Russian expansion: firmness, strength, consistency. And the greatest of these is consistency.

> (x) The one situation which might evoke war (apart from the Western powers 'compressing' Russia) would be if the Western Powers manifested such weakness, or such alternations between strength and weakness, that the Russians would feel compelled to advance to such a degree that the Western powers would feel that the menace was intolerable.

'Strength' in these contexts is not a synonym for 'military might', any more than 'consistency' is a synonym for 'obstinacy'. In the contemporary world, an appropriate amount of armaments is a component of strength, but strength cannot be reduced to a counting of lethal hardware and manpower in the forces. It is fortunate for us that this is the case; for, under present conditions, an authoritarian government in peacetime can always divert a greater proportion of its resources and manpower to military ends than can a democracy; were strength so simply defined, it would be well-nigh impossible for us to match the Russians over years.

Nor is strength manifested by threats, by rocketrattling, or by minor provocative actions. Here again, were this the case, we would be outmatched. With their conviction of being in the Truth, of being Justified by history in all their acts, the Russians can much more easily act in defiance of articulate world opinion (as was shown by their series of nuclear tests in October and November, 1961) than the governments of the West can or will ever be able to do while they honour any of the principles of democracy. We cannot, and by our standards we certainly should not, try to rival the Soviets in actions which, while they might strike fear in opponents, certainly do frighten and distress large and articulate sections of our own populations and of much of the rest of the world. The Russians can tolerate hate and fear which they have knowingly provoked with far less distress than we are able to do. We-- the Americans perhaps even more than the British--are dependent for our self-respect on the feeling that the rest of the world respects and likes us; the Great Russians are sure that the rest of the world is I objectively' hostile ('At least today Russians do not admit of neutrality: he who is not completely for them is "objectively" hostile, however friendly his overt feelings and behaviours.' p. 161). Therefore they feel few qualms in affronting other peoples' hopes or fears. A 'policy of strength' is, luckily, not synonymous with rocket-rattling or 'brinkmanship'; were it so, our chances would be poor. I think it Is quite certain that with displays of 'brinkmanship' we frighten ourselves far more than we frighten the Russians; the individual Great Russian is likely to have far less free-floating anxiety than the individual Westerner (in the colloquial phrase, they have 'steadier nerves') and, as is pointed out in maxim (vi), they find the strategical retreat a highly acceptable manoeuvre. It is pointless to play 'chicken' unless both parties accept the same definitions of the ways in which courage or fear are shown. For the Great Russians a temporary retreat is not a humiliation.

Military power is only one of the implications of strength', according to my intention in the maxims quoted above. Consider the implications of 'strongminded', 'strong-willed', a 'strong bead', a 'strong faith', I strength of character', and similar phrases in common use; these, I think, indicate the type of strength we need if we are to live with (rather than die with) the Soviet Russians. Above all, we need the strength of our convictions; and we permanently diminish our strength if, for the sake of a momentary advantage, we act in a way which affronts our strong consciences.

The greatest apparent threat to our moral strength is that we shall be seduced by overt fear and hidden admiration of the Communist system into copying those features of their system which are alien to our strongest-held values: free-floating suspicion, imputing guilt by intention or association, attempting to impose a formalized ideology, fear of heterodoxy.

Our moral strength, our strength of purpose are as important to us in dealing with the Russians as is our military strength. Not more important: 'My strength is as the strength of ten, because my heart is pure' is, unfortunately, only metaphorically true. But if our heart is not pure, if we sacrifice our moral principles for the sake of expediency or try to engage in a contest of amoral Machiavellism with the Russians, then our strength will be correspondingly diminished. If we are not to annihilate one another, we can look forward to a lifetime of negociations; and in negociations, strength of purpose is of comparable importance to strength of arms.

Strength of purpose is not the same thing as obstinacy and standpatness. It is foolish to assume that the state of the world is perfect, that any change is a change for the worse; or that there is automatic virtue in opposing any proposal that the Soviets may make. To believe that a willingness to negociate is a sign of weakness, that in negociations we have everything to lose and nothing to gain, is a mark of despair; it is the opposite face of that panic of submission--'It's better to be red than dead'--which--when it is honest, and not merely a mask of communism-be trays an equal lack of confidence in the values to which we at least pay lip service, an equal lack of moral strength.

In any situation, other than a demand for unconditional surrender, there are some elements which are negociable without the betrayal of moral principle and others which are not. Once these discriminations have been made, their maintenance is a test of strength of purpose. Great Russian negociators are not likely to make the same discriminations, even as an intelligence exercise, and will quite certainly try to get the maximum advantage at every point. When they finally recognize the strength of purpose with which some positions are maintained, particularly if there is consistency with which the positions are held from one context to another and from one set of negociations to another, there is every reason to suppose that they will withdraw their more extreme demands and reach a perfectly tolerable modus vivendi. The election of U Thant to replace Mr. Hammarskjold as Secretary General of the United Nations in November 1961 after the very persistent Soviet attempt to have the Secretary General replaced by a troika, is a good, recent example of this process.

In our somewhat atomistic short-term view of historical events, we may interpret this outcome as a 'defeat' for the Russians, since they gave up their previous demands. I do not think that the Russians see the situation in this way. They had gone to the limits of their strength in pushing their demands as strongly as they could. When they came up against the moral strength of those people and countries who would not allow the position of the Secretary General to be compromised, they made one more strategic retreat.

4

It may be thought that the last few pages have passed the boundaries proper to a social anthropologist; but I would maintain that they only make explicit ideas latent in the maxims of Chapter V, and that these maxims are directly derived from the evidence presented in the previous chapters. It seems to me inevitable that the study of the national characters of contemporary societies should result in maxims or generalizations which have political implications. Indeed, did they not have this result there would be little reason for accepting the difficulties of studying large and heterogeneous societies rather than the smaller and less differentiated 'primitive' societies which are our traditional field of work.

If we accept the fact that all the peoples of the world are human, with the same physiology and the same psychological potentialities, whatever their present level of technological development, system of values, or political organization, and that all human beings are organized into societies with distinctive cultures, then all human beings and human societies can be studied, at least potentially, by the scientific techniques which have been developed to these ends. Of these scientific techniques, social anthropology and whole-person psychology (including depth psychology and the developing data of ethology) are the most appropriate. Psychology has shown that in the life of any individual the process of learning is cumulative, so that earlier learning influences later learning; social anthropology has shown that culture is continuous over more than one generation, that the people who die are replaced by new members who have learned, by both conscious and unconscious processes, the values and customs appropriate to their culture and their position in it, or, in other words, their individual variation of the national character. This national character is susceptible to scientific study.

Whether or no there is articulate knowledge of the national characters of the representatives involved in international negotiations at any level, this factor of national character must play a continuous and influential role. Even on the most superficial level of vocabulary, there is little likelihood that abstract terms such as 'freedom', 'democracy', 'free elections', 'self-determination', 'compromise', will have identical referents for representatives of different societies, even when they have similar political forms and use variants of the same language. When political forms, levels of technology, and language are markedly different, it is quite certain that the words, and the values concealed therein, have different referents; and, unless this is explicitly realized, any agreement is likely to be shortly followed by charges of bad faith in the fulfilment of the agreement reached. All parties to the agreement are likely to feel that the others have failed in their undertakings, while they themselves have acted most loyally.

Today I believe that the only major risk of major war lies in exacerbated mutual misunderstandings. Though both the U.S.S.R. and the U.S.A. have groups who consider the other society so abominable, so divorced from common humanity, that the proper course is to destroy it forthwith, I think there is little likelihood of either of these groups of fanatics-the 'anti-party' group in the U.S.S.R. or the ephemeral right-wing anti-communist groups in the U.S.A. momentarily typified by the John Birch society-achieving political power; though it is possible that the internal necessity to placate these groups may lead the existing governments to displays of 'toughness' which incidentally exacerbate the tensions of the international scene. But genuine misunderstandings seem to me the real risk. It is in the hope that, at least to some degree, this book may diminish causes for misunderstanding, that I present it again to the public.

Sunte House,   G.G.
Haywards Heath
November, 1961

RUSSIAN CAMERA OBSCURA

Ten Sketches of Russian Peasant Life (1916–1918)

BY JOHN RICKMAN

NOTE: *On my return from Russia, where I was a country doctor with the Friends' War Victims Relief Unit between 1916 and 1918, the Editor of The Atlantic Monthly asked me for some articles. The sketches here called 'Peasant Officers' and 'Police' (and slightly revised and abbreviated) appeared in 1919 in that magazine under other titles.*

In 1937 the Editor of The Lancet asked me for four articles to appear, under a pseudonym, in his column 'Grains and Scruples'. They were to be a bit medical, about Russia but only mildly political, and to have journalistic interest. I wrote about a dozen Moujiks which I named 'Russian Camera obscura', and from among these he chose the jour here entitled 'The apology', 'The Threat', 'Snow', and 'Moujiks want Glasses', all of which appeared in The Lancet in 1938 under the pseudonym 'Vratch', which is the Russian for Physician.

IRON

*T*he peasants were desperately poor and their standard of living was low. When the crops were bad they starved, when good they filled out again; but even a succession of good seasons did not raise them out of their sunken condition of endless struggle for the barest living. Four factors in about equal degree united to keep them down. Their religion told them that suffering was acceptable in God's sight, and their Church, which fattened on their offerings, made return by an education better in Old Church Slavonic than in modern Russian and arithmetic. Their Temporal Rulers, even more rapacious than their Spiritual, taxed the poor almost to starving-point while allowing the rich to go almost duty-free—a business error which the Church never makes. In addition the Czarist regime opposed initiative on the ground that it was conducive to revolution, so that an enterprising villager who went about picking up ideas, even though only on farming, was suspect.

A third factor was their ill health. Undernourishment and lack of drugs, ignorance of hygiene and the belief that illness was from God, kept them more inert than they should have been. At times they rose like giants to great feats of toil, but like sick people the world over, they had not the capacity for a sustained activity which at the same time called for initiative. They were not lazy, but their grasp of new ideas, a new technique, was slow and feeble; the external world did not seem to them to be theirs to master.

A fourth factor lay in the unwillingness of the villagers to allow competition among themselves; as members of a community they must all think alike and act alike. The sharing of almost every task encouraged a certain handiness at many crafts but discouraged the development of outstanding skill in any one. It was against the village spirit to compel respect for any achievement that all could not in fairly close degree emulate. Peasants in other parts of Russia had village industries, here there were none. Those who felt an itch to be doing more or better than their neighbours found their way to the towns, returning for the harvests, and going their ways when country duties were over.

*   *   *

Here follows a small piece of amateurish 'field work', as anthropologists might call it which though not strictly medical, nevertheless could not easily have been carried out except by a doctor (or a priest) since no other persons had the privilege, accorded only to 'one of us', to enter the houses without knocking, and whose presence did not create a class-consciousness or sense of being Visited.

I set out to make a survey of the consumption of iron, and I will give at once my estimate of it in the poorest village that I visited, viz. about five pounds per head per generation! When I added the ounces up and divided by the number surviving in the village during the previous thirty years as near as one could estimate, that was the astonishing result. With this small consumption that community kept even in its struggle with nature. Through constant wear, loss by rust and burning away by heat, renewals of this (to them) most precious metal are needed from time to time. But iron is hard and elastic, it gives under strain and does not often snap, breakages were not common and such was the care lavished on the metal that very little was lost through carelessness and the consumption was due almost wholly to wear. When I add that on a rougher estimate but on the same basis, rather more than six hundred pounds of wood was used it will be seen how near the raw earth these people lived.

Let us watch a small house being built, all the time estimating the amount of material that goes into its construction and the durability of the product.

A peasant's hut of the poorest sort, if made on the steppe where you can drive all day without finding a stone large enough or hard enough to crack a brazil nut, will be fashioned out of clay and mud, puddled together by the feet of the girls, who fasten their skirts to knee-height and stamp and churn the slime to the accompaniment of songs until it reaches the right consistency, and then tread in straw as a binder, till the mixture binds on their feet, and however lusty they may be they can hardly move in it. It is a terrific labour and the wenches develop thighs of iron in the work, but it is a matter of pride to endure it. A girl of about seventeen came with a septic foot and begged me to get it healed quickly or she could not stand in with the rest. I told her she must not work her foot while the bandages were on, so sepsis or no she took the bandages off, and, confound it, she was no worse for it 11 found out later that not only is it a matter of pride before those of her own age to endure a long day in the clay, but the mothers urge them to it as the work is said to improve their ardour in embrace and to strengthen them against the pains of childbed. I can well believe it.

The stiff clay and straw mixture is then laid out on a smoothed piece of level ground, patted to an even thickness and cut with the edge of a spade. The blocks are about nine inches thick by twelve by eighteen and the spade cuts are renewed during the first stage of drying.

As soon as the sun has taken off the first moisture from the upper surface, and the level ground (powdered with a carpet of fine earth or dust to the level of half an inch, much as a cook powders a pastry board) has absorbed some of the moisture from the underside, the blocks are raised with a spade and carried to a drying ground. They are here laid on their side and turned from time to time till they are hard and dry and crumble like biscuit if knocked or cut.

The ground for the house is cleared during this time and also puddled and left to dry out, care being taken to screen it from too much sun with wisps of straw. A trench is dug about six inches deep in the hardened soil and the sun-dried blocks laid in to a width of about two and a half feet. This is smeared with a stiffer mixture of clayey soil and the 'courses' run to a height of about two to three feet from the ground.

I was not able to note any special technique in the binding of the blocks. Those that fitted nicely together were mated, an irregularity of spade cut matching another hump or hollow in a neighbouring block as near as may be. There were no hollows in the walls except such as came from careless laying of the blocks, and in the majority of instances no framework of wood; the walls were too heavy to need stiffening, and strong enough to carry the thatch and inner roof.

Except at the space for the door frame, the threshold being about a foot above ground, this thick wall is carried round the entire rectangle of the house; on this level windows will rest, but above this level the walls will be only eighteen inches thick, flush on the inside with the extra thickness without acting as an additional defence against the splash of raindrops from the thatch, and the sogging of melting snow.

At an inside height of about eight or nine feet, there will be laid a plate on the top of the wall near its outer margin. This is usually a pine tree with a sector cut off so that it lies flat. On this are laid the ceiling joists, and, notched into it, the foot of the rafters. These are left in the round, irregular in shape and meeting at the top, usually without a ridge plate, being notched and pegged together. As the roof will be thatched there will be enough lathing, tied and pegged to the rafters, to give lateral rigidity. The inner roof (it is more than a ceiling) is in the better houses boarded across from wall to wall; in the poorest it is a wattle and daub lashed under and another larger one lashed over the joists. On the top, above the ceiling and under the thatch—before the thatch is put on—is spread about four inches of sun baked clay dust and earth. This acts as a non-conducting layer against heat and cold.

Now that we have got the walls up and the roof on let us see what tools have been used. A spade for the clay, an axe for felling the timber, a saw for cutting the planks for the ceiling if planked, an adze for smoothing out the plates and notching the rafters, and an auger for making the holes. The weight of wood is about one and a half tons. In this fourteen by eleven foot house a family can have a roof over them and live for generations at the cost of three sledge-hauls from the forest and so far not an ounce of iron.

Now for the stove. Its outside dimensions are six feet by four feet six and nearly five feet high. It is composed of two arches above one another, the upper one is the oven, the lower one is for ashes, pot hooks, fire-raker, and such-like apparatus. The bed of the oven, which is placed at a convenient height from the floor, is oval and is two feet six from back to front and two feet wide in the short diameter. The arched roof curves down at the back to the oven-bed, and at the front lips down a bit so that the fumes and heat of the fire do not go roaring up the chimney too fast. The flue does not go straight up to the roof but rises to the ceiling, turns horizontally, descends, and ascends again (or it may take another double bend) so that there is at least nine feet of flue to absorb the heat of the burning before the final flight through the chimney stack is made. The flue takes up rather over a foot in thickness and rests on another arch, so that anyone looking at the stove from in front would see the mouth of this small cavern at waist height flanked with the curving buttresses that support the flue, like the shallow porchway of a Norman church, with the narrower round-topped arch of the oven behind.

The height of the cavern from oven bed to domed roof is about fifteen inches, so the 'brickwork' at its thinnest at the top is a foot thick, and the same at the sides; but as the stove is almost a cube (with this tortoise-shaped hollow in the middle of it) the thrust from a weight on its level top is taken by the more massive 'brickwork' of the corners rather than that of the thinner sides. The weight on the top is of course Grandpapa. Here through the long days and longer nights he and Granny and perhaps a grandchild lie in warmth, covered by sheepskins, and reach down for food.

Of the under arch nothing much need be said, but the flue has a complication. In order that the heated bricks should not continue to draw up cool air, warm it, and waste it into the cold of winter, it is necessary to have a damper of some sort-a piece of sheet iron rather thicker than the side of a biscuit tin suffices.

When building this stove there are three places where iron is used. A strip a twelfth of an inch thick and an inch and a quarter wide bent to an arch, and plugged in at its feet to the bed of the oven, forms a margin to that lip of the cavern I spoke of which comes down and curbs the outrush of flames and heat from the fire within to the flue without. It serves a double function, it prevents the licking flames from burning away the sundried bricks quite so fast, and by its greater hardness and elasticity it takes better than would brick the knocks of pots carelessly inserted or withdrawn from the oven. This piece of iron needs occasional renewing, say once every twenty years. That small strip is the first essential piece of iron in the structure of the house, and with the exception of the damper and the thin oven door, it is the last.

To use wood as fuel could only be compared for extravagance to burning one's Hepplewhite furniture. The fuel is dried manure. The farmyard droppings of the year are spread in a flat-topped circular heap and a few bucketfuls of water poured in the middle. The village girls then press it with their feet as they did the clay till it forms a smooth firm paste. Much the same procedure is adopted as with the clay except that less straw is used as a binder. The blocks are not more than four inches thick and six by nine in the other dimensions. These when thoroughly sun-dried are stacked in heaps seven feet high, tapering towards the top as peat is stacked in Ireland. This manure fuel behaves much like peat except that it has less 'life' in it but is better than the camels' dung which the Arabs burn in the desert. It makes a gritty ash from which it is hard to get a clean lye; accordingly the home-made soap obtained from boiling grease with the ash water is rough like sandstone.

*   *   *

Now a few details, for it is not yet a very habitable house. That thickening of the wall outside is, on the street side, usually made thicker still so as to form a seat. The stove is placed in a corner with a foot clearance all round so that no precious heat will be conducted away. Its mouth is near the doorway, because, I was told, if it should fume carbon monoxide the poison would soon blow away, and in this position there are fewer draughts across the room. The windows are never opened in winter, a film of water on a casement freezes the window frame as tight as glue. In summer one of the two eighteen by eighteen inch windows is opened or removed.

The door is heavily padded on the inside; a sheepskin stuffed with extra wool is stretched over it. It is held down with battens fastened usually with flat-headed nails, sometimes with wooden pegs. With these nails we finish the metal work of the house: the door swings on a peg of wood, fitting snug by leather-lined door jambs; the window hinges are of leather—ah, I forgot, a dozen tin-tacks to hold them on for the one window—if made to open. In sum.; 3 sledge loads of wood, 1 1/2 tons; iron, 3 lb.; and a house that will last for three generations.

We will furnish the house: a wooden bed frame five feet six long and two feet six broad for both parents, a table thirty by forty-five inches, three benches fifteen inches wide (more generous than most) and five feet long on which the boys will sleep, a wider bench twenty inches wide and also five feet long for two of the girls, a chest three feet long and two wide at the head of the parents' bed and against the wall by the back of the stove. No one sleeps on this, partly because Gaffer steps on it when he gets down from the stove. If the family becomes more numerous further accommodation for huddled repose will be needed. A deep shelf may be slung at a height of two to three feet from the ceiling if this will bear the strain. This shelf is up to five feet from back to front and four or five feet wide. It is in the warm and fuggy zone of air at the top of the room, the worst-ventilated part of the chamber; well out of the way the younger children sleep here.

A certain degree of privacy is sometimes obtained by erecting a partition parallel with the parental bed; this reaches to the ceiling but as it only juts out from the wall the same length as the bed which is in full view of the three on the stove it can only be described as a partial privacy. I have seen a curtain from partition to wall enclosing the tiny bedroom in fewer than half a dozen such huts (and remember that I visited patients without knocking at all hours of the twenty-four; and when travelling burst in with equal lack of ceremony for a few hours' sleep on the floor if the night was too dark even for Russian horses to pick their way in safety). Such curtaining was not considered decent; neither are the windows covered. Among adults I came across no prying—the children it was thought did not count. A child who peeped got his face smacked, but wasn't told not to do it again. He was slapped not for his good but because the grown-up was annoyed. (To go on with this aspect of their sexual life, the women above puberty bathed in their shift, the men went naked but when out of the water covered the pudenda with a hand. In the vapour baths the men and women bathed at different times.)

Thus far the house itself is finished, but to prevent a heavy in-gust of air when the padded door is open there is always a large porch outside, built of those same blocks of clay and straw but with thinner walls. The thatched roof is carried on over it but there is no ceiling. It has a wattle door and no windows. Add for this therefore three more hundredweight of wood but no more iron. The bytes which are built round the small court or farmyard will of course need more wood (but no more iron) for their construction.

Now for the farm implements: the plough was made of wood with an iron tip to the share weighing less than two pounds, the coulter was usually made of wood, though occasionally edged with iron; the axles of the farm carts were of wood, sometimes with a thin metal strip an inch wide and five inches long laid on the top to take the weight; the wooden wheels were usually rimless and bumped at each revolution as the gap in the rim hit the ground; the harrows were wooden, and so of course were the runners of the sledges.

So if the farmstead is on the same scale as the house, for the structure of the entire farmstead and contents (including carts, sledges, ploughs and tools) we shall need: wood about six tons; iron about thirty-five pounds.

SNOW

One evening just after tea in the middle of winter, the servants in my hospital came to tell me that a peasant wished me to pay a visit. A snowstorm was blowing up so I knew the matter was serious. In the hall a dejected peasant was standing waiting. He asked if I would go to a woman who had been delivered four days before, but was desperately ill. When he told me it was his wife a chill struck us as if the felt-covered door had blown open and let in the cold air. We were accustomed to tragic news from those thus facing possible bereavement; but in addition these words conveyed to us the fact that the snowstorm now raging was so terrific that the poor fellow could not persuade any friend or relative to face it. Though she was dying he had had to leave his wife and himself risk even disaster in getting aid. I made only one stipulation, that after my work for his wife was done he must get me driven back for the hospital duties next morning. He agreed and we set out.

As a sensible person when rations are uncertain will stuff into himself as much as he can eat, to make up for depleted reserves and lay in a provision for the future, so any sensible traveller leaving a warm stove and wrapped in sheepskins, still warm from the cupboard, would snatch a period of sleep before the frost began to cause distress. By the time the sledge had reached the end of the village I was asleep. It was an uneventful twenty miles. The night was terribly cold but it did not break through my layers of fur. Innermost was a closecropped sheepskin lining to a sort of melton greatcoat, outside of which was a coat of long-haired sheepskin, not buttoned but held together with tied thongs. Over all was a garment transcending tailors' terminology, shaped to be sure like a coat but so large that thirteen sheepskins had gone to its making. This vast envelope, showing to the world the white inside of the pelts, was kept in position by a girdle curiously patterned and woven in scarlet and white, half a yard wide and four or five yards long—a present from a grateful Tartar—wrapped round the belly of this mountain of hides. The collar when open fell over the shoulders like a mantle; when closed it crossed over the face and stood up like a conical dome over its wearer's head and was kept from falling by a narrow hand-woven braid tied in front with a bow knot for quick release in case of being pitched head-first into a snowdrift. The feet were protected with stockings made of camel hair, thick as blankets, and the legs were thrust into knee-high wide felt boots; there must be no pressure for if skin circulation is stopped even over a small area the result is frost-bite, and (since it may in the recoverable stage pass unnoticed) necrosis. It was indeed wise therefore to get one's sleep while one was still warm.

When I unpacked the instruments in the patient's house, which was larger and finer than most peasants' huts, the skin of my hands froze to the cold metal, after which warning I handled them through a towel to prevent a 'cold-burn'. The patient had been delivered of a dead child and some of the placenta had stuck. The village gamps had been at work with unwashed hands and a teaspoon; these measures proving unavailing the old women had used an S-shaped thick wire lamp-hook, rusty and besmeared with greasy soot. The lacerations produced by its use were dreadful.

The professional situation was a delicate one. If I told the gamps what I thought of their methods and of their choice of implements I should make enemies of them, and as I had to leave the patient in their care it was desirable to obtain their friendly assistance. As for instruments, I doubt if there was such a thing in the whole village as a metal tablespoon whose long handle might have served. The lamp-hook seemed to me inexcusable. However, it must be remembered that when face to face with a crisis, and ignorant of the least thing that will remedy the condition, when fear benumbs the mind and one loses contact with one's experience of past difficulties and the way in which to overcome them, then with nearly all of us a stupefy-ing hate surges up, and the crudest and most violent actions are per-formed in place of more gentle and skilful ones. I was half-sorry for that huddle of shrivelled old women as they passed the hook from one to another, showing it to me as if they felt caught in an evil con-federacy and could only excuse their action by giving it the sem-blance of a joint undertaking. Perhaps it would have been wiser to use their services but I could not trust their obedience; so they were sent to borrow samovars and prepare boiling water, which they could not very well infect.

The details of the gynaecological operation are immaterial. I had to sterilize the instruments three times because of the crawling infes-tation of cockroaches which ran over the table and dropped from the ceiling. (Cockroaches live on bugs, by the way, so many peasants prefer them in the house; but I, who grow quickly immune to bug bites, prefer these to the restless, rattling scurrying of cockroaches over face and hands when sleeping in the peasants' huts.) I organized as helpers the girls of between fourteen and eighteen who had been to school, hoping thereby to instil, though it be only by a few hours' example and instruction, something of the need for care, cleanliness, and gentleness of touch in these affairs. The village appeared to have about five or six girls of the right age and educability to choose from; they were all given duties.

Eventually the exhausting business was done, and I asked for food. No! I could not have food, did I not remember it was a fast day? I begged for it, said it was near midnight and I had to drive back to the hospital at once (they shuddered); I implored them to give me hot milk, eggs, and bread, saying that the priest had allowed me to give the indulgence of fast-breaking to patients physically in need of food, and I would make it right with their priest if they would give me some. They were adamant. Then I thought of a ruse. I moved the instruments into the kitchen and said I must pack them up myself. They readily agreed, but realizing I was going to steal some bread moved every eatable from the place first. For my comfort perhaps it would have been better if I had employed those old women round the instruments and the bed rather than in merely boiling water in the outer-world of the kitchen; for it was they who raised objection to my taking food, in the belief, I imagine, that it would go ill with the patient if I did.

After seeing about a dozen other patients in the village ('since you are here, doctor!') the patient's brother this time and I set off on the return journey still supperless.

There are two kinds of snowstorm: there is the fluffy kind we have in England, in which snow-flakes fall gently sloping through the breeze and delight us with their cool moist dabbing, and there is the *burran*. It is not only snow that falls in a burran, but also ice-crystals that have lain and become hardened on the ground are picked up by the wind and hurled through the air. The flying ice lashes the skin so that to the pain of cold there is added the torturing bombardment of these sharp, hard particles.

Within half an hour of our departure a *burran* in full strength was upon us. Swiftly it penetrated layer after layer of those sheepskins and the heat of the body was powerlesss to meet and throw off the onset of cold. Exhausted with the night's work, which besides being medically tricky had been socially difficult, I found myself overpowered with sleep. I seemed to be travelling in a curious luminous blue haze; it was cold, of course, but not unpleasant. Sensation was becoming numbed, indeed for some reason being a tiny island in an ocean of cold was not a bad experience. I began to feel an interest in sensations again, the blue haze was rather fascinating and there were faint lights floating or revolving before my sightless gaze. It was quite pleasant to watch their movement which one felt might go on for ever and for ever. Suddenly the faint lights raced in circles and exploded, and at the same time I heard a crash in my skull. I came to with the sledge on top of me in a snowdrift. I had fallen asleep, and so, I imagine, had the driver. In the upset a shaft had been broken.

It is a weary task to mend a sledge shaft by day in still air, there are never any tools but an axe and always too little rope; but in a *burran* at night it is torture. The ropes are stiff with frost, the fingers get so cold that they will not bend to grip the shaft pole, still less the thin hemp cords, and every movement of the limbs is hampered by the mattress-thick layer of sheepskins that one dare not throw off lest the low temperature congeal the muscles into immobility. However, the shaft was mended at last, the horse put back, and on we went; but soon we overturned again. The splice had worked loose, so that the pull of the sledge on the animal becoming suddenly lopsided, he had been thrown one way and we another. Again the struggle with the shafts and cords, and again the horse was put back into harness; but now its nerve had gone and it would not move. So by turns we walked at its head, tapping the snow with the butt of the whip to feel if it were solid under foot, patted the animal's nose, talked to it, and led it along yard by yard. Thus we progressed for, I judge, about an hour. At last the horse took to trotting without being led, so we both got into the sledge and once again dozed off, to be woken up by the stopping of the sledge. We had slid gently into a drift. The driver, having now given up hope, fell on his knees praying, and asked me to join him; 'We will pray and then die'. At this craven and fatalistic suggestion I flew into a rage and knocked him down, asking how he dared to talk about dying, and besides we were pledged to be back in the hospital at eight o'clock in the morning! Then I dumped him in the sledge and tried to stir up the horse. The poor creature was immovable; and although it would obey its master better than it would me I could not trust the peasant on the snow lest he started kneeling again, so I had to lead the horse myself using both the coaxing language and some of those half-Oriental curses which keep Russian horses on the move. By one or other persuasion the animal finally started to trot, so I got back into the sledge for a rest.

But the driver now seemed to have lost his reason. He kept on repeating 'It is foolishness to go on; better die, better die!' Every time he yielded himself to the thought of death my anger was roused afresh; each appeal to resignation was responded to with curses and blows. Under this treatment his view changed; I ceased to be human; it was obvious, he told the Deity, that I was a devil under the protection of Satan. The villagers had rightly called me 'The Great White Devil' (a name I had regarded as an endearment and had ascribed to my large outer coat); it was obvious, he went on in a sort of mixed prayer and conversation with God, why the church bells were never rung for me to guide me when I was out in a snowstorm, the reason why I was thought to be indestructible was now clear-the devil looks after his own. Alternately praying to God and cursing the fiend in the sledge behind him he jogged the horse along.

When he was silent I feared that he had resigned himself once more, so I stirred him up with kicks and oaths, knowing from my experience of anger at him how warming it was! Hour after hour passed in the cursing and fighting of two half-frozen mortals moving painfully over a vast empty expanse of snow under a canopy of hurricane and ice.

At length we saw stacks and hurdles and other outposts of human habitation. It was a khan on the track of a Tartar trade route. So far from our proper and ordinary road were we that I had not even known of the existence of the place. In the starlight we stumbled over sledge ropes and bumped into squatting camels in the courtyard of the khan. It was good to hear their contemptuous guttural grunts (though Russians usually loathe them). We burst into the great kitchen, hot as an oven, where a score of Tartars and Kirkhiz were snoring in their shirts. We took off our sheepskins, held the inner ones against the walls of the oven to warm them, and then, putting them on hot, lay on the floor for an hour's sleep.

The last few miles to the hospital were the worst. After a certain point has been passed the experience of freezing is not painful; the reverse process is an agony of mind and body. The hour's baking in the khan had been the turning-point, so that now, though dawn was breaking and the world was beginning to reshape itself as some external thing that would have to be dealt with, I felt that the task was insupportable through lack of inner strength, and that the pain would go on and on and the spirit sink down and down to an unstruggling and inevitable eternity of suffering. Eventually we arrived at the hospital compound; when passing under the gable end of my house I saw a Siberian crow, which had wintered under the eaves and which I had always looked for with pleasure every morning, frozen dead on the ground. I suppose that the 87°F. of frost registered that night had been more than it could endure. The sight of its stiff body was a shock, but I thought 'I am glad of it! If I know that it is dead I know that I am alive!' In some way that ruthless life-greedy thought produced a change in my mind.

The servants on our arrival were not sure whether it was us or our ghosts; I soon proved which view was correct, for by good fortune a ham had been boiled and was still in the pot, steaming hot. I ate such slabs of it as I thought not possible for a mere human being to consume. But it made no difference; though I knew I was alive my body still felt dead. The hot meat within soon seemed to cool down to the corpse-like temperature of my body; nothing seemed to give the feeling of heat and inner life which sustains our courage and gives a feeling of health though we do not realize this until it is lost. Three times that day the fires were lit in the great stoves and I would have had them relit again but the servants refused lest the overheated stoves burn the house. My table and bed were moved against them, but without effect. For nearly a day my skull felt like a helmet of cold steel under a layer of tepid and scarcely living flesh, the ribs were a chill cuirass which seemed to frost the drawnin air, the long bones of the arms and legs felt like cold iron bars inserted between the muscles, heavy and chilling from the inside. The horse was laid up for a week and it took the driver two days to recover.

The silly fellow, immediately on our arrival and before taking to his bed, went among his acquaintances in the village and spun them an astonishing tale of the horrors of the night; but it was not the agonizing pain of straining to bend frozen fingers round the shaft and gripping the stiff ropes to lash the broken ends, not the misery of that isolation in the very heart of coldness, no, nor the condition of his sister for whose sake the journey was taken. These were things of this world in which pain is natural. His tale was of having driven a devil who moved under the protection of Satan.

I walked across from my house to the hospital at 8 a.m. to start up work as usual; but this moujik with his yarn had so diverted attention from physical ills to far more interesting metaphysical-theological questions about demons and their like that at first I got nothing from the patients but gaping stares; but soon reluctantly, apologetically even (I am thankful to say not timorously—that nickname was not really taken seriously), they begin as usual to tell me of their ailments.

Later I heard that the woman died.

PLACENTA PRAEVIA

A note came one day from a nurse who was working in an outlying village to say that a patient under her care who was before long expecting a child had begun to bleed; the case looked serious and would I come at once.

An examination showed that her urgent summons was justified but that if we took immediate steps the woman could probably be delivered of a living child.

There was the usual crowd of old women in the room observing everything. When not murmuring of comparisons between this terrible event and the score of others they had witnessed, they consoled themselves with short exclamations of piety or with deep sighs which surpassing the physical emptied their souls to the very fundament of woe. These noises are not in themselves disturbing, on the contrary I find in them an echo of my own mood when engaged on obstetric business of unusual difficulty; the worry lay not in their interruptions but in the fact that they might in their ignorance imitate what they thought I had done. In this case all that they would notice was a plunge of the hand nearly to the elbow into the womb, some rummaging about there, then the withdrawal, legs first, of a child. What they would not notice was the careful cleansing of my hands and of the patient and further, what they could not even guess, was why just this particular time is chosen for the work. To their dull eyes and fidgety brains the important thing, the new piece of cunning which they might learn from watching me, would be that dramatic plunge into the interior. It was the master stroke which they would try out when opportunity came, and if they hadn't my magical formula to mumble while doing the trick they would substitute, despite endless failures, one of their own, till they too without harm could thus wrench new life from the bowels of the living.

But these beldames could not be turned away from a spectacle they craved to see, without risk. Among the affairs of men their voices, single or united, amounted to no more than a scranny interruption easily put aside; on matters of childbed, the management of infants, and lastly in the laying out of the dead, these old creatures held absolute sway. All the forces of their lost fertility were turned to a rapacious control of those who in the full heat of youth and maturity held the ardent desires of the present and the growth of the next generation of men in their power. The first question, then, was whether if the crones were turned out of the room they would hold a grudge against the mother and the babe on account of the affront to their position and their pride, saying in later days that an evil spirit had disturbed it in the womb, made the mother gush blood before her time and by another evil spell be delivered. Such a devilridden infant is in their view best left to the devil's care if the slightest thing goes wrong with it.

Had I been alone among peasants I should have chosen someone not as helper so much as guardian angel for the child, as guarantor of its true and honourable delivery, but I had with me-a rare event-a fully trained nurse who, of course, for them was a professional rival I To admit the amateur rabble would lower her status, a thing which could not be thought of as she needed as much authority as she could be given. Illness always upsets a home; either there are too few rooms in which the quiet offices of nursing can be performed without interruption or there is no one both suitable and available to watch and wait. Among these peasants there are nearly always helpers in plenty, bunches of them, but they take no individual responsibility, and to get a quiet room is very hard. The huts are small, in them are huddled together six, eight or ten of all ages without privacy of any kind. The personal impact of one person upon another, the desires, loves, hates, love-making, squabbling, clamouring children, discontented whining old age, cause a seething that makes illness doubly trying for the patient. When the occasion demands it the sick nurse must be in a position to requisition a room free from the continual urgency of human associations, she must be in sufficient authority to claim the services of those of her choosing, to inform the relatives (and convey to the patient) that if the house is given up to sicknursing, the rest finding their lodging elsewhere, it is not because the shadow of death is already darkening the entrance, but that by this seclusion the patient will find a safer and a speedier way to health.

The peasants had primitive ideas about health; there was good health; there was discomfort; and there was illness, this last a dreadful thing bordering on death. A sensible person resisted discomfort for as long as possible, 'went on as usual', until compelled by pain or disturbance of function to call a halt to his labours in the field. Then, and not till then, he lay low, expecting the end at any moment. Only the aged or the maimed allowed it to be seen that they were not capable of a full man's or woman's toil. In convalescence the stages were reversed. A sensible person lay low, brooding within himself and withdrawn until he felt well, then at a turn of time that no one could predict, least of all himself, he would rise and resume his place at the plough or with the axe in the forest. Yesterday he was ill, to-day well: there were no transitions.

Sick-nursing tends to smooth out the stages of recovery, it implies that a person can be ill and yet not nearly dead, can need help of a special kind and yet not be helpless; it introduces the notion of there being different kinds of illness and therefore of special ways of taking care of the body in sickness. Sick-nursing also implies *bodily* disease, and that is a notion which no Russian peasant can grasp; for to them all illness is the evil work of some bad *thing* inside, a foreign body. This alien thing within may be sent from God as a punishment for sins or may be picked up in folly as one gets pricked with brambles if heedless. Illness is an affliction and recovery a blessing—such forces cannot be controlled by man and he should not intervene in the fulfilment of the divine plan.

Such was their view, and this fatalism would have been their practice if another force had not worked on their spirit from within. The love they bore each other made the sight of illness painful and they were glad to get the skilled help of doctors and nurses for those they held beloved and (with inward reservations) for themselves as well. Such help was called only when the condition was past their comprehension, i.e. when the approach of death had been heralded by symptoms that were alarming, or if the patient behaved in an unusual way, as for instance this case of bleeding before labour. They leaned upon doctors for support when in great distress and their minds were ready for the dramatic work of surgery and obstetrics, but nursing in their homes introduced many new complications, it disturbed their ways of thought and needed both a tactful introduction and continual firm support. The chief obstacle, of course, lay in the prejudices of the old women whose emotional life centred on the misadventures of childbirth and the almost voluptuous excitement of laying out the dead. Their power was now twice threatened, first by the passing of their fertile years, and now by the introduction of younger women who neither claimed the affections of men nor brought forth children of their own, but by the exercise of knowledge and by their deft handling of the body in suffering, rose to a position of respect, and more, of affection in the village.

So the old women were coaxed out of the room with the promise that they would be the first to have the news and that they should have a description of what transpired. To make the place quite private, as it had fallen dark, I put clouts over some besoms which I found in an outhouse and propped them against the window panes.

This done I turned to the nurse with some satisfaction and said that with those old biddies out of the way and having the place to ourselves (us two and the patient) it made quite a cosy hospital atmosphere even in a peasant's hut. Nothing irrelevant to intrude, nothing we did would start false ideas going in these greedily curious people-the relief was prodigious.

From my first arrival with the nurse to the exclusion of the old women was perhaps the matter of a quarter of an hour. We now set to work busily; arranged tables, sterilizers, instruments and chloroform all neatly to hand, had lamps hanging in just the right place and everything ready.

The nurse and I worked together swiftly and in silence. The patient needed a whiff of chloroform, which acted I think more by suggestion than by its anaesthetic property, for she needed only a few drops, and its administration by the nurse was skilfully done. The delivery—after that plunge of the arm—was straightforward, and was followed by the afterbirth with very small delay. At this dramatic moment I heard a gentle but long-drawn-out 'k-k-oo-oo'. 'What are you saying, nurse?' 'Nothing, I didn't speak.' I was puzzled, for I could have sworn someone spoke, and that it wasn't the patient; it was an articulated sound, not the relaxed puffing or stertorous gargling noise of a person under an anaesthetic, and I did not think the mother was then fully under.

It was a finely shaped child, with no moles or other devil's marks upon which malice could fasten, and in a trice she was breathing. The mother was soon round and comfortable. I was sweating with the nervous strain, for it's a touch and go matter at the best of times, and it seemed to me a good day's work. I flung myself on a stool, leaned back against the wall and looked up at the ceiling while I wiped my forehead—and there only five feet above the bed in full view of it was a row of boys' and girls' faces. Half a dozen of them.

When clearing the hut of all but the nurse and the patient I had forgotten to look for the shelf which hangs about two feet from the ceiling and runs about five or six feet out from the wall. It is used for stowage, but often enough the members of the family old enough to climb and young enough to be wanted out of the way house themselves there for the night and lie chattering and wriggling, listening to their elders and watching all that goes on till sleep overtakes them.

I was mightily annoyed, at them without reason and at myself with some cause, for having overlooked the common hiding-place; so

I hauled them out and gave them a smack on the bottom apiece, telling them not to watch such doing again, and be off!

The nurse and I had a good laugh when they were gone and then ushered in the old women, but it was no longer possible for them to be the first to have details of the birth. They were not, however, angry at the children having been there, because they were only children, they did not matter, their turn had not yet come for the rub of birth and death.

Then in came the proud grandmother, chewing a rag in which was pocketed bacon rind and baked flour; this she was about to pop into the child's mouth to be the first intruding touch from the outside world when I stopped her, and asked her to consider whether it was as nice and clean a comforter as the mother's breast; and, besides, had she not got pyorrhoea (her gums were awash with pus)—in fact, the usual hygienic pleas. It was an ill-judged if not unkind interruption, because in any case the cosy rag would be thrust in the moment our backs were turned and by giving the babe something she had herself chewed she was in an animal sort of way binding her love to it as best she knew how.

There was no need to be worried over the nurse's status in the villages. The half-dozen young witnesses gave a full version of how she had killed the woman with a rag wet from a bottle while I had gouged the brat out with my arm, and then between us we had pulled both round to life again. With them the exciting spectacle would only give colour to their dreams; they were too young to crave for the details as a means of holding in their jealous grip the destinies of a younger generation.

*   *   *

An earlier experience had made me nervous of the use these old women would make of medical knowledge. One old woman came to hospital because her belly was becoming distended with fluid. She was admitted and was 'tapped'. The word, I suppose, is borrowed from the brewers; in this case the vast tun of her abdomen was broached with a medium-sized trochar and cannula. The patient was told to look away-for further security and to give her comfort a nurse kept her hand over her eyes; she was told 'It is just a prick', then came a quick jab, the silver tube was plunged up to the hilt, the trochar removed and a rubber tube put over the spouting jet of ascitic fluid-all in a matter of seconds. The rubber tube led over the bedside to a bucket and when the rate of flow had been arranged to be neither too quick nor too slow, and all was covered up, the patient was told to look round now and see how nice everything was I Indeed, she had hardly felt anything, a prick, that was all. The hours passed, and the full buckets were removed, measured and returned empty to the ward; meal-time came; bandages were gradually tightened, to haul in the slack; the orderly routine of a small hospital doing a small operation in an efficient, tidy way, was pleasing to the patient and to ourselves.

When the fluid was out of the way it was possible to make a proper examination; this done, she was told that the fluid would return-secondary growths were numerous-but that its removal would be no more unpleasant than on this occasion. She was to use her discretion, not to put off coming till the discomfort was unsupportable, nor on the other hand to come every few days, but say once a month or so.

In six or seven weeks she returned, staggering under her caskfal of fluid. Again she went through the simple procedure. She was put to bed, a nurse came and held her hand over her eyes, another nurse dabbed her belly with something wet (iodine), the doctor jabbed at her (a mere prick), then some fuss with buckets, the bedclothes rearranged, and finally with a 'there now!' all was over once more and she had an afternoon in a little whitewashed room, occupied besides herself by two or three other women. All settled down for a good chat.

A third time she came, at a rather shorter interval, and she was by now quite at home with us, full of praises for our help to her, and how great was our cleverness.

On the fourth visit she was more thoughtful. She asked to be allowed to watch the procedure; we told her that it would be exactly the same as before so she need not worry. Her head was averted, the procedure in all details carried out quite smoothly, but she was still worried. After a time, she said, 'You see, doctor, I do want to know just what you do to me.' She was told that nothing more was done but to drain the fluid away. 'Yes,' she replied, 'I understand that, but what I can't get hold of is the method you use. Will you show me the thing you do it with?' It is not a doctor's habit to do such a thing; but, overcome by her persuasions, another trochar and cannula was fetched similar to the one that was then in use but a size smaller, not that there was much in that. She handled it with great respect and began to give the reason for her curiosity.

She had been an object of interest in her village, leaving it in the morning so big and so inert, returning in the evening so slim and full of life. At the vapour baths she was an object of comment, and the other women there began with a spread of hands to ask if she could last out another week, and so forth.

On one occasion during this banter their sharp eyes spied a girl also growing big in the belly, and contrasting her with my patient they said that she was filling up in another way-and what wonder, a fine healthy wench ... and who was the father ... she had kept it pretty quiet-and so on, bathroom gossip. But the girl took it otherwise, swore to them that she had no relations with a man, it was no baby at all; to which they replied, 'We will wait and see!'

The patient turned the matter over in her mind and, after another bout of this teasing, approached the girl with an offer. She was by now an expert in this fluid business, and if it was as the girl said no baby at all, then from her experience she knew the remedy.

Next week at the baths the matter came up again. Again the girl denied before the company of women any connexion with a man; again the patient said that if it were so, then it must be fluid, and she knew how to drain it off. She had brought with her a kitchen knife. At the sight of it the girl's resolution almost broke, but, being reminded of her denials of pregnancy, she yielded to the view that it must be fluid. At this she was urged by the old woman to have it drained away. With the words 'It is just a prick', she drove the kitchen knife into the girl's belly below the navel, 'and doctor, she lay three days dying'.

There was a pause after she had said this. She turned the silver cannula and the fine-pointed steel trocher over and over in her hands, and added as if a doubt had now been cleared up, 'I thought you used a knife !'

There was only one question after that to put to her: 'Why, if you thought it fluid, did you not send her to the hospital?' She made no reply and gave no sign that she thought the question contained a good or bad idea. The situation was baffling; one was not sure whether this was ignorance more profound than one had dreamed possible or malice so infiltrated into the character that it left no stirring of remorse even after a killing she could not accommodate herself to her guilt.

THE APOLOGY

Some time before the Bolsheviks were even heard of in our part of Russia, I was driving at dusk through a village on my way back to hospital when a drunken peasant jumped on to the runners of the sledge and demanded that I should stop and treat his headache. He tried to drag me from the sledge by force, so I put my foot on the pit of his stomach and pushed him into a snowdrift. His manner and the strong language he used when he rose were such that a more exact diagnosis and a more medical treatment of his condition did not seem to be indicated. My driver, remarking that the fellow would have a worse head next morning, whipped up the horses and drove on. The trivial incident passed out of my mind.

One day, months later when the snow had gone, an unusual thing happened. A peasant in the waiting-room of the out-patients asked to be seen last, in contrast to the usual clamour to be seen first. When all the other comers had been attended to, the moujik, standing rather shyly by the door, said 'Doctor, don't you recognize me?' I looked at him carefully and said I did not, then turning to the out-patient register, asked when he had been before and what his trouble was. He said he had never been before and had no ailment, but before proceeding he must know that I recognized him. I told him to come to the point; if he had not been before and was not ill what knowledge had I of him, and what did he want of me in the hospital now? 'Doctor, if I tell you, you won't be angry with me, will you?' I searched my mind for possible wrongs received, things stolen from the hospital or my house, swindlings at the fortnightly fair where I had bought sheep and pigs; but remembered nothing amiss that I could associate him with and gave him my word I would not be angry.

'Do you remember months ago in the village of _____ a drunken man set upon you as you were driving through and demanded that you should stop?' The scene came back in a flash. 'And do you remember,' I said, smiling, 'the doctor who put his foot in that man's belly and gave a shove? Damn it all, man; we were quits.'

'Now doctor, don't make a joke of it. It's a serious matter.' I thought I must have injured him, so apologized and asked him to tell me all about it.

He then began a long story. He had been drunk and felt sick and thick in the head; so seeing me, he suddenly had the bright idea of demanding an instant cure. But his headache made him angry and he tried to do this by force. He had attacked me and that was wrong. Before he asked my forgiveness, it was necessary that I should know exactly who he was and recall the circumstances. He then very shyly produced a document which ran roughly as follows:

> This is to certify that I [here there was a space for my name] have received the apology of _____ _____, of the village of _____, on the [space for the date]. And this is also to certify that the elders of the said village of _____, after careful examination are convinced that _____ _____'s apologies are from the heart. [Date, signatures of village elders and crosses of attestation.]

The whole thing seemed fantastic; an apology was in the circumstances odd but understandable, but the certificate seemed all out of proportion. I made up my mind to see the village elders and try to clear the matter up.

A few days later my round lay through that village and I called on several of the elders. They said they had been horrified by the attack on me. I had done them no harm, on the contrary had been diligent for their good, and it was necessary to eradicate the evil disposition which had shown itself amongst them that night. I pointed out that my quite adequate physical defence had prevented injury to me being laid on the man's conscience, and also that I had attended patients in the village after the episode just as before, so they need not fear the loss of my assistance; but that was not the point. They felt the attack to be a stain on the honour of the village. They had reproached him next day and asked him to apologize. He was defiant in refusal (perhaps through the humiliation of having been rolled over in the snow) and finally brought forward in extenuation the obvious fact that he had been intoxicated. But this for them was no excuse; when sober one must make amends for one's deed when drunk. Then, since as a group they had not been able to persuade him to apologize, they changed their policy and approached him as individuals. They also got his friends to join in their efforts and for weeks the poor devil was followed wherever he went with reproachful eyes. One day he burst upon them with the news that he would go and apologize. But his manner of saying it did not satisfy them; it was hasty and still somewhat defiant; his heart had not changed. They accepted his consent to apologize as a good sign but not necessarily as an indication of true repentance. Gradually he became more passive and waited patiently to be 'released' by the village elders from the yoke of guilt. He then came to me with their certificate.

This narration left several things unexplained. This repentant sinner had been brought once more within their most sensitive and intimate circle, he had become again what the village calls 'one of us'; after months of communion with him he had been found to be pure in heart. Why then did they need my signature to the certificate of release? Did it mean, I asked, that they could not after all trust him to apologize? They said that they did not distrust him, but that they wished me to know that they felt themselves also to be involved in the insult and hence also in the restoration of the honour of the village.

This was their explanation. There were, of course, other reasons for dealing with me in this way. A physician was an object of value to them. They were helplessly dependent on him and his goodwill, and however familiar he might be as a visitor in their homes and at their councils, they *as a group* could not replace or reproduce him because he belonged to a different civilization, that of the metropolis and of international communications. Towards all members of this civilization they looked with abject submission, envy, and sometimes hatred; from the metropolitan civilization came to them tax gatherers, political police (civil order was maintained, as this story shows, by the villagers themselves in a most unbureaucratic way), landlords (for the most part absentee), priests, a few schoolteachers, and a very few doctors. These, one and all, belonged to the metropolis, not to the village. Over all loomed the distant and terrible, revered and incomprehensible figure of the Czar, who, however widely his characteristics ranged over everything Russian, certainly was not 'one of us'.

It was a sign of affection and trust in me that the village elders did not themselves come crawling to me with an apology, but a sign of latent fear that made them send the certificate. A not unfriendly representative of an alien world, I belonged to the town, distant from them though familiar with their village ways. The gulf between us narrowed when the relationship was personal, widened when it touched on the doctor's position in the social structure.

This little episode shows something of the way in which the villagers were bound together by ties of love and how they kept the spirit of their community intact. This spirit gave the members strength when they were in accord with it, and they lived in misery and isolation when they broke, in thought or mood, with the opinion and sentiment of their neighbours. The episode also shows how difficult it was for them to include a member of the alien caste in their way of thought and living.

*   *   *

Some of the social history of the next few years is well known. The Bolsheviks came to power and made all things new. The peasants were collectivized, many were I forcibly moved to public works, many more were driven by starvation to seek a living in the towns. The new social unit became the factory, and the old village organization ceased to be typical for the Russian people. But its spirit did not die.

Seventeen years passed, and an Intourist traveller brought back from one of the large new cities a collection of factory wall-newspapers (the placards on which anyone may freely criticize anyone and anything except the essentials of the new regime). Most of the contents related to the factory statistics, how the shock workers were breaking records, sport, the factory theatre, music news, and so forth. Down in a corner (always the same corner of each issue) there was a series of notes which at first glance seemed of the most trivial significance. But their spirit was reminiscent of the village I have mentioned, and heaven knows how many thousand like it. The notes ran somewhat as follows: 'We do not like the way Sonia _____ does her work. She doesn't show the right spirit; she slacks.' Several times was she thus publicly reproved. Later she was said to show signs of adopting the proper attitude. Finally Sonia was declared an enthusiastic worker who had entered truly into the spirit of the Revolution.

On reading this my mind went back to the peasant whose heart was changed by the silent but not harsh pressure of the group; the steps in this re-entry into the community seemed to be remarkably similar in the two cases; in spite of the greatest imaginable change in the economic and political life the behaviour of the group to a wayward member remained the same. The village spirit, the need to feel that everyone was 'one of us', had re-emerged; and I have no doubt that this plays its part in strengthening and consolidating a regime which often seems to us in the West to be based only on force.

The Threat

*C*linical work is much the same the world over because the response to physical disease is little affected by race or climate; but the doctor's work is greatly affected by the social conditions, the administrative complexity (or over-simplicity), and even the climate in the area of his labours. Sometimes difficulties arise from issues quite outside the proper limits of medical activity.

When I was acting as a county council doctor in Russia I had to cover single-handed an area about the size of Surrey and a population of at least 50,000 of half a dozen different races. The problem was to distribute the small amount of medical aid where it would be most effective and was most needed, irrespective of other considerations. A few outlying clinics were established (at about twenty miles from the central hospital) which I visited on weekly rounds so as to save patients the burden of travel; they were placed after careful consideration of the population and general healthiness of the neighbourhood. To prevent unnecessary delays I stopped at villages *en route* to these clinics only if I had previous notice of illness that must be seen at home, or if more than a handful of out-patient cases was reported.

One route passed through a small village of independent colonists from Little Russia, people of vigorous disposition and, as it happened, good bodily health. The headman of the village, who had seen me drive through several times, requested me to place a clinic in his village, but this was declined on the ground that his village was small, quite near another clinic, and, above all, remarkably healthy. He offered to provide a room free: 'And would you', I asked, 'let me see all comers there?'

'We certainly would not, it would of course be for out own people!' It would be a disgrace, he added, for his villagers to mix themselves with the ordinary peasants among my out-patients; his people were above such mud and desired special consideration. He admitted that one of his chief reasons for wanting the clinic was prestige, as he had promised his villagers that he would obtain it. I refused on the ground of medical urgency elsewhere.

The next time I drove through on my round I noticed an unusual number of dogs barking, and realized that they were being set on us. The horses, though frightened, kept up a good pace. One of the wolf-like beasts nearly got on to the sledge, but having to run after us it did not quite manage the final leap. Shortly after a note came from the headman. Would the clinic be opened? Again it was refused. I resolved next time to go through his territory prepared. A week later my driver asked if I would not make my round by another way; but this I would not do, and we set out.

There are few things pleasanter than a sledge drive across the Steppe on a sunny morning. There is a sting in the air, the snow under the runners squeaks crisply, and the muffled thumping of the horses' feet and the rocking of the sledge over the undulating ground produce a peaceful contentment. The best kind of sledge is one with a level floor big enough to hold a truss of hay, which, skilfully spread out and covered with sheepskins, is more comfortable than any contrivance of seats and springs. By jamming one's feet in one corner, sprawling diagonally across the sloping mound of hay, and bracing one's shoulders into the opposite corner of the back one can by a quick stiffening of the body grip the sledge, as it were, when it crashes into a deep bump or heels over on an incline, and one's arms are free to be tucked into the long sleeves of the sheepskin outer overcoat. The shaft-horse is attached only at the collar, the shafts being kept very wide apart by the great arch of wood on which the bells are hung. The traces of the leading horse are long enough to leave eight or ten feet between the leader's tail and the shaft-horse's nose, so that the leader can swerve round bumps and potholes and pull the forward end of the shafts into the right direction. This also permits the leader to pick a good surface by allowing him a wide lateral range of movement. But the leader must have good nerves, for if he runs wild the sledge will crash, the shafts be broken, and the curved-up front of the runners may break the shafthorse's legs. The distance between the horses necessitates two whips, one with a thong about six feet long for the near animal, and one about thirty feet long for the trace-horse. These whips dingle from the driver's wrists, and their long thin strands of twisted leather ride over the snow with an arching and rippling movement like attendant serpents keeping pace on either side of the sledge.

On this morning our horses slowed down at a hill and rested at the top. Below us lay the village we must pass through. The wall and fence that surrounded it were banked up with snow into sloping ramparts, cut by the road that passed through the middle of the village, which was guarded by a gate at either end. It was a quiet scene and I noticed that both gates were open. The driver started the horses and we raced down the hill at a full gallop. He went through the first gate superbly, and we were doing the quarter-mile of village street at a speed and in a style that Russians love. When we had gone part way through the village they let the dogs loose. This time the dogs bore down upon us from the front so that they had the advantage of a springing attack. They worried the horses, which slowed down enough to make it possible for the brutes to jump full on me and to get over the back of the low-built sledge. I had already disconnected the two portions of a cranioclast and held them in readiness. I got up and, standing by the driver, dealt with those that came upon us from the sides, while he with the whips tried to keep them clear of the horses. Then, to my surprise, the villagers, who had stood and watched the scene, whistled to their dogs; this caused a momentary distraction which allowed the horses to spring into a gallop.

But the villagers had not done with us yet. There was the second gate to shoot through, and some of them standing nearby released more dogs at us from the flank in order to head the trace-horse up the rise of snow that had banked up to the level of the top of the wall, where an overturn would have been inevitable, and a ghastly mauling by dogs a certainty as we floundered to our feet. The horses were in panic, the sledge was swerving from side to side of the road, but by masterly driving they were kept off that dreadful slope, and we made a clean exit through the open gate.

The rest of the day was uneventful.

Some weeks later I was called from supper. Would I go at once to a desperately ill woman? A fast sledge had been sent for me and the village was only twelve miles away. Without thought or discussion I stepped into the sledge, and was driven off at a fine spanking pace. I soon saw that the route lay towards that village. Then I noticed little details: the carriage of the driver's head, the cut of his coat, the shape of the sledge—all seemed familiar and yet made a pattern that was different from the usual one in my neighbourhood, and I realized suddenly that I was going not through but *to* that village.

We drew up at the headman's house and I was led straight to his mother who was certainly very ill with pneumonia. I did what could be done about diet, explained about nursing, and then wrote a pre-scription to be made up at my hospital. As soon as that was done the headman said, 'And now about that clinic !' I told him the answer was the same, and further that to set dogs on doctors was not the way to get a clinic. 'Very well,' he said, 'if you don't consent you can get home by yourself, my horses shall not take you and I am not going to be responsible for what the dogs do to you.' To his shame this was said in his mother's hearing. I saw only one way out of the difficulty, apart from agreeing to set up a clinic where he wanted it and not where it was needed. Acting instantly on the knowledge that a prescription is regarded by these people with superstitious reverence, I replied, 'The burden of that decision falls on other shoulders' and tore the prescription to pieces. To *my* shame this also was said and done in the patient's presence. He took the dreadful blow to his mother with steadiness and said quietly that I had beaten him. I immediately promised to send the medicine at once on my return to the hospital if he would have me driven back and no more dogs were set on me. I said I would visit serious cases in his village as I was doing at that moment and would stop on my way through if requested in the customary way; but no clinic, and no more dogs. He kept his bargain and I mine. I do not know what happened to his prestige.

These hardy independent people were a fine set of men, if somewhat rough. It is a misfortune for which individuals are not to blame that when an aggressive attitude towards life finds outlet in communal action the leaders of the group are often rich in cunning, though poor in wisdom. The people I have described had different, but equally admirable, qualities from the more numerous, more lazy, more gregarious village-peasants of Great Russia; unfortunately the two types did not get on well together. The world now knows such sturdy independent farmers in the heart of Soviet Russia by the name of *Kulaks*. And I for one, who saw something of their mettle, regret, though can understand some of the reasons for, their liquidation.

THE BRIDAL DRESS

One of my recurrent duties when on my rounds in a nearby village was to visit and watch the progress or the deterioration, as the turns of her illness took her, of an eighteen-year-old girl who had tuberculosis. She was of an amiable disposition and, knowing what ailed her and what was probably in store, met the changes of her condition with resignation. Before one of my holidays she was worse and I did not think it likely that I would see her again.

On my return I went to that village a day or so earlier than I expected, for I was called out late in the evening to another case. Being so near I thought I would look up the girl; I told the driver to wait while I went on foot, the better to enjoy the freshness of the summer night. From a distance I heard the hollow wooden sounds of carpentry, and the little house where the girl lay was lit up. The lamplight fell on the low whitewashed fence surrounding the little garden and the boughs of a silver birch dipped into the shafts of light and lifted again into the darkness as the wind swayed the trees. Within doors the scene was also one of brightness and animation. From a distance I could see people in festival dress moving about under the lamps, so many lamps that they must have been borrowed for the gay occasion. She must have turned the corner, I thought; quickening my steps I came to the little fence by the garden and saw her sitting up in bed, far prettier than of late, her hair in plaits hung down neatly, her cheeks looked plump, her posture, so different from the sunken invalid I had left, was trim and alert. She sat very still and her eyelids looked heavy—fatigue, I first thought: but she was dead.

The sounds of carpentry followed me down the village street as, not wishing to join in the wake nor share the labour of her brothers making her coffin, I returned to the waiting horses.

She lay in the dress she would have worn as a bride, and which if worn as a bride she would have treasured, kept tidy and neatly folded till its second bridal appearance, when she would enter the Kingdom of Heaven once more a girl, fresh in the glory of her youth, rejoicing in her Lord.

'Tell me, doctor,' I have often been asked by some old women as I have stood by their bedsides, 'how soon will it be that I wear my bridal dress?—this autumn, maybe; the spring perhaps?'—wheedling out of me if possible a date that they can look forward to. It will be *their* day once more; their hair will be done in plaits, their hands crossed over the blessed sign of Jesus, they will be carried aloft over the heads of men, to lie on the top of the hill for ever and ever in the holy company of angels.

POLICE

Soon after my appointment as Resident at a county hospital in the district of Buzuluk in the government of Samara, I was honoured by a visit from the chief of police of the neighbourhood. He was very polite, and offered to assist me so far as he was able. If I got into trouble with the peasants, I had merely to call on the constables, and everything would be put right. I was told that the police had genuine Tashkent horses worth six hundred roubles, and if I cared for riding he was sure everything could be arranged. Finally he mentioned that his daughter was dying of heart disease and would I see her.

During the frequent visits that that disease involved, I became acquainted with the family, and found the report true that the chief of police was as kind-hearted as any man in the province. The peasants respected him and no one had a bad word for him. His usual price was three roubles, but any work which he did for the people involving extensive silence called for a higher rate. People said that they respected the way in which he took money—he was friendly, easy, and gave confidence without 'stooping to the people' or lowering himself in any way.

One day the village postman burst into the outpatients' department with a notice. He said, with a meaning smile, that he hadn't time to discuss it then, but there would be plenty of time later. It was the last official manifesto from Nicholas the Second-his abdication. With it was a circular which began, 'At last. It has happened!' and went on to encourage the people by telling them that liberty lay in their hands, and that, if they used self-restraint, they would enjoy the privileges they had so long coveted.

I nailed the notice up on the wall, and proceeded with my work. The peasants came into the consulting-room beaming with delight. 'Well, so he's gone, just think of that: and he has been our Czar for God knows how many years, and when he leaves us everything will be the same as ever. I suppose he will go to manage his estates somewhere; he always liked farming'—and so on. Only an old woman cried, 'Poor man! he never did anyone any harm; why did they put him away?'

She was interrupted: 'Shut thy mouth, thou old fool! They aren't going to kill him; he's run away, that's all.'

'Oh, but he was our Czar, and now we have *no one*!'

In the village street I met the chief of police; he forced a grim smile and said, 'Now I'm unemployed. Look at this.' And he slapped his left hip, 'Unarmed! And I, chief of police, this morning gave up my sword to a woman! In *Russia*!'

He turned, and we walked down the street to the square; but he would not go into the village councilroom, as he still felt a little bit ridiculous in the presence of that fat woman. The person in question was a schoolteacher from a neighbouring village who, because of her executive ability and public service in the past, had been chosen to fill the post of Keeper of Public Order for the time being.

Several weeks passed without anything of note happening, till the time drew near for a local horse-fair which attracted thousands of people from outlying districts. In the old regime, this had always been a time of anxiety for the police, so we were anxious to see how the schoolmistress would cope with the situation. Going out to the fair, I noticed twelve old men, greybeards, walking with long staves very like a Greek chorus, each wearing an armlet of white linen. I went up to one and asked him who they were.

He said, 'We are the militia. It is my first day out and I feel a bit foolish, but it will be all right in an hour or two when I get to talking with some of the people.'

I asked what his duties were.

'God knows. I'll just do what they all do.'

This militia was in force for several months. One or two old men, when appointed by their village councils to the duty, wrote to me asking for medical certificates that they were too old and feeble. The matter became so pressing that I paid a special visit to one village council to inquire what I had better do. The elders said that my sole criterion was to be real physical disease; they told me that they specially selected old men because they had tact and judgement and were of all people least likely to antagonize a young man if he was drunk and disorderly; they said that no one would dream of knocking down an old greybeard, whereas, if they appointed a young man as militiaman, there would be trouble all the time. 'We don't need to be kept in order, we only need to be reminded.'

The deserting soldiers contributed with several other causes to produce a new militia. In my district I was told so many times that I should be shot if I did not give certificates of exemption from army service, that I wrote to headquarters requesting that a military tribunal should settle the cases in the villages. The threatenings among

Russian villagers are as a rule much more serious than the shootings. After a few weeks such a tribunal was instituted, and a military militia came into the district. In the middle of the summer several men in our village took exception to me because I was a friend of the expoliceman, and must therefore be a counter-revolutionary. I received 'warnings', and anonymous notes telling me of my danger were slipped under my door in the early hours of the morning (one written by the daughter of my would-be murderer).

Of course, nothing happened. The friends of my critic told the military militia of the danger I was in, in order to get the militia to take sides and so divide the village sentiments. But the militia said that it was 'all nonsense', and that the whole affair would blow over. About a week later the would-be murderer was admitted to the hospital for scalp wounds because he had told the villagers that they were not revolutionary enough. Perhaps he was the first Bolshevik we had in our village. Everyone was sorry for him—they said he was a bit 'cracked'.

The militia went away in the fall, and the village elected constables of their own. Not old men this time, but middle-aged men who were serving oil the council. On one occasion it was discovered that four men whom the village trusted had been robbing the village coffers. An enraged people, on hearing their confession, led them out into the public square and clubbed them to death. Next day they were buried at the public expense, and their families pensioned.

Under the latter days of the Bolsheviks, a few of the Red Army were put in charge of the villages—poor frightened boys armed and set against the trained fighters of the allied Czechs and Cossacks. When the writer left, the village was patrolled by Cossacks, and the villagers lived in terror. I asked the people why they were frightened and they said, 'Because they are Cossacks and we know them'.

When working for order in Russia there are two opposing agents between which we must choose:[1] the force of the police and Cossacks, and the influence of the village elders. A peasant said to me, explaining the police, 'When a Russian is armed by the government he is made into a brute. We do not use force in our villages because it stands between men; our way brings them together.' And judging from my own experience, the period when greybeards were clothed in authority was the period of greatest security and of fullest development of political and domestic life.

1. Written in 1919. (from pg 74)

Peasant Officers

One day after seeing a great number in the outpatient department, close on a hundred, I was poring over my notes with some attention and did not notice that I was no longer alone, for on chancing to raise my eyes I saw there before me not a villager but an apparition. The dull log walls of the out-patient room were lit by the presence of a handsome young Caucasian officer in full and shining uniform. When I looked up he clicked heels and saluted. I shook hands and waved him to a seat, asking what on earth brought him to visit me; for there was not a look of worry held firmly in the background which darkens the faces at consultation of the young and otherwise healthy when they come with venereal disease. He seemed at peace with himself and the world. His movements were swift, strong, and graceful, without a trace of the lumbering movement of the peasant. Their action seems as from habit to wait upon the common will, the motion of each limb follows the slow deliberation of a hesitating soul, whereas the gestures of the fine young animal before me were the muscular expression of a single independent mind. 'I was waiting till you had finished', he said, 'my business is not urgent. Two of my brothers are back from the front and we are all rather worried about my father's health; so I came to ask if you would look him over; he says there's nothing to bother about, but we don't like the look of things at all.'

This was altogether puzzling; first of all an officer who does not swagger or get impatient was in itself a rare event; then his voice, strong and quiet, was one I could not place, it had none of the clipped city-bred culture, nor the peasants' drawl; finally I wondered where his father could at this moment be lying. I knew most of the land-owners round about but he did not resemble them.

I got my case of instruments and went with him. A rather shabby carriage was at the door; we got in and, without a word to or from the driver, were off. He pulled up at a peasant's house, bigger than most, without a trace of luxury, but there was a shelf of books—an unusual thing. It had a single large room capable of being warmed in winter, and a cold outhouse in which lived the usual collection of chickens and calves.

In the room there were already nine adults; our three selves made twelve. Three of those I judged to be sons were in officers' uniform, a fourth in the ranks, all as clean, neat, well shaved, with trim hair-cut, polished boots, and as well-ordered, brushed tunics as you could find in all Russia. A peasant of about sixty-five lay on a bed, his wife and a girl of about twenty were busy by the stove, a young woman had a baby at the breast, and another rather more slatternly-looking stood about doing nothing. A peasant boy sat at a table finishing a meal and there was besides myself also the driver. Only one looked ill, the peasant on the bed, so I went over to him and after a greeting said, referring to the Caucasian officer, 'Is this your son?' He laughed and said, 'You look surprised. Yes, he is my son all right and these are his brothers.' I was introduced to the officers and the private, and with equal pride to the peasant chewing at the table and to the driver. He had daughters which he indicated in a general way.

Four of his six boys had gone to seek their fortunes in the towns. The war came and they had been drafted into the army; the pre-revolutionary chaos came, and by their ability they had risen to officers' rank, in two cases with transfer of regiment, hence the Caucasian accoutrements; the revolution came, and they had gone back to their village to see how things were faring there. This done they would go back to the army, and when the fighting was over they would return to the life of the city again, unless their help was needed in the village. Two of the officers were likely to settle down in city life, one was married to a town girl, another engaged, the ranker didn't know what he would do, the officer who came for me would continue in the army if there seemed likelihood of proper work, if not he was as content to follow the plough.

The father began by telling me of his sons, and of how popular they were in the village; but of none was he so proud as of the two who were farmers because they seemed the best natured; this was spoken, of course, aloud, and in the hearing of the other four. My discomfort at hearing these gentle family discriminations in Russia was slowly vanishing, because they appeared to be signs of solidarity and unity in the family, rather than occasions of bitterness.

I asked why he was not proud of his officer sons. He said the country could be proud of them, because their worth was shown in the country's wars; but his home-staying sons had shown their worth in the village and home; therefore he was proudest of them because he was a plain villager himself.

The old peasant was more communicative about them after his 'army boys' left. Their career and abilities were a source of pride, but he was more gratified by the fact that success had in no way altered their friendliness to their stay-at-home brothers, nor their interest (not mere curiosity) in the village. 'They can go away and they can come back; that is a great thing.'

It is indeed a great thing to be able to acquire the independence which city life brings, the capacity for quick decisions, to feel the emergence into consciousness of personal ambition, and then to shed these newfound instruments of satisfaction, to yield them up and lean with an utter reliance on the public will, becoming once more with perfect resignation 'one of us'.

Those who get bitten by the pushing egoistic life of the towns usually return at longer intervals to their villages, till finally they form part of that uprooted proletariat without a village (communal) life or an urban (mob) life, which though gutter-streaked and apparently degraded has sometimes a tradition and at all times an immense reserve of strength. Until they have found themselves again in politics or in an organized occupation these cultural no-man's-landers are the loneliest souls on earth.

I think the extent—and, indeed, the pain—of this cultural rootlessness may have contributed a good deal to the revolution. The brutality, not merely the bloodshed, of the revolutionaries could only have come about —at least, as far as I understand Russians—in the presence of much isolation in the minds of very many men from the corporate spirit of their fellows. The economic factor, about which much has been said, is there as well of course, but I have missed from the writings and the lecturings I have heard on the Russian Revolution a sufficient understanding of the part played by the interaction of two forces—the strength of personal ambition and the 'pull' of another force leading to submission to the group. The former is found in an almost pure form in the old régime bureaucracy, the latter, again in almost pure form, in the peasantry. (These two forces do not mix readily together; the task of the new régime,[1] to make a modern state out of Old and Holy Russia, was and is far greater than Western observers commonly realize.)

In the old régime there were two societies facing one another, the Bureaucracy and the Peasants, the Rulers and the Ruled. No position between these two was satisfactory, no Russian, to use the language of another culture, could really believe that it pleased God to call him to any other station but those of the extremes; there was no middle-class content; nor could there be when those of the middle looked above and below them with mingled yearning and moral or physical repulsion.

---

1. Written in 1919.

A Political Episode

*T*he political events in Petrograd following the abdication of the Czar and the setting up of the Provisional Government were much discussed in our village, but they did not affect our lives to any great extent.

One day a deputation came to me from the village; its members were shy about making their request but would I kindly stand as their candidate for the Constituent Assembly shortly to be summoned in Petrograd. The request filled me with an almost overwhelming sense of littleness and humility, and of compassion for the good folk who were driven to such an extremity. It was an endearing request and though the thought of being mixed up in city politics was most distasteful, that fact had to be concealed from the villagers out of consideration for their feelings. Then I thought of a way out: 'But I am an Englishman!' 'So was Tom Paine,' said a tousled-headed old moujik, 'but he sat in the Constituent Assembly in Paris'; several gave assent to this.

Interest in the distant events in the capital, however important they might be for the future of Russia, receded from my mind; a fact of major importance demanded immediate attention. How came this illiterate old man, shielded for generations from every political influence by an enormous force of political police, to know of Tom Paine? I knew the moujik and his villagers well, or thought I did, was invited to their weddings, baptisms, and funerals, and to the meetings of the *mir*, had often talked into the night on every sort of subject including politics (though of the latter much more after the abdication than before), but I never guessed such *knowledge* existed among them. They had questioned me at length about the political system in England, and I had explained about our two-Party system of Liberals and Conservatives, and of how sometimes the Conservatives passed measures which had been prepared and begun under the Liberals, and the other way round too. (On hearing this, which astonished them, one old gaffer said 'I'll go and tell that to my horse; if he understands I too will believe that there may be some sense in it'.) Of curiosity there was no limit and each point was discussed among them with thoroughness and a good deal of common sense; but the *knowledge* was another matter, of that they showed nothing until that remark about Tom Paine.

About forty years before this time an educated man had gone from village to village putting up in the peasant houses and telling them in the evenings of the liberation of the people in various countries and of the French Revolution in particular; he was probably a Narodnik. My informant had heard of this as a boy and had told his children: thus was history taught and passed on. Had the abdication occurred a half-century later and another Englishman had made a similar excuse in declining the invitation I have little doubt he would have received the same answer but from this old fellow's grandson.

From long habits of caution, the caution natural to peasants reinforced by the fear of the police, there was never a parade of knowledge, before me at least, of any facts that were not within the common experience of every member of the *mir*. But after this revelation I saw that the instances they adduced from their village experience were sometimes selected with respect to, but without reference to, other events of which they had knowledge. The peasants talked much and they gossiped freely, so that one got to know who was pregnant by whom, and where and when, and who had an abortion and whether it was to be hushed up or made a scandal, and who was a scallywag and why people thought so, who cheated and how everybody else's kopeks were spent. They talked freely even to a doctor about the woes of the soul, and before him they gave forth in the relaxation of spirit their terrific sighs—Lord, how the Russians sigh! But of their knowledge of political facts it was, and perhaps still is, hard to be sure. Possibly only when the situation is apt and the disclosure would clinch a point forcefully is their knowledge disclosed; but even then those who live under police must hesitate. At that time and place the people were their own police, their knowledge therefore was freed for public use.

MOUJIKS WANT GLASSES

*T*he first Revolution which overthrew the Czar did not immediately affect the medical work in my village; but within a few months aged patients came complaining of symptoms quite unheard of among the villagers before. Presbyopia had not previously affected the daily life of the peasant as he did no near work; when he cut logs to build his house or sawed wood to make the window frames he did not measure closer than an inch. But now old men came to me with aching eyes; for they were learning to read now that they could do so without incurring the suspicion that they wanted to revolt. They borrowed school books and took instruction from their grandchildren. Of their land-hunger there had been much talk before the Revolution came, but I never guessed that the craving for learning would be so strong. It goes to show that when people are denied opportunity for self-development their true level cannot be judged while they are still under subjection. What these good souls got from their reading, their slow fingering of each word, each letter, was certainly but little of the author's meaning; no matter, they said, their children would learn quicker than they did, and in time all would read as freely as the priest.

When a priest moves among his flock he carries with him inevitably something of another life than this of ours on earth, so be he ever so human he always sees men as they think they ought to be. But in the great crises of life as well as in the vexing little ailments and injuries, the doctor is called in to help his patients to cling to this morsel of flesh, to get over painful times, and get deeper into the present with its everyday activities and its round of duties and cares. For this reason I found my opinion more often sought by the peasants than was that of the priest. His views coloured by his professional attitude to the future were, they felt, not as gross and earthly as theirs or mine.

Much of the aggressive element in the Russian disposition had, in the old régime, been turned inwards under the influence of an unusually mystical religion and an exceptionally autocratic régime, so that the people were submissive—not docile, that is too passive a con-

cept—and unself-confident, but subject to outbursts of self-glorifica-
tion and indignation against their oppressors. Furthermore, they were
taxed so heavily that they spited their government by remaining
poor. When I asked why, with their communal ownership of lands,
they did not communally own a threshing-machine and so save
themselves the back-breaking work with the flail or the wasteful
treading of the grain by oxen, they answered that they would go on
as they were doing rather than give the tax-gatherers the excuse to
raise their dues because they could afford machinery.

It has puzzled many how the new régime acquired the power it
wields over the minds of the people, since it first taxed the peasants
as heavily as did Czardom and then liquidated them. Apart from the
important fact that a majority of the present citizens of the Soviet
Republic have never known another régime, I think the main source
of its strength lies in the new direction given to the aggressive
impulses of the people. When Lenin said 'Peasants! seize the land!'
many of them had already done so; when the Bolsheviks said 'Workers, exploit your every opportunity!' the message did not fall on deaf
ears. Work was to be their salvation and factories their new chapels;
here they could pit themselves against materials they had hardly
dared touch before, lest they call down on themselves an inquisition
from the Governing Powers. The tax-greedy bureaucrats had stood
between the energies of the people and the earth from which they
derived both their life and their strength.

In another direction also the new régime met a need of the people. The Orthodox Church had in practice (I do not speak of the theory) two ways of dealing with the aggressive impulse; if turned
outwards it must be at the service of the Czar and the State, but it was
better to turn it against the self by fasts of inordinate length and most
lowering to the physique (my Tartar patients were invariably fitter
men at the time of spring ploughing than the Christians), and by a
constant preoccupation with the worthlessness and wickedness of the
self in wretched contrast to the ineffable glory and kindness of God.

The brutal anti-God campaign of the Bolsheviks was an endeav-
our to tap sources of energy of the people. Do not wallow in guilt and
self-abnegation! they said in effect, there is nothing to fear but yourselves. Possess yourselves of Russia, master it by work, don't just pray
for strength to overcome evil, work to make this land and this life better. For the first time the people were both appealed to and given a
chance to turn their energies to constructive work. In the Czar's
régime, taxation, which gave a minimum return in the way of social
services-witness the scarcity of State doctors, in the country districts
there were no others-and political oppression lowered the productive

interests of the people and bred a hatred of the State. At the same time the hold of the Government was strengthened by suppressing education, freedom of movement, and the marketing of a man's own labour, and by using the Church as an auxiliary of the temporal power. But though the Bolsheviks pulled down the old gods they set up other gods in their places; the strong, half-Oriental, cynical portrait of Lenin, a Russian like themselves, was even in his lifetime offered for their worship and was accepted.

There can be no two opinions as to the extent of the change produced by the new religion of work and the new theology of dialectical materialism. The people were free to exploit their energies in a way undreamt of before. Gaffer comes for reading-glasses, the grandson goes to technical schools; the one has begun to give expression to his desire to know more of what is going on around him, the other to master a more complicated trade than his father-to become *skilled*. In the view of the new régime not only the wealth but also the happiness of the people depended on freedom to acquire and use skill. What applied to trades applied also to professions. Tens of thousands of 'medical assistants' were trained at short notice to bring medical help to the villages and towns. Their curriculum was sketchy but they were missionaries for better sanitation and a care for health. Only those who knew what conditions were like before should judge of the wisdom of that policy. It is not pleasant to think of the country being overrun by half-trained medical men, but they were better than gamps who used lamp-hooks on a retained placenta, and as the supply of better-trained doctors improved, these men could finish their studies.

The materialistic philosophy which guided the energies of the people to constructive work and to the acquisition of skill, and which therefore diminished the tendency to depression, introspection, and pessimism so common in the old régime in all classes of the community, may thus be said in a measure to replace the institutions which ministered to the spiritual needs of the people and furnished them with ideals. But the desire to employ science in the service of man is more readily fulfilled in the physical sciences than in the mental. It is easier to get men to improve their manual skill than it is to change their inner ways of thought.

The almost fantastic depths of self-abnegation and submission common in the days of the mystical Czardom is not in theory favoured as a national trait by materialist Commissars. But though, according to plan, the workers have risen in their pride, overthrown their oppressors, and asserted their rights as a free people, there is from time to time still an organized orgy of penitence-by proxy. In the State Trials the attitude of objectivity which characterizes so much of modern Russian life is laid aside and the accusers, the accused, and the 'organs of opinion' (the Press and the Platform) give themselves over to an exercise in moralizing and subjectivity that can only come from inner tension and self-distrust.

The service of the materialist revolutionaries has been great, they have opened out a new life to a people who were vilely oppressed, have raised them up and given them not only new hope but the means by which they can consolidate their gains; but the new materialist mode of thought has no rational way of dealing with the inner life of man. It denies the old gods and sets up new idols for worship. It lends the readiest ear to every discovery of science[1], except those which deal with the sufferings of the mind, and these it does not seem able to probe or even to acknowledge.

The Russian attitude towards feelings of guilt has always seemed strange alike to Western and Eastern peoples. In the religion of the old régime it was a central theme; in that of the new it is denied in relation to everything except the State. In the place of the old blasphemy -thoughts of hate against God and not believing in His goodness- there is now the sin of not believing in the perfect suitability of the present rulers and the present materialist philosophy for the needs of the Russian people. Discontent is taken as a sign of the unpardonable sin working in a diseased mind.

The materialism of the present rulers has put them into an awkward predicament; by attempting to eradicate every trace of superstition and bourgeois mentality and presenting the Socialist State and its founders as an object of adoration, they have given their people no alternative to either loving or hating the central power.

The psycho-analysts have pointed out one way in which the parliamentary government of Great Britain has overcome the problem: the constitution provides for a permanent or untouchable portion of the governing power (the king) and a removable portion (cabinet) which can be sacrificed without disturbing the loyalty to Authority. Thus discontent can find a safe outlet without disturbance or serious break in the function of government, and it is impossible for the executive to bedeck itself with the glamour of omnipotence and omniscience, which is always corrupting to wise judgment. Parliament may bestow enormous powers upon an individual for a special occasion, as in time of war or crisis: power thus freely bestowed implies the constraining force of a sense of responsibility. It is different when power is seized. Violence may be necessary in politics; but violence

---

1. Written in 1938

generates feelings of guilt which may be unconscious. It is foolish, and, I believe, in the long run politically imprudent, to deny a factor so important in mental—or political—life.

Every one of us in the village had mixed feelings on hearing of the fall of the Czar, nearly everyone rejoiced at the release from constraint, most of us felt that a great responsibility was laid upon us. Innocent though we were of the great political event, we felt obliged to shoulder the burden caused by our fantasied complicity in having desired it. The murder of the Czar deepened the sense of guilt because the image of the Little Father embodied a high ideal.

THE PSYCHOLOGY OF
GREAT RUSSIANS

BY GEOFFREY GORER

Chapter I

CHILDHOOD TRAINING

1

*I*n complex societies, in which there is a hierarchy of social levels, anthropologists distinguish between 'class' societies and 'caste' societies. The distinction between caste and class is by no means clear-cut, and is indicated more by the relations between the groups than by the behaviour or composition of the groups themselves. In a class society the groups are typically in a single linear relation to one another from the upper to the lower and there is a general consensus as to which groups are superior and which inferior; if a person is socially mobile in a class society his mobility is through an orderly and predictable series of positions. In a caste society on the other hand the inter-relationship of the different groups is far more complex and relative superiority and inferiority are less clearly determined; social mobility (which occurs even in the most caste-bound societies) is less predictable, and does not necessarily follow an orderly sequence. Typically, members of caste societies have fewer feelings of inferiority than members of class societies; each caste has its defined role in the society and provides assurance and dignity for its members. In caste societies, much more than in class societies, a person's rights, privileges, duties, and in the vast majority of cases occupation, are determined by the group into which he is born; and it is unusual—often illegal-for a person to marry outside his or her caste. In caste societies it is general for each caste to develop its own customs, attitudes, and behaviour (in technical language its subculture) to a point of much greater contrast than is usual in class societies.

By all such criteria Great Russia was a caste society at least from the imposition of serfdom to its abandonment less than a century ago. Social mobility was possible through education, wealth or religious dedication, but this mobility was not progressive through a single line; it was not, for example, necessary to be a merchant before becoming a noble. Despite the great change-, produced by the freeing of the serfs, the killing or exiling of most of the members of the existing upper castes after 1917, and the modifications in social structure produced by the changes of recent years, it still seems more accurate to treat Great Russia as a caste society. I shall therefore discuss the customs of child-rearing by caste.

2

The environment in which most Russian peasants live and work has probably changed very little in the thirty years since John Rickman was a country doctor among them. The climate certainly has not changed, nor the landscape; although electricity is available in some rural areas there is little reason to suppose the domestic architecture has changed, nor the general pattern of living. Most Russian peasants still lead extraordinarily isolated lives; few important new railway lines have been built in Great Russia, and there is an almost complete absence of usable motor roads, or of motors to travel on them if they existed. Communication is still almost entirely on foot or by horse-cart or sleigh.

Because of this static condition I am using the present tense to describe the customs of the Great Russian peasants, although the greater part of my most concrete material dates back twenty years or more. This is perhaps risky, and may describe the way in which the present generation of adults was reared, rather than the way they are rearing their children. I do know, however, that there have been no significant changes in those customs which are visible to an untrained observer.

From all the evidence we can get, it seems as though peasants accept the birth of a child as an inevitable portion of human life, rather than welcome it with very deep emotion. Parenthood does not seem to be psychologically necessary to Russian peasants to prove, or to complete, their masculinity or femininity; and it surely is not without significance that one of the most widely publicized transformations of the early revolution was the legalizing of abortions, and the sending out of propaganda trains and exhibitions on the right to abortion throughout the country. The later withdrawal of this right is congruent with the general withdrawal of the changes and privileges granted in the first years of the revolution; but it also suggests that perhaps excessive advantage was taken of it.

When a child is born it is normally very well treated, and protected from hunger, cold, and all other unpleasant physical experiences to the greatest possible extent, often at the cost of considerable parental sacrifice; but the attitude of the parents seems to be one of succouring protection, rather than of great emotional attachment.

Babies are fed by their mothers generously and frequently; whenever a baby cries the elders think that this means it is hungry. Normally a young peasant woman will be working in the fields within a relatively short time after having given birth; but she will return to the house or have the baby brought to her at frequent intervals. Russian women say that they know when the baby is hungry because their breasts ache; although this is physiologically accurate, I know of no other society which phrases the situation in the same way; and this can perhaps be interpreted as further evidence of the relative lack of deep emotional attachment to the child.

Apart from nursing, the baby is normally looked after by a woman of a generation older than the parents, typically a grandmother or great aunt, 'the old beldames who ... in the management of infants hold absolute sway'. These old women are usually called *babushka* (grandmother) whether that is their actual relationship or no.[1] Sometimes older brothers and sisters also take a hand.

If the mother is on a journey or working in distant fields a comforter (called *nib*) is made for the baby; this consists of chewed-up food tied in a rag and fastened round the baby's neck. My informants said the food consisted of black bread among the poorer peasants, and white bread sweetened with sugar among the richer ones; but in the incident John Rickman describes it is bacon rind and baked flour. This might be a local variation, or something special for the baby's first food. If the baby cries while the mother is away, whoever is looking after it will moisten the *nib* with water if it has dried and then pop

---

1. (From pg 96-7) On some few occasions throughout this study I have found it necessary to use Russian words, when no single English word or phrase will cover all the meanings. Thus, it is a saving of time to write '*babushka*' rather than 'grandmother or great-aunt or some other old woman who may be more distantly related or not related at all'.

Russian is an inflected language, and changes the endings, and often the form of the words according to case, number, person, and tense, like Latin or German. I am following common anthropological custom and not inflecting the words: nouns are written in the nominative singular, and verbs in the infinitive, whatever position they hold in the sentence. Where nominal and verbal forms of the same root exist I am only employing one form. Since these words are used to illustrate an English text, it seems reasonable to use them as though they were English words.

It may be remarked that Russians normally add case-endings, &c., to English and American words and names when they use them in Russian sentences, despite the fact that English is relatively uninflected.

it in the baby's mouth, so that the baby is, as it were, plugged and cannot disturb the adults with its cries. Most of the time the baby is in a cradle attached to a springing ash-pole fixed to the ceiling or inner roof; unless it is born in early spring it is not taken outside the house for several months.

From the day of its birth onwards the baby is tightly swaddled in long strips of material, holding its legs straight and its arms down by its sides. When Russians are asked why they swaddle their babies in this way, they give a considerable variety of reasons, but they all have one common theme: the baby is potentially so strong that if it were not swaddled it would risk destroying itself or doing itself irreparable harm, and would be impossible to handle. For one mother an unswaddled baby would risk developing a hunchback or crooked spine, others fear it would break its arms or legs or back by thrashing about, and would certainly have crooked limbs, others again that it would scratch out its eyes or ruin its nose. In the Ukraine (which of course may be different) in 1947 John Fischer was told by pediatricians, 'If a baby's hands were left untrammelled, he would wave them in front of his face, thus getting a fright which might permanently upset the nervous system'.[2] All Russians are agreed that an unswaddled baby is impossible to handle, and would jump out of constraining arms; Russians exposed to Occidental practices justified swaddling on the ground that Russians had no perambulators.

When swaddled the baby is completely rigid; one informant said the infants were like sticks, another likened them to sausages, a third to parcels. The baby can be held in any position and by any part of it without bending, and temporarily unswaddled infants are (according to the photographs) liable to maintain rigid poses which are very unusual in Occidental babies. The better the mother, the firmer the bandages (the term which all my informants used for swaddling cloths): 'With a neat woman the bandages would be harder, because she would have prepared in advance and made double layers of cloth and sewn them together, closing down the ends. But with an untidy woman any old pieces of material would be used. But anyhow, I would say that they were harder than the napkins ... which are wrapped round their legs and then tightly bound with strips of cloth to keep the legs straight so that they shouldn't bend.'

The usual method of swaddling is very impersonal and involves little contact between the baby and the swaddler. The infant is laid on

2. (From pg 98) John Fischer, *Why They Became Like Russians* (New York, 1947), P. 30; published in England under the title *The Scared Men in the Kremlin* (Hamish Hamilton).

its back on a table or other flat surface, and lifted from the ankles as the cloths are wrapped round. It seems possible that the concept of the baby's great and destructive strength is in some way communicated to the infant by the manner in which the adults handle it during the swaddling.

This swaddling is maintained on the average for about nine months though there may be variations according to the season. The baby is unswaddled, and wrapped in a loose shawl, for nursing unless the mother is too busy, and for occasional bathing in carefully adjusted tepid water, but for no other reason. In careful families the swaddling is removed gradually, the shoulders, chest, and arms being freed before the rest of the body; in more slatternly households all the swaddling is taken off at the same time. Informants say that the unswaddled baby crawls on all fours 'like a bear' before it can stand and walk.

Few other disciplines are put on the child before it can walk and talk. It is not expected to be clean before then; and later lapses are apparently treated lightly. We have very little information on infantile sexual play after the child is unswaddled (while it is swaddled there can obviously be none). The general picture seems to be that children are 'innocent' and 'sinless' and therefore nothing they can do can have any 'moral' or rather 'immoral' significance.

In most cases infants are nursed for a very considerable period, often up to two years or even more. This is done partly for reasons of economy—it is the cheapest way to feed a child—and partly as a device for postponing another pregnancy; the widely held belief that suckling prevents conception is subscribed to by the Great Russians. Even after the child has abandoned the breast as its major source of nourishment it will be allowed by its mother (if she has milk) to suckle occasionally, if it is frightened or disturbed or unwell. When the baby can sit up it is usually held on the knees of one of its parents during the adults' meal and is allowed to have a little of their food. Apart from their mothers' milk, children have exactly the same food as adults. This coarse fare may cause stomach-aches, and strong purges will be given to relieve these; purges are not reported as being normally given to relieve constipation.

Even before the child can speak it is likely to get its first training in the partly religious, partly magical, practices of Orthodox Christianity from the *babushka* looking after it; it will learn to prostrate itself, to make the sign of the cross to avert the evil spirits and dark forces which threaten to take possession of human beings; and, as it learns to speak, it will learn the ritual prayers. From about the age of five or six it partakes as fully in the ritual of the Orthodox Church as any layman, including confession and absolution.

This is not the place to discuss in any systematic way the many differences in dogma and ritual which contrast the Orthodox faith, as practised in Great Russia, with Roman Catholicism or other forms of Occidental Christianity. It is, however, necessary to describe Orthodox confession. The priest stands while the penitent kneels at his feet; the penitent makes a ritual statement of his great sinfulness, and the priest then cross-examines the penitent on his or her particular breaches of sin. Save in exceptional circumstances the penitent does not volunteer an account of what he thinks his sins are. With the belief in the universal sinfulness of human beings, it is not considered to be a lie to confess to sins one is not conscious of having committed; and priests may refuse absolution on the ground of contumely and spiritual pride if the penitent persists in denying sins of which his confessor accuses him. A number of Russians have told me of their first confession, and of how their parent or guardian instructed them to say 'I am guilty, father', every time the priest asked a question. Sometimes the children (perhaps not peasant children) did not know what the priest was referring to; in most such cases the priest would pass on quickly.

At the end of confession most penitents are in a highly emotional state, weeping and beating their foreheads; the priest may impose penances of fasts or other mortifications of the flesh; he then covers the penitent kneeling at his feet with the lappets of his ritual garment and pronounces the absolution.

Absolution gives a feeling of great psychological relief, and is very highly valued by most people. In a way, absolution seems to give a retrospective justification to sin; as a widely quoted proverb says: 'If you do not sin, you cannot repent.' Many Russians state that repentance is more highly to be esteemed than innocence; and this although uncontaminated 'innocence' in adults is valued and respected.

Great Russian peasants cleanse their bodies too, at regular intervals—usually once a week—in the village steam-baths, during which the body is violently purged of all impure matters by great heat. Young children go with their mothers; from about the age of five little boys go with their fathers and elder brothers. The glow—partly physical and partly psychological—which follows this cleansing is highly valued.

When small peasant children gain complete physical control they contribute to the household by doing various odd jobs, including on occasion looking after their younger brothers and sisters. The chief demand which adults make on young children is that they shall not be a nuisance; if they do become so, or if the father is drunk, they may get severely thrashed. It is important to note that such punishments are capricious. The child 'is slapped not for his own good, but because the grownup was annoyed'. Such punishments are likely to be spasmodically administered, and the community will not stand for their being too severe or frequent; I have a number of stories of villagers reprimanding a father who thrashed his sons too much.

In many ways the whole village community is likely to be treated by the young child as though it were a single extended family. A child will play with all the children of its own age and will be as free to enter other houses or gardens as those of its parents; it will receive from the neighbours the same kind of emotionally calm succour and food as it would do at home.

The normal relationships between parents and children would seem to be of low intensity. The child owes complete obedience, gratitude, and respect to his parents; and the parents, especially perhaps the father, get satisfaction from the child's growing strength and capacities. Childish precocity—the time at which children acquire new skills—is not valued, and there does not seem to be even a common Russian word to describe it.

The relationship between brothers and sisters would appear to be normally friendly and of the low intensity usual in Russian family relationships, on condition that they be equally treated by the adults and of more or less the same capacities. If one child is markedly more gifted or more favoured than his brothers or sisters, there is likely to be considerable resentment on the part of those who feel themselves disadvantaged. As the proverb says: 'If a son is cleverer than his father there is joy, but if one brother is cleverer than another there is jealousy.'

Russian peasants do not seem to feel any fear that a boy or girl will not fulfil its sex role adequately, and there is no record of anxiety being demonstrated if for a time children play with toys or engage in occupations more customary for the opposite sex. In adult life, the occupations of peasant men and women are generally different; but if unusual circumstances compel a man to do a woman's work or vice versa he or she is not thought to have lost dignity or status thereby. Women are felt to be strong; men's larger frames and bigger muscles may give individuals greater physical strength, but the difference is purely physical.

In the first years after the Revolution the Soviet government made considerable propaganda in favour of the type of child-training then current in the West (particularly the United States); but as far as the peasants in the villages were concerned, the only major change seems to have been some increase of attention to hygiene—for example, sterilizing the rag in which the comforter was wrapped, washing hands, and boiling drinking water—and earlier recourse to medically qualified people if the children got ill. During the period of active anti-religious propaganda—roughly from 1923 to 1940—participation in Church rituals was obviously limited, and some secrecy may have been necessary in the teaching of religion. The large crowds of young soldiers present at Church services after the ban was lifted—a fact recorded by many witnesses—suggest strongly that such instruction continued to be given. Many more children than before 1917 attend school between the ages of seven and fourteen.

3

Before 1917, there were very few factory workers whose parents had been factory workers also in Great Russia outside St. Petersburg and Moscow.[3] The great number of urban workers were reared as peasants, and in many cases they returned to their villages to marry and raise their children. Where children were born to urban workers they were (it would seem) raised on the same principle as peasants' children, though possibly less attention was paid in some cases to their religious instruction.

With the increase of industrialization under the Soviets, the number and proportion of children born to urban workers has greatly increased; and this is the group which the innovations of government policy and government-sponsored practice have the most influenced, with the possible exception of the large group of lesser government employees, about whom we have regrettably no knowledge.

In the cities expectant mothers are meant to attend clinics to receive proper medical instruction during their pregnancy and to get advice on the treatment of the young child. Owing to the general overcrowding (even by Russian standards) workers' babies are generally born in hospital, though the lying-in period is usually less than a week; and mothers are meant to consult clinicians about their infants' treatment at regular intervals. Particularly in the earlier years of the Soviet régime, and to a modified extent even to-day, the advice which the clinicians gave was in line with current American practice, and against the traditional Russian customs: they advocated scheduled nursing, early toilet training, light and unhampering infant's clothes. The way the advice was treated is exemplified by the remarks of one Russian mother who brought up her two children in Moscow

---

3.   (From pg 105) There were probably more 'hereditary' workers in other portions of the Russian empire: the Black Sea ports, especially Odessa, Baku, Kiev, &c.

in the late twenties and thirties, and who was very active in kindergartens, parent-teacher associations, and so on:

'Officially babies shouldn't be swaddled, and all sorts of explanations
were given as to why it was better not to be, but nearly all the babies I saw
were swaddled. The mothers were so busy they had to make the child
secure. You know they didn't have anything like straps or leading-strings.
In order to keep the babies safe even my intellectual friends would swaddle their children. You know there are no prams in Russia and people had
to carry their babies, and it's much easier to carry a swaddled child. And
then you know it's cold in Russia and swaddling the child keeps the baby
warm. Teachers used to teach mothers that it was bad to swaddle the
children and that they would develop much better muscles if their limbs
were free; they tried to teach more modern ways. In the exhibitions there
were pictures of the clothing children should wear, but nearly every baby
I saw was swaddled ...'

'The young mothers that I knew accepted the propaganda against
swaddling but explained why they did the opposite. In the same way
modern theory said that you shouldn't pick up a child when it cries and
carry it around all the time. The mothers said: "What can we do? If the
child cries, it will disturb the neighbours." Or another gave the story of
how her husband had to have quiet in the house. This treatment of the
children and why they couldn't follow the theory was a constant subject
of conversation ...

'Mothers were told that they should feed their children regularly, but
they didn't have time for this and didn't know about calories and vita-
mins. They were told they should feed them every three or four hours. But
many mothers couldn't do this because conditions did not permit this.
Mothers had to feed their children lest they cry and disturb the neighbours. Russians like their children very much and like to do this because
they thought this would be the way to save the new generation ...

'There is a good deal of propaganda to train [for cleanliness] early in
life; the Russians advocated it strongly. But mothers didn't have the time,
or the possibility to do it and so they did very little. They left the children
to themselves. Of course it was different in the government nurseries.
There they were trained early and fed on schedule, but at home mothers
don't do that ...

'Most of the mothers I'm talking about were a very loyal Soviet generation, and they didn't feel guilty [about not following the government
rules] because life was so hard for them. They didn't feel any personal
guilt. I remember one mother telling me that she was bringing up her
children in the old way because they were living in such crowded conditions, but if they got more room in a few years she would treat the children differently.'

Because of her professional interest in child-care and education,
this woman is a particularly reliable witness; and what she says is
borne out by the other informants who have lived in Great Russian
towns in recent years. Unless the mother worked in a factory which
had a day nursery of adequate size and equipment (and this is still

fairly uncommon) most workers' children were and are brought up in their earliest years in much the same way as peasant children.

The Soviets have established a legal holiday for a newly delivered mother; when that is up the mother normally returns to work and the baby is usually looked after by a *babushka*. The mother is meant to be given intervals for nursing the baby, either returning home for the purpose or the baby being brought to her. Many city *babushka* trained their charges in religious ritual; but there was much more militant atheism among the workers.

For most workers' children who have passed infancy the role of religion in the old régime is now replaced by the teachings and practices of communism. Nursery school and kindergarten space is planned for all workers' children and is probably already available for a large number; and in them supervised games, occupations, songs, and stories start instilling the approved attitudes and beliefs. The mother I quoted before told me:

> 'Children go to kindergarten from the age of three and a half; that is where it's possible; in Moscow many wanted to and could not because there was no room. But there are other institutions which take care of children when both parents work. In kindergarten they begin to get a complete Soviet ideological education. I remember a children's camp in the summer Of 1929, when the collectivization propaganda was going on. The kindergartens and summer camps got a directive, as it was called, to explain collectivization to the children; we mothers were indignant about it (a thing we couldn't have done later) and they asked me, as I was chairman, to protest. Well, one day there was a programme devoted to collectivization. I saw they were doing a marvellous job. They made sand games for the children, showing how they could do much more if they would work together; and I made a report that there was nothing to get indignant about. Of course, they made the children repeat a lot of hard words they didn't understand; but when a child leaves kindergarten he is quite an enlightened little Soviet citizen and full of devotion for his country.'

Besides kindergartens, there are supervised playgrounds attached to many of the big apartment houses, and in Moscow on the outer boulevards. Patriotic holidays are much used to drive home ideological lessons. From the age of seven children go to school and belong to the 'Pioneers', the communist organization for the young folk.

One of the areas in which there have been the most violent oscillations of Soviet policy is the officially approved attitude towards parents and teachers. A young woman who first went to school in Moscow in 1921 said:

> 'In Moscow in 1921 there was a positive Soviet approach. There were no melancholy poems read. I was nine and we were left alone. We worked on

the Dalton plan. The teacher had no authority whatsoever. We were broken into units of four or five of our own choosing ...

'The children in school all had the feeling that they couldn't rely on their families. There was no such thing. The government encouraged it and said it was the government who was supposed to take care of the children. We were completely liberated from our parents. We felt no responsibility to them.'

As her education progressed, Soviet policy changed; by 1928 or 1929

'the teacher's authority became greater and greater ... As time went on—my later experiences in school—the political situation changed and it became something that was imposed on you. The democratic method [of choosing student representatives] was abolished. The representatives of the Party were assigned to the school. There were lists of selected people from whom you could choose ... The third year [1931] they didn't let them choose but appointed a boy instead of me.'

During about the first ten years of the Soviet régime, parents had legally no authority over their children, and children were not meant to have any respect for their parents. Children could complain to the school and party authorities if their parents punished them; and then the parents would be punished in their turn, if they had disciplined their children for any reason except the infraction of the rules of the school or the Pioneers. These attitudes towards parent—child relationships were changed in the thirties; by about 1936 parents were made responsible for their children's delinquencies, even if these had occurred away from the parents' supervision, for example, if boys spoiled public property or engaged in any acts of hooliganism.

The most recent expression of the official attitudes that I know of is found in a text-book issued for teachers in 1946:

'The feeling of love for father and mother is the first noble feeling which arises naturally in a child and which plays a central role in the life of every individual ... Our children must appreciate how honourable is the title of mother in our land. Only in the Soviet Union has the state established the title of "Mother—heroine" and the bestowal of orders and medals on mothers of many children. And with the word "father" we address the Great Stalin when we wish to express to him the feeling of filial nearness, and of love and respect ... In our country there are no conflicts between fathers and children ... '[4]

4.   (From pg111) D. P. Yesipov and N. K. Goncharov, *Pedagogy* (Moscow,1946). Partly translated and edited by George S. Counts and Nucia P. Lodge under the title *I Want To Be Like Stalin* (NewYork, John Day, 1947, and London, Gollancz, 1948), PP. 72-5.

4

Although most of the members of the former upper castes—the greater and lesser nobility and the merchants—seem to have been either killed or exiled in 1917 and the years following, it is perhaps of interest to describe briefly the way in which they were brought up; this may explain some of the points of contrast with the behaviour of the present upper castes.

Whether an upper-caste mother nursed her baby or not was a question of fashion and individual temperament. In the first years of the twentieth century there was a more general tendency for such mothers to nurse their own babies; for those who did so, it was a very great tie, for the babies were fed every two hours during the day and for many months. During the nineteenth century nearly all upper-caste babies were suckled by peasant wet-nurses, *kormilitsa*; and in the twentieth century this was still very general. These wet-nurses were either poor women or unmarried mothers. It was very rare for the *kormilitsa* to be allowed to nurse her own child as well; it was feared that either she would favour her own child over the foster-child, or that she would be anxious concerning her own child and so 'turn' her milk. There was consequently no expected relationship between foster-children, such as is found in other societies.

In looking for a wet-nurse it was essential to find one whose own child was exactly the same age as the fosterchild, but the relative sexes were not considered. It was believed that these wet-nurses' milk would 'turn' or dry up very easily if the nurse became angry or disaffected or jealous; and consequently they were greatly indulged and their whims were attended to promptly. They were provided with the colourful. 'national' Russian costumes which are today so regularly featured in nightclubs and musical comedies in Great Britain and the United States.

Apart from the actual nursing (whoever did this) the child would be looked after by an old and experienced peasant woman called *nyanya*. *Nyanya* normally only had complete control over the infant during its first two years; but in many households the *nyanya* was permanent, looking after each child in turn, and frequently going on to the second generation. In such cases *nyanya* was often the chief authority in the household; I have stories of married men, fathers of families, being scolded by their old *nyanya* and meekly doing their bidding. *Nyanya* were expected to be temperamental, to be swept by unaccounted for moods; mothers would tell their children to respect such moodiness. On rare occasions men would play the role of *nyanya*, especially orderlies in military families, and sometimes devoted family servants.

In contrast to peasant children, upper-caste children were *always* expected to be unswaddled for nursing; and they were usually left unswaddled for half an hour before the evening bath when they could kick and exercise their limbs. After about 1900 a new style of wrapping up children became fashionable: they were put in 'envelopes'—large squares of material stuffed with down and typically quilted, which were fastened over both sides and from the bottom; the child's head and neck were supported by a pillow. This style allowed the child a little lateral movement of its limbs.

Most upper—caste children learned religious observances and beliefs from nyanya. It is very uncommon to find Russians who have clear memories of their early childhood; the few I did elicit dwelt on such subjects:

> 'Old *nyanya* was very religious, and there was always a fire in front of the ikon, and old *nyanya* used to pray for a long time and speak in words we couldn't understand, and she'd pray and bow down and pray and then go to bed herself. It was very, very peaceful.'
> 'The old *nyanya* used to place the child and point the ikon out to it from the word go. *Bog* [God] is among the first words the child learns to speak, and often the children could point to the picture of God before they could say a word. And then in each room there's the ikon with the lamp in front of it and the child sees the *nyanya* praying and bowing.'

All castes in Russia tend to connect Christianity with the peasantry. Peasants typically described themselves, and were referred to, as 'Christians'.

Another very important part of the *nyanya's* function was quieting and entertaining her charges with the traditional folk-tales and songs. Russians regularly repeat the fact that Pushkin learned his wonderful stories from his old *nyanya*.

From the age of two or three, and often till they had passed adolescence, upper-caste children were put in the charge of a variety of maids, governesses, and tutors of almost any Occidental nationality except Russian, often two or three at a time, to teach them manners and various accomplishments, especially foreign languages. These foreign instructors were frequently changed. As soon as a child's table manners were good enough it would cat with its parents, except on formal occasions; and in most houses children were free to go anywhere provided they did not disturb the grown-ups. Russian upper-caste children spent most of their waking life in those rooms from which the adults were temporarily absent, or out of doors.

Like peasant children, most upper-caste children grew up in the emotional equivalent of a very large family; though in their case blood kinship often played a more important role. In the towns relatives usually lived very close together, often having flats in the same buildings as their parents or married brothers or sisters; in the country summer-long visits were paid by whole families of relations. In the bigger households it was customary for there to be permanent additions in the shape of more distant poor or unmarried relatives and other dependants, who stood in a quasi-parental role to the child. In the case of families living isolated in the country with few children of their own caste it was customary to choose some of the peasant children from the village to be educated with the upper-caste children. The happiest childhood recollection reported by upper-caste men who were educated in the country is playing with the peasant boys, away from the super-vision of governesses and tutors.

The chief contrasts so far discovered between the typical experiences of children from the upper castes and from the peasant caste seem to have been the following: upper-caste children were not expected to manifest responsibility or to contribute early to the comfort or wealth of the household; and the presence of governesses and tutors of non-Russian culture often produced emotional conflicts, either by their demands, their attitudes or their sudden removal, which accentuated tendencies in later life to neuroses and character problems similar to those found in Occidental society, and different in form and content from those found among Russians not early exposed to non-Russian influence.

Officers can be considered a sub-caste of the upper caste, for the profession was in the great number of cases hereditary; there were special military schools exclusively for officers' children.[5] Officers tended to be poorer than the majority of the upper caste and to have smaller families. Orderlies often acted as *nyanya*.

5

One of the most exclusive castes in pre-revolutionary Russia was the 'white' priests, the Orthodox priests who married and did most of the parish work; the higher ranks in the hierarchy were filled by the 'black' priests, who had taken a vow of celibacy, and might be recruited from any caste. By ecclesiastical law priests were only allowed to marry priests' daughters; their elder sons had to become priests, but in large families—and priests' families were normally very large, for there were

---

5.   (From pg115) It is interesting to note that such schools were recently re-established in the U.S.S.R.

state bounties for children—younger sons would go into other professions, especially teaching.

'White' priests were considered 'outsiders' by the upper castes and peasants alike. In the villages priests ran the parochial schools, and their children would mingle with the peasant children during school hours; they seem to have had little contact with them or with other adults apart from this. Most 'white' priests were poor, and only had such domestic help as their straitened means allowed. Many 'white' priests were ignorant men.

6

I have not been able to get any concrete information on the methods of bringing up children customary to the caste called *meshchanye*— the '*petite bourgeoisie*', the small shopkeepers and white-collar workers, the stewards and overseers who play so large a role in many of the best-known Russian plays and novels. In the present régime their place seems to have been taken by the lesser government employees and bureaucrats; for that caste too I have no concrete information.

7

The castes so far described compose a stable society; the members of each caste have their probable life and occupation marked out for them from birth. What happens when an individual, through temperament or individual gifts, feels himself unsuited for life in his caste?

Till the beginning of the nineteenth century there was only one way of life outside the castes open: religious dedication as a 'black' priest or nun, whether for study or contemplation in the monasteries and convents, or, for men, in the upper hierarchy of the Orthodox Church, or in one of the numerous schismatic sects. 'Black' priests took a vow of celibacy (if the vocation came after marriage they renounced their families), and consequently the group did not perpetuate itself.

From about 1820 onwards[6] there developed an alternative career for those whose talent, interests or temperament rendered them ill at ease in the conventional life of their castes; this was the study and

6. (From pg117) 'The following statements are chiefly founded on D. N. Ovsianiko-Kulikovsky's exhaustive *History of the Russian Intelligentsia* (St. Petersburg, 1914, 3 vols.).

practice of science, technology, and the arts as they had developed in
Western Europe. A number of individuals acquired these techniques
with varying efficiency; there was, however, no place in the existing
Russian society for them, and they gradually formed a predominantly
urban group on the edge of the Russian caste system—if the habitual overtones of the term can be forgotten they could properly be
described as 'out-castes'—which was later labelled the intelligentsia.

The intelligentsia were always a very small group numerically,[7]
but their influence, both inside and outside Russia, can hardly be
overestimated. With few exceptions, the writers and musicians of the
latter half of the nineteenth century and after come from this group,
and they are consequently almost completely responsible for the
views on Russia held by non-Russians.

Whatever their views or pursuits, the intelligentsia differed from
their compatriots by the fact that they abandoned the automatic,
almost unconscious, following of traditional Russian culture; they
questioned current Russian behaviour in the light of the contrasts
which they established with Western Europe; and they claimed the
moral autonomy of judging their own society. From their origin,
and to this day, the intelligentsia have been divided into 'Western-
izers' and 'Slavophiles'; but the latter, no less than the former, are
influenced in their judgements and attitudes by the impact of alien
(Occidental) cultures.

Like the 'black' priests, the intelligentsia were recruited from all
castes, on the basis of education, talents, and individual temperament; possibly the children of the lesser nobility and of the 'white'
priests contributed the greatest number. As with the religious vocation, membership of the intelligentsia separated the individual from
the emotionally large and extended families in which most Great Russians lived all their lives. But unlike the black priests, the intelligentsia
married and had children.

The children of the intelligentsia were born into a setting which
contrasted sharply with that of the 'caste' Russians; instead of spread-

7. (From pg118) Russian authorities differ on the way the intelligentsia
should be counted. One of the favourite occupations of the intelligentsia was
an attempt to define itself and number its members. One of them,
Pyshekhonov, in his *Materials for the Characterization of Social Relationships in
Russia* (St. Petersburg, 1904), maintains that the best way to count them is by
the signatures received when some famous member of their group is honoured. At Mikhalovsky's jubilee 20,000 signatures were received in this way.
The all-Russian census of 1897, published in 1905, lists something under
200,000 for all the members of the 'intelligent' professions, including their
households, for the whole of Russia.

ing their emotions over a great number of adults and children they were most of them reared in small families, their most constant adult contacts being with their parents, and among children with their own brothers and sisters.

Together with other 'Westernizing' ideas the intelligentsia imported (at least, to the best of their ability) Occidental ideas of the proper way to bring up children. The children of the intelligentsia were not, as a rule, swaddled; older informants will explain, 'We were not swaddled because we belonged to the intelligentsia'. In most such families the mothers looked after their babies themselves, or had trained foreign nurses or governesses, and imposed feeding schedules and earlier cleanliness training. In many families the children did not receive conventional religious instruction.

The leading members of the various clandestine revolutionary parties were drawn almost entirely from the intelligentsia; the schools and universities were the chief recruiting ground for this group: for many adolescents conspiratorial politics played a role analogous to sexual experimentation in the West. In the vast majority of cases where one can trace the social development of Lenin's colleagues and collaborators—the 'professional revolutionaries'—they came from the same 'out-caste' group.

When the 'professional revolutionary' section of the intelligentsia achieved supreme power after 1917, they immediately instituted propaganda (as has already been pointed out) for contemporary Occidental-style pediatrics; all the traditional Russian methods of child-rearing were inveighed against; in this, as in all other spheres, the U.S.S.R. was going to 'equal and eventually surpass' the West. Despite the current Slavophile repudiation of the West in most other spheres, these attitudes to (relative) bodily freedom, scheduled nursing, and very early toilet training are still favoured and practised in the best state creches and children's homes, if one can judge by the photographs and the pamphlets and brochures. It seems reasonable to suppose that these approved 'modern' and 'scientific' practices are followed in the families of the present Soviet elites.

Detailed analysis of the photographs of children in creches shows that there are some significant differences between Soviet and Western practices; hand-mouth exploration is considerably impeded, and various devices isolate the child from its environment, its fellows, and the adults to an extent which is not customary elsewhere.

Chapter II

CHARACTER DEVELOPMENTS

1

*T*his chapter will be occupied by a description of what appear to be some of the typical characteristics of the majority of what may be called 'caste' Great Russians. Nothing which follows is meant to apply to any other of the societies of the U.S.S.R.; unless explicitly stated otherwise, it also does not apply to the *children* of the intelligentsia or of the Soviet elites, nor to children raised in institutions. I have not been able to study enough of these 'out-castes' to discover any positive regularities in their childhood experience; they are united negatively in not sharing—at least with any completeness—the earliest experiences of the majority of their compatriots.

2

Under normal conditions the Russian infant is not exposed to conditions which might be expected to give rise to any of the painful internal physiological feelings which often form part of the infantile experience of members of other societies. He is not expected to be hungry or cold, and no demands for the control of elimination direct his early attention on his gastro-intestinal tract. But except during the short periods when he is being fed or bathed he is completely inhibited in the free movement of his limbs; he cannot explore the external universe through the use of his hands or through carrying things to his mouth; the only way he can express emotion of any sort is through his eyes or by screaming; and the latter may be impeded by 'plugging' the baby with the comforter.

These facts are observable and verifiable; their incidence could easily be established statistically. The deductions which follow are unverified hypotheses, though verification could be obtained.

When human infants are not constrained they move their limbs and bodies a great deal, especially during the second six months of life; it seems probable that much of this movement is physiologically determined, as an aspect of biological maturation. Infants tend to express emotion with their whole body and not merely their face, for example arching their back or thrashing about or hugging. They also explore their own body and the universe around them with their hands and their mouth, gradually discovering what is edible and what inedible, what me and what not-me. While they are swaddled in the Russian manner, Russian infants can do none of these things; and it is assumed that this inhibition of movement is felt to be extremely painful and frustrating and is responded to with intense and destructive rage, which cannot be adequately expressed physically. This rage, it is assumed, is directed at the constraint, rather than at the people who constrain the infant. Since the infant's exploration of the universe is very limited it would seem that the identification of the people who constrain him is impeded; the more so since, as has already been pointed out, the actual swaddling is done in a very impersonal manner with little contact between the swaddler and the infant who is handled and turned around almost as though it were a rigid and inanimate object.

Teething normally starts while the infant is still swaddled; and evidence from Occidental children shows that this is usually a physiologically and psychologically important aspect of their development. It therefore seems probable that fantasies of biting and destroying by devouring play a major part in the hypothecated rage. Partial confirmation of the important psychological role of teeth and biting can be found from a number of sources. Russian folklore contains the figure (which I do not know of in any other folklore) of the Witch Baby with the Iron Teeth who devours her parents,[1] as well as the more common old witch Baba Yaga who also has iron teeth. In Russian swearing and invective animals with prominent teeth and tusks (hyenas, jackals, sealions, crocodiles, dogs, &c.) play a major and consistent role; Soviet propaganda frequently described the Nazis (and subsequently their later enemies) as cannibalistic. I have the impression that in Russian political caricatures hostile figures are drawn with exaggeratedly large teeth. It is perhaps relevant that the Soviet dental service provides false teeth of stainless steel.

1. Older ballet-goers may remember the figure of the witch baby in the Diaghilev ballet *Contes d'Enfants*, frighteningly mimed by Lydia Sokolova.

Psychoanalysis has coined the phrase 'omnipotence of thought' to describe the typical mental processes of infants and young children before they can distinguish between wish and reality. If this is the case the assumed destructive rage would appear to give the infant a feeling of overwhelming destructive strength; and this may well be one of the sources for the rationalizations given by adults for swaddling their children.

A second very primitive thought mechanism is technically known as 'projection'; this is acting as though the thoughts or wishes emanating from the self (whether conscious or unconscious) were emanating from persons other than the self. It is assumed that this mechanism is regularly employed by Great Russian infants who project on to the vague figures in their environment their own hostile wishes; in consequence they feel that they risk being bitten or devoured if they were to gratify their destructive wishes (or in retaliation for having gratified them in fantasy). It is worth noting that swaddling prevents the gross muscular movements of the limbs which accompany 'temper tantrums' in unswaddled children; and as a consequence fantasies of rage and destruction will not normally be accompanied by fantasies which involve the voluntary use of the large muscles. This may help account for the emphasis given by many Russians to the workings of the soul and the inner nature.

Because of this projection of their hostility and fear the painful restraints which exacerbate the destructive rage become at the same time an essential protection both for the Russian infants themselves and for those around them; for the restraint prevents the full gratification of the destructive wishes, and so saves the infants from the fantasied perils of retaliation.

It would appear that Russian adults generally do little or nothing to an older child in a rage or temper tantrum; but it is worth noting that Russian adults, though normally so impervious to outside disturbances, appear to feel very great discomfort at infantile screams, and feel that their fellows would be equally disturbed. Since adult intervention would appear to be limited to quieting the screaming infant by 'plugging' it with the comforter, it would seem that infants sometimes exhaust themselves physically and psychologically with unassuaged rage. This exhaustion to the point of impotence would seem to be accompanied by feelings of complete loneliness and helplessness. This feeling of impotent exhaustion would appear to be an analogue to the state of *depression* described in adult melancholics.[2]

2.   I developed this hypothetical linking of swaddling and the 'depressive position' of infants, as described by Mrs. Klein, on the basis of literary

If this depression is the nadir of infantile misery, then all other emotions and experiences, however relatively unpleasant, gain some positive value as a sign that one is 'alive', not overwhelmed with weakness, helplessness, loneliness; even the rage which is presumed to precede, and probably to follow, the attack of depression becomes also positively valued. A symbolic illustration of these feelings may be found in a lyric written by Pushkin in 1830 entitled *Imps of Hell (Bjessy)*.

Storm clouds are dashing on, storm clouds are whirling, the invisible moon lights up the flying snow. The sky is opaque, the night is opaque. I am driving, driving in the wide open field. The sleigh-bell goes din, din, din. Against my will I am afraid amidst the unknown plains.

'Hey, go ahead, driver.'

'It is impossible to bear it, it is hard on the horses, master.

The snow storm sticks together my eyes, all the roads are swept by snow. May I be killed, but no tracks can be seen; we went astray, what should we do? The imp of hell leads us, it seems, and makes us circle in all directions. Look—there, there he play—he blows and spits on me! Now he pushes into the ravine the horse that got wild! There he stuck before me like a non-existing mile-post, there he flashed like a small spark, and disappeared in the empty darkness!'

Storm clouds are dashing, storm clouds are whirling, the invisible moon lights up the flying snow. The sky is opaque, the night is opaque.

We have no strength any more to circle around. The sleigh-bell, all of a sudden, becomes silent, the horses stop. What is it there in the field? A stump or a wolf?

The snow storm is cruel, the snow storm is crying, the sensitive horses are snorting. There he jumps—only the eyes are burning in the mist.

The horses again tear away, the sleigh-bell din, din, din. I see the spirits gather amidst the whitened plains. Endless, ugly, in the opaque play of the moon, all kinds of imps twirl around, like leaves in November.

How many of them are there? Where are they driven? What are they singing so plaintively? Are they burying the house spirit, or marrying off a witch?

Storm clouds are dashing, storm clouds are whirling. The invisible moon lights up the flying snow. The sky is opaque, the night is opaque. The devils are dashing, swarm after swarm, in the limitless height. With their plaintive yelps and howls they wound my heart.[3]

It seems probable that, using the mechanism of projection, the infant considers that these depressions are produced by the external

---

material quoted and analysed by Dr. N. Leites after I had left the United States and written my first formulations on Great Russian character. (See Appendix 1, p. 218). I should like to express my sense of indebtedness to Dr. Leites for this material, as well as for much other assistance in the course of this study. I understand that Dr. Leites is preparing a study of Bolshevism.

3. Cf. the behaviour of the peasant in 'Snow', p. 40.

world, possibly as retaliation for his hostile wishes; and, as will be developed later, an unconscious fear of a return to such a state remains operative in adult life.

These feelings of rage and fear are probably made endurable, but also given emphasis, by the fact that the baby is periodically loosed from the constraints, and suckled and petted while unswaddled. This alternation of complete restraint without gratifications, and of complete gratifications without restraint, continues for at least the first nine months of life. It is the argument of this study that the situation outlined in the preceding paragraphs is *one* of the major determinants in the development of the character of adult Great Russians.[4]

It is *not* the argument of this study that the Russian manner of swaddling their children produces the Russian character; and it is not intended to imply that Russian character would be changed or modified if some other technique of infant training were adopted. Swaddling is one of the devices which Russian adults employ to communicate with the child in its first year of life, to lay the foundation for those habits and attitudes which will subsequently be developed and strengthened by all the major institutions in Great Russian society. It was through the study of swaddling practices that I discovered what appear to me to be some of the most important clues to the interpretation of Russian behaviour;[5] and the derivatives of the swaddling situation became for me as it were the thread which led through the labyrinth of the apparent contradictions of adult Russian behaviour. The thread is not the labyrinth; but it is psychologically almost impossible for the explorer, who has relied on a thread, not to overemphasize its importance. Individuals have a childhood, but society does not; child-training practices are one of the devices through which a culture is maintained through time.

4.   I should like to stress as forcibly as possible that I consider the hypothesized derivatives from swaddling as only one of a presumably large number of antecedents to the development of Great Russian character. Further investigations would almost certainly develop others of similar importance. The vulgarizations and misinterpretations of my paper 'Themes in Japanese Culture'(Transactions of *the New York Academy of Sciences, New York, March 1943, and Penguin Science News No.* I, London, 1945) have falsely imputed to me a belief in a monistic antecedent to Japanese adult character. I trust that a similar error will not be committed in the present instance.

5.   See Appendix I.

3

For several months, at least, the Russian infant experiences intense but relatively undirected rage and fears deriving from his projection of this rage on to the external world; as a result of this he develops a feeling of pervasive though unfocused guilt. So pervasive is this unfocused guilt for some Russians that they can (or did) feel responsible for the sins and miseries of the whole world, an emotion most graphically and beautifully described by Dostoievsky in his major novels. This feeling of diffuse guilt presumably underlies the Orthodox dogma of the universal sinfulness of human beings, and accounts for the admission in confession of sins one is not conscious of having committed; it would also help account for the great feeling of psychological relief which accompanies confession and absolution for the devout, and also for the role which confessions outside religion have continuously played in Russian public life. The sensational confessions of the purge trials Of 1936-8 and the recantations of error in communist self-criticism are modern examples; an older example, dating from 18qz, comes from one of the most hostile critics of Czarist Russia, E. B. Lavrin:

> 'Nothing is more striking or characteristic in the annals of Russian criminal justice than the almost mathematical certainty with which one can predict that a person arrested on suspicion, even though there be no legal proofs of guilt, and no likelihood of their ever being obtained, will take the Juge d'Instruction into his confidence and glibly relate every detail of his share in the transaction. Out of sixty-five criminal cases taken at random, I find that in forty-eight the prisoners were convicted on their own confession, and in most of the remainder there was no need for self-accusation, as the malefactors were caught red-handed.'[6]

Although I have described the general Russian feeling of responsibility for evil and apprehension of punishment as 'guilt'it is important to bear in mind that this 'guilt'is of a different nature to that commonly manifested by the members of Occidental Protestant cultures. In the Occident guilt-feelings apparently become formalized considerably later in life, and are perceived as fear of punishment from specific external (or later internalized) parental or quasi-parental figures for having contravened specific ethical rules.[7] Among the

6. E. B. Lavrin, *Russian Characteristics* (London, Chapman & Hall, 1892), p.115. 'E. B. Lavrin'is the pseudonym of the Times correspondent of the period, Dr. Dillon.
7. The internalized figures, with their autonomous control over the ego's behaviour, are termed by the psychoanalysts the superego. The portion

Great Russians, however, these guilt-feelings apparently arise before people in the external world are clearly differentiated, and indeed before the acquisition of adequate speech, and are felt, not as fear of punishment from specific figures, but as fear of dark forces *(tyomniye sili)* which might overwhelm one. These dark forces might ,arise either inside or outside the individual.

The common practice of Orthodox Christianity made this fear concrete as the fear of possession by an evil spirit or devil who would take up its abode in a person's heart; and there were a number of ritual practices designed to avert this psychic disaster. Many children, for example, were taught to make the sign of the cross over their mouths every time they yawned; should they fail to do so, the lurking evil spirit would jump through their mouths into their hearts. The extent of these fears can be illustrated by the reminiscences of a young woman, who was looked after by a *nyanya* when she was separated from her parents in the first years of the Revolution:[8]

> '*Nyanya's* religion was rather on the negative side, and she was frightened of the devil. The devil is part of the folklore-something like a household god, an evil spirit. She expected to be punished at any time, at any minute. You must be extremely careful not to provoke the evil spirit. Every time you do something wrong you get punished immediately because there was something waiting for you to do it. I was a very obedient child but when I did do something wrong and then later bumped myself or hurt myself, it was the punishment So you see it was all very convincing ...
>
> 'The devil gets in through your mouth. He gets into a general location [saying this she made circular movements round her chest]. That was part of the threat. [Makes sign of the cross over her mouth.] That was why you made the sign of the cross over your mouth, like this, to keep him out. The devil provokes you to be bad and if you are sufficiently bad he can get into you and then you are possessed. My nurse was in constant fear of being possessed and she made me feel that.'

Later in the same interview, when this girl was talking about her life as a Komsomol in Moscow in the late twenties she said: 'To be appointed [to an official position in the Komsomols] to the task was a great honour. The more you did, the more honourable your position was. We were considering the welfare of all humanity, not only of the Russian people. You felt the fate of the whole world depended on you.'

---

of the super-ego which is available to consciousness corresponds to the 'conscience'of popular and religious parlance.

    8.   This informant has already been quoted on pp. 109-10.

4

While the Russian baby is swaddled, the only way it can always express its emotions is through its eyes, for its mouth may be stopped by the *nib*. It is only with its eyes too that it can explore the outside world; speaking metaphorically, one might say that Russian babies grasp or touch with their eyes. The very great importance of the eyes is maintained in adult life; all non-Russians tend to notice the great expressiveness of Russian eyes, and it is perhaps significant that the song which is often considered to be most 'typically Russian' is entitled 'Dark Eyes'*('Ochi Chornie')*.

Those Russians who believe in the soul nearly all consider that it is located somewhere inside the thorax and is expressed through the eyes; one analytically minded woman said the soul 'must be partly in the brain, because the brain is connected with the eyes and the eyes show the soul'.

Great Russians feel that they can communicate love and hate, passion and disapproval through the eyes. In folklore and fairy stories it is common for the hero and heroine to have fallen mutually in love before they have addressed a word to one another; they look into one another's eyes in the church or some other place where they can see but not speak. In the words of the proverb: 'Love finds its beginning in the eyes.' The ideal Soviet school-teacher can enforce discipline with his eyes: 'Fortunate is the teacher who is able to influence the Pupil by silent reproof, by reproof of a glance or a hint. Thanks to such ability discipline is quickly restored without waste of words or time.[9]

5

The inhibition of exploration of the surrounding world during the swaddling period would seem to be one way in which the lack of sharp distinctions between other people in the environment, and (on an unconscious level) the distinction between the self and the not-self is perpetuated. This tendency is probably reinforced by the fear of separateness arising from the feeling of isolation and helplessness in infantile depressions.

This concept is one of the most difficult to convey, for English possesses neither the language nor (save exceptionally) the experience which the language designates. A few illustrations may possibly make the idea clearer.

9.   Yesipov and Goncharov, *op. cit.*, p. 118.

The central sacrament of Western Christianity is Communion, the intimate connexion between the individual worshipper and Jesus Christ; in the Orthodox Church the central experience is *sobornost*, the Pentecostal descent of the Holy Ghost on the whole congregation simultaneously. Whereas a solitary Western communicant loses nothing by his solitude, an Orthodox believer cannot participate in *sobornost* without the presence of his fellows and peers.

In one type of old Russian *mir*, the village collective, all decisions had to be unanimous:

> 'The decisions of the *mir* are achieved by unanimous agreement of all the members. If at the time of the meeting there are a few who are opposed, the meeting is considered incomplete and a failure. Peasants do not understand decisions by majority vote. They know in each case there can only be one proper decision and it should belong to the most clever and truthful of all. To find the truth, all members are supposed to join, and if the solution is found all the members have to comply with it. As a consequence, a member who is in disagreement with the general consent has only one outlet-to separate from the *mir*, which means that he will not be a member of the village any more.'[10]

The proverbs which play such an important role in Russian peasant thought emphasize the same point: 'The *mir* is like a wave; one man's thought is everybody's thought.''The *mir's* conclusion is God's decision. '*Mir* is a great man.' 'The voice of the *mir* is the voice of God.'

This stress on unanimity and the merging of individual differences is so well known in contemporary Russian life that it does not need illustrating; the young Komsomol whom I quoted earlier said, 'I say "My generation" all the time and not "I" because we never thought of ourselves individually, but always as a whole group'.

This feeling of being merged into a larger group undoubtedly gains strength from the fact that most Great Russian children are brought up in the emotional and psychological equivalent of a very large family—all the members of a village or courtyard, uncles and aunts and cousins who all stand in nearly the same relation to the growing child as true brothers and sisters, mothers and fathers. This probably helps account for the fact that most Russians accept as a natural unit in which to live and work very large groups, by Occidental standards. In the same way a constant feature of their great plays and novels is an extremely large cast of characters compared with their Western equivalents. judging by their literary productions, one could

---

10. N. P. Semenov, *The Liberation of the Peasantry in the Reign of the Emperor Alexander III* (St. Petersburg, 1894).

say that the Russian imagination (or unconscious) is very densely populated, and often by not very sharply differentiated figures. I do not think it is merely the unfamiliar names which make it so difficult for most non-Russian readers to identify all the characters in the larger novels.

Once a child is finally weaned, it does not seem as though its relationship to its own parents (at least among the lower castes) differs much in kind (though it naturally does so in degree) from its relationship with other older people. To all such people the child is meant to show gratitude, respect, and obedience. Parents do not normally impose unexplained decisions on their growing children; the Russian father is generally pictured as a succouring and protective, rather than stern and frightening, figure. The relationship between parents and older children generally approximates to a mutually respectful equality. Even in early childhood the chief disciplinarian is likely to be the moody old *babushka* or *nyanya*, a generation older than the parents, in the decline of life, and not a model which the growing child would be likely to take for his or her own development.

This does not mean that the parents and the other adults of the parents' generation do not punish or scold the child; but the punishments they inflict, though severe, are likely to be capricious, because the child has done something to annoy them, not on account of his breaking some rule.

Comparative research from a number of contrasting societies appears to demonstrate unequivocally that the development of a strict conscience, so that people will behave according to ethical imperatives (or feel guilt if they do not do so), is dependent on the parents rewarding and punishing their children, giving or withholding their love, on the basis of conformity to consistent principles that the child can understand. Without such consistency the child cannot judge how the parents would view a given act when they are not present, and so cannot incorporate the parents' approval or disapproval. In other words, he will not develop a strong ethical conscience; without such incorporated rules he cannot feel the type of guilt which produces internal discomfort for specific transgressions of specific rules.

Guilt is only one of the devices which human societies have developed for controlling their members; other devices include fear of direct reprisal; shame (the fear of disapproval from the community, or some portion of it); and pride (hope for approval of the community, or some portion of it). Most societies place their chief reliance on one of these devices; but it is unusual not to find at least traces of the other mechanisms.

The evidence suggests that Great Russians rely heavily on public shaming for social control: the *mir* controlled its members by this device[11] more recent developments can be seen in the communist party's public purgings and 'self-criticism', and the holding up of individuals to public obloquy in the press and in factory newspapers.

The very unusual aspect of Great Russian character would appear to be the fact that this control by external shame is superimposed on more archaic diffuse guilt; the Great Russians neither possess the internalized ethical control which guides the conduct of most Occidentals [12] nor the relative freedom from unpleasant autonomous internal emotions which seems to be characteristic of these non-European societies which place their chief emphasis on shame, such as the Trobrianders, the Lepchas, and probably the Chinese. Great Russians manifest considerable interest in large ethical problems, but are apparently little occupied with moral rules of conduct.

6

Constriction would appear to be the only consistently painful experience of infancy and early childhood that Great Russians undergo. They are fed bountifully and regularly, they are fully protected (perhaps over-protected) from cold, and no disciplines beyond their physical capacity are demanded of them. Following this physiologically contented childhood it would appear understandable that little evidence can be found in adult life of anxiety about the attainability of physical gratifications; and it seems that they can postpone eating, drinking, rest (which is conceived as a positive pleasure), and other similar physical pleasures with ease and without psychological disturbance. Even under conditions of very great deprivation, most Russians maintain their optimistic belief that 'things cannot get worse, so they are bound to get better'.

What Russians value are not minimum gratifications—enough to get along with—but maximum total gratifications—orgiastic feasts, prolonged drinking bouts, high frequency of copulation, and so on. Nearly all Russians would seem to prefer a huge feast, followed by months of meagre fare, rather than a little improvement in their daily diet. These preferences were institutionalized in the religious observances of peasant Russia: the prolonged ritual fasts and the Gargantuan feasts with which Christmas and especially Easter were celebrated.

11. See p. 55, 'The Apology'.
12. See also below, p.147.

I think it is legitimate to trace a connexion between the total pleasure of the orgiastic feast,& c., and the total pleasure which the infant can be supposed to feel when it is unswaddled, nursed, and loved. Such gratifications are not merely pleasurable in themselves; they are patent and concrete reassurances that the projected rages and feared retaliation are not real, that the complete abandonment feared in depression has not taken place; total gratification—the orgy—provides an absolution for the diffuse guilt.

It seems probable that an unconscious search for such absolution underlay the prolonged drinking bouts which have been a feature of much peasant and working-class life (and also of the former merchants). Such drinking bouts were, it appears, periodic, lasted for several days at a time, and typically ended up with the destruction of much property; in the upper-caste drinking bouts a regular feature was the smashing of the mirrors in the restaurant.[13]

A very alert observer, Mrs. Oriana Atkinson, who spent several months in Moscow with her husband in 1946, relates the following suggestive anecdote about Russian drinking:

'The Russians have a story that they tell on themselves that really needs a Russian to tell it, but it goes like this. It is on the three stages of Russian drunkenness. (I) The Russian leans his head on one hand, his elbow on the table, holding his vodka glass in the other hand. He has been drinking but he is not drunk. He looks at his friend and he says, with deep sincerity, "You are my friend. You are the best friend that I have. I love you and trust you with all my heart. Yes, you are my best friend." And they have a couple of drinks on this. (2) Then the Russian continues, still leaning his head on his hand, his elbow on the table: "True, you are my best friend and I love you deeply. Although it is well known that you are a rascal, still 1 love you. I do not trust you, you and your sneaky friends. Everybody knows what a dastard you are, but I love you. Yes, I love you anyhow"; and they have a half-dozen drinks on that. (3) Then the speaker continues, his head still leaning on his hand, a little more heavily now: "My best friend!" he cries in scorn. "A fine friend you are! I am surrounded by enemies! Every man's hand is against me! Why do I not die?" And his head slips off his hand, his elbow slips off the table, he slips off his chair and falls on the floor. His friend regards him silently for a moment, and then carefully lies down beside him. They sleep.'[14]

13. A possible explanation of this smashing of mirrors might be that it represents a safe method of turning aggression against the self. As ego control becomes diminished under the influence of alcohol there might arise some sort of realization that the hostile and destructive wishes emanated from the self, and not from the others on whom they were projected. By destroying the mirror, which reflects the self, it may appear that the evil self is destroyed.

14. Oriana Atkinson, *Over at Uncle Joe's* (New York, BobbsMerrill Co., 1947), P. 36

7

Psychoanalysts have found that some people are 'compulsive' in respect to a group of character traits which are often linked together (though in varying force)-the traits of neatness, orderliness, economy,, punctuality, cleanliness, and the like; when such people have been psychoanalysed it has been found that a quite consistent aspect of their childhood experiences has been early and severe cleanliness training. By the standards common in the Occident the mass of Great Russians pay too little attention to these 'compulsive' traits; usual complaints of people who have to work with them is that they are chronically unpunctual, wasteful, careless, and so on.

This is one of the aspects where the contrast between the Soviet elites and the mass of the population is most marked; the Soviet leaders consider these traits of great social value and demand them from and, within the limits of possibility, impose them on the rest of the population. There is no evidence to show whether a conscious connexion is established between the high social value accorded to these traits and the Soviet demand that cleanliness training be started early (one of the recent child-rearing manuals demands that it should be imposed from the age of three months) and the imposition of such early discipline in the state-controlled clinics and creches.

8

We have practically no direct evidence concerning the vicissitudes of sexual life in childhood; but all the evidence from adult life suggests that this is not an area of psychological stress. Among the lower castes potency seems to be taken for granted, and there is little evidence to suggest that sex identification is a problem or that there are fears of an individual derogating from his or her sex. Outside the directly sexual sphere the physical differences between men and women are very little stressed; it could almost be said that the difference is restricted to the presence or absence of a phallus. In the case of necessity, Russian fathers appear capable of taking over all maternal activities other than actual suckling; in general the Russian father is far more 'maternal'in his treatment of his young children than the fathers of the other societies of north-western Europe.

Because of the certainty of sex identification, and the apparent lack of psychological involvement, Russians of the lower castes do not appear to develop strong psychological defences against homosexuality; in situations where they are separated from women for considerable periods they will indulge in homosexual practices with ease, and without apparent guilt.[15] In ordinary life tenderness between men is given free verbal and physical expression.

It is perhaps worth noting that the last two paragraphs do not apply to members of the former upper castes (nor, it would seem, to many of the intelligentsia). Possibly because they were chiefly brought up by governesses and tutors belonging to different cultures and with different standards, people of these castes tended to treat sex with deep affect and considerable ambivalence; neurotic disturbances and true inversion occurred and some parents seem to have been conscious of this risk. Havelock Ellis, quoting Tarnovski, says that, at the end of the nineteenth century, the lower castes referred to homosexual practices as 'noblemen's games'.[16]

Among the upper castes there was a fairly widespread belief in what might be called patrilineal and matrilineal characteristics. Women tended to describe their husbands and all their husbands' families as gross, inconsiderate, lustful, and coarse, and to describe themselves and all their own families as fine, delicate, sensitive, and spiritual. It should be noted that this is not identical with the ascription of certain qualities to all the members of one sex, such as is usual in the Occident; a man who will be seen by one woman as a delicate and sensitive brother, will be described by his wife as a coarse, inconsiderate, and sensual husband. When these characteristics were recognized, mothers, it would appear, were pleased when they could discover the 'matrilineal' characteristics in their sons, fathers when they could discover the 'patrilineal' characteristics in their daughters; mothers were pleased if their sons were spiritual, fathers if their daughters were sensual.

Together with this emotional complex of attitudes about sex there was generally very considerable verbal prudery in the upper castes and some of the intelligentsia; compared with their Continental contemporaries most Russian plays and novels are notably reticent, and even prudish. In some portions of the upper castes postmarital love-affairs were apparently frequent and passionate, becoming for some groups the chief occupation of adult life.

In the earlier years of the Soviet regime members of the communist party were required to be very abstemious in all physical indulgences; subsequently the laws and regulations were modified.

---

15. This fact is regularly noted in the many books (especially French) dealing with prisoner-of-war and concentration camps of mixed nationalities in Germany during the last war.

16. H. Ellis, *Psychology of Sex* (London, John Lane, 1936).

9

Although Great Russians can enjoy physical pleasures with great gusto and without apparent guilt, it seems as though they felt that nothing which happens to or with their bodies is of really major importance. The stoicism and endurance of the Russian peasant and Russian soldier have been often described, and often admired. John Rickman recalls that when he was doing medical work as a country doctor boys and girls, men and women would have two or even three teeth pulled out in a single session without any anaesthetic, and without showing a quiver of fear.

It seems comprehensible that people who pay so little attention to their own physical sufferings should also ignore those of others; and I think it probable that a good deal of behaviour which, if performed by Occidentals, would be deliberate cruelty, should rather be described as indifference when performed by Russians.

The vicissitudes of the body are of relatively little importance; the vicissitudes of the soul and of the emotions, on the other hand, are of overwhelming interest and importance. While swaddled, the Russian child has no control over his body; he can do nothing but endure the pains of constriction; all his attention is inevitably concentrated on his emotions.

At least until recent years, one of the greatest and most consistent pleasures that Russians enjoyed was giving verbal expression to the emotions momentarily possessing them, by talking in the presence of a 'sympathetic' listener. The presence of a 'sympathetic' listener is essential for the pleasure to be felt at its fullest; and by 'sympathetic' Russians do not seem to mean a person feeling the same or similar emotions, but a person who listens with feeling and understanding and without condemnation. Many Russians deny the possibility of non-Russians being 'sympathetic'. There are a number of expressions to denote this communication of emotion; one of the most common is 'pouring out the soul' *(izlivat dushu)*. The ideal situation of love or friendship is when two souls are poured out together so that they mingle-in some ways a worldly analogue of the Pentecostal *sobornost.*

Although a 'sympathetic' listener is ideal, any listener at all is better than none. The person to whom no one will listen is a constantly recurring pathetic figure in the works of Chekhov and other Russian writers; and the most consistent complaints from Russians who have left Russia since the beginning of the purge trials is that one can no longer say what one feels. This privation seems to bulk very much larger than the merely physical privations, which many Occidentals would find unbearable.

Of course, the desire to have a listener when one wants to talk is universal, but the psychological urgency with which Russians desire to express their emotions to another appears unusual and specific. It seems plausible that this urgency derives from the psychological de: fences against the infantile depressions, with their in tolerable feelings of numb loneliness; the presence of others is a patent sign that one has not been abandoned. In John Rickman's telling phrase, it is an 'unswaddling of the soul'. It is probably the same defences which make the cultivation and exploration of emotions, which most non-Russians would regard as painful, relatively pleasurable and rewarding to Russians: feeling, any feeling at all, becomes valuable in contrast to the agonized apathy of depression.

Nearly the whole of Russian literature bears witness to the intensity and zest with which Russians probe their thoughts and feelings; the common Anglo-Saxon parody of Russian plays stresses this point almost exclusively. The sitting-rooms of many Great Russians outside Russia which I have seen seem as though they were chiefly arranged to facilitate the pouting out of the soul: chairs grouped round small tables (for tea and vodka) with bright and usually unshaded lights immediately above them, so that nothing shall impede the flow of soul through the eyes.

Common Russian speech has a large vocabulary to describe emotions of varying degrees of intensity; and most Russians are articulate concerning the techniques by which unpleasant feelings can be removed or alleviated. The list which follows is illustrative, rather than exhaustive.

(I) Except for deeply religious people, and possibly the intelligentsia, the least important of the unpleasant states Russians recognize is the reproach of conscience *(soviest)*. Although this term is used for the religious concept of the 'internal voice', in common speech it generally refers to minor transgressions of politeness or etiquette. This depreciation of the concept of 'conscience' is congruent with the hypothesis of the low potential of internalized ethical parental figures. For the laity faults of conscience can be removed by formal apologies which need not be sincere.

(II) An infraction of the law or of social usage is termed *vina*. This is absolved by the appropriate punishment, without any necessary emotional change on the part of the transgressor. In this it is distinguished from

(III) a sense of sin *(grekh)* which can only be removed when the sinner has reached a state of highly emotional repentance and is then given absolution by the priest or other appropriate figure. In the case of sin the absolver's emotions are not taken into account.

(IV) To get rid of a sense of shame *(stid)* however, it is essential to induce the appropriate emotions of understanding and 'sympathy' in the person or persons wronged before they can absolve you; this is usually produced by long demonstrations of the 'sincerity' of the transgressor's repentance. The 'sincerity'refers to the strength and unambiguity of the transgressor's emotions, and not necessarily to the truthfulness of his explanations.[17]

The states so far discussed arise from actions, whether intentional or not, on the part of the sufferer; those that follow are either seen as spontaneous or as due to the behaviour of others.

(V) *Stradanyie* can probably be best translated as 'mental'suffering'. It is the emotion felt for unrequited love, for the unfaithfulness or coarseness or lack of understanding of lover or spouse, and similar situations. It can be removed by a change in the emotions which gave importance to the person provoking stradanyie.

(VI) *Skuka* corresponds in some ways to boredom, ennui, the 'spleen' of Baudelaire and his contemporaries, a feeling of loneliness and uselessness, perhaps an attenuated version of depression. *Skuka* descends on the sufferer autonomously, without being provoked by any conscious action; if he can change his situation and start 'driving on' again, *skuka* may disappear.

(VII) There does not seem to be a single English word to correspond to the feelings described by *toska*, though the Latin word *desiderium* carries many of the same meanings. O'Brien's dictionary gives 'anguish, affliction, pain, grief; weariness, boredom, oppression, homesickness', and as an adjective or verb 'afflicted, grieved, anxious, melancholy, sad, to pine away, to long for'. The feeling of yearning for the unattainable is probably the most common aspect. *Toska* descends on a person autonomously, and there is nothing that the sufferer can do, except wait for it to pass away.[18]

(VIII) Finally, there is the concept of *pozar*, disgrace. This is really in a rather different category; it is the feeling of shame and humiliation resulting from the behaviour of other people whom one feels to be akin with oneself. It is indelible unless, or until, the situation is reversed. On the personal level it is produced by the dishonourable conduct of a person near and dear to one—a brother embezzling, a sister (in the upper castes) having an illegitimate child. This emotion can also be felt on a national scale; Stalin's speech on the defeat of Japan in 1945, when he recalled what 'we of the older generation' had

---

17. 'The Apology', P. 5 5, seems to illustrate this situation very concretely.

18. Many of Chekhov's characters illustrate *toska*; the Three Sisters is perhaps particularly clear.

felt after the Russo-Japanese war, illustrates the final wiping out of national *pozor*. Before the Revolution the feeling of *pozar* was not much cultivated or dwelt on; it is an emotion to which the communists have publicly appealed a great deal; and they have probably lessened its impact by too frequent recourse to it. The communists have also greatly extended the pre-revolutionary use of the emotion of shame, *stid*, and appear to consider this emotion of great social value.

Before the Revolution, schools for the upper castes gave what amounted to lessons in the cultivation and expression of the emotions, by laying great stress on the evocation of the appropriate moods in the pupils when they were confronted with different works of art, above all literature. The enjoyment of such expression was not, however, confined to the upper castes; peasants had little else to do during the enforced idleness of the long Russian winter.

The Soviet élites have always been most deeply opposed to this proclivity of the mass of the Russians, and have done everything possible by education and edict to force its abandonment. Their objections seem to be founded on two arguments. It is absolutely bad for a communist to allow his will to be subordinated to his emotions, such as occurs when the soul is filled with suffering or ennui; and it is socially undesirable that attention and emotion should be directed inwards, on the feelings which cannot be modified, instead of outwards, on the material objects of the environment, when thought can be the prelude of purposeful action. Although this training and propaganda has probably been successful among the more disciplined elites there is good reason for doubting whether the behaviour has been abandoned by the mass of Great Russians, although some of the vocabulary may no longer be generally current.

10

A trait of Great Russian character which has been frequently commented on by Russians and non-Russians alike are the sudden switches and alternations from one type of behaviour to another in complete contrast to the first. One of the great Russian character actors illustrated this trait with great vividness:

'In Russian nature there's only the breadth of a split hair between cruel, coarse, abject brutality and the greatest warmth and tenderness. The peasants will curse the Virgin Mary and a moment later kiss the hem of her dress. In the Civil War, which was in many ways more cruel than the war of the Vendee—and that was on both sides—a friend told me about a Red Company in South Russia which was cleaning up the area, one of the most cruel and pitiless groups in the whole Red Army. Well, one day this group came to a burnt-out village, without a living soul, and suddenly they heard a baby crying; they looked and found a baby just a few weeks old, alive, lying beside the corpse of his mother. Well, half-drunk and dirty bandits though they were, they took the baby and then they asked, "Who will nurse the baby?" So they invaded the next village and took a woman with a baby of the same age and killed her husband and said to her, "Citizen, you must serve the Revolution". They dragged this woman round with them several weeks, and made her nurse her own baby and the baby of the company. They took a pair of scales and used to weigh both babies on the balance every day to make certain she was feeding the company baby properly. If the company baby weighed less than hers did, they used to beat her for cheating; but during the fighting they would all protect this woman and her two babies and keep them in the rear. When they finally returned to Moscow they gave the woman one of the highest awards and made her chief nurse in an institution for orphans … This is just one example of the mixture of brutality and cruelty, and sympathy and warmth. In the midst of battle they were more engaged in protecting the babies than their own selves.'

A young girl who was in Danzig when it was conquered by the Russians gave a number of other examples. The soldiers would 'go and steal anything which was left in one house and then go to the next house and give everything to the children there, beaming as if they'd given the most wonderful presents'. After they'd raped girls, 'they'd often pat them gently on the shoulders and talk consolingly to them, as if to say "Now you've done your duty"'. She told of letters she had received from girl-friends who had returned from forced work in Russia: 'They [the girls] were made to do very hard work in enormous heat with nothing to eat or drink except one tin of watery soup until they broke down. But if they broke down or got ill they were taken to a hospital and treated with the greatest care and given every possible luxury-lots of cream and cakes and everything like that. But the second they were fit to work, they were turned out again and put back on the starvation regime.'

These switches from kindness to cruelty, from brutality to gentleness could be endlessly illustrated. They are very disconcerting to most non-Russians. There is a frequently repeated prototype to this dramatic and sudden change of feeling in the infantile experience of most Great Russians. At one moment they are lonely, filled with rage, constricted by the swaddling; the next moment their limbs are free, they are held in warm and strong arms and given the bountiful breast. Then this freedom and bliss in its turn comes to an end; the babies are wrapped up as though they were unfeeling parcels and left alone with their emotions.

Chapter III

THE ENEMY AND HATE

1

*I*f the arguments advanced in the last chapter are correct, it will follow that the majority of Great Russians have a diffuse feeling of guilt, which is largely or entirely unconscious, and a diffuse feeling of fear, derived from the projection of their infantile hostility. This fear would appear to take the form of an emotional conviction that there exists in the external world an enemy (or enemies) who plan to constrict and destroy them, but no sort of certainty concerning the identity of the enemy.

The theory and practice of the Orthodox Church took these feelings into consistent account, and gave relief to them; the malicious enemy was identified as the devil and his minions, and minute ritual instructions were given for warding him off; the pervading sense of guilt could be at least temporarily assuaged by a full confession (or, more properly, admission of guilt) followed by ritual absolution. The practices of the Orthodox Church fulfilled a most important function in Russian society by making tolerable the greatest psychological stresses; as is common with such institutions, it also maintained these stresses and induced them (though perhaps to a somewhat attenuated degree) in those whose individual experiences or constitution differed from the norm.

Russians who believed in and practised Orthodox Christianity received enormous psychological alleviation from the absolution which followed confession; they felt freed from their guilt, and could believe that other sinners who confessed and contritely asked forgiveness could also be freed from guilt. In every Orthodox household, before the Easter confession, each member would solemnly ask the forgiveness of every other member, irrespective of age or status.

When, however, Great Russians ceased to practise Orthodox Christianity they had no technique left (with the possible exception of the orgy) for ridding themselves even temporarily of the oppression of unconscious guilt; and consequently they could not admit that others could be absolved, however completely they confessed and repented. If one's own guilt cannot be alleviated, then an enemy who has been identified appears to be irremediably wicked, and almost without human qualities, as though he were an incarnation of the scriptural devil no longer consciously believed in. As an exceptionally high-minded and religious noblewoman said of her schoolteachers, 'We thought of many of our teachers as enemies, and because they were our enemies all sorts of things were allowed. If you are my enemy I can cheat you and lie to you.' When the most high-principled persons could hold such attitudes towards people they had decided were their enemies without conscious guilt, it is understandable that atheists should deny almost all human qualities to enemies who are 'unmasked'. Only complete abjection, followed by prolonged and rigorous 're-education', can permit such near-devils to go on living.

2

The Russian language is a very rich one on nearly every level; and it therefore seems significant that there are very few common-speech terms (as opposed to literary words) to identify the enemy. Perhaps the most usual phrase is *tyomniye sili*—dark or sinister forces.[1] This term is completely vague; the dark forces might be anywhere and anyone, inside or outside the individual, the group, the country. All that can be certainly known about these dark forces is their plan (conspiracy, intention) to constrain and destroy.

The most straightforward identification of dark forces in the real (as contrasted with the supernatural) world is the contemporary secular authority or forces responsible for existing constraints. Russian history, up till recent years, contains a considerable number of conspiracies to assassinate and actual assassination of figures of authority. Perhaps even more revealing is the fact that Russians in positions of authority seem to expect those they control to attempt assassination and take very elaborate precautions to ward off this eventuality.

---

1. *Tyomniye* means in the first place dark, but by implication sinister, suspicious, evil. To a certain extent the antonym is *Krasniye* which means in the first place red, but by implication beautiful and bright. in Russian the terms 'Red Army', 'Red Square', and so on, have also the overtone of beauty, brightness, the opposite of dark and sinister.

If it is believed that authority is evil, suspicious, and pervasive, attempts to overthrow it must be masked with very elaborate techniques of conspiracy. These techniques are gradually becoming known to the nonRussian world through the imitative practices of contemporary communist parties. Besides secretiveness and dissimulation, they include the testing of aspirant members by ordeal instead of by investigation, public and covert authorities, and the use of *agents provocateurs*. These techniques of conspiracy seem to be Russian rather than specifically communist. To illustrate this assumption I propose to give a long excerpt from an interview with a man who was a member of the Social Revolutionary party[2] when he was a student at Kazan University and the Moscow Institute during the first decade of this century. My informant was a younger son of a 'white' priest.

'My father's brother belonged to the People's Will party and spent many years in prison, but father was friendly with him and showed no animosity when he was free. The People's Will party was the mother of the S.R. party. … For me and my older brother it was as though my uncle were a founder of the S.R. party so it was natural for me to join that in out Real school. Despite many friends among the Marxists, I never thought I could become one and I never was. I read Marx but he didn't impress me. The road I followed was a very natural one. It began in Réal school with schoolboys being organized into small groups to combat the régime. Generally they were cultural groups, but all were filled with politicians. …

'It's difficult to tell the principle of selection. The life of a revolutionist was very short. … If a group of eight or ten, say, were organized, after a couple of years some of these would have run away or been arrested. And then you've got a smaller group, and then you take in new recruits and the older ones inevitably become kind of leaders. The police used to plant agents everywhere, not as leaders, and then they would arrest most of the leaders and the police agent would become more important to the new people as an old revolutionary. And by such tricks they promoted their agents. And that applied to all close revolutionary movements. With general student organizations, they were about 10 per cent. legal and go per cent. illegal. Usually the leaders would come from the secret party groups. It was impossible to build leadership up in any normal way. Membership in small revolutionary groups was more important than position in bigger public groups …'

Q. 'How did that work?'

A. 'For example in Kazan University there were about 5,000 people in some of the big student organizations, and then there were the small secret organizations. … If there was a general meeting of, say, one or two thousand people, the revolutionary organization would present its most eloquent people-not usually a regular member of the organization for fear of the police. If you found a person who was ready to promote the

2. The programme of the S.R. stressed agrarian reform, and distrusted the urban workers.

ideas which the party believed in, he would be authorized to become
the public speaker. ... He had influence on the public but not on party
members. ...'

Q. 'Exactly how did you become a member of the S. R.?'

A. 'My older brother was a member. He never told me but I felt it and
knew it when I was thirteen or fourteen. Then I became a member of a
group which listened to lectures on economics-the lecturer was an S.R.
man who was supposed to be very dangerous and very revolutionary. We
met secretly in one another's apartments, and then later on he—no, it
was somebody else showed me secret leaflets, very badly mimeographed,
and I began to read those. Next somebody gave me a secret mimeographed book to read. It was a book by an American journalist, what is his
name?—a man who was invited by Count Witte to inspect Siberia and see
that the exiles were not badly treated, and he became converted to their
views. It was a book on prison and exile—oh, yes, the author's name was
George Kennan. He showed sympathy but no more. That book was terribly secret and dangerous and I was just given it to read for two or three
nights. Later on I was given literature and pamphlets to disseminate to
others. And little by little I was offered to become a party member after I
had performed some difficult tasks. We were living in a conspiracy so the
general rule was: never tell, if you had no need to tell, with whom you
have connexions, or who belongs to the party. In that way the police
could be isolated.'

Q. 'What sort of people were the police spies?'

A. 'I am happy to say that I only met two *agents provocateurs* and they
were not my friends ...

Q. 'Have you any idea how these student agents were recruited?'

A. 'Mostly by intimidation. The police would arrest a young person
who was very successful and with whom everything was going all right,
but who was a party member or close to the party. They would catch him
with leaflets, and that would mean three years' detention in an honourable prison, and then he would inevitably be sent for three, four or
five years to exile in Siberia. Such a boy would be involved because he
would be betrayed by a gendarme and then they would give him his
choice. [Informant suddenly changed his voice and manner, till now
rather loud and jovial, very markedly. His voice became very gentle and
insinuating and almost feminine, and at the same time he seemed to
hunch up his body.] "It's a pity for a boy like you to wreck your life in this
way, and we could easily come to an arrangement. We don't want you to
do anything bad, but tell us . . ." And so the boy became an agent and was
given assignments, usually very easy ones at first, and then little by little
they would spoil him. They used to go to committee meetings and then
report back. Some became nihilists and would kill a gendarme to clear
themselves of guilt.'

3

At about the turn of the twentieth century (if not earlier) the Russian
authorities extended the employment of a technique for diverting

from themselves the free-floating unfocused hostility of the mass of the population. This technique consisted in pointing out to the masses that there were other groups who were planning to oppress, constrain, and destroy them, with the implication (usually tacit) that the removal of existing authorities would lay the masses open to even greater constrictions. These malevolent dark forces can be discovered anywhere; they may be any foreign nation, Jews, Trotskyists, fascists, capitalists, and so on endlessly; they may be vague and far away, or they may be people very near to one-fellow-students, fellow-workers, managers, generals, high officials. This technique has been very highly developed in the last thirty years; and to-day one of the chief functions of authority is to 'unmask' and point out to the rest of the population who their enemies are.

If the hypothesis of free-floating unfocused hostility is correct, it would be understandable that Great Russians would be relieved, rather than disconcerted, by being informed that individuals or nations whom they had formerly considered friends were really 'masked' enemies;[3] they would also probably not be disturbed by the 'unmasking' of former allies and associates which has characterized Soviet foreign policy in recent years. From such evidence as is available, it would appear that many Russians were disconcerted on the unique occasion when the reverse situation took place (the Ribbentrop-Molotov pact) and an enemy was revealed as 'really' benevolent. At least to-day Russians do not admit of neutrality: he who is not completely for them is 'objectively' potentially hostile, however friendly his overt feelings or behaviour. Implicit in much current Soviet writing is the belief that no praise of the U.S.S.R. on the part of non-communist foreigners is sincere and spontaneous. If it is not hypocritical and intended to deceive, it has been extorted grudgingly and unwillingly. It is almost certainly significant that the only complicated psychological concept which is employed consistently by Russian Marxists is the concept of unconscious hostility.

4

Once an enemy has been 'unmasked' and identified, what should be done? It would appear that this is a question where the Soviet elite and the intelligentsia tend to give a different answer to Great Russians belonging to the traditional castes.

3. For a schematic illustration of this process, see the account of the phases of Russian drunkenness, quoted on p. 140.

For the latter the proper response to the identification of an enemy Is an attack of destructive rage, *zloba* which may involve the exercise of violence, but which is quickly over. For the intelligentsia and the Soviet elites the proper response is hatred-persistent, conscious, cold negative feelings which should not be allowed to lapse. It is significant that the only word for hate—*nyenavist*—is a learned, literary word which apparently has little currency in ordinary speech.

It would seem as though an attack of rage had a somewhat cathartic effect (perhaps similar to the 'righteous anger' recognized by Anglo-Saxons) and is not avoided; and that violence—especially emotional violence—becomes valued *as an instrument* in liberating one temporarily from the diffuse unconscious guilt and fear and destroying the confusions produced by the dark forces. In the infantile situation postulated in the previous chapter, the infant was not overwhelmed by depression as long as he was raging and pushing against the constraints; and the depression would cease with the return of the feelings of rage.

On an unconscious, or at least on an unverbalized, level, lower-caste Russians would appear to establish some connexion between violence and sexual potency. Wife-beating would appear to be a not unusual phenomenon in lower-caste marital life; and it would seem as though beating bore some relation to copulation, for beater and beaten alike. Numerous proverbs stress the point: 'Love your wife like your own soul, shake her like a pear tree'; 'Blows from one dear to you don't hurt for long'; 'I like him, so I beat him'.

In so far as violence is positively valued as an instrument for liberating one from the feelings of guilt and fear, it tends to be treated like directly physical pleasures in which quantity becomes of great psychological importance. It seems as though Russians felt a continuous psychological compulsion to go all the time to the limit of their strength and endurance. One can only know that one has gone to the limit of one's strength (done all that one should do) by a feeling of complete exhaustion, or by coming against an indestructible barrier and being repulsed and pushed back. This may be an analogue of the infantile situation in which depression is warded off by constant pushing against the constraining bonds of swaddling. It is probably this feeling which makes the tactical retreat so acceptable to Russians, Czarist and Soviet alike.[4]

---

4. It should be noted that although the notion of being pushed back, after one has exerted all one's strength, is acceptable, the notion of weakness, of riot having the strength to exert, is almost intolerable. I have never interviewed willing informants from any other society who were so incapable of recalling incidents from their own childhood; it is as though all memories of the period of physical weakness were suppressed.

The objection of the Soviet élite to attacks of rage which are quickly over would seem to be of the same nature as their objections to the cultivation of the emotions: the feelings should be controlled by the will for useful social ends. Consequently in their view while anger is individualistic and undesirable, hatred is a valuable quality in the Soviet citizen and should be cultivated. The teaching of hatred plays a major role in the 1946 text-book for Soviet school-teachers already quoted:

'A morally educated individual, according to our understanding, is one who in his conduct subordinates his own interests to the service of his Motherland and his people. Such service presupposes wrath and hatred towards the enemies of the Motherland who imperil the battle-won rights of the people and all that has been created in the realm of material and cultural life by both the old and the younger generation.'

'The pupils of the Soviet school must realize that the feeling of Soviet patriotism is saturated with irreconcilable hatred toward the enemies of socialist society. Hatred gives birth to class revolutionary vigilance and creates a feeling of irreconcilability toward the class enemy; the weakness of such vigilance undermines the cause of the socialist revolution. It is necessary to learn, not only to hate the enemy, but also to struggle with him, in time to unmask him, and finally, if he does not surrender, to destroy him.'

'In all educational work devoted to the preparation of future citizens to defend the Motherland, it is necessary to remember that to vanquish the enemy is impossible without the most burning hatred of him. Passionate love of the Motherland breeds inevitably strong hatred of the enemy. Enslavers of people, destroyers of culture, and stranglers of liberty are hated by all to whom the freedom and independence of the Motherland are dear.'

'Stalin links the question of education in patriotism and in friendship between peoples with education in hatred toward enemies of the people and enemies of the Motherland.[5]

I should like to draw attention to the vagueness with which the target for this cultivated hatred is described The enemy 'imperils battle-won rights', 'enslaves people, destroys culture, strangles liberty', is filled with malevolence; but, save that he does not devour the soul, what human traits does he possess? The Soviet schoolchild should be taught to hate; but this hatred appears to be as free-floating and unfocused as the guilt and fear which I have postulated for their earliest experiences.

5.   Yesipov and Goncharov, op. cit., PP. 42, 62, 70, 146.

Chapter IV

THE LEADER, LOVE, AND TRUTH

1

Since the later middle ages, and with a certain amount of interruption in the earlier years of the Soviet régime, political authority in Russia appears to have possessed two components: a Leader who is held to be allwise and all-knowing, the embodiment of Truth and Foresight; and a minutely graded hierarchy of officials to carry out the wishes, plans, and revelations of the Leader and to transmit and interpret them to the mass of the population.

The emotional bonds between the Leader and the mass of the population have always been of a very different nature to the emotional bonds between the officials and the mass of the population. In the former case there is the greatest emotional closeness; in the latter very great emotional separation.

The Leader, whether Czar, Lenin or Stalin, has always been completely idealized by the mass of the population which loyally adheres to the régime; he is, in the most literal sense of the word, superhumanly perfect in knowledge, truth, and foresight. This belief is beyond the reach of conscious criticism. The girl who was in Danzig during the Russian conquest said of the Russian soldiers: 'They are terribly patriotic and worship Stalin, and when they get drunk they say this even more loudly'; other observers report similar behaviour; a "white" priest spoke of 'The Czar who is the hand of God Himself'; and a passionate anti-communist said 'Stalin is the conscience of the Russian people, but in a very perverted way'.

This idealized Leader is an aspect of the mass of the Great Russian people, and in some fashion as it were a part of them, in so far as they accept him. This is illustrated for example by the fact that formerly peasants addressed the Czar with the familiar 'thou', instead of the honorific phrases they would use to officials; on ceremonial occasions to-day millions of marchers carrying huge pictures of Stalin march past Stalin, so that Stalin salutes himself as he marches past in millions of bodies. Similarly, Stalin joins the mass in applauding what he himself has just said. Stalin's constant use of the rhetorical device in which he both asks the questions and gives the answers may reflect the same concept.

Although the Leader is as it were a projection of the mass of the population, he is so idealized that the ordinary person cannot imagine himself thinking or feeling as the Leader would do, when he does not have the necessary information. This point can perhaps be most clearly seen by means of a contrast with the typical attitude of the Japanese (before their defeat) to their Emperor. Although the Japanese regarded their Emperor with the greatest veneration, it was always theoretically possible for a Japanese to know (as it were by introspection) what the Imperial will was, and to act accordingly. The typical excuse for political assassinations was that the persons assassinated were 'failing to carry out the will of the Emperor'; this implies that the assassin, his judges, and the public opinion to which he appealed, had means of knowing the will of the Emperor which were not dependent on the Emperor's pronouncements on the situation or person in question. On a less marked level, an English or American ship's captain, for example, can make decisions as the King's or President's representative without feeling (in many cases) the necessity for prior consultation and concrete authorization. With the mass of Great Russians this is not the case. They cannot know the Leader's will, in small things or great, until the Leader has declared it. Once the Leader has made the declaration, the Russians will dedicate all their energies, and easily their own lives, to the fulfilment of the expressed commands, wishes or plans. No ordinary considerations can stand in the way of carrying out the Leader's will; a course of action so started can only be stopped or reversed by the Leader himself making another statement of his will. The excesses and sudden reverses of Soviet domestic policy in recent years illustrate this situation clearly.

It would seem as though this very great idealization of the Leader were a psychological necessity to the mass of Great Russians. With the all-pervasive unconscious hostility and guilt engendered by their infantile experiences, their psychological well-being (perhaps on a certain level even their sanity) depends on preserving in the external world at least one figure completely uncontaminated by the all-pervading suspicion and fear, a figure which has no human frailties, which stands as a safeguard against their own guilt and its consequences.

It has been a commonplace of psychoanalytic thinking to trace a correspondence between the social figures of authority, and the earlier familial figures of authority in childhood, so that the king, or officer or policeman, can be viewed as a 'father-surrogate'. Despite the use of the term 'little father'to address the Czar (and, on occasion, Stalin) I do not think this is a major component in the figure of the Leader; to a great extent the Leader represents the idealized self rather than any figures in the child's environment. This concept is impossible to prove with the evidence now available, and difficult to substantiate; it was first suggested to me by such phrases as the one already quoted about Stalin being 'the conscience of the Russian people', and the consistency with which former Imperial officers spoke of the duty of the army to 'mother the Czar'. Such an idiom from martial men about their martial duties appeared very unusual. The mother is a strong, protective, and succouring figure to the young child; if the officers feel that they stand in a similar relation to the Czar, then, on an unconscious level, the Czar is a child, but a completely idealized child.

This hypothesis is not merely of theoretical importance. If it is correct it would imply that it would be psychologically intolerable for Great Russians to live for any length of time without an idealized Leader, that a Leader is necessary to save them from political anarchy and personal disintegration.

2

The Leader guides and directs the mass of the population through the agency of a minutely graded hierarchy of officials who are under him and over the people. On occasion the Leader will by-pass this official hierarchy to enter into direct communication with some of the people and right wrongs perpetrated by his agents in his name (but without his knowledge); but such interventions can only be occasional and spasmodic, for otherwise he would be distracted from his most important work. As Lenin once remarked, 'You mustn't stroke anyone's head-you might get your hand bitten off.'[1] (Stroking the head is the conventional way in which a Great Russian father demonstrates his love for his child.)

During the greater part of Russian history, most of the positions in the hierarchy of authority were determined by heredity, but even

1. M. Gorky, Days with Lenin (New York, International Publishers, 1932), P. 52.'

then there were some (especially in the ecclesiastical hierarchy) which were achieved by personal abilities and ambition, even though the competition was generally within a restricted group. Since 1917 the great majority of positions have been achieved; in the early years of the Soviet régime heredity counted negatively, inasmuch as individuals might be disbarred from positions of authority, whatever their personal qualifications, if their parents were of a disapproved social class; there are some slight signs to-day that heredity is again being counted positively, for example the military cadet schools reserved for the sons of higher officers in the Soviet army.

There are at least two prerequisites for the achievement of positions of authority: knowledge through education (which is consequently extremely highly valued by those who seek or respect authority); and the renunciation of immediate pleasures. Among the pleasures which must always be renounced to achieve authority is the feeling of oneness with one's fellows, and the indulgence of emotions for their own sake; both must be replaced by conscious internal discipline. Other types of renunciation which have, or have had, power to give authority are the renunciation of sexuality and all worldly goods (which gave the 'black'priests their authority) and the abandonment of the exercise of free will and judgement, the ascetic life, and the shortening of life itself by overwork (which gave the members of the communist party their authority).[2] It is perhaps justifiable to suggest that the current policy of the leaders of the Soviet Union is to achieve authority for themselves and their country by the renunciation on the part of the mass of the population of all direct gratifications, and by using these renunciations to forge the weapons of conquest.

It is interesting to note that the Great Russians apparently do not hold the belief that authority is more suited to people of certain character types than it is to others. Such notions as 'potential leadership', 'initiative', and so on, which bulk so large in Anglo-Saxon thinking, have no place in theirs. Education, obedience, and the will-power to renounce present pleasures should, it would seem, automatically bring with them the other necessary qualifications. In the Czarist military cadet schools 'authority among the cadets in the classes was given by marks, not by physical appearance or proficiency in drill, or marksmanship or anything like that. Of course, if a person got good marks, he should get the other qualities later, even though he might

2. Scattered evidence suggests that in contemporary Russia the rank-and-file members of the communist party no longer have special authority nor enjoy special respect. This may be connected with the tripling of the number of party members during the war years.

not be a good disciplinarian ... Prestige was given directly along intellectual lines, and then you should climb up to proficiency in the
other branches.'Another informant, who was in a position to know,
said that in current recruiting for membership in the communist
party and some of its branches 'the first quality looked for is pliabil-
ity, that is to say, people who will do what they are told without argu-
ing or questioning. Too much book-reading, unless it is directly
connected with professional work, is considered, an undesirable quality. So, too, is initiative, except in direct connexion with work.'

There is even some evidence to suggest that 'natural leaders' who
create circles of students and so on around themselves are looked on
askance; their ascendancy is likely to be due to their defiance of existing authority. Thus school-teachers are warned 'Sometimes friendship between children is formed on the basis of negative interests or
even harmful mutual "enterprises". On noticing such a development
the teacher should take measures ... to destroy the friendship by dis-
pelling the halo of the "friend-leader" ...'[3]

As has already been said, people who become members of the
hierarchy of authority abandon all feelings of identification with their
fellows, and as a consequence all feelings of equality. An illustration
of this can be found in the use of a pronominal adjective; ordinary
nonofficial Great Russians habitually speak of 'our peasants'; officials
speak of 'the peasants'. Somewhat similar is Stalin's instruction to
teachers: 'People must be grown carefully and tenderly, just as a gardener grows a favourite fruit tree.'[4] A gardener may give his favourite
fruit trees the best possible care, the most ideal treatment; but this can
never imply a feeling of identity or equality between the gardener and
what he cares for.

Among those in authority, the feeling of equality is replaced by
the most rigid insistence on hierarchy and one's relative position in it;
members of the governing elite show the greatest intellectual contempt for the concept of *urapnilovka*-egalitarianism, the attempt to
make equal those who are naturally unequal. It seems probable that
one reason why communists are so much more hostile towards and
contemptuous of social democrats (Labour) than of more right-wing
parties abroad is because of their adherence to this despised doctrine.

The preoccupation with relative status in the Russian official hierarchy would seem to be a major source of the 'bureaucratic spirit'
which is so constantly inveighed against and satirized in Czarist and
Soviet speeches, books and periodicals.

3. Yesipov and Goncharov, op. cit., p. 61.
4. Ibid. p.38

3

The relationship between the elite in authority and the mass of the population they constrain and guide is ideally one of complete superordination and subordination, of activity on the one side and of passivity on the other.

This is the ideal, but it is only attained under certain conditions. just as those in positions of authority abandon their feeling of 'oneness' with the mass of the people over whom they are placed in authority, so do the mass of the people apparently feel that those in authority are 'apart' from themselves. This would seem to be a derivative of the fact that the earliest constraining 'authority'-the swaddling-is not part of the self, and is not personified.

The analogy of swaddling illustrates very clearly the relations that exist between people in authority and people under authority. The qualities most demanded from authority is that it should be firm and consistent, neither too tight nor too loose, and, above all, not shifting capriciously from excessive severity to excessive lenience. There seems to be a general tendency to'test' authority; if it is not firm and consistent, it will be first disregarded and then cast off.

For obvious reasons, it was impossible to do consistent interviewing on attitudes to accepted political authority; it was a subject fraught with too much danger in the greater number of cases. I therefore concentrated on what appeared to be the nearest 'safe' and nonpolitical analogue to political authority, the attitude towards teachers and schoolmasters. These attitudes, both from informants brought up under the Czarist régime and from those brought up under the Soviets, fell into two sharply contrasting groups: an attitude of mutually respectful equality, indicated by the fact that teacher and pupil addressed one another in identical terms (first name and patronymic); and the treatment of the teacher as somebody alien and potentially hostile. The most eloquent illustration of this latter attitude was given by the Czarist cadet, already quoted; similar attitudes were expressed by people brought up under the Soviets, but with less clarity. He was talking about cliques among the students, and said that some of them had their chief interest in fighting authority. I asked what he meant:

A. 'It all depended on who was in authority. If it was a weak person advantage was taken of him very cruelly and unfairly. If he was strong, he was respected and liked, odd as it may seem. And if there was a strange man, life was made hell for him. He was just hounded.'

Q. 'What happened?'

A. 'Cadets used to see how far they could go. There were some specialists in the fight against authority, and the class would observe what happened to them. In my clique, we were intellectual challengers, and we would argue and resist on an intellectual plane.'

Q. 'And what would happen if it was a strong man?'

A. 'Oh, he would slap down opposition. What we liked above all was consistency. We hated people who were strong one day and weak another.'

Q. 'Was there friendship between the professors and cadets ?'

A. 'No, you'd never say there was any real friendship; it was very formal.'

Q. 'And when you say you made life hell for a stranger, what does that mean?'

A. 'Oh, we'd tease him and shout and wouldn't listen to him. We'd turn our backs when he spoke.   We'd put pins and thumb-tacks on his chairs, smelly nutmegs on the end of his pencil, and anything else.

Q. 'Could you tell lies to the teacher?'

A. 'Oh, sure. We all lied to our teachers. It was all right to lie to any of our superiors, but not to other students. There was a feeling that teachers were, you might say, fair game ... You could lie to defend yourself. A few didn't but most of them did if they were accused. There was a lot more lying than one would have thought. In Russia there was much antagonism to the teachers as such. The teachers never took the students into their confidence. You could say it was really a battle of wits against authority. No co-operation was attempted. It was a warfare.'

Thus far the Czarist pupil of more than thirty years ago. Note how closely his attitudes correspond with the instructions given to Soviet school-teachers in 1946:

'Moral demands must always be made upon schoolchildren in a decisive form and be carried into life with firm insistence. It is entirely inadmissible for a teacher at one time to punish pupils strictly for errors, and at another "not to notice".'

'Consistency must be observed by all adults who share in the rearing of the young. The several teachers of a given child should not contradict each other, but rather should follow a single line. As his teachers change, provision should be made for an orderly and consistent sequence of influences. When a child passes with age from certain teachers to others, he suffers injury if he encounters an entirely different treatment, if, for example, mildness changes sharply to severity, or if *firmness changes to weakening softness.*'

'An individual possessing volitional qualities of character is consistent; with him words do not contradict deeds and acts harmonize with convictions. Children form their convictions in school and become habituated to conscious and definite consistency in their actions. These traits of character are developed gradually and in the face of serious difficulties.'[5]

---

5.   Yesipov and Goncharov, *op. cit.*, PP. 46, 49, 122. My italics.

4

In all relations which are not defined as leader and led, superordinate and subordinate, Great Russians who are not in the authority hierarchy demand the most absolute equality in their personal relationships. It would appear that Russians do not conceive of any intermediate positions: there is either complete equality, or complete superordination and subordination. This may derive from the situation in which the infant experiences weakness as the absolute weakness of depression, not the relative biological weakness of being smaller. For the Great Russians, weakness, like power, is absolute.

Some examples of this demand for equality, until it almost becomes a merging of personalities, have already been given, and more could easily be found: the village mir and the Soviets and collectives formed on the same model, the Pentecostal experience of sobornost. Situations which outside Russia are viewed as competitive or exhibitionist will often be rephrased by Russians as positions of symmetrical equality. Thus the great actor, already quoted, compared the relationship between actor and audience to that between tennis partners! 'I don't play for the audience-that is cheap and bad-but with the audience. There is no rivalry, no looking for effect, but pure sport. You send the ball to the audience and they send it back to you. If you lose the ball that is your fault. But if the audience misses the ball, you win. The audience misses the ball when you place it where they don't expect it and they are surprised.'

Many of the dramatic changes which have taken place in the organization of the Red Army can, I think, be traced to the fact that the Russians can envisage no alternative between the most complete superordination and stress on rank, and complete equality. An observer who saw something of the Red Guard in the early days of the Revolution wrote:

'The Bolshevik recruits were familiar with the village form of government. It was therefore natural that they should introduce into their army the same type of administration and discipline which obtains in the mir or village council. In our sense of the word, discipline was lax, but the spirit of brotherhood was strong, and the men were accustomed to acting upon the compelling force, not of orders from a superior officer, but of the will of the meeting. Putting this into other words, the men obeyed a committee of the regiment or platoon, which was elected by themselves and which took its authority solely from the will of the regiment or platoon expressed in mass meetings ... The Bolsheviks were good at guerrilla warfare.[6]

6. John Rickman, An Eye-witness from Russia (London, People's Russian Information Bureau, 1919), reprinted from the Manchester Guardian.

It would seem as though the only alternative to this type of organization, which could not possibly be effective on a large scale, is a hierarchy of officers with rights and privileges far greater (relatively) than those enjoyed by officers in any Occidental army.

I think the same principle—the idea that the only alternative to complete equality is complete subordination—can be seen operating in much of the Soviet Union's foreign policy. The proposed establishment of the United Nations' police force, for example, was nullified by the Soviet's insistence that the contributions of all the great powers should be absolutely equal (so that the navy and air force could not be greater than four times China's contribution). Similarly, the dispute with Marshal Tito of Yugoslavia would seem to have as a major component the fact that, while paying the Soviet Union every respect, Tito was not willing to concede its absolute, but only its relative, superiority, that he would admit his country to be only relatively, and not absolutely, weaker. Whatever their conscious intentions may be, it would appear that the Soviet elites find it psychologically impossible to permit their satellites relative independence, because it is a state they cannot envisage. The moment the balance is tipped, to the slightest measurable degree, from complete equality, they seem to fear that they will become completely subordinate; the moment a subordinate shows the slightest independence they seem to fear that the process will not stop until the subordinate is in a position of complete equality or else completely superordinate. In the expressive metaphor of Dr. Leites, the Soviet elites have avalanche fantasies. It would seem legitimate to make a connexion, on an unconscious level, between these fantasies and the horrible experience of being overwhelmed by the impotence of depression; and also with the feeling of destructive omnipotence when the depression gives way to rage.

5

With the partial exception of the relationship between a parent and a young child, the most tender emotions which Russians express are those between complete equals. Of these the most dramatic is passionate love; but Great Russians seem to regard this emotion with some ambivalence, because it is conceived as being so completely outside individual control or the dictates of reason; in the words of the proverb, 'Love is evil; for you can even fall in love with a goat.' Overwhelming passion-*strast'*-is thought likely to lead to disaster.

For many years, one of the most popular forms of amusement (especially among factory workers) has been the singing of comical or ironical quatrains called *chastushki* to the accompaniment of an accordion. Many of them are traditional; but new ones are constantly being invented to suit new circumstances. In their function-though not in their contents-they somewhat resemble the limerick. One of the most constant themes of the traditional *chastushki* (the new ones are chiefly political or technological) are the defects of the beloved.

> I have a sweetheart
> And it's a shame to walk with her in the streets;
> All the cab drivers are angry
> Because all their horses bolt when they see her.

> My darling weighs seven *pood*
> And she's afraid of camels.
> But the camels got so scared
> That they ran away from her for miles.

> Behind our house
> All the grass is trampled.
> It's not a horse and it's not a cow;
> It's all damned love.

> My darling sits on the stoops
> With an expression on his face.
> I did not think long;
> I came close and spat.

> I suffered and suffered
> And threw myself from the bridge into the river.
> On account of you, you devil,
> I swam for three hours.

> On the far horizon
> A cloud humped its back.
> My darling girl jumped with a parachute
> From behind the cloud.

> I am yours and you are mine;
> Do anything you want with me.
> If you want, you can lose me at cards,
> And if you want you can give me to your comrades.

Out of a very considerable collection of chastushki this last one is the only one of those dealing with love between the sexes which does not express some negative feeling about the beloved. And even in this case a number of people who were discussing it thought 'the girl wouldn't mind going to his comrades for a change'!

These *chastushki* it must be emphasized are exclusively lower-caste, and only refer (in the main) to lower-caste emotions. As far as I could discover, none are obscene; and obscenity appears to play little part in Russian humour (though a major role in Russian invective). In true literature and poetry (as opposed to folk-poetry) there are many lyrical and whole-hearted descriptions of passionate love, though even there (I have the impression) such love is likely to be tragic and disastrous.

6

The most widespread tender emotion that Great Russians value can perhaps be called sympathy-pity. English possesses no single word which covers the connotations of the Russian terms (*zhalitsia, sochustvovat', otzivchivost*), though 'pity' is the most usual translation. But the emotion described is both less and more than pity (as it is used in English or American); it is less than pity because it generally excludes the feeling for the mentally and physically handicapped, the maimed or the physically sick; it is more than pity because it is as desirable-perhaps more desirable-to be the recipient of another's sympathy-pity, than to offer this sympathypity to another. Mutual sympathy-pity is often the forerunner of successful and happy love. It can perhaps be defined as 'a sympathetic understanding and feeling for the moral and spiritual anguish which others are undergoing'.

This emotion can be felt for everybody undergoing moral and spiritual anguish, whether they are known and seen or not. An often-quoted poem by Alexander Blok on this emotion tells:

> A girl was singing in the church choir
> Of all the tired in foreign lands,
> Of all the ships that went to sea,
> Of all who lost their joy …

It is the emotion felt for the down-trodden and oppressed, for criminals and convicts. It is above all on this emotion that the Soviet leaders play to mobilize the Great Russians to the missionary task of liberating the down-trodden and oppressed in the rest of the world.

The common use of the reflexive form *(zhalitsia)* and the connotations of the emotion suggest that, on an unconscious level, the object of pity-sympathy is felt to be similar to, or 'the same as', the person feeling the emotion. But to be a proper recipient of such an emotion the object must be already suffering mental and spiritual anguish. This has two implications: the Great Russian thinks of himself as suffering, and the suffering of the other is not the fault of the pity-sympathizer, is not produced by his acts or wishes. If the hypothesis of diffuse unconscious hostility and guilt is correct, it is understandable that there is reassurance in the certainty that one is not responsible for the other's unhappiness; and also that this emotion (unlike the passionate love portrayed in the *chastushki*) is not contaminated by negative and hostile feelings.

Similar reasons may be the cause for the fact that the same terms are not normally used for the feeling for the physically incapacitated or mutilated, the maimed, the halt, and the blind (nor for such positive feelings as exist for other people's children); the physical differences prevent the feeling that these sufferers are 'the same as' oneself, and it is possible that these gross physical misfortunes arouse too much unconscious guilt. The common terms used to describe the emotion felt for such unfortunates are comparatively lightly toned; for example, *shchadit* to take care of, to tend.

It would seem that the feeling that the Leader and his associates have for the mass of the people is nearer to tending than to sympathy-pity. The Leader looks after the masses, but he controls his feelings for their moral and spiritual anguish; he 'grows them carefully and tenderly, like a gardener growing a favourite fruit tree'.

7

The Leader and his associates cannot indulge their feelings of sympathy-pity, just as they cannot indulge in any other emotions for their own sake; for to do so would distract them from their occupation in the most important activity of mankind-the gradual discovery and application of the Truth, *pravada*.[7] In the Russian conception of the universe, their concept of Truth holds an extremely important place.

The concept of Truth can be likened to a circle which surrounds one; it is analogous to the horizon which bounds the limitless and featureless Russian steppe. This steppe is, for very many Great Russians, the 'typical' Russian landscape, no matter what sort of country or town they may actually have been reared in; and it is often used, both by them and by non-Russians, as an illustration and explanation of Russian character.

A distinguished Russian said:

'I think you can say that Russian psychology is conditioned by their geography and their history. In Russia there is no rational shelter from the ever-present threat from outside. The Russians are brave in the face of disasters they expect, but all the time they are looking round for ways of avoiding their enemies. You must keep in mind that they grow up in those enormous steppes with nothing to prevent them galloping mile

7. Much of this analysis of pravda is founded on concepts developed by Dr. Margaret Mead and Mr. N. Calas.

after mile in any direction in a literal fashion; and figuratively you have this great width of character with no restrictions, no limits on what they think they can have ... Russians are rather lost in those vast spaces where they live. They have nothing to cheer them up. ... Russians are always living on the same level, seeing everything from the same aspect. Mountaineers have songs glorifying the storms and new impressions and new thoughts, but on the plains life and the view are monotonous. There is nothing but monotony and loneliness ... In Russia the soul plays a great part ... there are no mountains, no sea; only agriculture, the forest, the marshes, and the endless plain, and there are long periods of winter rest which give time to consider things of immaterial interest.'

In actual material fact, the great plains of Russia are not-at least to the casual traveller-more immense or featureless than the plains of the Middle West United States, or large areas of India, China, Indo-China, or Argentina; but Great Russians (and, as already said, very many non-Russians) consider this featureless landscape relevant to the understanding of the Russian character, in a fashion quite different to the relevance commonly attributed to the other areas named in the formation of the characters of their inhabitants. Possibly a connexion can be traced between the belief in the relevance of the limitless plain bounded by the horizon and the fact that in the typical childhood experience intense feeling is diffused (not concentrated) on the periphery of the body where it is bound by the swaddling, and the interior of the body is felt to be 'featureless' without objects on which the attention can fasten.

The concept of Truth can be likened to a circle which surrounds one. Truth exists, one and indivisible, and it can be discovered and applied. There is not a 'core' or 'heart' of Truth with a series of applications which may be more or less correct. Truth is rather a system of interconnected items, arranged in a hierarchy, but in such a way that the destruction of one item jeopardizes the whole system. There is no concept of relative truths or of the possibility of various 'aspects' or 'versions' of truth. As a consequence compromise is inadmissible (except perhaps as a tactic); and there is no possibility of a 'loyal opposition'. All men of good will must recognize the Truth when it is pointed out to them; if they refuse to recognize it, this shows their wicked characters and evil intentions. To accept the decision of the majority, without the appropriate internal convictions, is for Great Russians the abandonment of all honour and self-respect; to submit willingly to those you are convinced do not possess the Truth is an act of baseness.

Although Truth is a coherent system, it is not consistent according to the usual standards of Occidental logic. Truth embraces contradictions both in space and time; the fact that the truth revealed to-day, or the application of the truth demanded to-day, is not the same as the truth (or application) of yesterday, does not mean that one or the other ceases to be part of Truth. Truth is so great that it contains all contradictions; Russians do not reject these contradictions, nor is it certain that they perceive them as contradictions, in the way non-Russians would do.[8]

The Leader and the hierarchy of authority under him see the Truth more clearly than the led, and they impart their discoveries and applications to the latter. But all Great Russians, however ignorant and however humble, feel that they are part of the Pentecostal Congregation and have partaken of sobornost and so live in the Truth and follow it to the extent of their capacities. It is this conviction that they live in the Truth and pursue it as do the people of no other nation which gives the mystical overtones to the phrase 'Holy Russia' and the newer form 'Soviet Motherland'. It is this conviction which binds the Russians in the sure belief of their righteousness and superiority and gives them their seeming unyielding rigidity, whether the present aspect of the Truth be Orthodox Christianity, or the latest version of Leninism-Stalinism.[9]

8. In his book *The Russian Idea* (London, Bles, 1947) the famous theologian Nicolas Berdyaev documents the manner in which Hegel's dialectic-the philosophy of contradictions-was eagerly embraced by 'us Russians'from the moment it was published. It was felt to be particularly congenial to all shades of Russian thought, both in its idealist and its materialist (Marxist) versions.

9. Note these two quotations from Berdyaev (op. cit., pp. 2, 8). 'The Russians have not been in any sense a people of culture, as the peoples of Western Europe have been, they have rather been a people of revelation and inspiration.'

'In what respect was the conception of Moscow as the Third Rome twofold? The mission of Russia was to be the vehicle of the true Christianity, that is, of Orthodoxy, and the shrine in which it is treasured. This was a religious vocation. "Orthodoxy" is a definition of "the Russians". Russia is the only Orthodox realm, and as such a universal realm like the First Rome and the Second.

Chapter V

CONCLUSIONS

*I*f the views expressed in the previous chapters are correct, the following statements can be made about Great Russians. Most important of these perhaps is the fact that there are very marked differences in character between the Soviet elites on the one hand, and the mass of the population on the other. The mass of the population is oppressed by diffuse feelings of guilt and hostility, but shows very little anxiety. They tend to oscillate suddenly and unpredictably from one attitude to its contrary, especially from violence to gentleness, from excessive activity to passivity, from orgiastic indulgence to ascetic absterniousness. They endure physical suffering with great stoicism and are indifferent about the physical sufferings of others. They also tend to oscillate between unconscious fears of isolation and loneliness, and an absence of feelings of individuality so that the self is, as it were, merged with its peers in a 'soul-collective'. They have deep warmth and sympathy for all whom (at a given time) they consider as 'the same as' themselves; they direct their vague and unconscious hostility on all whom they consider 'different to' themselves, paying little attention to which figure is momentarily the focus for their hostility. They seem to expect hostility from all who are 'different'. They consider themselves superior to the rest of the world, because they and their country are the special repository of the Truth, one and indivisible; it is their duty to make this Truth prevail. They have a tendency to confuse thought and action. They pay little attention to order, efficiency, and punctuality. They are much preoccupied with the exploration and verbalization of the feelings momentarily possessing them. They submit unwillingly but resignedly to firm authority imposed on them from above, and merge themselves willingly with an idealized figure or Leader.

The intelligentsia and élites seem to share the diffuse guilt and hostility and to see potential enemies all around them, including the mass of the people they control. In contrast to the mass of the population, they value and cultivate the power of the will, as opposed to the emotions; they pay great attention to order, efficiency, and punctuality. They consider that people (and peoples) are fundamentally and naturally unequal, but that equality can be precariously preserved by paying attention to every minute detail. The only alternative they conceive to this precarious equality is complete superordination or complete subordination, complete power or complete weakness; and they are haunted by fears that they will be in the position of complete subordination, complete weakness. They consider themselves to be in possession of the Truth to a greater degree than the mass of the population, and would appear to have esoteric versions of the Truth which cannot safely be communicated to outsiders.

All Great Russians seem to feel the psychological compulsion to exert their strength to the limit, and to place value on violence as a means of liberation and producing order out of confusion; but here, as in all other domains, the elites consider that both efforts and violence should be subordinate to the will, while the mass of the population consider that they should be responses to appropriate autonomous emotions.

On the basis of these generalizations, it would seem possible to derive the following political maxims:

(I) It is useless to try to make friends with, or win the sympathy of, the mass of the Great Russian people, in the hopes of producing transformations of policy. The mass of the people never have had, and (in any foreseeable future) are not likely to have any appreciable influence on the policies their leaders adopt. Policy, both foreign and domestic, is determined by a very small group.

(II) The leaders suspect that those they lead are hostile towards them, and they seek to divert this hostility on to other figures. If the leaders were to feel convinced that the mass of the population (or a sizeable portion of it) were becoming disaffected from them and favouring some outside power, this might well exacerbate the leaders' fears and induce them to precipitate a war, as the most efficacious way of diverting hostility from themselves.

(III) No techniques are yet available for eradicating the all-pervasive suspicion which Great Russians, leaders and led alike, feel towards the rest of the world. This suspicion springs from unconscious and therefore irrational sources and will not be calmed, more than momentarily, by rational actions.

(IV) Great Russians, leaders and led alike, will continue to go all the time to the limit of their strength. They will expand their boundaries like a flooded lake, and this flood will only be contained by the political equivalent of a firm and solid dike. To continue the analogy one step further, the Great Russians will always seek out weak places or gaps in this dike; and if they find them they will exploit them.

(V) The analogy of the dike describes the only type of political behaviour which will contain Russian expansion: firmness, strength, consistency. And the greatest of these is consistency.

(VI) It should be remembered that the strategical retreat is a highly acceptable manoevre to Great Russians. (We have no information as to how this is viewed by the other peoples of the U.S.S.R.) To be forced back means that one has gone to the limit of one's strength and endurance, done one's utmost. It is not necessarily a humiliation.

(VII) In negotiations with Great Russians, a successful outcome is most likely if negotiations are phrased in the terms of the most concrete and symmetrical equality: man for man, ton for ton, acre for acre, town for town, and so on. In the view of Great Russians, the only alternative to the most rigorous equality is for one of the parties to be completely subordinate; and they always have the fear that they may be forced into the position of absolute weakness.

(VIII) Ideological arguments, notes of admonition and disapproval, and the like, are a complete waste of time and energy, as far as the Great Russians are concerned. With the Great Russian concept of Truth, pravda, it is impossible for them to admit error in any one instance, for that would destroy their whole system of Truth, and their self-esteem. If one action or attitude is wrong (incorrect) then all are wrong; and such an admission is only forthcoming in a religious conversion or political purge trial. Neither of these is likely to happen on an international scale.

(IX) There is no likelihood of Great Russians voluntarily engaging their country in any form of international organization which might conceivably give to other countries the possibility of constraining them. Consequently, it is a waste of time to discuss, for example, the abolition of the veto in the Security Council of the United Nations. There is no possibility of the development of a 'world state', as now conceived, except under complete Russian domination, while the U.S.S.R. is an independent power with Great Russians in most of the positions of authority.

(X) Although the Russians will resist every encroachment, while themselves encroaching to the greatest possible degree, there would seem to be no necessity for war between the Western Powers and the U.S.S.R. The one situation which might evoke war (apart from the Western Powers 'compressing' Russia) would be if the Western Powers manifested such weakness, or such alternations between strength and weakness, that the Russians would feel compelled to advance to such a degree that the Western powers would feel that the menace was intolerable. If Russia is faced with *permanent* strength, firmness, and consistency there would appear to be no reason why a tolerable and durable *modus vivendi* should not be maintained indefinitely.

APPENDICES

Appendix I

DEVELOPMENT OF THE SWADDLING HYPOTHESES

BY GEOFFREY GORER

NOTE: Although in what follows I am presenting the development of my own views, I should like the reader to be as sharply aware as I am that these ideas could never have reached this degree of clarity without the constant assistance of and exchange with my collaborators on the Columbia Research Project. These ideas could never have been developed at all without the help and knowledge of my teachers and friends in anthropology and psychology the late Dr. Ruth Benedict, the late Professor Bronislaw Malinowski, Dr. Margaret Mead, Professor Clark L. Hull, Mr. Earl Zinn, Dr. John Rickman, Dr. Harold Lasswell. I also owe an inestimable debt to three thinkers whom I never met (and have read the works of only one of them with any consistency): I. P. Pavlov, Franz Boas, and Sigmund Freud.

1

As far as my reading and inquiries have gone, there is no precedent in the literature of anthropology, psychology or psychoanalysis to the hypotheses developed in the previous chapters on the derivatives of muscular restraint by swaddling. It therefore seems as though it might be of some interest to outline briefly the steps by which I was led to develop these hypotheses.[1]

---

1. For a review, analysis and bibliography of the existing literature see: Phyllis Greenacre, 'Infant Reactions to Restraint' (American journal of Orthopsychyiatry, Vol. XIV, No. 2, April 1944)

I should like once again to reiterate the fact that I have undoubtedly over-emphasized the importance of swaddling because, as the following pages are intended to make clear, it was one of the chief clues which I used for interpreting Russian behaviour. For me it is a clue, not a cause, of Russian behaviour; but without this clue I do not think I could have made the deductions I have. Other workers might well have reached the same results by a different route.

I approach the attempt to describe the national character of a society without being in the territory of that society by the assumption of a highly self-conscious ignorance. This ignorance has to be much more selfconscious than in the case of field-work; in the field every sight and experience emphasizes this ignorance and also produces material to modify it; when one is relying on interviews with exiles and emigrants and symbolic material (books, pictures, films,&c.) this ignorance must be constantly kept in the forefront of the mind. By ignorance I mean that I ignore, for the time being, any ideas, impressions or prejudices I may have acquired through visits to the country in question, acquaintance with members of the society being investigated, experience or recollections of their works of art, literature, and music, reactions to newspaper reports of the behaviour of that nation's government, and so on. Subsequently, I may use any or all of this material to test hypotheses developed in the course of the work; but my initial position is that I know nothing whatsoever about the society I am investigating.

Although I assume that I know nothing about the society under investigation, I assume that I know certain laws about societies in general and about human beings in general, and that my task is to discover the particular manifestations of these general laws in the present instance. Following Malinowski, though maybe with modifications, I assume that every society, from the simplest to the most complex, possesses the same basic institutions and cultural imperatives, and that these institutions are intelligible only in terms of the needs, basic and learned, that they satisfy; following what I believe to be the basic underlying assumptions of Freud and Hull, I assume that human behaviour is understandable, and is derived from the operation of the laws of learning on the innate biological drives and processes of physical maturation which are common to all human beings. When I made the initial study of national character away from that nation's territory (the study of the Japanese in 1940 1 developed a set of twelve postulates; with the possible exception of postulate (VII) (the assumption that fear and anger are not innate) my subsequent experience and study have not led me to abandon them; and I will therefore repeat them here.

(I) Human behaviour is understandable: with sufficient evidence it is possible to explain any observed behaviour, however incongruous isolated items may appear.

(II) Human behaviour is predominantly learned. Although the human infant may be born with some instincts and is born with some basic biological drives whose satisfaction is necessary to its survival, it is the treatment which the infant receives from the other members of the society into which it is born, and its experiences of its environment, which through the gratification or frustration of its needs enables it to learn new needs and new methods of gratification. (In this context I should perhaps state that I assume that, in a large society, genetic peculiarities do not involve any major inherent psychological differences in comparison with other large societies.)

(III) In all societies the behaviour of the component individuals of similar age, sex, and status shows a relative uniformity in similar situations. This is equally true in unformulated and unverbalized situations.

(IV) All societies have an ideal adult character (or characters, depending on sex and status) which is of major importance for parents and other adults in authority in selecting which items of children's behaviour to reward, and which to punish.

(V) Habits are established by differential reward and punishment (indulgence and deprivation) chiefly meted out by other members of the society.

(VI) The habits established early in the life of the individual influence all subsequent learning, and therefore the experiences of childhood are of predominant importance.

(VII) The chief learning in early childhood consists of the modifications of the innate drives of hunger, thirst, optimum-temperature seeking, pain avoidance, sex and excretion, and of the (possibly secondary) drives of fear and anger (anxiety and aggression) and of the biological derivatives of maturation, which are demanded by the adult members of the society; consequently a knowledge of the types of modifications imposed, the means by which they are imposed, and the times at which they are imposed, is of major importance in the derivation of adult behaviour.

(VIII) Since, in the greatest number of societies, it is predominantly the parents who reward and punish their children, the attitudes of the child to his father and mother, and, to a lesser degree, to his brothers and sisters, will become the prototypes of his attitudes towards all subsequently met people. In societies where the disciplinary role is normally taken by adults other than the biological parents, the attitudes towards such adults also become of major importance.

(IX) Except in situations of the greatest physiological stress, adult behaviour is motivated by learned (derived, secondary) drives or wishes superimposed upon the primary biological drives.

(X) Many of these wishes are unverbalized or unconscious, since the rewards and punishments which established the habits of which these wishes are the motives were undergone in early childhood, before the acquisition of speech, or because the verbalization of these wishes was very severely punished; consequently people very often cannot express their motives in words, and the motives have to be deduced from the observation of what satisfactions are actually obtained from different courses of behaviour.

(XI) When these wishes, acquired through early learning, are shared by a majority of the population, some social institutions will eventually be developed to gratify them; and institutions which originate in other societies and are then subsequently adopted will be modified to congruence with these wishes (to the extent that this is possible without impeding the gratification of the primary drives).

(XII) In a homogeneous society the cultural patterns of superordination and subordination, of arrogance and deference, will tend to show a certain consistency in all institutions from the family to the religious and political organizations; and consequently the patterns of behaviour demanded in all these institutions will mutually re-enforce each other.[2]

A reproach to studies of this nature which is frequently voiced is that they ignore the influence of history, economics, geography, and similar 'impersonal' phenomena. To my mind, this reproach would only be justified if any claim, overt or implied, were made that studies of national character were meant to describe all the phenomena of a nation's life; as far as the studies I have made are concerned, all that is attempted is the isolation and description of the main motives of the majority of the population over and above those rational ones which are gratified by the operation of the institutions which historical accident and technological development have produced at a given time.

For example, marketing (the exchange of goods or services) performs similar basic functions in all societies; I try to isolate what specific functions, beyond the acquisition of articles of use, prestige or

2.   Originally mimeographed, late 1941, in the Institute of Human Relations, Yale University; subsequently printed in the *Transactions of the New York Academy of Sciences* (Series II, Vol. 5, March 1943) and *Penguin Science News No. I* (London, 1945). I have made a few verbal modifications here.

profit, marketing has for members of a given society. Anybody who has done shopping in a number of different countries will know that these are very various: in one society the pleasure may be in skill in bargaining, so that the vendor feels defrauded if his first asking price is paid without demur; in another the vendor may feel gratified if he has passed off an imperfect article at a high price, while in yet another he may get greater satisfaction from an experienced and discriminating buyer who manifests his appreciation and knowledge of the vendor's skill and taste; and so on, with a very great number of variations and permutations. I consider it my business to isolate this psychological 'surplus value' and to attempt to bring it into relationship with other similar manifestations; the description of the operation of the market as an economic institution I leave to the specialists in such matters. If it is necessary to the development of my argument I may quote from some recognized authority on the subject; but I have not the training to conduct independent research; and I assume that the recognized authorities are as available to interested readers as they are to me.

The case of history is parallel. I do not question for a moment the importance of historical developments, but the study of these is not my speciality. I am interested in how members of a society interpret their own history, and in some cases have made great use of this;[3] but I have nothing original to contribute to history as such. In the course of this Russian study I have read more than half a dozen Histories of Russia for my own instruction; but this is reflected in only two or three phrases in the text.

The history of religion and theology will tell how and when Roman Catholicism, for example, was adopted in different countries, and the formulation of its dogmas: I want to understand why, in the religious pictures and statues of one country, great emphasis is placed on Jesus as an infant or child, and the Virgin Mary as a young girl; in another on Jesus as a mature and bearded man, and Mary as a mature and maternal woman; in a third on Jesus as tortured and crucified, Mary as an older and grieving woman. All these figures are contained in Roman Catholicism; my interest is to discover what psychological mechanisms have influenced the choice in any given case.[4]

---

3. In the case of the Russians, I think the century-old complaint that other countries are keeping them from a 'warm-water port' probably has important psychological implications; but I have not, so far, been able to discover what these are.

4. I have not made any exhaustive study of Russian iconography; but my impressions of what I have seen are that there is an almost complete

2

My usual, and preferred, method of modifying my total ignorance of the national character of the people I am investigating is by long interviews with members of that society. Although clues can be found and hypotheses developed by an analytic reading of books and other symbolic material, I personally prefer to use such material for confirming (or disproving) hypotheses deduced from interviews, and for providing additional evidence.

Who my earlier informants are is usually a matter of chance. I have been fortunate, so far, in always having friends who have had friends or acquaintances of the nationality I am interested in, who have given me introductions. These first informants in turn give me introductions to their compatriots. As the research progresses, I may feel the need for interviewing people who occupy (have occupied) certain positions in their society; in that case I enlist the assistance of anybody whom I think capable of helping me; or, if I know that a person of the type I am interested in exists, write directly. (In the later stages of this current study I combed the Northeast United States for wet-nurses-unsuccessfully-for nyanyas and for people who had been in a position to make political and commercial appointments.)

Since studies of this nature are inevitably qualitative and not quantitative-to use an analogy from biology, they are anatomic, not taxonomic-and since it is impossible to produce any reliable quantitative and statistical results,[5] I do not pay much attention to the 'sociological' representativeness of my informants, though I try to get them from as many varied social milieus as possible, and of all ages and both sexes. I try to get as much of a 'scatter'as possible, but make no attempt to make this scatter proportionate. In most cases the risk I have to guard against is 'reverse'proportions; often the largest portion of the resident population-the peasants and factory workers-is quite inadequately represented in the migrant population.

---

absence of representations of Jesus as a child or adolescent, or of Mary as a young girl. (The usual method of referring to Mary is not as a Virgin but as the bearer of God, Bogorodyitsa.) Jesus is usually portrayed as a mature, bearded judge in regal robes, Mary as a younger but mature mother, often with an almost unsupported, rigidly erect, and swaddled Infant Jesus. There are many representations of God the Father, again as a bearded man of early middle age, and some strange triune pictures of the Trinity, consisting of three merging and identical faces, occasionally reduced to three noses and four eyes. This choice of sacred images appears congruent with my hypotheses.

5. Statistics gathered by technicians for other purposes are of course employed when available.

I work on the assumption that any individual who has passed his or her childhood and adolescence as a full participant of his culture[6] is a typical representative of his culture and manifests its national character, whatever his or her individual characteristic attitudes, quirks, vicissitudes or occupation may be. This may appear paradoxical, since we are all deeply and intimately aware of the differences between individuals; but in the same way and at the same time, as people acquire their mothertongue, they acquire their national character. To pursue this analogy further, different people have very different vocabularies and different manners of speaking, sometimes different accents; one may use the language fluently and skillfully, while another may barely make himself understood; one may use the language poetically and imaginatively, whereas another may only make flat and dry statements; some may stammer, some lisp, some speak ungrammatically; and each speaker has an individual voice and intonation which his friends usually recognize without ambiguity. It needs a very analytically minded person to be conscious of the fact (so obvious to a foreigner) that he and his friends and family all speak the same language, with its highly complicated and idiosyncratic rules of grammar and syntax, and probably speak it in a way which identifies them by class, or region, or both. Without perhaps full verbalization, people recognize and stress the *differences* of timbre, speech rhythm, and turn of phrase which give each person his speaking individuality; but they completely ignore the far larger *identity* of language and accent which characterizes everyone in the group and the group itself and (linguistically speaking) completely differentiates it from groups of very similar social and individual composition in other societies, and often from similar groups in other regions or classes of its own society.

The fact that a person has learned Russian (for example) as his mother-tongue means that his thoughts and concepts will be limited and defined by the vocabulary and syntax of the language; in certain important ways he will view and interpret the universe differently to the way he would do if he had been brought up with English or Chinese or Esquimaux as his mother-tongue. Further, every Russian is an informant (technically a linguistic informant) on the Russian language; one may have a specialized technical vocabulary, another may speak with a peasant idiom, and so on; but if you want to learn Russian, and know none, any native-born Russian can be your informant

6. Because of this stress on full participation I refused all informants who were not born members of the Orthodox Church; or, in the case of atheists, whose parents were not born members of this Church.

or teacher, though you may learn more, and better, and more easily, from some than from others.

Analogies are dangerous traps for the unwary; but I am convinced that in this case the analogy is fundamentally accurate; that every deviation and variety of personal character is a deviation from the norm of the national character; even in the case of the neurotic and the physically handicapped this axiom holds good. Though 1 know of no work on the subject, I feel convinced that a study of deafness, for example, would show significant differences in different societies in the manner in which this affliction is endured and interpreted, and the way in which the sound of hearing respond to the deaf.

When I have a first interview with an informant, 1 always give briefly my reasons for troubling them, and on occasion a little of the theoretical background; in many cases I state my sincere belief that the study I am engaged on will tend to promote mutual understanding between their country and ourselves; and I always try to convey, even if I do not state it in so many words, my conviction that each informant has unique and valuable knowledge which only he (or she) is capable of providing. Then, unless the informant has specialized knowledge on which I want to concentrate, I ask some quite general question: usually, in the case of mothers or grandmothers, how they brought up their children; in the case of men, or women without children, details of their schooling. From then on, I let the informant take charge of the conversation, filling in pauses by demands for further clarification; in the main part of the interview I only direct the conversation if the informant is indulging in excessive generalizations or entering political arguments. After a number of interviews, I always have a series of subjects which I want to check with every appropriate informant; if they have not come up spontaneously during the course of the interview, I bring them up at the very end, usually after the interview is formally over, and we have risen from our seats. I count the interview a failure, whatever the information gained, if it has not been for the informants an interesting and stimulating experience, which they wish to repeat in the near future. In most cases the informant's response is rather like Monsieur Jourdain's delighted discovery that he had been talking prose all his life; people are pleased to discover that their 'ordinary' life can be so deeply interesting to a stranger.

Unless I have excessively nervous informants, I take the fullest possible notes (I do not know shorthand); I either have my notebook out at once, or use the first excuse of a foreign word or phrase to bring it out of my pocket. I have acquired the technique of writing almost illegibly to others, I must confess-without looking down at the paper on which I am writing; none of my attention is distracted from my informant by this note-taking, and, as far as I can tell, it never worries the informant. My preferred situation is to interview two or three or more (up to about six) informants at once; they stimulate and correct one another, forget that I am there, or nearly, and often evoke material which I would not envisage, or of a depth I should be unlikely to reach; and their behaviour towards one another gives valuable additional data. In the case of professional people interviewed alone I like to have a shorthand typist (seated behind the informant and out of sight) to take down the interview *verbatim*. When I have taken down my own notes, I dictate or write as full an account of the interview as possible at the first opportunity.

I take these extremely full notes, always indicating my own questions, and any interruptions, whether from other informants or mechanical causes (telephones, doorbells, &c.), because two of the chief sources for getting hypotheses (as contrasted with data) are metaphors and the free association of ideas;[7] the juxtapositions of ideas or figures of speech have quite different significance if they are spontaneous or if they are elicited. When they are elicited, the means by which they are elicited may also be significant. This concentration on metaphor and association of ideas bears a slight resemblance to psychoanalysis, and would not have been developed without the practice of the psycho-analytic interview; but it is also not unlike the work of the classical detective of fiction, hunting for significant clues among the mass of data presented.

As far as possible, I avoid asking leading questions; but an elucidating technique which I have often found useful is the presentation of cross-cultural illustrations, either from the society in which the interview is taking place or from other societies which I know of from reading or investigation, and asking whether the informant's experience contains anything similar.

3

I first became aware of the existence of the practice of swaddling among Great Russians not from an interview, but from a discussion in our group of typical Russian gestures and body movements. In the

7.   Other topics which I find suggestive are jokes of all kinds, swearing, religious observances, obscenity, preoccupations about health, judgements or criticisms made of other individuals in the same society, criticisms of concrete aspects of foreign cultures.

course of this discussion Margaret Mead interpreted the movements or one of the gesticulating Russians in a way I had failed to and, turning to her, asked, 'X, were you swaddled as a child?' It then developed that all but two of our Russian collaborators (these were children of intellectuals) had been swaddled. It may be of interest to note that, though I failed to interpret the gestures at this meeting, I could, after three months' interviewing, tell at a glance, and with practically no errors, if a Russian had been swaddled as a child: the square set of the shoulders, the 'resting position' of the upper arms against the side of the body, further back than is habitual with people who have not been swaddled, and many symmetrical gestures with the forearms and hands, the upper arms being kept in the resting position-these are the chief indicators of which I am conscious.

I did quite a little interviewing before I got much further information; I found that I had not made my ignorance of Russian character complete enough and had assumed-incorrectly-that mothers would be able to tell me how children were brought up. This delusion was finally shattered one evening when a Russian mother, who was absent from the room watching her little son be put to bed when I arrived, had to go into the child's bedroom a couple of hours later to see if his arms were inside or outside the swaddling. I then discovered that the only people who know articulately about infant care are grandmothers;[8] and the curious fact developed that the birth of a grandchild brought back into conscious memory the treatment the grandmother had given her own children. I also found that though Russians could normally recall very little of their own childhood, if they had a brother or sister some six or more years younger (particularly if of the same sex) they could recall a great deal about the childhood of this younger sibling, and often by deduction of their own.

Once the fact of swaddling appeared of importance, it was only a matter of application to discover the extent of the practice by exten-

---

8.   The social arrangement of linking alternating generations (grandparents and grandchildren) occurs in many parts of the world; it is often symbolized by grandparents and grandchildren using the same term of address to each other. Often the grandparents have the major care of the child after weaning. I do not know of any field-work which has studied societies with such arrangements from a psychological point of view. It would appear that the old and very young are equated by their equal distance from full strength and maturity. Great Russian peasant life would seem to show an echo of such arrangements, with the role of the grandmother, babushka, and (to a lesser extent) the grandfather caring for the grandchildren. In the words of the Russian proverb, 'A daughter's children are dearer than one's own'.

sive interviewing, the analysis of text-books on child-rearing, photographs of children in creches and the equivalent of questionnaires.[9]

The first thing I noted about the swaddling was the series of rationalizations concerning the injuries that the child would do to itself if it were not swaddled; and from this I developed the hypothesis that 'restraint is unbearable; yet one has enormous strength and one must be restrained in order to keep from breaking oneself and others'. I had also noted the orgiastic nature of adult Russian gratifications, and made the connexion between this and the fact that babies were unswaddled for nursing. I also noted that, apart from the swaddling, Russian children did not appear to be deprived or disciplined, and connected this with the lack of apparent anxieties in adult Russians of the type to which we were accustomed in Occidental society.

My chief theoretical preoccupation in the first months of interviewing was an attempt to establish a connexion between the attitudes towards political authority and their prototypes in the familial situation. My first interviews were chiefly with people in the upper castes, and from them I got the account of what I later called the belief in 'patrilineal 'and 'matrilineal' characteristics, the fact that the father loved the daughter for her 'masculine' characteristics and so on. I pursued this as far as it would go, but did not get any results which seemed satisfactory, nor any which explained the social and political phenomena I was documenting. Furthermore, continued interviewing showed the lack of deep affect (judged from an Occidental point of view) of the emotional relations between parents and children, and the fact that the father was a friendly and succouring figure in nearly every case, whereas 'authority' was severe and distantial.[10]

I then developed the hypothesis (which I abandoned with great difficulty) that the prototype of authority in childhood was the *babushka* or *nyanya*, a moody and somewhat sexless figure, distant from the parents in age or caste or both.[11] This might account for the lack of feeling of 'loneness' between those in authority and those under authority and the 'unpredictability'of authority, and I built a

9. It should be kept in mind that, except in these late studies on the extent of the practice, information on swaddling was never given in isolation.

10. I was puzzled for a long time by the figure of the father in *The Brothers Karamazov*. I now think that Father Karamazov is a symbol of 'authority', in its feared and hated aspects, rather than a representation of a 'typical'father. This interpretation of characters as symbols would seem to be valid in a number of cases in Dostoievsky's major novels.

11. It was at this period that I searched so eagerly for wet-nurses and *nyanyas* to interview.

number of constructs on this hypothesis. Russians, however, never accepted it willingly; and it left many aspects unaccounted for.

Meanwhile I had collected from interviews, and other sources, a good deal of evidence for what I have called unfocused guilt and hostility; and also the very great use of the eyes for conveying emotion, love, &c. Somebody reminded me of the rather heartless experiments conducted on children by behaviourists during the twenties, when it was found that holding children's legs straight-that is in the swaddling position-made them cry and also made them angry. I then developed the hypothesis that swaddling was painful, as inhibiting spontaneous movements of the limbs,[12] and that the infant responded to this pain with rage. I further suggested that this rage was projected and produced guilt or fear; I almost certainly derived this from my contacts with Mrs. Klein, Dr. Rickman, and other psychoanalysts interested in Mrs. Klein's developing ideas some months previously. This hypothesis seemed to account for the diffuse guilt and fear, and suggested that swaddling was psychologically important. I then re-read my interviews to see if I could get any further leads from metaphors or free associations.

On swaddling itself two free associations seemed to me important. Russians refer to swaddling material as 'bandages'; and shortly after talking of children being 'bandaged', more than one informant referred to 'Lazarus lying three days bandaged in the grave'; this connexion of the swaddled baby with a corpse[13] seemed to suggest that there was very strong negative emotion about (being) a swaddled baby. Another woman, trying to explain to me about swaddling, stuck out her legs and crossed her arms on her breast. I asked if the arms were crossed as she held them. She hesitated and then said, 'No, I think flat, like this [again sticking out her feet and putting her arms flat against her sides] *You know the Russians put a lot of emphasis on every point.* The young mothers that I knew accepted the propaganda against swaddling but explained why they did the opposite ...'

The italicized phrase was one starting-point for the hypothesis of the 'circle of truth' and the importance of the periphery as contrasted with the centre. It made a link with the hypotheses on Truth developed by Dr. Mead and Mr. Calas.

12.   When I first produced this hypothesis I was reminded that one of the alleged tortures imposed by the Russian secret police is to insist on several hours'complete immobility in a rigid position

13.   1n fact, with a resurrectible corpse; but I did not see the full significance of this until after I had developed the hypothesis of infantile depression (see below) and was discussing the evidence with John Rickman.

I did not get further clues from the descriptions or discussions of swaddling; but when I re-read my material on authority, particularly on school-teachers and schoolchildren, both interviews and excerpts from Soviet textbooks, I was much struck by the wealth of metaphor applied to teachers and their authority which could equally well be applied to swaddling: firm and consistent, weakening softness, neither too tight nor too loose, and so on. The most striking examples out of a great deal of evidence are presented in Chapter IV, section 3. It was from this material that I produced the most novel (theoretically speaking) of the hypotheses: that the prototype of authority was not any figure in the familial environment but the impersonal swaddling. In Chapters III and IV I have presented the conclusions and some of the evidence from my own material; but one of the most telling illustrations was produced by Dr. Leites from his fund of political knowledge; the fact that the chief theoretical quarrel between Lenin and Rosa Luxembourg was on the question whether the workers could develop 'straight' without the tight 'swaddling' authority of the Central Committee.

Once the attention was focused on the importance or swaddling it was possible to make some other deductions directly—e.g. the role of the eyes, the inhibitions on exploring the universe, the role of teething and fantasies of devouring, &c., and others, such as the reason for the apparent enjoyment of unpleasant emotions, more tentatively.

When I had reached this point my work in the United States had to be terminated. I wrote a paper developing the hypotheses in that state, and it was only through a series of accidents that it was not published in that form. In one paragraph in this paper I still clung-rather halfheartedly, it is true-to the figure of *nyanya* or *babushka* as the prototype of authority. I found it difficult to make the intellectual jump of abandoning every human figure in the infantile world; and also I was probably unconsciously loath to consign so much work to my files.

Back in England I did a good deal of further reading and re-reading of Russian literature and history for my own edification; but I did not think of modifying my hypotheses until Margaret Mead came to England for the Mental Health Congress, in August 1948, bringing with her a generous selection of the material which had been collected after my departure by the Russian group in New York. Included in this material were a number of excerpts Dr. Leites had made from classic Russian literature on the exhilaration of rapid movement, the unpleasantness of motionlessness, and the joining of these two emotions in Pushkin's lyric *The Demons*, quoted in Chapter II, section 2. This material struck me as odd and difficult to interpret; pondering on it, I thought I saw an analogy in the misery of motionlessness to the misery of depressives, and the concepts of Melanie Klein on the infantile 'depressive position'; and I then produced the additional hypothesis of infantile depression as a result of exhaustion from unassuaged rage. This hypothesis seemed to account more adequately for three sets of facts for which we had plenty of data: the pleasure in painful emotions, the fact that Great Russians viewed weakness as absolute and not relative, and 'avalanche fantasies'.

Some weeks later I was invited to participate in an international seminar convened by the Centre Cultural International de Royaumont. Also taking part in this seminar were two young French psychoanalysts of altogether exceptional qualities, Professeur Daniel Lagache of the Sorbonne and Madame Dolto-Marette. I gave them my Russian hypotheses to read, and was enormously encouraged by their response to such unconventional material. Professeur Lagache told me of an analysand he had had who, on account of a childish skin disease, had been swaddled from his fourth to his tenth month, with psychological responses very similar to those I had hypothesized, and which Professeur Lagache had only been able to interpret at the end of the analysis,[14] and Madame Dolto-Marette was married to a Russian, who had also been psychoanalysed, and she told me that she thought the construct of the character was correct, though she had explained it on more conventional Freudian lines. Monsieur Dolto subsequently gave me a great deal of most useful confirmatory material.

With this theoretical support, aided by John Rickman's encouragement and collaboration, and egged on by Professor Edward Shils, I decided to suspend the work on which I was then engaged and rewrite the hypotheses in a longer and more detailed form. It was while I was engaged in this task that I produced the latest development (to date) of the swaddling hypotheses: the interpretation of the

14. This is the only case I have discovered of the psychoanalysis of an adult swaddled in infancy. The only reported case of the psychoanalysis of an Orthodox Russian (the reported presence of Jews as servants makes it uncertain if the patient were a Great Russian) is Freud's 'wolf man'. ('From the History of an Infantile Neurosis'(1918): S. Freud, *Collected Papers* (London, Hogarth Press, 1933), Vol. III, pp. 473 ff.) Apart from the information that the patient was born in a caul, this paper tells nothing about, and makes no deductions from, the experiences of the first year of life. There is too little social information to decide with any certainty which caste the patient belonged to; what does appear untypical in the account given is the (apparently) very small household in which the patient grew up. It may be of interest to note that, in discussing the difficulties of analysing this patient, Freud writes of his I national character that was foreign to ours'(p. 5 8 5). As far as I know, this is the only place where Freud uses the concept of national character.

role of the Leader as a projection of the 'idealized self'. This was developed under the stimulation of Melanie Klein's *Contributions to Psycho-analysis, 1921-1945*[15] which I was reading in the evenings for a review. In her paper on *Mourning and its Relation to Manic-depressive States* (p. 316) she writes:

> 'In the infant the extreme character both of his sadistic and of his constructive fantasies is in line with the extreme frightfulness of his persecutors—and, at the other end of the scale, the extreme perfection of his "good" objects. Idealization is an essential part of the manic position ...'

I do not subscribe to all of Mrs. Klein's views by any means, nor do I wish to suggest that all Great Russians are manic-depressives-it seems to me nearly meaningless to apply psychiatric terms developed to describe deviants in one culture to the norm of another culture—but under the stimulus of this passage I reconsidered my evidence concerning the Great Russians' attitudes towards their Leader, and developed the hypothesis which can be found in the first section of Chapter IV.

4

I was first appraised of the existence of swaddling among the Great Russians by a sudden insight of Margaret Mead's; but had I held more firmly in my mind the concept of the 'culture-area'I should have expected it, instead of being surprised. Swaddling—wrapping the young infant in strips of cloth instead of enveloping it in a loose piece of cloth, clothing it in fitted garments, or letting it be naked-is a very widespread custom; it apparently spreads almost uninterruptedly[16], from the North polar regions to the Mediterranean, the Himalayas, and the Mexican border.

A frequent—and natural—question in response to my hypotheses on the influence of swaddling on Great Russian character is to ask why it does not produce similar results on all swaddled peoples. This is a difficult question to answer, for I know of no other comparable researches on societies employing swaddling; all I can do is to point out how, in the instances on which I have some information, Great Russian swaddling is different.

15.   London, Hogarth Press, 1948.
16.   I write this without the complete checking of the data which should ideally be performed.

(I) *Amount of body swaddled.* In Central Europe, including France, apparently only the trunk is swaddled; movements of the limbs are not impeded. The Italian bambino of classical painting and bas-reliefs has his hands and arms free, and his exploration of the universe is not much impeded.

(II) *Length of time swaddled.* In Central and Western Europe the swaddling is replaced by clothing which allows free movement very much earlier. According to some travellers the swaddling is removed much latertowards the end of the second year-in Albania and Southern Yugoslavia; we know very little about these people; but the stories of blood-feuds, & c., suggest that this swaddling may produce psychological responses of a simila nature to those I have postulated in Great Russians.

(III) *The absence of hunger and other unpleasant internal sensations.* According to one trained informant, Polish peasant babies were as completely swaddled as Russian babies in their first weeks of life, but they also suffer a great deal from hunger, the mothers leaving them behind in the house for many hours while they work in the fields, and, when they do feed the babies, feeding them hurriedly and ungenerously. On theoretical grounds I should expect unpleasant internal sensations to outweigh (psychologically) unpleasant peripheral sensations; it is the Russian baby's physiological contentment which gives such relative psychological importance to the restraints of swaddling.

(IV) *The impersonal handling of the infant and the treating of the infant as strong.* Eastern European Jewish babies are swaddled; but the reason given for this is that they are so weak and fragile that they might otherwise be damaged by clumsy adults, especially the father. This would imply that the child—both swaddled and unswaddled—is handled in quite a different way to the Great Russian infant; and therefore probably has quite different emotional relationships to the adults around him.

(V) *Great Russian babies are unswaddled or nursing.* The contrast between restraint without gratifications and gratifications without restraint is not experienced by those American Indian tribes who employ cradle boards; the infant is only removed from the board for very short periods; all his infantile experiences, pleasurable and painful alike, are connected with restraint.

There are other societies which employ swaddling, about which I know nothing relevant except this one fact; the field of research in national character—or, if every hypothesis is rejected, in the variations in childcare and child-training—is still almost totally unexplored.

Appendix II

A NOTE ON THE SWADDLING HYPOTHESES

BY JOHN RICKMAN

*T*he swaddling hypotheses[1] break new ground in the field of psycho-dynamics. I have no recollection of having read about the influence of swaddling in psychoanalytical or psychiatric literature, nor heard it discussed. In the former there is much reference to frustration of gratification at the, breast and in toilet training and so forth, but the effect of the restriction of movement as a specific factor in influencing the development of the personality is, I think, new. Though I am not in a position to criticize this general deduction of a national character largely influenced by very early experience of individuals I am prepared to accept it pending further evidence. I certainly know of no single factor which affords a better explanation of the Russian character. In addition to the swaddling factor there are others which work in the same direction. The 'diffuse guilt reaction', i.e. guilt not focused upon the relation to one person, may in part be explained by the fact that save for breast feeding the infant is cared for by any one of up to a dozen persons who may be near. Three or four generations usually inhabit the *izba* and anyone from any generation gives a

---

1. Naturally one of the first things I was asked by the originator of the swaddling hypotheses, after he had evolved the idea, was what I had seen of swaddling in Russia. I had to confess that I had not noticed it. The explanations that occur to me are these: first, at that time I had no interest in the treatment of babies, so it was not a detail that would stay in the mind; secondly, the death of babies was so much taken for granted by peasants that they rarely brought them to hospital. (I do not think this was due to my lack of interest.) This supports the author's view that the attitude of the peasants to their children is not the same as in the West. When I did see babies in the hospital or in the peasants' homes they were unwrapped for examination and wrapped up afterwards either in another room or after I had left the house; my ignorance on this point is therefore of no special significance.

hand, thus the infant grows into a relationship with a community far
more than he does in the West. But because of her breast feeding the
mother is a central figure as regards gratification. The 'dietetic weaning' is usually ended at about two years, but I have seen children
scared at my sudden entry (in that vast mountain of hides) even up to
the age of four or five years rush to their mother usually (or to any
woman if the mother be not by), and pulling apart the blouse hold
the nipple in the mouth, eyeing me the while as I pulled off the layers of fur coats; when satisfied that there was no danger they dropped
the nipple and went on with their play.

It is probable that the two factors interact, viz. the swaddling and
the fact of being brought up by three generations simultaneously.
Since the latter is common to many cultures it is well to give special
consideration to the former. Some day we should have a full survey of
the influence of swaddling on national character in which record
would be made of the following points:

(a) the extent of the body restricted, or, in terms of action, the
freedom allowed to the various parts of the body. To take but one
obvious instance, and that not the most important, the fact that Russian babies can scarcely move any part of their bodies except their eyes
helps to answer the question why it is that Russians use their eyes so
eloquently. I have not noticed the same use of the eyes in other
nationals. I think the swaddling hypotheses have given us an answer.

(b) The timing of the swaddling in respect to feeding and its ces-
sation in respect to what I call 'dietetic weaning' would provide
another 'scale' by which the 'swaddling cultures' can be arranged.

(c) the influence of the swaddling on the parents' relation to the
child; I say 'parents' for short, meaning here the people who unswad-
dle and attend to the child. If the child is turned into a sort of cocoon
the impulse to intrude upon it-to see whether it is wet or not, to
adjust its pillows, tuck it up, untuck it, and so forth-is obviously in
some measure checked. From the point of view of the parents' psychology swaddling prolongs one feature of the intra-uterine state-you
can't get at the child or play about with it.

Geoffrey Gorer makes special reference to his debt to Pavlov, Boas,
and Freud. All three authors have influenced his swaddling hypotheses. The alternate constriction and then relaxation with gratification
has in it something of reflex conditioning which we associate with
Pavlov; the anthropological approach we associate with Boas, the
interweaving of guilt with the texture of the personality (which the
other two authors ignore) we associate with Freud. From that cork-

lined physiological laboratory in St. Petersburg which Pavlov ruled like a Czar an idea which has heretofore been largely unassimilable in Western psycho-dynamics-though often uncomprehendingly quoted-is brought into relation with the work of Boas and Freud.

Appendix III

TRUTH AND GUILT

BY JOHN RICKMAN

NOTE: The late H.W. Massingbam, Editor of 'The Nation', with some mis-givings publisbed in 1919 two articles of mine, the content of which is incorporated in this Appendix. His misgivings were justified, for it was more than twenty-five years before anyone but myself showed any interest in the ideas expounded in them.

The feature of this book which has in my opinion most immediate social importance is the clarification of the *Russian attitude to Truth*. Because there is so little understanding of the profound differences between the Russian and the Western way of looking at Truth there is a tendency for people on both sides of the cultural frontier to ascribe obscurantism and even malice to the other. I have had some experience of the difficulty in getting Western people to see the Russian way of looking at things.[1]

On my return to England from Russia at the end of 1918 I found great confusion of ideas about Russia but very little curiosity about the origins of the striking differences between the Russian outlook and that of the Western Powers. My replies to questions put to me about Russia were listened to with attention, until I suggested that an adequate answer required equal attention to Western ideas for comparison. Then interest lapsed.

It may perhaps be useful to outline briefly how the matter appeared to me at the close of the First World War, since it is unlikely, if the ideas put forward in this appendix are at all correct, that the

---

1.   I should add that when Geoffrey Gorer wrote this book he had no idea that I had written or spoken on a somewhat similar theme thirty years before.

broad differences which have existed for two millennia will have changed completely in three decades. The view then put forward in many political speeches and in some articles[2], is here expanded (and modified in a few points) because it has relevance to this important problem concerning the difference in attitude towards truth in Russia and in the West.

The argument can be summarized briefly thus:

> *The Western attitude was greatly influenced by Rome-the Eastern by Athens: Roman lawyers-Greek philosophers: Pauline Christianio-Johannine Christianity: developing individual ownership of the means of production-retention of Communal ownership of the land: Eucharist-Pentecost: Bi- or Multi-party Government-the Mir (Collective opinion) Government.*
>
> *At the end of the First World War the Central European Powers were attacked from the West and split by 'vertical' (national) divisions, from the East by 'horizontal' (class) divisions: at the end of the Second World War the political rearrangements show signs of following old patterns.*

The activities peculiar to man may be viewed as techniques of adjustments made necessary because of his inherent instability. The instability within himself as an individual is mainly the field of study of the psychiatrist, the instability arising through his membership of a communities within the subject-matter of the anthropologist, the sociologist, and the historian. Neither of these disciplines alone can give a full account of the process of adjustment to the instability and, since the adjustments of the individual and the group are interconnected, neither discipline even in its own special field can lay claim to completeness. Out of the full range of possibilities one community, for reasons that are in essentials still obscure, chooses one way of dealing with conflicting tensions, another another; there is probably, if we did but know it, an inevitability in the choice characterizing the community in each case, but this does not imply that one type of community (or national) character can be used for assessing another as being 'right' or 'wrong', 'good' or 'bad'.

With this in mind, and as an exercise rather than as a finished thesis, let us examine the forces other than the purely military that were operating in the First World War to split up the Central European Powers. These forces may be grouped under the names of the two frontiers that were being attacked, Western and Eastern (the latter in this case does not mean Oriental); the two kinds of force have each a long and different history.

Western ways of thought and action have been largely characterized by the inheritance of Rome. In Rome the mental activities of the

2.   E.g., in *The Nation*, 29th March 1919, and 19th April 1919

educated classes employed the mode of thought which characterizes lawyers. The influence of this approach to the problem of human adjustment found its expression in the religious field in the writings of St. Paul[3] where the handling of the problems of spiritual life were thought of in terms of property law, which included in those days the ownership of slaves and their manumission.

In the most sacred rite of the Roman Church, the Eucharist, the thoughts of the devout were directed, when the Divine Essence entered the individual, on the notion of Redemption through the sacrifice on Calvary.

It is unnecessary to stress the general influence of Roman Lawyers on Western culture, but particular attention may be directed to the attack on the Central European Powers in the First World War. The lines of cleavage were 'vertical'; state was separated from state with promises of separate treatment in separate treaties of peace. Two thousand years ago the Roman Senate in its political dealings with foreign states used a similar technique.

We can make a generalization by saying that whatever the activity it could always be argued about; basically, intellectual (and spiritual) activity was treated as if it were a step-by-step process of negotiation between contesting clients appearing in the same court. It is not surprising that Western Socialism is commonly thought of as coming gradually.

3.   Romans i. 14, Paul as a debtor to both Greeks and Barbarians; i. 18, truth held down in unrighteousness; i. 2.5, the truth changed for a lie; ii. 2, the judgement of God is according to truth; iii- 7, if the truth of God through my lie abounded unto his glory why am I not still judged as a sinner? iv. 4, reward not reckoned as of grace but of debt, ix. i, I say the truth in Christ, I lie not my conscience bearing witness with me; 1 Corinthians i. 30, redemption through Christ, Galatians ii. 14, when they saw that I walked not according to the truth of the gospel [here a point is argued like a lawyer]; iii. 18, contrasting the inheritance of the law and of promise; v. 3, a debtor to the whole land; Ephesians i. 7, redeemed through blood; i. II, on being a heritage foreordained; i. 14, on the inheritance through Christ; v. 5, naming what bars a person from inheritance; Colossians i. 12, partakers on inheritance; i. 14, redemption and forgiveness of sins; iii. 24, inheritance as a recompense; Hebrews i. 4, on inheriting a name; ix. 15, Christ as the mediator of a new covenant; 1 Peter i. 4, an inheritance reserved. Though the Acts of the Apostles was probably not written by Paul but was almost certainly influenced by him it is not inappropriate to refer to Chapter xxvi, verse 18, where there is reference to remission of sins and the inheritance of those sanctified by, faith. The list is by no means complete but it may serve to show how much St. Paul's thought was influenced by Roman Law.

In contrast to Geoffrey Gorer's point about the Eastern approach to the Truth we might say that in the West the approach is individual, it comes by a slow process of adjustment, that though at moments the grasp of Truth may be felt to be complete, for the most part the notion of 'Living in Truth' is an aspiration rather than an experience, and that we are usually ready to find in other people elements of the Truth which will form the beginning of a negotiation with them. To say this is not to deny the fact that individuals in the West occasionally, but usually only temporarily, experience an 'oceanic feeling' in which their identity with other participants in the Truth is felt to be complete. Above all, the discovery in other people of characteristics which seem alien or even antagonistic to what is regarded as the Truth is accounted for by their imperfect approximation to a viewpoint. The relation to Truth admits of the notion of *quantity* of gradual approximations, whereas the Russians exclude these steps and plump for quality—you are in the Truth or else you are outside it, you 'belong' or you don't.

Turning to the Eastern ways of thought and action the comparable point of origin to Rome is Athens. The mental preoccupation of the Greeks was with philosophy and metaphysics, and Christianity derived from this source a different pattern of thought. The relation to God had but little of the personal bargaining which has characterized so much of the spiritual life of the lawridden West. In Russia the mystics 'belong' in the community to a far greater extent than in the Roman area of influence. The burden of sin is shared by the group of believers and is dissolved by a religious act in which everyone participates simultaneously. Pentecost for the peasants of my acquaintance was the moment in history of supreme significance, not the Last Supper. The Gospel of St. John was their favourite text.[4]

4.   This Gospel shows no sign of Roman influence, at least on my reading of it. To be sure its precision when describing a train of events is lawyer-like, e.g. Chapter ix, where the blind man was made to see, but no use is made of legal ideas. Ile concepts are almost entirely spiritual or metaphysical: 'The Word was with God and the Word was God', 'The Word was made flesh', 'full of grace and truth', 'the true light which lighteth every man that cometh into the world', 'God is a spirit'. The relation between God and man is expressed in terms of love and identification, belief in the Truth springs from love, and the Truth makes man free from the yoke of sin. The commandment is this: to love one another, 'henceforth I call you not servants … but I have called you friends; for all things I have heard of my Father I have made known unto you.'

If one takes the behaviour of the peasants (for instance, that described in 'The Apology' given above) and sets it alongside these quotations from St. John and those given earlier from St. Paul one can see which matches well and which does not.

The conduct of the village *mir* is comparable in the social and economic plane with Pentecost on the spiritual. There is first a discordance of individual opinion in which everyone expresses his personal views, sometimes stridently, sometimes gently; the lack of unanimity to begin with is most striking and there is no sign of party organization. Then with an increasing number of silences (such as occur in groups of chattering people in any part of the world) defined courses of action are mentioned (the speaker claiming no prestige for voicing a policy and none being accorded him) and policy opinions are received with assent or else the hum of talk continues, meaning that opinion is not united. Once opinion is united there is a profound sense of satisfaction and of village solidarity, and the members of the village assembled at the *mir* disperse without a vote having been taken, with no committee formed and yet the feeling that each man knows what is expected of him.

Returning to the end of the First World War: the Eastern attack on the Central European Powers had none of the sharp lawyer-like bargaining characterizing the Western attack but was a diffuse emotional appeal to the masses to join the Brotherhood of Socialist Revolution. Self-abnegation and participation in a mass movement were asked for and in return the peoples of Europe (eventually the world) would receive the strength which comes of human solidarity and eventually communal possession of the means of livelihood. Of course, there were many reasons for the Bolsheviks adopting the world-revolutionary policy; the suggestion here made is that it fitted in with the Russian *mir-sobornost* (Pentecostal) way of thought. It is not surprising that Eastern Socialism is commonly thought of as coming suddenly.

Geoffrey Gorer's theory about the Russian attitude to Truth seems to be supported by the ideas outlined above, but I should like to add that I do not think because of this that the Russians have inevitably a fanatical aggressiveness to foreigners. At present in Russia the people have but little opportunity to measure themselves and their material progress against standards other than their own, for despite the surging oceanic feeling of their political and religious life (I am speaking definitely of the old regime and surmise things have not altered in essentials since) there was a considerable curiosity as to how others lived and thought. I would remind readers of the 'Political Episode' in an earlier section of this book; at the time of the Constituent Assembly there was among the villagers I served a desire to use the political experience of the West as a model. Subsequent events seem to show that the materialistic Kremlin has, like Peter the Great, 'opened a window to the West' but only in respect to physical, not sociological or psychological, techniques. In order to keep their control over the masses the Kremlin rulers have to paint foreigners as beings who are black and themselves as beings who are white.

The greatest difference as I see it between the old regime and the new is in relation to guilt. In the old regime though the Church was so much in the service of the Czar it nevertheless gave the people a different scale of values to that supplied by the Autocracy; Czars could be measured against the myths about the saints. In the present day the Kremlin (carrying One Party Rule to its logical conclusion) tries to be both State and Church. It decries any pangs of conscience except for breaches of its own rules and denies that its own destructiveness can carry a load of remorse; so far as my experience goes this sounds to me un-Russian and therefore I am not surprised that the political police are busy.

My next point is that the new regime in Russia is far further from an understanding of Western culture than the old. In the old, though there was this mass-action, an all-or-none approach to Truth, the body of Truth, with its acceptance of internal contradictions, included an acknowledgement of the complexity of guilt (one of the points in common between the old regime and the West): the Kremlin, on the other hand, allows of only one kind of sin—disbelief in the complete correctness of its system.

The gulf between the leaders and the led is in certain important respects greater than ever; the internal tension—witness the strength of the political police force—is as great as in the old regime despite a 'people's revolution'. Geoffrey Gorer has outlined a policy for keeping the Russians within bounds, but neither he nor I nor anyone else has put forward a plan to lessen that tension-creating gulf. But perhaps in time the effect of early upbringing, which the Soviet Authorities are trying to westernize, may produce a change in the national character. A peasant, after asking how we did things in the West, said to me when discussing the new regime, 'We peasants will give them thirty years and then see what they make of the job'. We too must exercise such patience before passing judgement upon a way of life that is difficult for us to understand and that conflicts with so much we accept, perhaps uncritically, as right. It is the Russian attitude to Truth that is, of all things, the most baffling. For the Russians, this attitude to Truth is at once a source of strength and an inspiration: for us it usually seems mere confusion. Nothing is harder than to move into the ways of another culture; few things are more important, particularly in a world influenced by a rapid increase in the rate of communications, than a realization of the restrictions which our own culture imposes upon our tolerance of human differences.

SOVIET ATTITUDES TOWARDS AUTHORITY

by
Margaret Mead

Chapter 1

QUESTIONS WHICH THIS STUDY SEEKS TO ANSWER

A primary task of the mid-twentieth century is the increasing of understanding, understanding of our own culture and of that of other countries. On our capacity to develop new forms of such understanding may well depend the survival of our civilization, which has placed its faith in science and reason but has not yet succeeded in developing a science of human behavior which gives men a decent measure of control over their own fate. This book is a report on an interdisciplinary-group approach to the study of certain aspects of Soviet attitudes toward authority. My role as director has been to help to integrate the approaches of my colleagues within an anthropological framework and to prepare this report of the work which we did together.

The problem of forming reasonably accurate estimates of social and political conditions within the Soviet Union, of calculating directions of change, and of assaying the significance of single events presents peculiar difficulties because of the impossibility of attaining direct access to the Soviet people, because of the highly centralized ideological screen through which all public materials have to pass, and because of the strength of feeling for and against the political system of the Soviet Union which has resulted in the positive or negative coloring of almost all first-hand reports. It is these obstacles to direct observation which justify the use of the type of analysis which will be attempted in the following pages. Ideally, the anthropologist works on the spot, and, to attempt an understanding of the areas which have been covered in the background for this report, field workers would have been placed in plants and factories, in collective farms and Machine Tractor Stations, on Party committees, in the editorial rooms of journals and newspapers, in the schools, in Komsomol meetings. Not only the contents of a book or a film, but the response of the readers and of the audience would have been investigated. The proportion of the Population who read a propagandistic pamphlet or followed in detail a governmental injunction would have been determined by sampling methods. Hypotheses regarding the character structure of different groups, the Party Members, the skilled workers, the managerial class, etc., would have been tested by interviews and observation, by data from the clinic and the consulting room.

These methods cannot be applied to the present task. It has therefore seemed worth while to collect such data as were available and to analyze these *as if* one were giving an anthropological analysis of authority problems within a society which it had been possible to study by direct field methods. Such a procedure has the advantage that it uses the anthropologist's training in relating isolated items of behavior to a systematic whole, in remembering that abstractions like "The Party" or "Soviet agriculture" are convenient ways of describing certain of the institutional activities of Soviet men and women, but that the same Soviet man may be a Party member, the manager of a Machine Tractor Station, a father, a reader of a novel, a man who responds or falls to respond to a cartoon in *Krokodil*, who takes the mandates of the Party with extreme seriousness or executes them with his tongue in his cheek. If this focus on the individuals who appear and reappear in the different phases of Soviet life is maintained, then it is possible to outline certain regularities in their behavior and to trace these regularities through the organization of the Party, the way in which a collective farm functions, or the admonitions given to teachers of small children. The words which a novelist puts into the mouth of an approved heroine, or the scolding which is given in *Pravda* to collective farmers who steal grain, or the methods used to recruit skilled labor by appropriate political prosecutions can all be used as data on the behavior of the Soviet people who live within the Soviet Union.

With such data, we can attempt to answer such questions as the following: What are the patterns of behavior between those in authority and those over whom they have authority? Are these patterns of behavior congruent with the ideals of behavior which are constantly preached in the schools and in the youth organizations? When we analyze the attempt to remake the old type of Great Russian into "the new Soviet Man" through adult education, political indoctrination, new forms of organization, and the attempt to bring up children to fit the new ideals, do we find contradictions which may be sources of weakness in the present, of revolt, or of change in the future? Can we form an estimate of the type of devotion or acceptance of the Party and the State which is characteristic of the great mass of Soviet citizens who do not emigrate against which we can interpret the testimony of those who do emigrate?

If we can form hypotheses on problems such as these, they will have direct bearing on such questions as the type of loyalty which may be predicted for border populations or the sorts of pressure exerted upon a chairman of a collective farm by central authorities on the one hand and the members of the collective on the other. An informed estimate of the response of Soviet citizens at different levels to changes in the Party Line coupled with our historical knowledge of the shifts in the Line should make it possible to estimate the morale differential and resistance to propaganda of different age groups or of individuals with different status in the Party, armed services, or industry.

Americans are daily forming opinions regarding the public behavior of Soviet officials or events in the Soviet Union which hinge directly on the answers to such questions as these: What is the Soviet attitude toward compromise? What types of behavior are regarded as permissible and ethical which we would regard as impermissible and as involving those who practiced them in depths of cynicism? At what level, for what purposes, can we say that Soviet officials are sincere? How does this sincerity differ from our sincerity?

A second group of questions concerns the internal structure of the Soviet Union: the meaning of organizational changes, the extent to which different parts of the "apparatus" are rivals, the relationship between the actual clique formation and the official ideal picture which is given to the average Soviet citizen and to the world.

Many of these questions might be summarized briefly in the following manner: What is the nature of the hold which the contemporary authority system in all of its ramifications—Party doctrine, centralized organization, economic rewards and punishments, censorship, political police, and educational system—has on the population? What are the conditions under which this hold may be expected to get stronger, to remain the same, to get weaker?

It is toward answers to these questions that the following analysis is directed.

Chapter 2

METHODS AND MATERIALS

*T*he method used in this study is one which has been developed during the last decade for the study of cultures at a distance, using individual informants and written and visual materials where field work is impossible. The anthropologist brings to this approach his training in preliterate societies, where he has had experience in the use of living informants and in tracing regularities among many disparate elements of a culture small and simple enough to grasp as a whole. While it is quite impossible ever to obtain the same grasp of the culture of a great complex literate society, and while it is always necessary to rely on the combined research and experience of many disciplines, the anthropologist's way of looking at the materials can still be used.

This particular anthropological approach goes beyond the mere identification of such regularities in different aspects of a culture. It attempts to integrate these observed patterns of behavior, as reported by historians, economists, political scientists, and other specialists, with our knowledge of the growth and development of human beings and with the findings of the psychologist and psychiatrist on the functioning of human personalities.

Probably because this method has been developed as an applied science to deal with problems of great human urgency without the protection of an ivory tower, it has been subjected to a very large amount of misrepresentation.

(1) It has been asserted that this method attempts to trace political and social institutions back to events of infancy. This is not so. Events to which the growing child is regularly subjected in any society are invoked to analyze the way in which the child learns his culture. The critic has confused here three kinds of statements about origins: (a) the origin of the particular anthropologist's insight (in the sense that a study of the way a child is taught to cat may give a clue

to cultural attitudes toward scarcity or responsibility; (b) the origin, within the life span of the individual, of that *individual's* understanding or appreciation of an institution, in the sense that a child's religious view of a Heavenly Father may be shaped by the behavior of its human father; and (c) statements about origins of political and social institutions. The anthropologist does not differ from other students of social institutions in his recognition that social and political institutions have long histories and have been shaped by many generations of human beings within changing social, physical, and technological environments. Though the origins of all social institutions are complex and cannot be traced to any *single* cause, institutions persist by being embodied in each generation, which must learn the appropriate behavior and acquire the appropriate character structure, and changes in any society of any duration must be expressed in changes in these learnings, in which case the accompanying character structure will change also.

(2) It has been asserted that in this approach caste, class, occupational and regional differences are ignored. Where the material is available and relevant, these differences are taken into account; but this method has been used primarily to deal with behavior in national and international contexts, in which it is possible only to know the national culture from which a given newspaper or propaganda leaflet, broadcast, army, or mission comes. We may be able to identify the particular region or subculture or class which plays a dominant part in shaping some or all aspects of national policy—for example, the role of men with public-school education in traditional British foreign affairs, or of Great Russian culture in contemporary Soviet culture—but primarily we are concerned with those regularities in the behavior of citizens of a nationstate which can be attributed to the fact that such citizens were reared or have lived for a long time under the influence of a set of nationwide institutions. Knowledge that a man is a Soviet citizen does not make it possible to tell what language he speaks, what food he prefers, or to what place names he responds with nostalgia, but it does make it possible to state certain aspects of his relationship to the police system, to rationing, and to his available reading matter.

Such a statement regarding "national character" is necessarily bare and schematic, omitting the nuances of region and class and unable to do justice to the unique ways in which individual personalities express their culture. When an anthropologist describes a whole primitive culture, or a historian a whole period, the description is richer than the actual content of any individual personality, as no one person, however precise his class and regional representatives, ever embodies all the intricate detail of his culture. So where reading a full account of one's culture is felt to be ennobling, reading a schematic description of a certain set of regularities which one shares with every other national of the same country—a description which is not a composite portrait, not even a snapshot, but only a diagram—is felt to be impoverishing. When such a diagrammatic statement also includes references to parts of the character which have become unconscious—either as a child learning to reconcile its impulses with cultural demands, or as an immigrant, sternly repressing memories of the past—the resistance of the reader may be even stronger. Yet such diagrammatic statements have proved useful for special purposes: to predict the behavior of members of one culture as compared with another and to comprehend and allow for large-scale changes which are taking place in contemporary cultures.

(3) It has been asserted that anthropologists assume that the character structure of a people is static and unchangeable, which is equivalent to a form of racism. This is not so. This assertion confuses the methods used by anthropologists in dealing with primitive societies when there are no records and for which, therefore, change can only be inferred from indirect evidence and so cannot be studied systematically, with anthropologists' approach to modern societies in which they recognize rapid change and profound discontinuities between generations as being the rule. However, we also recognize that changes are made by human beings, themselves reared within the existing culture, and that the new character structure will therefore be systematically related to the old, sometimes as a deviation at only one level, sometimes as an extreme counterpoint, as a new class or a special segment of the population comes into power. The more rapid the change, as in successful revolution or when large numbers of individuals emigrate as adults, the more conspicuous are the relationships between the old and the new character. This book is an attempt to examine contemporary Bolshevik character, which may be seen either as a new, special version of old Russian character or as a new Russian character, and the institutions which Bolsheviks are developing to shape the next generation.

In this approach it is assumed that human infants begin life in every human society—of comparable size—with a comparable range of abilities and potentialities. It is assumed that differences reported by all students of human societies as existing between one culture and another—differences in language, social organization, religious belief, etc—are in no way to be related to any racial characteristic of the members of these societies, but must be learned by each generation. It is further assumed that, while the particular form of the culture of any society—the United States, or the Soviet Union, or the Republic of Indonesia—is to be related to a long sequence of historical events within a given geographic context, the fact that a given group of adult members of a society embody an historically developed culture is to be referred to the circumstance that they either have been reared in those particular cultural forms or have emigrated and subsequently have mastered them. Because of man's common psychophysiological equipment, it is possible to explore the way in which different cultures are learned by human beings with comparable abilities and so to learn something of the cultural character of those who perpetrate a culture and participate in revolutionary or evolutionary changes which take place within that society. When changes occur, especially the drastic changes which accompany a successful revolution, it is possible to relate these changes to the existing learned behavior and to ask, How will individuals who embodied the old culture behave within the new revolutionary forms? To what classes, or personality types, or sorts of experience can we relate the insistence on new behavior and the repudiation of the old? How does a knowledge of the way in which the old culture was learned or of how the new emerging culture is acquired—when placed against a comparative knowledge of how all children and adults learn—add to our ability to understand and to predict?

Throughout such research, emphasis is laid upon combinations rather than upon single items, upon configurations of widely diffused or universal aspects of human behavior. just as every language is made up of sounds shared with other languages, of grammatical devices shared with whole families of languages, so the patterns of learning within any culture share many single items with neighboring cultures or with cultures which derive from common historical roots. In identifying the regularities within any one character structure, the anthropologist attempts to show how the particular combination of interpersonal events by which parent and child or old resident and new immigrant communicate with each other is organized to produce a character which can be identified as American, or Russian, or French, or Greek, or Siamese.

Furthermore, this new approach has to work out relationships with other disciplines which have been the traditional ways of studying historical societies.

This approach is meant to supplement rather than to replace the findings of other disciplines by relating the mechanisms within the individual to wider descriptions of social process. The social sciences have already made outstanding contributions to our understanding of contemporary Russia by analyses in terms of such organizing abstractions as revolution, the pace of industrialization, and the characteristics of dictatorships. Such analyses can be given additional usefulness if such large-scale changes can be described in terms of what has happened and is happening to the Russian people who are participating in them. Findings from this method should not be expected to contradict any other analysis of the Soviet Union which is based on scientifically viable hypotheses, but they should reveal hitherto unidentified connections, open up further lines of research, and thus increase our capacity for prediction.

This report concentrates on the special contribution of this method without continually repeating the interpretations which other disciplines place on the same phenomena. For example, the success of the centrally controlled police state may be related by historians to earlier models in Russia or in Asia or in the Near East, and the functioning of the NKVD may be compared with that Of the Janissaries; political scientists may discuss twentieth-century totalitarian models; political philosophers, the role of Marxist philosophies of power; and economists, the peculiar Soviet methods of solving problems of full employment by methods which call on the political police to provide a specified number of politically suspect skilled carpenters. This report will stress the relationship between a police system which does not seek to fix responsibility accurately for a particular crime but which operates with diffuse terroristic methods and a characteristic of Russian behavior which, by equating treasonable thoughts and treasonable acts, makes the acceptance of such a police system, both by those who execute it and those who live under it, *different* from the acceptance of such a system in another society. Where the other disciplines will invoke as explanatory concepts "Russia's peculiar historical position," "the level of industrialization," and "the Hegelian dialectic," this approach will invoke the learned behavior of Russians, particularly of Great Russians, and more particularly those Russians who became Bolsheviks, not in opposition to these other explanatory concepts, but in addition to them. The comparative anthropological approach lays stress upon differences between cultures, upon the basis of an acceptance of a common humanity, in comparable situations—such as revolution—and upon a recognition of the diffusion of ideologies, such as Communism, beyond the limits of one culture. But it is the distinctively Russian version of humanity, the distinctively Russian aspects of the Revolution, the distinctively Russian interpretations of Communism upon which the anthropologist would expect to throw additional theoretical light. When we stress these distinctively Russian characteristics, we do so in recognition that there are many formal resemblances among revolutionary situations, that Communism is found in other countries, and that totalitarian regimes have certain organizational aspects in common. These considerations have been systematically taken into account with the help of the historians and political scientists in the group. This discussion of certain aspects of Soviet attitudes toward authority thus proceeds within the context of historical and political scholarship on the Soviet Union but will limit itself to such aspects of the question as are not dealt with in this form by the other disciplines.

In an undertaking such as this it is necessary for the reader to have a record of who did the work and of how it was done.[1] We were a staff of nine with two consultants; all but two—of whom I was one—were familiar with Russian culture and the Russian language. Each research worker assumed responsibility for the selection and analysis of materials in specific areas within a framework provided by individual consultation and group seminar.

Six areas were chosen for analysis: (1) the Party, the two youth groups which prepare for the Party—Komsomols and Pioneers—and the records of the trials of the Old Bolsheviks in the late thirties (selected as a part of the most recent material on communication within the top levels of the Communist Party of the Soviet Union); (2) leadership in agriculture; (3) organizational problems of industry; (4) education, especially official standards for parental behavior and school practice; (5) contemporary literature, both adult and juvenile, especially direct and indirect expressions of disapproved attitudes and behavior; and (6) the new folklore concerning Lenin and Stalin. The published materials used—having been published within the Soviet Union—must be assumed to have been, at the time of publication, approved by the regime. They may therefore be taken as indications of what the top echelons of the CPSU would like the lower Party echelons—the worker, or the member of a collective farm, the parent or teacher—to believe and do, and of what types of thinking and acting were or are disapproved. These materials provide no direct information on the extent to which those to whom they are addressed believe

---

1. This project was originally suggested to RAND by Professor Ruth Benedict, who was also directing a series of researches on contemporary cultures, under a grant from the Office of Naval Research, known as Columbia University Research in Contemporary Cultures. When Professor Benedict died in September, 1948, I succeeded her as director of Columbia University Research in Contemporary Cultures and was asked to assume in addition the direction of this project, which was then reorganized as Studies in Soviet Culture under the American Museum of Natural History. Dr. Nathan Leites, a member of RAND's scientific staff, acted as research coordinator, with special reference to the political relevance of the material.

what they read or on the extent to which they act upon it. This is pre-liminary research to construct hypotheses concerning the responses of the Soviet population to these materials and the way in which the enjoined ideals are carried out in practice.

In order to interpret further these materials, the following steps were taken: (1) Recent emigrants were interviewed. (2) The personal experience of members of the research group who had worked at various times and in various capacities within the Soviet Union or with representatives of the Soviet Union was thoroughly exploited. (3) There was a systematic inclusion of hypotheses on the character structure of different groups in pre-Soviet Great Russia, especially of peasants and intelligentsia, which had been developed in the Russian section of the Columbia University Research in Contemporary Cultures by Geoffrey Gorer.[2] These had been derived primarily from interviews with adult Great Russians, using methods of interpretation based on our present knowledge of human growth and the educational practices of a society as embodied in the character structure of adults. (4) Parallel hypotheses on the special Bolshevik version of this older Russian character structure, as developed by Dr. Nathan Leiter[3] through a detailed analysis of the works of Lenin and Stalin, were included and systematized with reference to our present knowledge of the less articulate aspects of human psychology. (5) Critical use was made of comparative anthropological studies of social structure and of the relationship between certain types of social structure and certain types of character structure.[4]

Within this apparatus of interpretation, selected materials were analyzed in detail by methods of tracing connections and delineating patterns which are used by anthropologists, linguists, clinical psychologists, and psychiatrists. Every effort was made to use this approach (which has been developed on a known context) against a critical historical background.

This report does not attempt to document the findings of the Studies in Soviet Culture project. Appendix D presents a detailed

2. Geoffrey Gorer and John Rickman, *The People of Great Russia, a Psychological Study* (see pp. 3-159 above); Geoffrey Gorer, "Some Aspects of the Psychology of the People of Great Russia," *The American Slavic and East European Review*, Vol. 8, October, 1949.

3. *The Operational Code of the Politburo*, The RAND Series, McGraw-Hill Book Company, Inc., New York, 1951.

4. M. Mead, *Cooperation and Competition in Primitive Societies*, McGraw-Hill Book Company, Inc., New York, 1937; G. Bateson, *Naven*, Cambridge University Press, London, 1936.

account of the large amount of published source materials which was systematically examined by different members of the research team who specialized in materials of a given order; for example, pedagogical literature, letters to the press on a given subject, and literary controversy, during a specified period of time. The selections which each research worker made were processed as working papers and made available to the entire research group. Each member of the group participated in developing hypotheses for further exploration of these particular materials. The choice of illustrative material used in this study was checked by the specialist who originally contributed the particular quotation. It therefore seems valid to draw illustrative materials from sources covering the whole life of the Soviet Union without in each case giving an account of how the contextual relevancy has been established. The varieties of experience in the group are the guarantee that material has been used only with full and systematic consideration of the date, the particular setting, the type of publication, and the local historical situation, etc. The problems in this report have been considered against Soviet society, seen as a whole, and against a conception of traditional Great Russian character and emerging Soviet character. These cannot be discussed in full in a report of this length, and only such aspects as fall within the range of this inquiry will be dealt with; but in the discussion of Soviet police terror, for instance, although the state of transport, record-keeping, fingerprinting, etc., will not be elaborated, it will have been taken into account.

Nor are the hypotheses suggested here meant to be complete explanations of particular events—as providing, for example, an explanation of the great purges of the late thirties, which have their very special historical context. If the hypotheses presented here are to stand up, then nothing which we know about the great purges should conflict with them, but there is no expectation that the entire course of the great purges should be derivable from them. Studies of culture provide better bases for prediction the larger the number of members of a culture involved in the prediction: they are more valid for the behavior of a group of critics than for the writer of a single work of fiction; for the response of the populace than for the writer of a single broadcast or the behavior of a particular political leader. While the behavior of the single writer, the particular editor, or the political leader must be systematically related to the culture to which each belongs, it cannot be specifically predicted from it, although the limits within which it may fall may be established.

In attempting to describe that particular version of human behavior which may be represented as being contemporary Russian, and showing how contemporary Soviet political action may be referred to such characteristics, there is no suggestion that the political behavior of the Soviet Union is solely selfgenerated and in no way responsive to and influenced by political events in the world outside the Soviet Union. Nevertheless, in this political situation within which the Soviet leaders are responding to internal and external events there should be considerable usefulness in discriminating the special Russian character of these political behaviors.

I have prepared this report on the basis of the materials developed by the research staff and with criticism and consultation from members of the group, especially from Geoffrey Gorer, Nathan Leites, and Philip E. Mosely. I am not only not a Russian specialist, but I do not speak Russian and I have been able to do only a minimal amount of interviewing or first-hand analysis of materials. I have had twenty-five years of experience working on comparable problems among primitive and contemporary people and several years of experience in relating researches of this sort to specific national and international problems. This book must be understood as an attempt to point up some of the implications of the work of the project team. The members of the research group are responsible for the selection of the concrete materials which have been used and for criticizing the contexts within which I have used them, but I alone am responsible for the theoretical phrasing, based as it is on the insights, research, and formulations of the members of the two Russian projects with which I have been associated.

This was a pilot project. Hypotheses which have been developed during a year and a half of systematic research await elaboration and further verification.

Research Team of Studies in Soviet Culture and Their Areas of Research

Margaret Mead, Director, anthropologist; integrating, working with, and supervising the research staff with special emphasis upon a cultural frame of reference.

Nathan Leites, political scientist; specializing in an analysis of the trials of the Old Bolsheviks; integrating, working with, and supervising the research staff with special emphasis upon political relevance. Member of the Social Science Division, The RAND Corporation.

Elena Calas, psychiatric social worker; specializing in Soviet child-training ideals and ideas of authority in Soviet children's literature.

Elsa Bernaut, Slavic linguist; specializing in analyses of the trials of the Old Bolsheviks and of conflicts within the Party.

Herbert Dinerstein, historian; specializing in studies of Party unity and organization and case studies of the way in which Party ideals of organization work out in agricultural management. Member of the Social Science Division, The RAND Corporation.

Leopold Haimson, historian; specializing in studies on Party unity and organization and case studies of the way in which Party ideals of organization work out in management of industry.

Nelly S. Hoyt, historian; specializing in analysis of Soviet youth training ideals and Communist synthetic folklore about Lenin and Stalin.

Vera Schwarz (Alexandrova), literary analyst; specializing in delineation of images of types of conformity and nonconformity in contemporary Soviet literature.

Nicolas Calas, literary analyst; working on the relationship between attitudes toward authority in the Greek Orthodox Church and contemporary Soviet attitudes.

Ralph T. Fisher, graduate student in history; making a special study of the Eleventh (1949) Congress of the Komsomol.

Consultants

Geoffrey Gorer, anthropologist; scrutinized the concepts developed in Studies in Soviet Culture in the light of the basic hypotheses concerning pre-revolutionary Great Russian character structure which he developed for the Columbia University Research in Contemporary Cultures in 1948-49.

Philip E. Mosely, historian; has provided historical orientation and criticism in the light of his experiences with contemporary Soviet political behavior.

Chapter 3

BACKGROUND OF THE
SOVIET SYSTEM OF AUTHORITY

As a background for this study, certain broad historical tendencies in pre-Soviet Russia must be taken into account. In the nineteenth century, Russia, hitherto a caste society, developed a group recruited from various castes known as the "intelligentsia," defined by education and attitude rather than by birth and without the definiteness of place in society which the old castes occupied. This group reacted strongly against many tendencies in the old Russia, such as the miserable conditions of the lower castes in country and city and the backwardness of the whole life of the country. During the decades in which members of this group came out both openly and secretly against the status quo, a rapid industrialization set in. While most of the industries were in the hands of private capital, Russian and foreign, the State played a major role in fostering industrialization through direct subsidies, guarantees of interest to investors, loans, guaranteed. contracts for purchase of output, free importation of equipment, and high tariffs on competitive imports as well as through preventing the formation of trade-unions and punishing the outbreak of strikes, thus assuring to the new industries a supply of unorganized and cheap, if not always docile, labor. The new capitalist class was small in number, weak in prestige and subservient to the autocracy, and it provided little if any support for the growth of liberal and democratic demands for reform. Under these conditions, Marxist doctrines imported from the industrialized West had to be adapted to a society in which the enemy consisted of an amalgam of Tsarist bureaucrats, large landowners, foreign and domestic capitalists, etc. With no trade-union movement of a character such that labor leadership might have grown out of it, leadership became largely the task of a small group of self-dedicated intellectuals. Despite the widespread feeling of solidarity among the intelligentsia, many diverse programs developed, surrounded by furious controversy.

Lenin and the group of Bolsheviks around him had the task of shaping from a group of fervent, talkative, impractical intellectuals who had been mainly concerned with reacting *against* tyranny and exploitation rather than with the development of any practical program, a group capable of seizing power and of holding it once it was seized. At the same time, everything—institutions and persons, they themselves as much as the rest of the population—had to be remade into something different from the old.

Strict forms of political control, centralization of government and industry and political police who watched over a people adept at indirect forms of resistance, did not need to be invented but had merely to be shaped to new purposes. For example, under the peasant commune, or *mir*, which was the dominant form of rural life in Great Russia until 1928, the peasants were accustomed to regard the land as owned by the community or by the Tsar, not by the individual peasant, to decide on the joint planning of village work (times of planting, harvesting, stubblegrazing, etc., had to be uniform), and to perform some forms of community work together. Conscription of community labor for state needs had long been a tradition, which was gradually abandoned only after the 1860's; and, in fact, the peasants usually clung to the custom of providing free labor for this purpose in preference to paying additional taxes.

Russian Communism, using Marxist theory but grounded in Russian conditions, developed by men imbued with a Russian attitude toward life, has had a double emphasis. It fought against certain aspects of old Russia but also against certain aspects of the West seen from Russia. It opposed the sluggish apathy and the tendency of old Russia to accept fate and also opposed the romantic, despairing, or overoptimistic adventurousness of those who reacted against resignation; it turned against those who wished to go too fast as well as against those who wished to go too slowly. This double character of Russian Communism (which in future will be referred to as Bolshevism) has become familiar to the world in the picture of a struggle around a central position from which the "rights" and the "lefts" are always "deviating," with those in power always trying to overcome both deviations, sometimes by absorbing parts of one deviating group, sometimes by using one group to destroy the other, sometimes —when strong enough—by lumping rights and lefts together and destroying them both.

The use and ideology of supreme power in the Soviet Union have certain unique characteristics, in addition to the circumstances that they were developed directly following a hereditary monarchy with a highly centralized bureaucracy and that the Soviet Union is a dictatorship which shares with other dictatorships the totalitarian demand for control over every aspect of life. The very considerable tightening of controls in the Soviet Union, as compared with the Tsarist regime, may be explained in part by the fact that a traditional regime reacts to overt signs of rejection; a new regime demands active proof of loyalty.

There are also certain aspects of the Bolshevik version of Marxism which must be held in mind. One of these distinctive aspects is the theory of the Party Line. The Bolshevik concept of the Party Line sums up the doctrine that the policy-making group knows the "correct" course to take. Krupskaya, Lenin's widow, said at the 14th Party Congress in 1925:[1]

> For us, Marxists, truth *(istina)* is that which corresponds to reality. Vladimir Il'ich *(Lenin)* said: The teachings of Marx are immovable because they are true *(verno)*, and our congress should concern itself with searching for and finding the correct line. It is impossible to reassure ourselves with the fact that the majority is always right. In the history of our party there were congresses where the majority was not right *(neprav)*. ... The majority should not get drunk *(napivat'sya)* with the idea that it is the majority, but should disinterestedly search for a true *(vernyi)* decision. If it will be true *(vernyi)* it will put our party on the right path.

The Line, as understood by the policy-making group, represents absolute Truth; therefore, while temporary retreat before a strong enemy may be necessary and in fact dictated by the Line itself, true compromise—in the Western sense—is not comprehensible to the Bolshevik leadership. As one American negotiator reported in an unpublished memorandum:

> During negotiations they feel that appeals to public opinion are just a bluff. If American public opinion is contrary to what they want to do, our government or some hidden body, a "capitalist Politburo," must be manipulating it. We think of compromise as a natural way to get on with the job, but to them "compromise" is usually coupled with the adjective "rotten." They are puzzled by our emphasis on the desirability of compromise. They think we can be pushed around when we propose compromises prematurely, i.e., before they have fully tested the firmness of our position. When we or the British advance a series of compromises, we confuse them by changing our position so often.

The Anglo-American idea of political compromise is based on the expectation of there being at least two sides to a question, so that a

---

1. N. Krupskaya, 14th Congress of the All-Union Communist Party (XIV *s'ezd Vsesoyuz- Kommunisticheikoi Partii*), stenographic account, Moscow, 1926.

workable compromise represents a position somewhere between or among a series of positions each of which is sincerely believed in and stoutly defended. But the Bolshevik idea of the Line is more accurately represented by the figure of a lens which is correctly focused; there is only one correct focus for any given situation, and this is not seen as arrived at by finding some mid-point between lens readings which are too open and those which are too closed; rather, all settings except the correct focus are seen as deviations from the single correct position.

The absolute Truth embodied in the policy of the leaders had to be reconciled with the need for change. An autocratically organized society may meet the changes resulting from technological change, relative military strength in respect to other national states, etc., by simply handing down fiats from the dominating group for or against large families, universal conscription, or any other practice that it is considered necessary to initiate or alter. Such autocratic leaders may invoke, on behalf of their demands, patriotism, religion, loyalty, or fear of reprisal. Tsarist Russia and Japan previous to World War II were traditional societies of this type, and Nazi Germany was a hastily assembled twentieth-century model.

The Bolsheviks have drawn on historical autocratic models and, in phrase(109y, partly on Western democracy. But it has become clear that Western democratic practices, with their emphasis on the direction of government being derived from preferences which the majority of the people express among alternative courses of action, are hard to combine with the idea of a single Truth or with the overriding importance of a single power center. In the United States and Great Britain there is usually no dominant feeling for some single course's being the inevitable line of action. In Anglo-American democracy it is recognized that each next step must be felt out: "Only one link in the chain of destiny," said Churchill, "can be handled at a times."[2]

But according to Lenin, as quoted by Stalin[3] "it is not enough to be a revolutionary and an adherent of socialism or communism in general. What is needed is the ability to find at any moment that particular link in the chain which must be grasped with all one's might to gain control of the whole chain and pass without a hitch to the next link."

The political forms of the Soviet Union today are related to this Bolshevik belief that those in power should and do have a correct

2. Excerpt from a speech on the Crimean Conference delivered by Winston Churchill to the House of Commons, February 27, 1945.

3. J. Stalin, "Foundations of Leninism" (*Osnovi Leninizma*), as in Stalin, *Leninism*, New York, 1928, p. 156.

diagnosis of the total historical situation and must use this power to the utmost. Authority is thus, in Bolshevik dogma, held to be justified by Truth and is to be exercised by those most able to perceive and to be most vigilant in combating, in themselves and in others, tendencies to deviate from Truth, either to the right or to the left. As the Soviet Union developed, the group of leaders allowed to express, first publicly and then behind closed doors, conflicting views as to what the correct position was, was steadily narrowed—down. But the theory and its expression in purges, in political discussions, or, for example, in literary criticism seems not to have changed. At any given moment in history there is only one course of action which is right; the Party, through its leaders, perceives this right course; all must acknowledge the leaders' monopoly of the Truth at all times and the rightness of the Line at any given time, whether it concerns the tempo and method of collectivization, making a pact with a former enemy power, or shifting a metallurgical policy. The implementation in action of each change in the Line commits large numbers of people to a policy which has the authority not only of power but also of Truth. Such a policy may be evaded or revised in practice, but its over—all formulations cannot be questioned by its implementers. The ordinary channels of communication through which, in the West, the lower ranks of any complicated organization—the army, a large industry, a foreign service—question the wisdom or the practicability of a policy are closed. The Western expedient of new elections which can brand the policy of the group in power as wasteful, blind, leading straight to depression, inflation, or war is also not present. Individuals in important positions below the top level who execute a given policy seek to build up subsidiary power centers, insisting on the exact following of the Line, for the execution of which their present powers are held to be granted. But the very zeal which it is appropriate to show in following out the Line decreases the possibility of such lower administrators making corrections which would prevent a course of action going too far in one direction, and tends instead to push it even further along the path inaugurated at the original shift. Sooner or later, because conditions change so rapidly in an economy devoted to change, and within the present structure of world politics, it becomes necessary to shift the Line. This, according to Bolshevik theory, can be done very easily by the leaders, whose every position is justified by their ability to recognize the time at which the Line should change. However, the problems involved in a thousand subsidiary parts of the huge bureaucratic structure are not so easily disposed of. The adjustments required in different fields may take months or even a year or so to carry out, and the discrepancies in timing between different areas may themselves become a source of confusion.

Many subordinate officials who came into power at the last shift in the Line began their terms of power or office by loudly disagreeing with those whom they replaced, strongly emphasizing their allegiance to the new Line. The jobs under them were filled by those who would rigidly carry out their orders. In every field of administration, whether it be the school system or the industrial system, the editing of magazines or agricultural research, there is an accepted doctrine. These doctrines are superseded by the new Line.[4] Under the formula of displacing those who have been either too slow or too fast in adjusting to the new Line, a political house cleaning can take place. If there has been an argument within a section of the apparatus as to the exact direction to be given, for example, to work in literature, biology, or social science, and a major or even a minor shift in the Line occurs, the losing side goes out. In other words, changes in Line are usually reflected in most aspects of Soviet life, even in those which appear to have no connection with the point at issue, while shifts in the Line will be reflected in changes of personnel all down the lines of command which regulate every aspect of Soviet life. It is often hard for an outsider to see why a change in evaluation of a theory of Shakespeare's poetic method should have any link with, for example, a theory of selecting Young people to be directed into factory work; and such a link may be, and is usually, expressed in denunciatory terms, by such general words as "objectivism," "formalism," "kowtowing before the bourgeois West," "equalization," "campaign style of work," etc. Meanwhile the personnel shift will express some change in the relative positions of the advocates of opposing theories, and the side which wins will work out the relationship to the Line. As many of these ideological links are very thin, it is not surprising that something which is forbidden, or out of date, or declared to be no longer correct is often more clearly stated than that which is positively approved. Even where a directive is clear, it is likely to be negatively stated. Thus a directive to document Russian precedence in intellectual history may be conveyed by a general directive against "kowtowing before the West."

4.   For examples, see P. Mosely, "Freedom of Artistic Expression and Scientific Inquiry in Russia," *Annals of the American Academy of Political and Social Science*, Vol. 200, November, 1938, pp. 254-74; Ivan D. London, "A Historical Survey of Psychology in the Soviet Union," *Psychological Bulletin*, Vol. 46, No. 4, July, 1949, pp. 241-77; and "Theory of Emotions in Soviet Dialectic Psychology," *Feelings and Emotions*, edited by Martin L. Reymert, McGraw-Hill Book Company, Inc., New York, 1950.

Examples of the way in which changes in Line are interpreted in particular fields may be found in the professional literature of the field in question. So, in the *Teachers' Gazette*,[5] the article, "Against the Overburdening of School Children," states:

> One must accustom students to guard their own and other people's time, to give up excessive link gatherings, publishings of meaningless newspapers, albums, etc. ... Often komsomol regional committees evaluate the activity of squads and troops not according to real educational results but according to purely superficial showing: is an exhibition handsomely presented, are wall—newspapers artistically put out, how many albums and placards are made by the pioneers. ... It is time to protest against *formalism* in educational work. [italics ours]

Here the damning word "formalism," always an epithet of disapproval, is used to describe and condemn a particular set of educational practices. The same condemnation occurs in an article on "The Pioneers," in *Family and School*,[6] which describes the way in which a disapproved type of leader is represented as thinking:

> "Why entrust this to a new link or squad which may fulfill the task one has no idea how? It is better to give it to the one which has repeatedly proved itself in other matters," some leaders figure. "Why should I let the pioneers repair, decorate or make installations in the pioneer room when a professional worker can do it better?" so sometimes thinks a director of a school. It is such people who adjust pioneer gatherings exclusively to dates of the Revolutionary and school calendar. The needs and interests of the pioneers do not interest them. The Central Committee of VLKSM demands a decisive end of *bureaucratism* and *formalism* in pioneer work. [italics ours]

Even the way children's games are taught in school will be scrutinized and attacked:[7]

> Probably janitors in all countries need the same "instruments of production," but one cannot create an image of a Soviet janitor, postman, mechanic, talking only of his implements. One must show his attitude to his work. But no games show this. Such "neutrality" of games, limitation of their subject-matter, may be justly considered as *ideological lack (bezideinst')* and *political lack (apolotichnost')*. [italics ours]

5. "Against the Overburdening of School Children" (report on the meeting of the Collegium of the Ministry of Education), *Teachers' Gazelle* (*Uchitel' skaya Gazeta*), November 11, 1948.

6. V. Khanchin, "The Pioneers," *Family and School (Sem' ya i Shkola)*, September, 1947.

7. A. P. Usova, "On Ideology in Educational Work of Kindergartens," *Pre-School Education (Doshkol' noe Vospitanie)*, May, 1948.

The Party leadership is held, in Bolshevik political dogma, to owe its right to rule and its relation to Truth to its ability to foresee the future, to "hear the grass growing under the ground." The rightness of the Line is a sanction for the exercise of power, and the successful maintenance of power is a sign that the Line was true. This has meant in practice that the success of any policy assumed enormous importance in passing judgment upon it. So an informant's report of a conversation between a member of the CPSU and a German communist in 1926 was as follows:

> I said to him: "How was I to know about Germany, about its economic conditions, about the ramifications of the socialist party?" (That is, that the Soviet leadership's plans for the revolution in Germany were made in ignorance of the real situation.) "I was only a young Communist. But you, you should have known." And he, twenty years older than 1, said: "I did know, but who was I to tell them? They made a revolution. They made our dreams come true."

The overwhelming effect of Soviet success in stifling such criticism among non-Soviet communists in the late twenties and thirties was paralleled within the Soviet Union by the effect on the Oppositionists of Stalin's predictions coming true instead of their own. The Oppositionists had believed that catastrophe from within and from without would follow from the Line taken by the Party leadership. When this did not happen, the Oppositionists were forced to reconsider their entire position. Radek gives an account of this:[8]

> "In 1934, we considered that defeat was inevitable. We proceeded from an overestimation of the difficulties in the countryside. In industry we considered that there was a transitional period when even the newly-built factories were only just being put into operation. The position on the railways was at that time considered to be catastrophic, but now, towards the end of 1935, could we consider that the situation on the railways was catastrophic? ... I ... knew of the opinion held of our railways by foreign intelligence services who considered that our railways were prepared for war. Could I, towards the end of 1935 ... consider that our industry was doomed in the event of war? ... I ... knew that everything required for the prosecution of war would be supplied. In the case of agriculture, I myself did not have a wide field of observation: every year I went to the same collective farms, in the Kursk Guberniya ... in 1935 [they] represented ... something absolutely different from what they were in 1933. ... And so, if in 1933 or 1934 we proceeded from the

8. Report of Court Proceedings in the Case of the Anti-Trotskyite Centre heard before the Military Collegium of the Supreme Court of the USSR, Moscow, January 23-30, 1937. Published by the People's Commissariat of Justice of the USSR, Moscow, 1937, pp. 123-24.

assumption that defeat was inevitable ... we now saw that the idea of the destruction of the USSR by western fascism and by the military-fascist circles in the east, which Trotsky took as his starting point, was now, from the standpoint of objective reality, a fantasy, that all the conditions for victory existed."

And Bukharin stated at the Third Trial:[9]

> ... everyone of us sitting here in the dock suffered from a peculiar duality of mind, an incomplete faith in his counter-revolutionary cause. I will not say that the consciousness of this was absent, but it was incomplete. Hence, a certain semi-paralysis of the will, a retardation of reflexes. ... Even I was sometimes carried away by the eulogies I wrote of Socialist construction. ... There arose what in Hegel's philosophy is called a most unhappy mind. ... The might of the proletarian state ... disintegrated its enemies from within ... it disorganized the will of its enemies and American intellectuals begin to entertain . n doubts ... in connection with the trials taking place in the USSR, this is primarily due to the fact that these people do not understand ... that in our country the antagonist ... has ... a divided ... mind. And I think that this is the first thing to be understood. I take the liberty of dwelling on these questions because I had considerable contacts with these upper intellectuals abroad. ...

Radek looks back on his 1930-31 belief in the catastrophic consequences of rapid and forced collectivization :[10]

> I dissented on the main question: on the question of continuing the fight for the Five Year Plan. ... History's joke was that I overestimated the power of resistance, the ability, not only of the mass of kulaks, but also of the middle peasants, to pursue an independent policy. I was scared by the difficulties. ...

The effort to discern the Line becomes endowed with all the emotion generated by the desire to remain in power, and by individual commitment to the future of the Soviet Union. (For the purposes of this argument it is not necessary to attempt to assess the degree to which Stalin and his associates are influenced by one consideration as distinct from the other, or the degree to which these considerations are felt as distinct.) The smaller the group at the top, the more monolithic the structure, the simpler a shift in the Line becomes. But the

9.   N. 1. Bukharin, Report or Court Proceedings in the Case of the Anti-Soviet "Bloc of Rights and Trotskyites" heard before the Military Collegium of the Supreme Court of the USSR, Moscow, March 2-13, 1938. Published by the People's Commissariat of Justice of the USSR, Moscow, 1938, pp. 776-77.

10.   Report of Court Proceedings in the Case of the Anti-Trotskyite Center, Moscow, January 23-30, 1937, pp. 85-86.

problems at lower administrative levels remain. Because of the tie-in with the Line of particular administrative and technical procedures, scientific schools of thought, etc. —subjects about which substantive differences of opinion exist—the administrator who has geared his practice most articulately to the Line becomes the most vulnerable when the Line changes. We should expect to find, therefore, two trends: a demand from the top for ever more flexible, unquestioning obedience, ever more explicit establishment of links between a particular practice and the general Line, and a tendency at lower levels to avoid the ideological tying-in of special procedures or issues with the Line. In a sense, the politicizing of the whole of life leads to a sort of attempted counterdepoliticization. But this depoliticization in turn is condemned by the Bolshevik leadership as a shortsighted policy which "lags behind life." So, in a discussion of current Soviet literature on the organization and planning of industrial enterprises, S. Kamenitser delivers a characteristic rebuke for such attempt to escape the dilemma. He says:[11]

> The basic defects of the … books examined … is the attempt to depart from class examination of problems of the economics and organization of enterprises, and to hide in the technical, practical side of the question. Technicism in works on production organization is not a chance phenomenon. This tendency to emasculate the class content of the work organization of the enterprise (is a tendency) to gloss over … the superiority of socialist enterprise.

The way the Truth, which is to be applied in every area of life, is derived, when expressed in the Line, has changed through the years. In the first years of the Soviet Power it was assumed that the Truth was arrived at through collective deliberation of the Party rather than through the deliberation of any one organ or person within it. In those years and, with diminishing effectiveness, back to 1929, "Party-democracy" was supposed to mean that all members of the Party, acting through cells and then through regional and finally through All-Union Party meetings, would help the leaders "at the center" to formulate the "correct Line." Accordingly, each Party member was supposed to exercise full freedom of discussion (within the general program of the Party) until a decision had been reached by a Party Congress, and only after that was he expected to abandon all differences of opinion and work with all his strength to carry out the decision reached by the Party.

11. From *Planovoye Khoziaistvo*, No. 3, 1949. Quoted in *Current Digest of the Soviet Press*, No. 33, p. 25.

As early as the 10th Congress of March, 1921, Lenin expressed strong doubts as to whether the Party could any longer afford the great amount of effort expended in reaching decisions in this way. During the twenties, the reinforcemerit of control from above over Party' personnel went on rapidly, and, by 1928, decisions were already reached by this means before a Party Congress was called to approve them. Thus, in official histories of the Party today, the period of the twenties, in which there were still many factions each giving an interpretation of the Truth, is passed over very rapidly, and the whole emphasis is placed on the importance of applying known Truth.

The appropriate behavior of the Party member today is to know the principles of Marxism-Leninism and to apply them as directed by the Line, not to think about them. But application must occur in every field.

Stalin, as the perfect exemplar of such detailed and pervasive application, is described in a statement by Kaganovich at the 17th Party Congress, 1934:[12]

> The work on the literary front was unsatisfactory. Stalin studied the problem and he did not limit himself to pious generalizations or orders to the workers on the literary front. He went to the core of the problem. He put the question differently: It is necessary, he said, to organizationally change the situation and the question was laid down of the liquidation of RAPP [Russian Association of Proletarian Writers], of the establishment of a united Union of Writers; after this organizational solution of the question, the writing forces rose, developed, and things in literature improved. The solution of the organizational problem thus secured the application of the Party line to literature.

It follows almost inevitably, so strong is the emphasis upon the correct application of known Truth, that those who are able to apply the Line, to act in accordance with a definite directive, in terms of a body of doctrine, would seem to be more likely to survive and to arrive at positions of leadership than those who have any tendency toward questioning or doubt. This is, of course, an outstanding aspect of Stalin, that he has been able to concentrate on the application of his conception of Leninism in a state of what appears to be undisturbed orthodoxy. All doubt is pictured in contemporary Bolshevik doctrine today as leading finally to complete loss of faith, and the inevitable accompaniment of loss of faith is to become the active agent of the enemies of the Soviet Union. The threat, dramatized in

12. L Kaganovich, 17th Congress of All-Union CPSU (XV11 *s'ezd Vsesoyuznoi Kommunisticheskoi Partii*), stenographic account, Moscow, 1934, p. 565.

the trials of the mid-thirties, and expressed over and over again at every level in the official literature, is that belief and practice are inextricably joined.

Muralov tells as follows of his development in prison :[13]

> Muralov: I reasoned that if I continued to remain a Trotskyite I might become the standard-bearer of counter-revolution. This frightened me terribly. ... Was I to remain in opposition and continue to aggravate the affair. My name would serve as a banner to those who were still in the ranks of counterrevolution. This was what decided me.
>
> Vishinsky: There were no prospects in the struggle?
>
> Muralov: The danger of remaining in these positions, the danger to the state, to the Party, to the revolution.

And Grinko says in his last plea:[14]

> I refer to my inner feeling of satisfaction ... my happiness at the fact that our ... conspiracy has been discovered and that the ... calamities which we were preparing and partially carried out against the USSR, have been averted.

Radek concludes his remarks at the second trial with remarks addressed to "those elements who were connected with us."[15]

> ... the Trotskyite organization became a center for all counter-revolutionary forces; the right organization ... is just another center for all the counterrevolutionary forces in the country.

In Bolshevik theory one cannot be a passive doubter and merely go away quietly into political oblivion and simply sit, having lost one's faith. It is considered that an individual who was once trained as a member of the Party will have so learned to combine belief and action that, if he changes his mind, he is potentially more dangerous than one who never underwent Bolshevik training. (There is always a danger also that, in the West, security agencies may act in response to this Bolshevik view and insist that individuals who leave the Party perform extraordinary services against the Party before they can become rehabilitated as repentant members of a democratic state.

13. Report of Court Proceedings in the Case of the Anti-Trotskyite Centre, Moscow, January 23-30, 1937, pp. 232-33.

14. Report of Court Proceedings in the Case of the Anti-Soviet "Bloc of Rights and Trotskyites," Moscow, March 2-13, 1938, P. 721.

15. Report of Court Proceedings in the Case of the Anti-Trotskyite Centre, Moscow, January 23-30, 1937, p. 550.

Such a response to this Bolshevik view tends, on the one hand, to strengthen the absolutism of Communist Party membership and, on the other, to strengthen the Soviet belief that it is unsafe to leave backsliders alive.)

This belief provides the rationale of the relentlessness with which the Soviet Union persecutes any Party member who appears to have faltered, deviated, or doubted in the slightest degree. This is not to be compared with the attitude of the Spanish Inquisition, which tortured the erring soul for that individual erring soul's sake to save it from Hell, for the individual is not regarded as valuable within the Soviet system. It is rather to be compared with the calculation of the Holy Office that, since all men "partake of one another," each erring soul would inevitably produce other erring souls and would thus contaminate the entire body of the faithful. So, by Bolshevik doctrine, the backslider cannot be let alone, because such a one will not merely backslide into harmless activity but will become transformed almost instantaneously into an active enemy. The insistence, in the Moscow trials, on the active and dangerous role of former Opposition leaders, who had actually been leading lives of political retirement and meaninglessness for several years, served to dramatize the belief that there is no neutral position for those who have once committed themselves to the Party.

The few records we have suggest that the only course of action which seemed open to Soviet foreign service officers who wished to break with the Soviet Union was to get in touch immediately with some anti-Communist or anti-Soviet group. Each dissenter who does this dramatizes in practice the Soviet leadership's belief that those who are not wholly with them are actively and totally against them. The belief that all who differ must implement their enmity leads to practices in the Party which in turn force all deviators to more extreme steps than they would otherwise have taken. Total commitment to the Party includes the acceptance of the Party's right to sentence to death—not only as any soldier is prepared to face certain death when his commanding officer so orders, but to the point of accepting the rightness and probability of being court—martialed in disgrace and shot, although every effort was made to obey every order. This attitude can be documented most vividly from the behavior of the old Bolsheviks, such as Krivitsky. Krivitsky claims that he did not break with Moscow,[16] even when he was ordered home during the height of the Purges and knew that he would be purged. He

16.   W. G. Krivitsky, *In Stalin's Secret Service,* Harper & Brothers, New York, 1939, p. 260.

planned to return, although he was certain that he would be liquidated. However, after he had actually boarded the train for Moscow he received a remand which made him feel that the Party had been testing him, that his willingness to return and be shot had been doubted. Then he broke. Our best material on this requirement of absolute acceptance of the Party's right to dispose of the individual comes from Old Bolsheviks. Recent interviews with Soviet DP's suggest that Party membership today often does not carry such completeness of dedication.

The emphasis appears to have shifted from the absolute devotion spontaneously accorded by the Party member to the absolute devotion demanded by the Party leadership. This demand for devotion in turn appears to be accompanied by an extreme fear that it will not be met, that the Party membership will yield to temptation.

Unless this conviction of the almost immediate and inevitable transformation of a doubting adherent into an active enemy is kept firmly in mind, the disciplining of Party members, the "reconditioning" of those returned from Western countries after the War, and the distrust of every Soviet citizen who lived under the occupation[17] are likely to be interpreted as signs of greater fear and instability in the regime than actually exist.

Americans are likely to equate the Soviet fear of the slightest expressed preference for anything Western, even the most innocent remark about some superior gadget, such as an electric switch,[18] as showing the same degree of hysteria which would have to be postulated if American officialdom became as worried by slight statements that child care or public health regulations were good in the Soviet Union. But the basic United States political position is that those who are not actively *disloyal* can be counted on to be either loyal or neutral. The Soviet denial of the possible existence of such neutral ground makes all these apparently hysterical reactions to the smallest doubt or the slightest criticism take on a very different coloring than would be the case if they occurred in the United States. It is not that such suppression of criticism does not express fear but that the degree of the fear cannot be measured by the minuteness of the deviations which arouse the whole paraphernalia of political suppression. In the United States, on the other hand, the size of the slip for which individual citizens or government officials are placed under suspicion at

17. Louis Fischer, *Thirteen who Fled* (subeditor, Boris A. Yakovlev; translators, Gloria and Victor Fischer), Harper & Brothers, New York, 1949.

18. P. Antokol'sky, "About Poetry, Education of the Youth and Culture" (*O poesivospitanii molodykh, o kul'ture*), *Znamya*, January, 1947, p. 141.

a given period may well be regarded as an indication of the political climate and of the amount of fear present at some echelon, possibly not the highest or the most central echelon.

It is important to distinguish between power conflicts among different sets of administrators, on the one hand, and on the other hand, between conflicts arising from originally nonpolitical issues as, for example, between the advocates of one laboratory method or another, or between two manufacturing processes, or between cotton monoculture and diversified agriculture. The political victors, after a shift in Line, are able to back up their side of the controversy, while the political losers will see their technical views go into the discard, at least temporarily. In the United States the same sort of thing occurs, within the services, when advocacy of a particular technical policy becomes associated with a contest between two different groups. When a new top appointment determines which group has won, either because the technical policies advocated by that group have been accepted or because the group itself has greater political acceptability, the policy of the other group will go temporarily into the discard, and the men who advocated it are likely to be frozen at a lower level than their service records promised. What is accomplished in the United States by the advancement of one group in preference to another is done in the Soviet Union by the liquidation (sometimes execution, sometimes only dismissal and banishment) or demotion of the group which was formerly in the saddle. Since 1938-39 there has been less physical liquidation and more temporary banishment or demotion.

This, in outline, is the relationship between the structure of political power and the political dogmas of Bolshevism expressed in the Line, which is an invention for reconciling the absolute rightness of the leaders at any given time with the need for change, and the repercussions at lower administrative levels, where the struggle for power often includes actual differences on technical matters.

Bolshevik Assumptions about Human Behavior as Abstracted from Theory and Practice

The following discussion is based on the hypothesis that the group of political leaders who founded and shaped the Russian Revolution represented, in ideal if not in actual character, a particular variant of the traditional Great Russian character. This Bolshevik ideal draws upon both Russian culture and that of Western Europe, but it had to be put into practice by a Party leadership which shared in various degrees, with the people whose behavior was to be altered, the traditional character. In the first two decades of the Revolution we thus have the spectacle of a group of adults who themselves varied in different ways from the traditional character-some of them having been deviants from childhood, others assuming the new ideal late in life—deliberately enforcing upon themselves a style of new behavior, at the same time trying to establish this behavior in the next generation.

In the course of this development, certain new behaviors, such as self-enforcement of ideal behavior combined with continual scrutiny by members of the group—methods appropriate to a transitional stage in the development of a new character type—became institutionalized as correct behavior. Self-criticism and mutual criticism, originally devices for maintaining behavior which had no history in the life experience of the individual, became established as consciencequickening procedures. Also, many of the traditional orientations were displayed in new and disguised forms in the emerging behavior patterns of the Bolshevik. Among the people of the Soviet Union today we find (1) preSoviet traditional behavior, (2) Bolshevik behavior taken on in adulthood, and (3) new Soviet behavior grounded in childhood exposure to behaviors (1) and (2). Without intensive studies of individuals it is impossible to give complete descriptions of the way in which these three character orientations are combined in any one individual, or class, or group.

We can give an internally consistent, although limited, account of the traditional Russian character structure, which developed individuals prone to extreme swings in mood from exhilaration to depression, hating confinement and authority, and yet feeling that strong external authority was necessary to keep their own violent impulses in check. In this traditional character, thought and action were so interchangeable that there was a tendency for all effort to dissipate itself in talk or in symbolic behavior. While there was a strong emphasis on the need for certain kinds of control—by government, by parents and teachers—this control was seen as imposed from without; lacking it, the individual would revert to an original impulsive and uncontrolled state. Those forms of behavior which involve self-control rather than endurance, measurement rather than unstinted giving or taking, or calculation rather than immediate response to a situation were extremely undeveloped. The distinctions between the individual and the group and between the self and others were also less emphasized than in the West, while the organization of the *mir*, the large, extended families, and religious and social rituals stressed confession and complete revelation of self to others and the merging of the individual in the group.

With little capacity to plan, work for, and execute a long series of steps toward a goal, the traditional Russian showed a large capacity to endure adverse conditions and to respond with great completeness to the particular conditions of the moment.

Traditional Russian character assumed the coexistence of both good and evil in all individuals, and, in attitudes toward individuals, an expectation that friends could behave like enemies was combined with an expectation that this behavior could also be reversed—by confession, repentance, and restoration of the former state.

With little interest in man's particular responsibility for particular acts, the traditional Russian emphasized instead a general diffuse sense of sinfulness in which all men shared. Little distinction was made between thought and deed, between the desire to murder and the murder itself. All men were held to be guilty, in some degree, of all human crimes. Against this lack of distinction between thought and deed there was a strong emphasis upon distinctions among persons, on a purely social basis, an intolerance of any ambiguity as between superiors and subordinates. This rigidity in matters of deference and precedence, however, was relieved by a strong countertendency to establish complete equality among all human souls and to wipe out all social distinctions.

Against this description of traditional Russian character, it is possible to place a description of Bolshevik ideals, in which description it is necessary to rely a great deal more upon written statements of purpose or upon the analysis of political acts and, where there are fewer data upon the actual character of the Bolshevik leadership. In assessing the regularities in the character of the traditional Russian, it is possible to use materials pertaining to a relatively slowly changing situation, where some data on the behavior of parents and grandparents can be used to understand the behavior of children. The Bolshevik leadership group, on the other hand, were assembled from diverse backgrounds and welded hastily and painfully together; and they must be considered in terms of a set of ideals on which the effect of such personalities as Lenin and Stalin and the importance of an imported ideology, that of Hegel and Marx, both have to be taken into account. It is possible to show very striking continuities between old Russian and Soviet political behavior, as in the demand for written confessions, the demand for the confession of sins which were not committed, the relationships between leader and people, the forms of political expansionism, etc. But even here it is impossible to assay how much a new leadership, of a different character, is taking models from an old historical situation—as a man who had sat cross—legged all his life might adopt the sitting behavior appropriate for chairs when he found himself living in a house—and how much these continuities are given their form by a persistence of certain aspects of traditional Russian character in the present Bolshevik leadership.

With our knowledge of the traditional Russian character and a systematic use Of the. theories of dynamic psychology and cultural analysis, it is possible to ,elate the utterances and public behavior of the Bolsheviks to their expressed goals on the one hand and the probable persistence of traditional Russian character on the other so as to construct hypotheses about contemporary Soviet behavior.

The Bolshevik ideal personality can usefully be seen as an attempt to *counteract* tendencies in the traditional Russian character which were seen as preventing the establishment of Bolshevism and as an attempt to *introduce*, or at least to accentuate, tendencies which were recognized and admired in Western civilization. In this ideal, the individual must be goal-oriented; all acts must be seen as instrumental in reaching the final goal—the triumph of Communism—and no act must be valued only in and for itself or be judged without reference to a goal. Instead of lack of internal control, surrender to impulse, and dependence on external authority, the Bolshevik is expected to develop a strong internal conscience, an ability to produce the highest level of activity without external prodding or stimulation. By constantly pressing against the limits, by "swimming against the stream," he can establish and maintain the necessary organization of his own personality. There must be no diffuseness in his behavior, it must be continually focused and purposeful, measured, calculated, planned, and appropriate. Within his behavior there must be a rigid subordination of personal and private feeling to the demands of the final goals of the Party. Whereas the traditional Russian culture valued rest and relaxation, the Bolshevik ideal distrusts both. Rest must be transformed into a means for more effective work or be suspect.

So far, this statement of the Bolshevik ideal will be recognized as a rather generalized ideal, one which, with a very few changes, could be ascribed to the Puritan fathers of early New England or to many Protestant groups in Western Europe at periods of high self-conscious religious ferment.[19]

We may now come, however, to the more specifically Russian aspects of the Bolshevik ideal, which can in turn be related systemat-

19. This view of the Bolshevik revolution, as embodying a kind of delayed Protestantism, together with the particular psychodynamics which accompany such changes, was developed by Erik H. Erikson. See E. H. Erikson, *Childhood and Society*, Chap. 10, "The Legend of Maxim Gorky's Youth," W. W. Norton & Company, New York, 1950.

ically to Russian history, and to theories of dynamic psychology. Ideologically, Russian Bolshevism demands a complete subjection of the individual, by an act of individual will, to the control of the Party. The individual is to have a strong, internal conscience, yet the perception of the correct line of action is delegated to a small group of leaders, and the will of the individual is to be used first for the voluntary act of initial subjection and then to execute this Truth perceived by the leadership. In organizational terms, the ties between the leader and the led reflect the older relationships between people, bureaucracy, and Tsar. In ideal political behavior, the rigid self-criticism and mutual criticism necessary to maintain a new and difficult way of life has become a regular pattern, enjoined even on those among whom, if the Soviet educational system had succeeded, such efforts to overcome the old character type should have been unnecessary. In administrative behavior, the feeling that the whole structure is newly erected upon and only partially related to the earlier base is found in the fear of the leadership that any slip, any deviation, however small, will bring the whole shaky edifice crashing to the ground. Although the new character structure calls for an individual who is extremely clear about his own responsibilities and duties, Soviet administration of justice still shows a lack of interest in the actual connections between a particular criminal and a particular crime, operating instead on a theory that all are to some degree guilty—in thought if not in deed—of something. In regular administrative practice, a great deal of the cumbersomeness and inefficiency of the Soviet system is due to a failure to make individuals accountable only for that for which they are given real responsibility. Instead, an accounting is demanded from officials, agencies, or party organs of the success of a harvest or of the fulfillment of a manufacturing plan over which those held accountable had no real authority.

When we come to the third group—those who have been educated in explicit accordance with Bolshevik ideas, but by individuals, parents, teachers, older brothers and sisters who shared to a greater or lesser degree an acceptance of the new ideal character—we again have to erect our hypotheses on a structure many aspects of which are unknown. We have, however, considerable systematic knowledge of the functioning of the educational process in other cultures.

We have a description of traditional Russian character. We have an account of Bolshevik ideals. We have formal accounts of Soviet pedagogical practice, youth organizations, expected family relationships, and we have a certain amount of data, from records of DP's, on actual educational situations. Any statement regarding the character of Soviet youth, educated wholly under the Soviet regime, has to be qualified by our lack of knowledge of proportional relationships between the new ideal and the actuality. For example, present—day Soviet pedagogy stresses the importance of the biological family of father, mother, and several children, of firm parental discipline, and of responsible cooperation in the home on the part of the children, who are to be reared with a strong emphasis on strict hygienic training. It is possible to say what effects such a family structure will have—when it exists. It is also possible to outline the differences which may be expected to result in the character of children whose parents, reared in a different way, apply new educational precepts, as compared with the character resulting from the application of the same precepts by parents who have had earlier experience of, and have given complete allegiance to, the new regime. We do not, however, have enough information to know in what proportion of homes the conditions approved and propagandized by the regime actually obtain. Crowded housing, inadequate provision for the care of .children of working mothers, and persistence of older attitudes toward children may to a great degree nullify the attempts of the regime to change, by education and propaganda, the character of the rising generation.

This, in brief, is an outline of the theoretical structure on which the following discussion is based. These are the three points of reference: (1) the traditional Russian character, as expressed in historical records and as analyzed by psychological methods; (2) the Bolshevik ideal character, as expressed in writing and political behavior; and (3) the emerging Soviet generation, as it can be hypothesized from our knowledge of (1) and (2), above, of Soviet formal patterns of education, of inexplicit materials from literature, and of interviews. On the basis of this general framework, particular points in Soviet attitudes toward authority have been selected for illustration and elaboration in terms of their political relevance.

On the context of these three points of reference, we have to consider the tasks confronting such a self-conscious governing group, which is attempting to maintain a society of the size and heterogeneity of the Soviet Union and at the same time to make over the character of the people. Here again the Bolshevik leadership was presented with a double problem, one outside the Party and one inside. It had to deal with the great mass of the peasants (including the small number of urban workers seldom a generation removed from peasantry), who had centuries-old habits of work and of response to authority. Inside the Party there was the problem of making over the intelligentsia, who were only to some extent westernized and who, during the last century, had built up their own peculiar forms of behavior, many of which were very antithetical to emerging Bolshevik ideals.

Among the intelligentsia, from whom the Party leadership was drawn, two trends in attitude toward the peasants can be distinguished: one toward idealization of their potentialities and the other toward an impatience with their backwardness. This latter attitude of impatient hostility toward the peasants, as being obstacles to the reconstruction of the society, was expressed in endorsements of the harshness of the forced collectivization.

In the case of the peasants, the problem was one of transforming people, who had very little interest in time, a great capacity for endurance, no experience with machines, very special habits of working in groups, a limited time perspective and a limited mobility, into competent workers in a society which was to be rapidly industrialized, workers who would have an allegiance to and mobility within the nation. The conspicuous problem with regard to the intelligentsia was one of shifting the emphasis from speculative talk to controlled action, from an interest in a vague eternal Truth, ever to be sought and never found, to a concentrated, unflagging, effortful attention to one urgent and immediate task after another. There was, of course, a relationship between the peasant who, as factory worker, had to be threatened with six months' imprisonment for coming late to work in order to impress him at all with the importance of punctuality, and the intellectual who was more interested in long discussions of Bolshevik theory than in the question of organizing propaganda for increased production in a certain industry at a certain moment. The Bolshevik demand made on both was for a new focus, a new definiteness, a new stiffening and particularizing of purpose and behavior.

An important element in contemporary Soviet practices designed to make Soviet citizens into new types of men and women is the assumption that each individual carries within him a whole series of disallowed attitudes. Selfcriticism, an essential Bolshevik practice designed for continuous scrutiny of motives and behavior, covers two activities: the criticism of the self and the criticism of any member of a group by other members of the group. In both cases alertness against the appearance of evil is enjoined. Each individual (outside of the condemned "classes") is seen as having capacities for great goodness—currently, the capacity to submit all of himself voluntarily to that perfectly wise, foresighted authority, Stalin and the Party, and to exercise a maximum of initiative in the context set by the Party—but, equally, each is seen as having the capacity to become an "enemy of the people."

This belief in the possibility of the Soviet citizen's having within him the capacity to be a complete enemy is vividly dramatized in the Soviet film *Frontier*. The hero, a tiger hunter on the Manchurian border, kills four kinds of enemies in the course of the picture: six Russian traitors who have helped two Japanese to smuggle dynamite over the frontier to blow up a new industrial development, the two Japanese who have brought the dynamite and plotted an uprising, a maniac leader of a sect which has opposed Collectivization, and his best friend, a tiger hunter like himself, who has been his closest comrade for forty years and who in the end turns out to have betrayed the Soviet Union. In this film, the enemy without and the enemy within are identified together. The hero and the traitor he executes look almost exactly alike, have been companions all their lives, and have the *same* life history. Ibis same theme is expanded in the postwar Soviet film *The Young Guard*, in which the whole group of young partisans are destroyed because they trusted one of their number who had been a schoolmate and whose family were all Communists.

Instead of a conception of character in which, through a long period of maturation, the individual becomes permanently attached to the Good as his society sees it and so becomes permanently incorruptible and reliable, the conception is that every individual maintains the capacity for complete betrayal of all those values to which he has hitherto shown devoted allegiance. The "enemy of the people" is the replica, in every detail, of the most devoted Soviet citizen or Party member. This gives the whole problem of authority a very special character in the need for continuous watchfulness over adults as well as children, over the high Party official as well as the humblest non-Party member, in a never-ending effort to hold the personality attached to the Good—to the Partyand to prevent the treacherous, destructive elements which are *always there*, in all personalities, from obtaining any degree of, and hence complete, control. There is no real distinction made between the watch which one should keep upon oneself, the vigilance with which the slightest doubt should be identified and extirpated in one's own mind, and the watch which should be kept upon others. This gives the peculiar collaborative tone to Soviet domestic espionage, the expectation that he who is denounced and he who denounces him are joined together. In the film mentioned above, *Frontier*, it is the victim, the enemy of the people, who is to be executed by his best friend and near double, who chooses the spot where his best friend is to execute him.

The interweaving of the ideas of watchfulness over the self and watchfulness over others is well illustrated in an interview with an informant who had been a Party member living in special quarters in Moscow, who described the method by which a member of each cell was appointed to spy on all the other cell members:

Question: Did you try to find out who *was* the watcher?

Answer: No, there was always a kind of respect for everything done by the Party. There is respect for the decision of the cell which is the decision of the Party and there is the conviction that you would do the same if they would ask you, so why should you find out? As soon as you feel insulted by the Party you are on the way out, morally.

Question: But wouldn't it be better to know so that you don't have to worry about all the people ?

Answer: No. NO You had better worry, engage in self-criticism, watch yourself, and if there is anybody [watching you], you don't know who it is. It is none of your business to find out. And if they tell you there is something wrong with you, you will believe it. After all you are only good so long as the Party says so. So if the Party says you are no good there must be something to it.

To the Western mind, political trials in which some highly placed official is not only accused of present deviation from the Line but is also "exposed" as having always been a professional agent for a number of foreign intelligence services sound absurd. In Soviet language this is simply a way of saying that this particular accused person shall not be allowed a political comeback. Hence the indictment is phrased in such a way as to insist that there never was any good in him. The appropriate sequel to an official declaration that an individual is completely evil is his removal from society by physical liquidation.

At lower levels, purges and removals from office may be a way of stating that the individual who has so enthusiastically executed a past Line is not capable of changing to the new Line. His very commitment to the previous Line becomes the ground for alleging that he has always been an enemy, which ground is often paradoxically expressed by an accusation that his previous activity was the exact opposite of what it actually was.

The intricacies of the path by which Stalin gained control of the entire Party apparatus reflect the interrelationships between the changing Line and the possibility that any given individual may at any moment be wholly loyal or wholly an enemy. One of the steps by which Stalin gained control of the Central Committee was to keep in the Committee members of the opposition who thus became involved in unanimous decisions in favor of policies which they were denouncing in confidential discussions within high Party circles.

The way the Line is operated means that behavior which was true and loyal yesterday may be branded as false and disloyal tomorrow. The assumption that every human being is potentially and continuingly wholly good *and* wholly bad throughout life is grounded in traditional Russian character and complements political practice very neatly. All those who are unable to shift satisfactorily when the Line changes can be seen to be those in whom evil has become dominant. But this change is not irreversible. A man whose particular scientific dogma has been in disgrace for a period of years may be suddenly brought back from an ignominious sojourn on the periphery—a mild form of exile—and made the head of an important institute or bureau. He may be publicly described as being entirely good, while the man he replaces, who may have received the same appointment with a comparable statement of his absolute loyalty and goodness five years before, is now unmasked as having always been an "enemy of the people," or whatever the official terms of vilification may be for the exponent of the previously approved and now abandoned course of action.

In fields less specialized than the arts and sciences, a capable man who has been displaced from one position and demoted or banished to the periphery but not physically liquidated may reappear later in some quite different field. Since 1938-39 there appears to have been less physical liquidation and more banishment to the periphery with possibilities of return to positions of importance at a later date. This relaxation may be due partly to the extreme shortage of trained personnel, especially since World War II, partly to some relaxation in the Soviet demand that individuals be defined as wholly good or wholly bad at any given time, and partly to a partial return to the more traditional Russian acceptance of the inherent goodness and badness in each individual.

This belief, that each individual is capable simultaneously of all good and all evil, is also associated with a great deal of confusion in role. In Soviet behavior there may be seen an extreme defense against this mixture of roles, a struggle between the attempt to keep each individual's role clear and a tendency, to treat each individual as capable of playing any part—from hero to traitor, from prosecutor to defendant, or from victim to executioner. The interrogators in the great trials were, to a considerable extent, persons who knew that they themselves would be liquidated very soon, and yet it was felt at the top that this knowledge would not materially detract from their efficiency as interrogators. There is a conspicuous lack of official executioners in the political police; members of the apparatus of many different levels might have to officiate as executioners. And within the Party cell, an individual might be selected to spy, but, if not so officiating, he would be spied upon.

In the film, *Frontier*, which is primarily concerned with this confusion of roles, there is not only the drama of virtual identity between the faithful Soviet citizen and the traitor, but also a ragged little peasant, who plays the role of inspirational speaker, of spy and informer, and who describes himself as "a little bit of a GPU.

There have been a variety of devices used to deal with the problems which arise from confusion of roles and the continuing possibilities of treachery. One device is to simplify the demands made upon the rank—and—file Party member, who is no longer expected to understand as much of the ideology as he was in the past. This makes the role of rank—and—file member simpler; it is easier to treat him like a sentry, taking him off one assignment and giving him different orders for a new turn of sentry duty. The narrowing of authority at the top, from Party Congresses through Central Committee to concentration in the Politburo, also serves to reduce the diffusion of possible treachery at upper levels. The narrowing of authority, however, also increases the demands made on each individual in authority and, by increasing the scope and range of his activities and responsibilities, increases the gravity of a breakthrough of disallowed behavior. So an individual, such as Yezhov, who is entrusted with great power to liquidate others must in turn be liquidated.

The contrast between the potential dangers inherent in any whole personality and the greater safety involved in rigidly prescribed and specialized functions is repeated over and over again at the organizational level. A complete range of functions is assigned to such large, unmanageable groups as Party Congresses, Plenums, District Committees, which break down into factions amid mutual accusation and suspicion. An attempt is made to correct this by setting up a narrower group which can exercise a particular function without breakdown. This organizational characteristic was used by Stalin to gain control of the Politburo: when he wished to reduce the power of the Plenum of the Central Committee, he increased its size, at the same time giving it more functions to perform and so making it less capable of performing them. Many of the functions of responsibility for political security, which were part of the regular duties of Party members in the twenties and thirties, seem now to be delegated to the political police (in the Ministries of Internal Affairs and State Security), who therefore are in the position of watching the Party. There are also special Party cells within the political police to watch them in turn and to keep them under the control of the Party. The political police force is now said to contain over 1,500,000 members and to have doubtfully adequate methods of checking on new recruits. This inadequacy is presented as being compensated for by the close watch that the political police keep on one another. The question immediately arises: "Who watches them?" Of course, this continual tendency of the specialized function of preservation of security to break down is partly associated with the very nature of any security system, but the types of confusions and reversals—characteristic of Soviet assumptions regarding human behavior exacerbate it.

One of the most curious features of the Soviet system has been the combination of the ' willingness to condemn an individual to death, to define him as totally an enemy, in terms of some small past action, and the absence of any really functioning modern system of keeping track of suspected persons. Generalized terror, mass arrests, indiscriminate accusations take the place of careful modern police work which might actually identify a particular saboteur. The, actual nexus between any given crime and any given person is exceedingly weak. For all crimes there must be identified criminals; but the accused need not have committed the particular crime, since they are, at all events, capable of any crime and have probably committed—at least in intent—other crimes. Because of the looseness of the police system, and the willingness to pin any accusation on to any convenient breast, sabotage, espionage, and temporary escape from the vigilance of particular police are comparatively easy, so that the need for more terror as a controlling measure which also makes any final escape less possible is intensified. The most recent evidence suggests that the system of police controls is being tightened although not necessarily made more specific.

The complications involved in assuming that every individual can be held accountable for anything which occurs, regardless of his specific responsibility, are shown vividly in Soviet theories of industrial organization, especially when these theories are compared with contemporary press accounts of failures and malpractice in factory organization. Soviet theories of industrial organization insist that organization is something which can be imposed upon a group of individuals, each of whom will be totally involved in the particular role he has to play, whether that of worker, foreman, or manager. This means that not only the particular parts of the personality needed for the particular task, but also all the other always present and contradictory elements in the personality are regarded as present. Then, in accordance with Bolshevik demands, organizational theory also insists that each individual must be presented with clear—cut goals and responsibilities. Clear-cut responsibilities are necessarily limited responsibilities, involving carefully defined lines of command and subordination. Thus Soviet organizational theory and practice struggle continually to devise an organizational chart which will define and limit responsibility. But within such an organizational scheme the worker is expected to respond, not with a careful delimited measured response to the particular demands of his job, but with total devotion and spontaneity. This spontaneity, which is fed by a desire to identify with the leader, holds the danger that this is in effect identification with someone who is unrestrained by the restraints which are binding on his immediate superior. In terms of such devotion he is expected to be able to criticize his superiors and to surpass them by displaying more initiative and more activism than they.

In contrast, American theory, based on a belief in the individual's capacity to adjust to an economic role and that this will involve only part of his personality, one clear role among many roles, tends to concentrate initially on the technical aspects of the activity itself. An American organizational blueprint therefore tends to be concerned with the mutual adjustments of various technical roles.

Furthermore, in Soviet theory there is very little differentiation between different kinds of organization, as they all are seen as expressions of universal principles which combine subordination to authority with the expression of spontaneity, and every group therefore presents the same problem and the same need for organizational control as every other group. Organizational absurdities which attempt to deal with this dilemma result. Kaganovich, at the 17th Party Congress, 1934, gave the following example:[20]

> A factory in Dnepropetrovsk had 75 paid workers in the Party organization which had 5 echelons and I I sectors. Each shop cell had 11 sectors: (I) culture propaganda, (2) mass agitation, (3) cadres, (4) verification and fulfillment, (5) work with Party *activ*, (6) works with Party candidates, (7) sector for learning vanguard role of communist for production, (8) work among komsomols, (9) work among women, (10) sector of cooperation and (11) Party dues. The matter went to such an absurd level that a link cell which had 7 Party members and 5 candidates established a bureau of the cell into which all the Party members went, and for these 7 Party members, 10 sectors were established.

Thus we see that the attempt to narrow and simplify particular functions came into continual conflict with the acceptance of the total involvement of the whole personality, so that, after eleven separate tasks had been defined in order to separate them, the same people were then required to perform all eleven.

Another illustration of the confusion of roles and of the conflict between specialization of function and the attempt to make everyone responsible for everything can be found in the management of collective farms where separate organizations, (1) Raion[21] party secretary, (2) MTS,[22] (3) Raion section of the Ministry of Agriculture, (4) Raion soviets, (5) Raion party committee of propaganda and agitation, and sometimes (6) the local bank are accountable and hence are forced into attempting to take responsibility for the harvest.

This Soviet assumption that the opposite of any form of behavior is also always potentially present is significant in interpretation of

20. Kaganovich *op. cit.*, p. 556,
21. District.
22. Machine Tractor Station.

Soviet behavior in international relations. Those who have dealings with Soviet officials in international negotiations or in joint occupation councils have been struck by the sudden reversals of policy which affect every aspect of every relationship, every echelon from general to chauffeur. These sudden switches are often explained in terms of the great centralization of power in the Soviet Union or the small amount of leeway allowed to any individual in the system. But while the perfect synchronization of such switches in behavior from extreme uncooperativeness to the sudden semblance of cooperation may be thus explained, the disposition to engage in sharp reversals needs further study. When the behavior of members of different societies is compared, we find that the capacity for reversing a position differs very much, from the Japanese prisoner, who is willing to broadcast on behalf of his captor within a few hours after being taken prisoner, to a people like the Poles, who remain actively intransigent in spite of drastic changes in circumstances. What is there in contemporary Soviet character which makes sudden reversals of policy sufficiently congenial that they can be carried out swiftly and easily?

We have already seen how abrupt changes in the Line and the accompanying liquidation of those persons who have most zealously and rigidly carried out the former Line are congruent with the Soviet assumption regarding human nature. Reversals are part of the mechanism of shifts in Line. Throughout the theory of Leninism-Stalinism there is an allowance for sudden sharp reversals rather than for slow gradual adjustment. There is a tendency to state extreme alternatives and to view both alternatives as part of the same system. It would be reasonable in judging, from the American point of view, for example, the expected behavior of Great Britain as an ally to say: From such and such a degree of present friendliness and cooperativeness we may expect no more than a given amount of coolness to develop, given certain conditions, over a given period of time. But a different type of estimate has to be made in the case of the Soviet Union, where the possibility of an extreme reversal is always present. As opposite and seemingly completely contradictory attitudes are already present, there is no need to allow for a transition from one to another in the behavior of officials who Must execute the new policy. The typical Soviet figure of speech is to unmask, in one gesture; one position, that of friend, is replaced by a diametrically opposite one, that of enemy.

Fadeyev, in *The Young Guard*,[23] published in 1945, describes the new generation as follows:

---

23.   Fadeyev, "The Young Guard," in *Znamya*, February-December, 1945.

The seemingly most incompatible traits, dreaminess and efficiency, flights of fancy and practicality, the love of good and relentlessness-mercilessness, depth wideness of the soul and judicial calculations, passionate love of earthy happiness and reserve—these seemingly incompatible traits together create the unique countenance of the new generation.

Whereas for many Westerners the existence of one attitude—trust, cooperativeness, reliance, etc.—toward a co-worker, a superior or a subordinate, makes the expectation of the occurrence of the opposite attitude less likely, in Soviet expectation the closer the relationship and the greater the trust, the greater the danger, the more possible a betrayal, and the greater the need for suspicion. This seems to be a specific Stalinist trend. During the Leninist era there was an attempt to treat the world as being divided into two rather distinct parts: the world outside the Party, which was to be regarded with maximal suspicion, and the world inside the Party, where such suspicion was to be held in abeyance until proof of betrayal was provided. This Stalinist trend toward suspicion of those within can be seen as expressing, in a new form, the traditional Russian assumption that all individuals are potentially both good and evil.

This whole view of human nature is so very unfamiliar to Americans that only by the greatest attention can it be held in mind. In interpreting Soviet behavior toward the outside world, there is a tendency to say that only negative feelings are real, or, conversely, that only the periodic accommodation attitudes are real. Actually neither is real in our sense of the term, that is, in the extent to which they exclude their opposites. The situation is further complicated by the fact that Soviet policymakers require of themselves the subduing of both positive and negative feelings in the service of maximizing their power and fulfilling their exalted mission in the world. All they can admit to themselves is that they are deliberately making pretenses of friendliness or hostility.

This complex of attitudes, a habitual expectation that contradictions will coexist in such a way that any feeling may at any moment be completely replaced by its opposite, combined with the Bolshevik insistence on the subordination of both types of feeling, makes for attitudes in the leadership which seem lacking in consistency, integrity, and sincerity.

As consistency and sincerity are regarded by Americans as essential to integrity, and as both are lacking in the behavior of the Soviet leadership, there is a temptation to continue to apply American standards of judgment and to regard Soviet behavior as insincere, cynical, in the American sense, and so without integrity. This interpretation is strengthened by those Russians who reject the Bolshevik ideal and themselves accuse the Soviets of insincerity and cynicism. But from the Bolshevik point of view the essential virtue consists in being so goal-oriented *(tseleustremenyi)* that no contradiction can arise between behavior demanded by changes in the Line and the individual behavior—in a diplomat or officer on a border—needed to implement the Line. When, in attempting to interpret abrupt changes in the degree of friendliness or of distrustful reserve expressed by individual Soviet officials, we invoke ideas which attempt to distinguish between *when* they are sincere or when they are insincere, or when we regard Soviet high officials as *only* ruthlessly seeking positions of power quite regardless of any ethical implications, we lose sight of the Bolshevik ethic. In this ethic, all acts commanded by the Party are ethical because of the long-term ethical goal of a good society. In such a pursuit of ethical goals, there is both a degree of self-justification and a need for continuous self-rejustification which does not exist for those who have no such goals.

In contacts between the Soviet Union and other nationals, officials at various levels are required by the exigencies of the Line to assume different and contradictory forms of behavior. The more flexible they are in doing so, the more integrity—or perhaps "integralness" would be a better word—they have as Bolsheviks. Assumptions which Americans make about the significance of the behavior of individual Soviet officials become imponderable but very important elements in shaping the course of relationships between the United States and the Soviet Union. If judgments of Soviet official behavior by American officials are related, not to the degree of sincerity or of cynicism in our terms, but, instead, to the degree to which each Soviet official is more or less a real Bolshevik, a much higher level of sophistication is introduced.

In the above discussion, we have dealt with the Bolshevik demand that Party members and high officials subordinate their beliefs to Party goals to such an extent that any prescribed belief can easily replace another, the convictions for either being based not on the personal feelings of the individual, but on the extent to which he is prepared to act in the interests of the Party. When we examine published propaganda materials directed at the general population, we find a decreasing tolerance here also for the coexistence of contradictory and potentially oscillating attitudes. Films such as *Frontier*, made in the thirties, and *The Young Guard*, made in the forties, reveal that the fear of such coexisting feelings is still present. However, the educational propaganda attempts to direct one set of attitudes, the positive ones—absolute loyalty, devotion, and love toward the State, the Party, Stalin—and to channel hatred toward the enemy. Instead of the diffuse hatred centering on generalized qualities and impersonal forces which characterized the pre-Soviet Russian, there is an attempt to fix these attitudes on specific individuals or nations. The assumption of coexistence' is still found, however, in the insistence that love and hate are in fact inseparable. Yermilo[24] comments thus:

> The heroes of the play know that the feelings of hatred towards Fascism are sacred. They are the reverse of the love of mankind. One who is not able to hate is not able to love.

In an article[25] in the Leningrad monthly *Tridtsat Dnei*, the writer watched

> … faces, new faces. The passions of the revolutionary, the elan of the fighter, the grit of the commander, and then love, love of life, love of its classes, of people who are builders, then the hatred of the enemy, furious, irrepressibleall this lay in new fashion upon the faces. All this penetrates deeply and organically into the faces of our men, the new men—l watched the eyes—they began to *burn* but the faces are *cold*, [italics ours]

An article in *Molodoi Bol'shevik* declares:[26]

> Soviet patriotism includes—carries in itself (*vkluchat*) the feeling of hot hatred towards the enemies of our native land.

The pupils in Soviet schools must

> … realize that the feeling of Soviet patriotism is saturated with irreconcilable hatred towards the enemies of Socialist society … It is necessary to learn not only to hate the enemy, but also to struggle with him, in time to unmask him and finally, if he does not surrender, to destroy him.[27]

This official attempt to direct active hatred toward the enemy as a way of keeping love for the Soviet Union clear has its repercussions in the feeling of these same officials that people of other countries hate

---

24. V. Yermilov, "Test through Peace" (*Ispytanie mirom*), *Literaturnaya Gazeta*, December 15, 1946, p. 2.
25. "People of the Thirties" (*Lyudi tridtsatykh godov*), *Tridtsat Dnei*, 1935.
26. "Educating Soviet Patriotism in the Schools," *Molodoi Bol's1revik*, December, 1947.
27. G. Counts and N. Lodge, *I Want to be like Stalin*, The John Day Company, New York, 1947. (Translated from V. P. Yesipov and N. K. Gocharov, official Soviet textbook on pedagogy, published with approval of Ministry of Education, RSFSR, 1946.

the Soviet Union. "Comrade Lenin himself said: 'Are we not in an ocean of hatred?'"[28]

The official insistence on the success of this effort to separate out feelings which are believed to coexist goes to further lengths. An educator boasts:[29]

> In all epochs children play war, usually presenting cruelty and violence. But our children's play at the Patriotic War reflects the noble role of the Soviet Army and calls forth noble feelings. There is not a single game in which children attacked, exhibited cruelty, violence. They always free and defend the motherland, chase the foe. These games express hate of violence and cruelty, of invaders.

For some peoples, ardent patriotic love of their own country is compatible with moderate affection for other countries, which only extreme conditions in the midst of war can turn into hatred. Even at the height of the Blitz against Britain there was very little expressed hatred for Germany or attempt on the part of the government to build hatred. Hatred of the Japanese grew gradually among American troops, accompanying battle experiences. The Soviet leadership seems to be seeking a way of directing coexisting love and hate. Strength of love and strength of hate are treated as functions of each other, so that, as hatred is directed against the enemy, love of country will increase, and vice versa.

Related to this habit of including opposite types of feeling within a single wider attitude, of always allowing for the coexistence of opposites which makes Soviet domestic and intra—Cominform behavior so baffling to the West, is the type of thinking which can be described briefly as "all or none thinking." We have already discussed the belief that if anything is wrong, then everything is wrong, or will be almost immediately. If someone is not completely a friend, then he is completely an enemy. The smallest slip will lead to total betrayal. Says *Komsomol'skaia Pravda*:[30]

> The Komsomol must in every way improve the ideological work among the young ... ! ... *any* belittling of socialist ideology, Lenin teaches, any departure from it, signifies the same thing as strengthening bourgeois ideology. [italics ours]

28. V. Ozerov, "The image of a Bolshevik in the Post-War Soviet Literature," *Bol'shevik*, No. 10, May, 1949.

29. D. Menderitskaya, "Influence of the Educator on Content of Children's Play," *Pre-School Education* (Doshkol' noe Vospitanie), August, 1948.

30. *Komsomol, skaia Pravda*, March 31, 1949, p. 2.

There are no stable intermediate positions: one little slip from total loyalty, and nothing can stop the change from friend into enemy, from loyal Party member into traitor and spy. This lack of belief in the stability of any middle position is accompanied by the impermissibility of referring to it in any way, in contempt for the Social Democrat idea of a "middle way," and in statements that "There is no third way."

The good Communist, Basargin, in Simonov's 1947 novel, says:[31] "I wonder whether you know that all our friends with reservations become in the end most often our enemies."

The inevitable final transformation of those who begin to deviate then follows. Stalin,[32] on March 3, 1937, said:

> It should be explained to our Party comrades that the Trotskyites who represent the active element in the diversionist wrecking and espionage work of a foreign Intelligence Service have already long ceased to be a political trend, in the working class that they have turned into a gang of wreckers, diversionists, spies, assassins, without principles and ideals working for the foreign Intelligence Services.

And he continues: "Against such total enemies ... not the old methods, the methods of discussion, but the new methods, methods of smashing and uprooting, must be used."

There is a very natural tendency in the West to interpret these accusations and denunciations as nothing but political rhetoric. There is abundant evidence that the particular charges made in the trials of the Old Bolsheviks, of sabotaging the railway system, of putting glass in the butter, or of espionage for foreign intelligence services, were palpably untrue. But what Stalin (or Vishinsky, in the trials) is saying is that those who are not totally for us are totally against us. The accident that they have not committed the particular extreme act which is used illustratively in accusing them is irrelevant. American misunderstanding of this type of thinking shows up sharply when American spokesmen waste their energies in getting angry at the inaccuracies of Soviet accusations and spend heat and time in denying and disproving particular points. When a Soviet speaker in the United Nations accuses the United States of particular acts of espionage, warmongering, etc., he is saying, in effect: We are at present classifying you as a total enemy who is, if serious, undoubtedly doing,

---

31. K. Simonov, "The Smoke of the Fatherland" (*Dym otechestva*), *Novyi Mir*, November, 1947.

32. Stalin, *Mastering Bolshevism*, report to the 1937 Plenum of the Central Committee of the CPSU, printed in *Bol'shevik*, April 1, 1937.

or should be doing, everything in your power against us; as we, when we classify you as a total enemy, are doing everything in our power against you. If this is recognized, the accusations can be taken as a catalogue of the hostile acts which the Soviet Union is either engaged in, or wishes us to think it is engaged in, or wishes it were able to execute. Answering speeches can be directed to the issue in dispute, while specific denials of charges can be made for the benefit of those other peoples who, like ourselves, think it necessary to deny false charges from any national group with which they are not actively at war. Such denials are, of course, exceedingly important in countering Soviet anti-American propaganda outside the Soviet Union.

Soviet assumptions about transformations from the position of total goodness to total evil may also be found in Soviet treatment of allies. All rival power centers in the world are regarded by the Kremlin as basically hostile, centers which can at best be temporarily negotiated with for truces or for purposes of combined pursuit of limited goals. And within the area of Soviet domination there is always the possibility of a formerly dutiful part of the Soviet side being transformed into the total enemy, as in the case of Yugoslavia at present.

Even with a sound, practical recognition that national states are self-interested groups, moved by considerations of power, there is a widespread expectation in the West that it is possible to set up relatively lasting good relations with other nations, and that difficulties may be overcome within such a generally good understanding. This is particularly true when relations between states have reached the formal treaty state which Americans take exceedingly seriously. The spectacle of a Soviet Union which makes a fifty-year pact with one of its satellites and denounces it two or three years later seems to us so shocking, so completely unethical, that it is likely to lead to the conclusion that there is no possibility of negotiating with such an unprincipled leadership. If it is once recognized that the friendly, nominally independent power within the Soviet orbit, with which the Soviet Union at a given moment negotiates, is also-at that moment—recognized as being potentially an extremely hostile power, it can almost be said that the Soviet Union is signing a pact with the other power as a totally loyal ally and is simultaneously including the possibility that this power may—at any time—require as formal a denunciation as a total enemy. This simultaneous acceptance of loyalty and treachery is self-evident to the Soviet leaders. it remains for further research to determine to what degree the Communist—dominated parties of neighboring countries, with cultural expectations about human nature which differ from the Bolshevik assumption, find this expectation to be either natural or monstrous.

However, this expectation, of possible transformations of allies into enemies and of the most extreme and drastic transformations following from the smallest slip, the least doubt, the slightest disloyalty, is accompanied by the possibility that they may be transformed back again. This expectation was much stronger in the early days of the Party, when the emphasis upon repentance, confession, and conversion, now reserved for the lower ranks of the Party and the Komsomols, existed at top Party levels. (What appears to be—though material on this is very scant—a recent tendency for demoted persons to have some sort of a comeback seems to apply only to the lower and middle levels of officialdom.) From the middle twenties to the middle thirties, Party behavior expressed a belief in the possibility of being an Oppositionist without becoming automatically an enemy of the Party. This expressed belief shifted in the middle thirties to an expressed belief that the transformation of an Oppositionist into a wrecker, spy, and traitor was inevitable and irreversible. This belief in irreversibility, unthinkable in the twenties, made mass liquidations within the Party possible. There have been recent signs that the process could be reversed posthumously, as in the recent interchanges between the CPSU and the Communist Party of Yugoslavia, in which Trotsky is no longer described as having been totally bad from the beginning. So, in the letter of March 27, 1948, from the CPSU to the CPY, we find this passage:[33]

> Again we might mention that, when he decided to declare war on the CPSU, Trotsky also started with accusations of the CPSU as degenerate, as suffering from the limitations inherent in the narrow nationalism of great powers. Naturally he camouflaged all this with left slogans about world revolution. However, it is well known that Trotsky himself *became degenerated, and when he was exposed, crossed over* into the camp of the sworn enemies of the CPSU and the Soviet Union. [italics ours]

Here a possible reversible period in Trotsky's early disaffection is implied by way of suggesting the possibility of a reversal in Tito's catastrophic progress toward becoming a total enemy. On the other hand, Soviet publications during late 1949 also quoted frequently from Stalin's 1938 denunciatory speeches.

We have already mentioned the tendency to banish and later to recall individuals who have shown signs of deviation. This is another instance of a possible relaxation in the extreme attitude of the thirties and a return to an older Russian expectation that, as possibilities of

---

33. *Soviet-Yugoslav Dispute*, Royal Institute of International Affairs, London, 1948, P. 15.

both total good and total evil are always present, transformation may proceed in either direction and need not be permanent. This older attitude was characteristic of pre-Soviet friendship but altered markedly after the Soviet regime was initiated. The way in which individual deviations are regarded—as committing the individual to a course of unredeemable villainy or as merely one step on a road from which full return is possible—will be one of the decisive elements in the development of the Soviet system of authority during the next decades, and every effort should be made to obtain as much material on the subject as possible.

Within this framework of attitudes, the Soviet leadership is often involved in what looks to the West like exceedingly contradictory behavior, between their acceptance of those conditions which are believed to be absolutely given by History and the Nature of Man, on the one hand, and, on the other hand, their acceptance of their responsibility to exercise complete control, both over themselves and over others. While the Line is merely an expression of correct perception of what already exists, the execution of the Line becomes something completely within the power of the Party. If the Line is correctly perceived, then the Party is acting within the course which History must take and so has, theoretically, complete power to realize the course which has been perceived as all objectively possible." This view lends itself to fantasies of omnipotence, of invincibility. But the opposite face of these fantasies is strengthened also by the fear, of the perfectly perceived, absolutely controlled situation getting out of hand, if the perception should be spoiled in execution, if a single slip between cup and lip occurs: The overestimation of power over events and over persons is thus balanced at every turn by an overestimation of the forces which may also be arrayed against the Party, against the leadership, against the Soviet Union. The burden of being perfectly right must be carried like a precariously balanced container of water, from which one drop spilled will be fatal. It is in this sense that it is possible to say that the Soviet leaders are sincerely convinced that every single thing they do is right and necessary and also that there is danger in questioning any particular act: they are frightened that they or those who follow them may, by such questioning, lead the Party and the Soviet Union to total destruction.

Bolshevik Willingness to Accept or to Fabricate Token Events

In Tsarist Russia there were attempts to give an appearance of reality and solidity to matters of dubious truth, as in the great insistence on written confessions as early as the seventeenth century or in the Potemkin villages specially set up to satisfy the demands of Catherine the Great for speedy development of the newly acquired province of Novorussiya.

These earlier customs of theatrical enactment of that which was desired by those in power or by their subordinates have become very marked characteristics of the Soviet regime. In Bolshevik doctrine, what the leadership decides shall be done is what History has already ordained is going to happen (although it is also what needs the utmost effort to make it happen). Hence, any gap between what is ordered and what occurs is proportionately less bearable. Although Bolshevik doctrine also includes stern exhortations to sobriety and recognition of facts as "stubborn things," and although romantic overoptimism is one of the condemned characteristics of the Left, nevertheless a great variety of falsifications and theatrical enactments of the ardently desired or deeply feared do occur.

This acceptance of falsification shows itself in the sort of reports which are passed up through channels in a bureaucracy reporting overfulfillment of a plan, when the overfulfillment of, for example, the readiness of the machines in a Machine Tractor Station is of such a nature that half of the tractors may break down within a week. The Machine Tractor Station will, however, already have celebrated its overfulfillment and the appropriate higher levels will have been able to include its success in their reports of their successes. Although bureaucratic conditions are particularly favorable to the tendency to believe what it is most comfortable to believe, this particular type of belief goes to special lengths in the Soviet Union. As so many of the reports are concerned with real events —the amount of grain harvested, the number of trucks turned out by a factoryfalse reporting has very real repercussions in actuality and so can be branded as sabotage. But as failure to overfulfill a plan may also be regarded as sabotage, the possibility of such repercussion hardly discourages the practice of inaccurate reporting.

The falsification takes many forms, even within a single factory. One informant described his wife's experience: she worked in a silk artel which listed itself as a whole as overfulfilling the plan by 110 per cent, when actually the plan had been only 65 per cent fulfilled. Within this artel, his wife's unit had actually overfulfilled by 250 per cent, but this was only credited as 121 per cent, since over 120 per cent warranted a premium. Such attempts to establish groups within which the weak can lean on the strong, as when one kolkhoz borrows from another, are very frequently reported.

Periodically the falsifications produce difficult situations. An informant described a province in which one county showed a. grain delivery of 131 per cent, and, as a result, Moscow ordered that more white bread should be baked and sold in the county center. The county started to obey this order, but by the middle of the year there was no grain left. The province looked over the invoices and pointed out that several thousand kilos of grain should be left. In order to straighten out the matter, the county party committee took grain away from some of the collective farms in the county.

Even with the extreme frequency with which this type of falsification occurs in the Soviet Union, it might be regarded as merely a sign of inefficiency or corruption or graft, if it were not for many other Soviet practices which make it advisable also to consider other hypotheses.

These practices must be placed beside the device of staging political events which serve not only as propaganda for home and foreign consumption, but probably also as ritual proof, somewhat on the order of the pleasure which a certain type of woman takes in wearing flowers which she has sent herself on a public occasion. In reply to a question about reports that peasants wrote letters to the newspapers accusing the chairman of a collective farm of being a thief, an informant said:

> No peasants write letters voluntarily. If the Party has an eye on the chairman, they go to a peasant and say: "Ivan, you know the chairman is a thief and he has to be removed. We want the whole of Russia to know about it." Then the peasant writes the letter. The whole thing is a comedy like a theatre. The term for this is *inspiratsiya*. State loans are engineered in the same way.

There are, of course, jokes about these synthetic successes. A DP informant tells about a meeting:

> The lecturer made a point that in Tsarist days ten ships a week left a certain port and now 100 did. A man from the port stood up and said it was not so; only two ships a week left the port. The lecturer was a little taken aback and then he said: "You are a fool. You do not read *Pravda*."

The trials may be seen as elaborate demonstrations that traitors existed in the Soviet Union, and that the most drastic measures were necessary to suppress such dangerous forces. Whether or not the Old Bolsheviks who actually confessed had committed any of the particular acts attributed to them was essentially irrelevant. They could be persuaded—as a service to the Party and out of their own knowledge of their political opposition, which in Party theory was itself a crime— to confess and receive punishment for a large number of crimes which they had not committed, thereby "proving" that such crimes were in fact being committed or at least plotted, and that measures must and had been taken against them.

A high NKVD official is reported to have explained his own arrest during the great Purge as follows:[34]

> The highest leadership and the People's Commissar U. ... in particular, know my activity very well; they also know that I could not be a political criminal; and if, despite this, they have arrested me and have accused me of this and that, there are obviously weighty political grounds, and it is not the business of a small person to go against the party line; on the contrary it is necessary to help its accomplishments.

Krivitsky[35] refers to attempts to stage trials outside the Soviet Union, notably in the United States and in Czechoslovakia, which would give further verisimilitude to the charges of foreign espionage. The attempt to construct a demonstration trial in Czechoslovakia, as further described by an informant, included approaching a large number of highly placed persons, journalists, etc., and finally planting documents on a former Communist refugee from Nazi Germany after he had been denounced to the Czech police as a Nazi spy. The belief that it would be possible to stage such trials successfully even outside the Soviet Union is an example of the lengths to which the sense of their being the executors of History can lead Soviet imagination in viewing the outside world as included in the audience. The 1949 trials in Hungary, in which plotting with Tito was confessed, is a continuation, within the area of Soviet control, of the type of dramatization found in the trials in the late thirties.

Another excellent recent example of the willingness of the Party leadership to take part in a drama which to the outside world looked like a very poor fake was presented by the elections in Czechoslovakia, which had the contrived appearance of there being several political parties who were competing freely among themselves, when, actually, all the "permitted" parties had agreed in advance to join in a single bloc with the Communists and to leave to the electors a choice of voting for this single ticket or of running the risk of voting against it. Dr. David Rodnick, who was doing field work in Czechoslovakia at the time, describes the procedure as follows:[36]

34. From an unpublished manuscript by a former Soviet historian.

35. W. G. Krivitsky, *In Stalin's Secret Service*, Harper & Brothers, New York, 1939, pp. 168-70.

36. David Rodnick, "Czechs, Slovaks, and Communism," excerpt concerning the Communist "Election" of May, 1948, taken from Chap. XVI of unpublished manuscript. See Appendix E for further details on the Czechoslovakian election.

Some weeks before the so-called "election" every storekeeper was required to put in his front window a poster urging support for the unity list. In all public offices and railroad stations there were banners or placards with the words "He who loves the Republic will vote for the Republic," of "White ticketblack thoughts," and so on. It took courage for an individual to use the white voting slip in the "election" on May 30th. In almost all polling stations, the box for the white ballots was out in the open and surrounded by watchers from the local Communist Party. Each voter had been given two ballots beforehand; a red ballot which had the government list inside and a white one which was blank. Each ballot was in an envelope and could be marked at home, sealed, and brought back to the voting station. There a voter's name was checked off the list and he was permitted to go to the back of the room where the ballot boxes were theoretically supposed to be behind screens. No screens were in any of the polling stations we heard of; both boxes were out in the open. The voter was supposed to drop a ballot in either the government box or the white-ballot box, and to discard the ballot he did not use in either the waste basket for the red ballots or the one for the white ballots. As many "paper" Communist watchers told us later on, it was very difficult to get by them. They were supposed to mark down the names of all individuals who voted the white ballot and to try to intimidate them by asking them if they weren't going in the wrong direction when they approached the white ballot box. It was impossible to cast a ballot without everyone knowing how one voted. Many individuals who wished to cast a white ballot but were afraid of the consequences used their red envelope, but instead of putting in the red ballot they inserted pictures of Thomas G. Masaryk, President Benes, Jan Masaryk, Franklin D. Roosevelt, Winston Churchill, caricatures of Josef Stalin, Gottwald, Hitler, toilet paper, or nothing. Many also wrote notes attacking the Communists. Official counters from various parts of Czechoslovakia told us later on that the Ministry of Interior in Prague confiscated ballot boxes without permitting them to be counted, or if they had already been counted, gave out abnormally low figures. One counter in a city of 35,000 told us that in his district alone he counted 860 white ballots, and friends of his who had also served as counters in other parts of the city told him afterward that they counted as much and sometimes more than in his district. The official count for white ballots in the whole city was 216! In other parts of Czechoslovakia we were told of similar instances, where the total white ballots for a whole town or city would be given out as much smaller than had been counted in only one district.

Whereas the American commentator is concerned with the degree of manipulation, the Soviet propagandist is concerned with the appearance of complete control as the essential point.

Less spectacular, but even more revealing, are the details of the trials which are held year after year within the Soviet Union, in which the politically suspect are convicted through dramatizations of crimes which they might have committed, confessions of which are obtained by pressure and torture.

The same manuscript referred to above[37] discusses a rationale given by high officials in the secret police, called "social political prophylaxis," for the apprehension and elimination of potential criminals:

> In practice social prophylaxis presupposes as a consequence not only the apprehension of the criminal but also the establishment of criminal mood, criminal position, and criminal readiness, three degrees preceding the actual criminal act or the attempt at one. This is attained by systematic observation and study of the appropriate objects on the basis of objective signs (social origin, objective activity, relatives and personal connections, attitude toward work, etc.) with the help of secret informants. ... After the criminal position or readiness of a certain person is established with details which do not evoke doubts—thence the conviction of the "infallibility" of the NKVD—there follows, not always, but when it is useful, an arrest. ... The preliminary inquiry does not serve the purpose of discovering who is the real criminal since he actually has already been discovered. ... not for the clarification of the circumstances and details of the crime *since it has not yet occurred* [italics ours] but only for the socalled "formulation" which comes down to the categorization of the potential crime according to the criminal code, putting it under the proper article and giving it all the appearance of a real action; then the court which issues the sanction (permission to hold under arrest) views the potential crime as real one.

It is furthermore of great interest that this same investigator, who had an opportunity for discussion with many high NKVD officials thoroughly familiar with all the details of "the composition of accusatory fables," could find no one who could give an answer to his question as to why all these "social fables" were necessary in order to eliminate "potential criminals." Yet the fables occur at every level on the world stage, in a satellite country, and also in remote regions of the Soviet Union. The staged trials in Bulgaria must be considered together with an informant's description of a trial—in a lower court— of a man who refused to make the required confession. Another man who looked like the accused was brought in to make the confession, and the accused was shot.

If we understand that these apparently different pieces of behavior—willingness to accept a report from a Machine Tractor Station that it is 100 per cent ready for Spring work although half of the tractors break down the first week, the routine handling of prisoners, and such elaborately contrived events as the great trials, the confessions in Hungary, and the Czech elections—and consider them together as instances of a willingness and a need to accept or, if necessary, to concoct proofs of what the leadership believes to be "true" if not factual,

---

37.   See footnote 38, page 46.

we are given more of a clue to Soviet behavior than is obtained from an attempt to explain one part of the behavior as mere inefficiency and graft and the other part as mere crude attempts to deceive.

The great religions of the world are characterized by comparable ritual representations of that which is most ardently believed, and religious wars have been fought over the degree of reality in the ritual and over how much of what was re-enacted was actually true. Those who denied the truth of the ritual were always likely to believe that the priesthoods who claimed belief were simply consciously deceiving the people. It is extremely easy to pass the same judgment on the leadership of the Soviet Union and to fail to take into account their genuine fanaticism.

The Party leadership in Russia is building, very quickly, as complete a semblance as possible of the world as they wish to see it. Production records in which the true and the hoped for are intermingled, prisoners who confess to crimes which they did not commit, lines of tractors reported "in full repair" and unable to get to the fields, voters who are forced by every possible manipulative trick to vote for the Communist Party-all these are dramatizations by and to a leadership who believe they are the custodians and executors of historical Truth.

The mechanism of belief, even in one who was fully aware of what lay behind the trials and of the accused's actual innocence of the acts to which they confessed, was described by a former member of the CPSU:

> The first time you are told that X is a traitor, you resist. But on your way home you have to build up a faith for yourself. You have to believe in something.

To brand these dramatizations as simple fakes—as many anti-Communists in Czechoslovakia did—is to throw away an opportunity to evaluate them more accurately. Rodnick reports on the Czech attitude:[38]

> No one thing that the Communists have done since their assumption of complete power in February antagonized the non-Communist Czechs and even many within the Party as much as the hypocritical building-up of an artificial public Opinion that was created for the Party to manipulate as puppets. Nothing showed the megalomania of the Communist Party leadership more than this tendency to project its desires onto paper organizations and a synthetic public opinion—a move which assumed a lack of critical intelligence on the part of the non-Communists. It was a striking example of the amorality of the Communists who cynically

38. Rodnick, *op. cit.*

assumed that by throwing words to the people, the latter would accept them as realities. The level of rationalization which this political campaign employed was one that could have appealed only to psychotic individuals. The only possible motivation was that the Communists had the power, expected to keep it, but wanted to cloak their intention with a synthetic "legality" which they assumed would satisfy the Czechs. Only the Nazis could have equalled the contempt for the dignity and common sense of the human being that the Communists displayed in their crude maneuvering. At the same time, they assumed a naivete on the part of the outside world which would be willing to accept such an obvious hoax.

To fail to realize the possibility of loss of faith in the Party by young Communists who have taken part in these ritual rearrangements of facts would also be a mistake. But it is important to note that it was not the *falsifications* involved in the trials, as such, but the wholesale destruction of members of the Party who had been outstanding in their devotion which seems to have caused the loss of faith of highly placed Communists in the thirties. One of the problems which needs investigation is the dynamics of loss of faith today. It is possible that the great emphasis on empirical science which has been stressed in Soviet education makes it much more difficult for a young Communist, who is also an engineer, to accept these dramas without great skepticism. On the other hand, some sort of compartmentalization between science and political faith may be as possible a solution here as the *modus vivendi* which is often set up between religious faith and scientific method. The most cogent argument against this possibility is the existence of the Soviet intolerance of any compartmentalization, any reservations, any area in the personality which is not drenched in faith. Recent evidence suggests also the possibility of an emerging character structure in which absolute belief in the omniscient power, rather than in the ideals, of the Soviet system is crucial; doubt of the power of the system thus becomes a break in individual allegiance.

It is within this background—the political device of the Line, which is absolute and changing, the continuing fear of the coexistence of opposites within the personality and of the possibility that loyalty may be transformed into treachery at any moment, the struggle always to involve the personality and yet to develop functioning systems of organization, the fear that the smallest mistake may lead to catastrophe, and the tendency to accept ritual rather than actual demonstrations of a Truth-that the Soviet efforts to develop a new type of Soviet man will be discussed in this report.

Within these articles of faith and fear there is an indomitable belief in the power of the leadership to make Russians into a new kind of people, to hold in a firm mold that Russian character which they simultaneously see as so fluid, so likely to transform itself before their eyes. To the present possibility of recurrent transformation of good into evil which it is beyond their power to prevent, except by extraordinary and unremitting acts of will, they oppose the picture of a future in which all will be transformed purposefully and irreversibly.

> Each day lifts our people higher and higher. Today we are not those we were yesterday, and tomorrow we will not be those we are today. We are not the Russians we were before 1917, and Russia is not the same. We have changed and grown, together with those immense transformations which in the very root have changed the countenance of our country.[39]

39. A. Zhdanov, *Report on the Magazines "Zvezda" and "Leningrad,"* Gospolitizdat (State Political Publishing House), 1946, P. 36.

Chapter 4
SOVIET IDEALS OF
AUTHORITY RELATIONSHIPS

Expectations from Different Leadership Levels

*I*n order to obtain a picture of the way in which the regime has looked at the question of transforming not only the social structure of Russia, but also the very nature of Russians, into the "new moral countenance of Soviet Man," is useful to discriminate between the demands which are made upon three classes of people: (I) those who are responsible for everything (2) those who are seen as assistants or lieutenants of those who are responsible for everything and who are also responsible for almost everything; and (3) those who are seen as acted upon, being educated, led, supervised, instructed, etc. This three-fold division is repeated again and again, in Soviet official literature.

Speaking of the Party itself, Stalin said, in 1937:[1]

> How do things stand with regard to the Party, In our Party, if we have in mind its leading strata, there are about three to four thousand first rank leaders whom Ac would call our Party's General Staff Then there are thirty to forty thousand middle rank leaders, who are our Party Corps of Officers. Then there are about a hundred to a hundred and fifty thousand of the lower rank Party Command Staff, who are so to speak our Party non-commissioned Officers.

Within this division, the leadership on any one of these levels is described as having, and is required to have, certain characteristics, The Leader himself is assumed to have all of the desirable characteristics—he is a model for everybody else. Whether any other leader is automatically and continuously endowed with all the ideal traits car)

---

1. J. Stalin, "Mastering Bolshevism," report to the 1937 Plenum of Central Committee of the CPSU, printed in *Bol'shevik*, April, 1937, p.45.

become a subject of embarrassment, as in the recent retraction of a Chinese Communist newspaper which had quoted General Chou En-lai as saying that even Mao Tze-tung "cannot be considered faultless."[2]

SHANGHAI, Sept. 10, 49—The editor and the Peiping correspondent of tile pro-Communist *Ta Kung Pao*, apologized today for the publication on Aug 22 of an article allegedly misrepresenting statements made in it speech by Gen. Chou En-lai, vice chairman of the Communist Revolutionary Council. Chou En-lai, vice chairman of the Communist Revolutionary Council.

In a front page notice in the *Ta Kung Pao*, the editor, Wang Yunslieng, and the correspondent, Hsu Ying, also declared that they had been guilty of an "irresponsible attitude" in publishing a story that had not been submitted for revision in advance to 11 the person involved."

The newspaper's original report on General Chou's Peiping speech, which concerned "a new mode of life," quoted him as saying in part: "A man cannot be completely faultless and even Mao Tze-tung (chairman of the Chinese Community Party) cannot be considered faultless. Even Mao Tze-tung had to leave out complete portions of his works while compiling the 'selected works of Mao Tze-tung.' Should we not be more strict with ourselves and know our own shortcomings ?"

Today's *Ta Kung Pao* notice stated that this was a misrepresentation of General Chou's remarks. Thus, for instance, Mr. Chou pointed out that "it is difficult to achieve perfection," the notice explained. "Even within the Communist Party of China only chairman Mao and comrade Liu Shao-chi (another top-ranking Communist) and a few other leaders have achieved the state of perfection."

The claims of perfection and faultlessness for Party leaders in other countries are bound to come into conflict with the CPSU doctrine of the inadmissibility of more than one power center within one's control area, but they provide an interesting illustration of the kind of leadership principle embraced in contemporary Soviet theory, a theory of the Party leader who has gained a perfect ability to diagnose the situation, to predict the course of History, and to develop a plan which will take maximum advantage of this situation.

The perfect models at the top of the Party, Lenin and Stalin, are to be imitated in, of course, descending degrees of perfection by all Party leaders down to the secretary of the smallest cell or the youngest Komsomol member. This newer, Stalinist belief in learning from perfect models contrasts with the earlier, Leninist belief in learning from a less perfect model who could err. Stalin, at the 13th Party Congress, in 1924, said, replying to Trotsky:[3]

2. *The New York Times*, September 11, 1949, p. 41.

3. J. Stalin, in *Report of the 13th Congress Russian Communist Party (B) (XIII s'ezd Rossiiskow Kommunisticheskoi Partii)*, stenographic report, Moscow, March, 1924, p. 244.

"The Party," says Comrade Trotsky ... "does not make mistakes." This is not true. The Party often errs. Il'ich taught us to teach the Party leadership by its own mistakes. If there were no mistakes in the Party there would be nothing to teach the Party with. Our task is to catch these mistakes, seek out their roots and show the Party and the working class how we erred and how we should not further repeat these errors. Without this the development of the Party would be impossible, without this formation of leaders and cadres our Party would be impossible, since they are formed and educated by their own mistakes.

But today the approved attitude stresses the perfection of the leader. Molotov speaks Of Stalin's: "... profound knowledge of the history of nations ... versatile experience as leader ... ability to fathom and to discern in time the strategic plans and tactics of ... states ... boldness and flexibility ..."[4] This is expressed at a popular level in Mikhailov's address at the 11th Komsomol Congress, March, 1949:[5]

Millions of Soviet boys and girls carry in their hearts the images of the great creators of our Party and State, Lenin and Stalin. Millions of our youth are learning to live and work, to fight and win after the manner of Lenin and Stalin.

The letter to Stalin from the 11th Congress includes a poem:[6]

And your life, your road, Comrade Stalin,
Is taken as an example by all youth.

Of the Party it is said:

The Party is a unity of will, which excludes all factions and splits in the power of the Party.[7]

Not a single important political or organizational question is decided by our Soviet and other mass organizations without leading directives from the Party.[8]

Comrade Kaligina said here that the Moscow organization in its own territorial unit felt daily the nearness of the leadership of the CC and of the

4. V. Molotov, "Stalin and Stalinist leadership," quoted from *Pravada*, December 21, 1949, p. 3, *in Current Digest of the Soviet Press*, Vol. 1, No. 52, January 24, 1950, p. 8.

5. Mikhailov addressing the 11th Congress of the VLKSM, *Komsmol'skaia Pravada*, March 31, 1949, p. 3.

6. From a poem quoted n the 11th Congress' letter to Stalin, in *Komsomol'skaia Pravada*, April 10, 1949, p. 1.

7. J. Stalin, "Foundations of Leninism" (*Osnovi Leninizma*), as in Stalin, *Leninism*, New York, 1928.

8. *Ibid.*

chief of our Party, Stalin. I must say that we who are situated in the Don-
bass felt just as closely the concrete leadership of our struggle, of our construction, by the CC and Stalin.[9]

The whole system of centralized leadership is stated in the Report
of the Central Revision Commission of the VLKSM (Komsomols):[10]

> The Komsomol has come to its (Eleventh) Congress ... rallied solidly
> (*spolochennyi*), as never before, around its mother, the Communist Party;
> around the Central Committee of the VKP (B); and around the leader of
> the Bolshevist Party and the Soviet people, the Great Stalin.

As Stalin and the central organization in whose name Stalin's
decisions are phrased are to the whole of the Soviet Union, so also is
each smaller leader to those he leads. The functions of the Party Secretary at the provincial level are therefore described as follows:[11]

> ... to know the plants exactly, to visit them regularly, to be directly in
> contact with the plant managers and the corresponding People's Com-
> missariat, to support them in fulfilling the Party's plans and decisions
> concerning industry and transportation, to control systematically the ful-
> fillment of those decisions, to reveal the defects in the work of the plants
> and to aim at their removal.

In other words, the Party secretary is to be all-knowing, all-direct-
ing. Examples of appropriate behavior for Party activists are sometimes published as models in which each step in the problem of
inspiring a group is outlined.[12] Similarly, Komsomol leaders "must
show to all youth an example of the socialist attitude,"[13] "set the
example for all students,"[14] and young Pioneer leaders are still charged
with the task of being "models of honesty, idealism, and industriousness."[15] But while each leader, no matter how humble or how young,
is acting as a model for those who know less than he, all, from the

9. Sarkisov, 17the Congress of the All-Union Communist Party (B),
(*XVII s'ezd Vesoyuznoi Kommunisticheskoi Partii*), stenographic account,
Moscow, 1934, p. 161.

10. Krivtsov, "Report of the Central Revisory Commission," *Komsomol'skaia Pravada*, March 31, 1949, p. 4.

12. See Appendix F.

13. Rules of the Komsomol, in *Rezoliutsii I Dokumenty XI s'ezda VLKSM*,
pp. 51-52.

14. From 11th Congress' resolution "On the Work of the Komsomol in
the Schools," in *Rezoliutsii I Dokumenty XI s'ezda VLKSM*, p. 28.

15. From speech to the 11th Congress by a Komsomol member who was
serving as Pioneer-leader, in *Komsomol's skaia Pravada*, April 3, 1949, p. 2.

lowest leader up, look all the way to the top for their models. Although there is continual exhortation to be a model, the complementary instruction to youth, to the average member of a collective farm committee, or to a factory committee is to look to Stalin and Lenin, not to the Komsomol leader or to the Party secretary in the farm or the factory.

There is a rigid realistic demand for subordination of one level of the Party to another, in which each higher level enforces its will upon the lower in the name of the Party, but this is not accompanied by a demand for personal loyalty or friendship. All such personal relations are stigmatized as "family relations." This organizational ethic provides a weak basis for organization because it includes no ties of loyalty, either from local units to local leaders or from local leaders to district or provincial leaders. There is no dogma to support any person-to-person relations of leadership and followership. Each leader is confronted with the impossible task of being a model for those who look over his head to a model higher and more perfect than he, although he is wholly accountable for them.

The implications of this peculiar leadership structure can be visualized if one imagines an army organized in such a manner that each officer is completely responsible for and accountable in regard to all those under him, both officers and men, but whose subordinates are expected to keep their eyes only on the leads given by the Commander-in-Chief as a model of perfection. Meanwhile the fact that Party officials at each level are accountable for the acts of those at lower levels stimulates the arbitrary exercise of power by all those in authority, always in the name of the Party. This makes it possible for members of each echelon within the hierarchy to see the *next* highest echelon as behaving bureaucratically; and this, in turn, may be one reason for the kind of betrayals which occur when men lose their belief in the Party.

This same demand that each individual who is responsible for others should play a model-setting role is extended to parents, who are, however, accorded much more explicit rights to direct obedience and affection from their children. While there seems to be no requirement to love a Komsomol leader or a Party secretary, affection for parents is enjoined upon children and "sons know that the love of a Soviet mother is not all-forgiving love but is exacting and proud, demanding responsibility *to her* for conduct and deeds."[16] In this respect, parents in regard to children bear a closer resemblance to Stalin's relationship to every Soviet citizen, as their right to receive

16. A. Sergeyeva, "Love and Obligation to a Mother," *Family and School* (*Sem'ya i Shkola*), November, 1947.

love and respect is as explicitly stated as is their duty to deserve it; "Fortunately, in the majority of Soviet families, between father and children exist the very best of relations based on mutual love, respect and understanding. For the authority of the parents to be really high, a strong, well-knit family is necessary first of all. ... If the parents are socially valuable persons and honest workers, if they share with their children their achievements at work, recount the life of their collective and events in the country, their authority will always be high in the children's eyes. ..."[17]

Nor is any time limit put on the responsibility of parents for children or of children to parents. In a model of an exemplary family, a Soviet mother is made to say: "All the children obey me. My eldest son, who returned from the front a lieutenant, will do nothing without asking my advice, will go nowhere without having told me."[18]

This use of individual examples is one further aspect of model-setting in which a model mother, a model collective farmer, a model worker are described for the whole Soviet Union. The emphasis is on the way in which a given individual discharged a particular role, not on the individual himself. This stress on a role, illustrated by the behavior of someone half the country away, is again an interesting way in which personal loyalty to individual teachers and managers can be muted into impersonal idealism. American observers comment upon the fantastic quality of these models, the description of the perfect agitator or of the perfect collective farm. However, they will seem less fantastic if understood as manifestations of the perfection already attained in vision by the Leader rather than as if they were intended to be taken as real descriptions of sober facts.

The direction of all eyes toward the top makes it possible to block out a line of spiritual ambition not unlike that available in those religions without a priesthood (a characteristic of Russian sects), in which each true believer can approach nearer and nearer to perfection. It appears probable that this insistence on the possibilities of becoming a better and better Communist, better imbued with an understanding of Marxism-Leninism, may play an important part in persuading men to assume the dangers of any sort of conspicuous role in the Soviet Union. It must, of course, be realized that there are great material rewards available to those who are able to rise, that it is difficult to refuse advancement when it is offered, and that behavior

17. N. Udina, "Parental Authority," *Family and School* (*Sem'ya i Shkola*), 1946, Nos. 4-5.

18. A. Alekseyev and M. Andreyeva, "Report of a Working Mother," *Family and School (Sem'ya i Shkola)*, April, 1948.

which is necessary to enable one to maintain any position on the advancement ladder is very similar to the kind of behavior which will single one out for promotion. Nevertheless, and in spite of the decrease in the danger of actual physical liquidation (after this danger to those in leadership roles had reached such a height in the late thirties that it endangered the entire trained Party leadership), it seems necessary to account further for the existence of this willingness. It is possible also that, as the latitude allowed to individual thought and initiative narrows, it is even more necessary to explain at least why men of very mediocre ability, picked out by the Party leadership as safe and reliable, are willing to run the risk of exercising their so inconsiderable talents. But the persistent propagation of the double doctrine—that it is possible to grow in the right to leadership, and that those who are purged or demoted failed to guard against some heresy—con tributes to making it possible for a man who rises in the apparatus to believe, despite such overwhelming evidence to the contrary, that he will succeed. (This would be in a way comparable to the persistent American belief in success, which is held by millions of men whose real chances of making more than two or three thousand a year can be demonstrated, statistically and by their own everyday experience, as being almost nonexistent. But because, in the United States, success is believed to be "making good," to be the reward of hard work and effort, each man who strives may believe that, statistics to the contrary, he will fulfill the Horatio Alger story, he will succeed where his fellows fail.)

It is suggested that the belief that those who failed deserved to fail plays a comparable role in the lives of those who are willing to assume office in Soviet society. There is considerable evidence that, in Nazi Germany, office attracted individuals who had unusually strong desires to bully, to hurt, to torture, to control the lives of others, for the sake of the pleasure that it gave them. Thus the revelation of the Nuremberg Trials and other studies of Nazism give us a Picture of administration which drew disproportionately upon the power-seeking, ruthless, cruelty-loving element in the population. If we look only at the outward political structure of the Soviet Union, with its increasing monolithic character and the great rewards in power over the lives of others which are offered to those who are able so to manipulate the power situation as to rise to the top and to stay there, we might be tempted to expect that the same personality type would obtain in the upper bureaucracy of the Soviet Union as in Nazi Germany. All material which makes it possible better to assay in more concrete detail the theories by which given men justify their attempt to reach and keep positions of power and influence in the Soviet

Union assumes significance. It is also necessary to realize that the man who reaches a position of great influence and importance in the belief that he has done so because of his superior understanding and application of the principles of Marxism-Leninism rather than from a sheer openly expressed belief in the right of the stronger to dominate the weaker will not be the less ruthless in exercising the power. He may be much more ruthless, because his conscience will be entirely on his side; he will not be subject to the sort of moral collapse shown by some of the top Nazis when faced with the expression of contempt for their ideas of power by represensitives of nations which had proved themselves more powerful than they. The Soviet leader seems to be of a different caliber and subject to very different sorts of pressures. His own failure may convince him that *he* was wrong but not that the political faith in which he believed was wrong. His own failure, his demotion or liquidation by his own Party, may serve merely as a reinforcement of his belief in his Party's rightness.

It is in this way that contemporary Soviet literature portrays the Communist who is exposed and demoted. So Tverdova (in Virta's play, *Our Daily Bread*[19]), chairman of the executive committee in a small locality, who has been a Communist for many years and is an experienced and able administrator, is "unmasked" by the new Party secretary. She first exclaims:

> Twenty years I spent for this cause and now I am politically bankrupt, shaken out of the calesh.

Then after a pause, she continues:

> And so what! In what I am guilty I will render account, looking straight. I have to think it all over, I have to think hard.

This attitude, expressed in a 1947 play, continues that dramatized in the great trials. At the January, 1937, trial Radek discussed his misgivings concerning the First Five-Year Plan:[20]

> Already ... in 1931 ... I thought it was necessary to hold back the economic offensive ... I dissented on the main question: on the question of contin-

19. N. Virta, *Our Daily Bread* (*Khleb nash nasushchnyi*), *Zvezda* (*The Star*), June, 1947.

20. Radek, Report of Court Proceedings in the Case of the Anti-Trotskyite Centre, heard before the Military Collegium of the Supreme Court of the USSR, Moscow, January 23-30, 1937. Published by the People's Commissariat of Justice of the USSR, Moscow, 1937, p. 84-85.

uing ... the Five-Year plan. To analyze these disagreements from the Social angle of course, I then believed the tactics which I regarded as correct to be the best Communist tactics— ... history's joke was that I overestimated the power of resistance ... of ... the Kulaks ... (and) of the middle peasants to pursue an independent policy. I was scared by the difficulties and thus became a mouthpiece of ... forces hostile to the proletariat.

This hypothesis, that the discipline of others is believed to have been deserved and that one's own discipline is accepted as a proof of uncorrectness, would provide an additional explanation of the way in which those who have been disciplined, demoted, or banished go to work again with apparent zeal, apart from the calculus of external rewards and punishment.

Characteristics of the Ideal Leader

We may now consider the way top leadership is officially said to gain and maintain its superior capacity to lead. Materials on this subject come from a variety of sources—the statements of Lenin and Stalin to the Party, the continual admonishment and exhortation in the Party press, exhortation to Komsomol and pioneer leaders, and the popular pictures of the leadership presented to the average citizen and to children. These will be considered together, since they may all be regarded as officially inspired, although the details may differ as to whether Stalin is presented in a synthetic folk song as the direct descendant of the Bogatyri, to the educators as the Perfect Educator, to the Literary Front as the master of organization of literary activity, etc. The basic intent, the virtues emphasized are fundamentally the same, and their reappearance in different forms should serve as reinforcement of faith in the dogma of the regime. (There are very few data available on the degree to which the beliefs of the top leadership about their own roles differ from the beliefs considered suitable for the masses of the people. What little evidence there is suggests that the difference lies not so much in the actual belief, in, for example, the superior capacity of Stalin to lead the Soviet Union, as in the tone of the belief. To the populace he may be presented as a loving, kind leader, to the inner circle of the elite he may appear as being much more interested in personal power, yet to both he will be *the* Leader, with any present alternative regarded as impossible. That is, the chain of reasoning which forms the connection between the Leadership and History may be quite different, but the belief in the absolute connection may nevertheless be there. The same informant who will relate a gossipy report in inner circles that Stalin decided on the Line first and then said, "Let the theoreticians justify it," will also report on Stalin's stubborn fidelity to his view of Leninism, and Stalin's personal fanatical devotion to building a state which will stand after his death.)

In tracing the details of this leadership role, it will be useful to consider Lenin and Leninist Marxism as given in the sense that the original founding prophet and the scriptures might be present in any ongoing religious system. World History as it is presented to the young citizen of the Soviet Union is divided in two: before 1917 and after 1917. After 1917, the picture is of an all—embracing way of life, with a Truth, a form of organization (the Party), the embodiment of that organizational form in a leader (Lenin and Stalin), and a way of life—difficult, all demanding—to which every Soviet citizen should feel called, to at least some degree, as a vocation. In these respects it is far closer to the familiar picture of a religious movement in its early, all-inclusive form than to the sort of political picture presented by contemporary Western democracies.

Some of the most vivid material on the leader comes from the large amount of folklore which was developed during the late twenties and early thirties and in which Lenin and Stalin were fitted into poetic forms of Great Russia, the *byliny*, and into the folklore forms of some of the non-Russian peoples of Asia. These poems were published with the specific statement that they represented spontaneous outpourings of the common people who had adapted the new Bolshevik figures to their idiom. They are quoted here as evidence of what it is considered desirable for the people to think.

In the folklore the people are pictured as gathering together, "from the old to the middle ones, from the middle ones to the young ones, and asking 'Who should be ruling?' " And they all "spoke the same speech," they all chose one "Vladimir Il'ich, the Leader Lenin," and they "entrusted all of Russia to him, to the leader Lenin and his helper, with the entire Bolshevik Party." Another revision of an old folktale, about three brothers searching for Truth, tells how one went to the factory "to seek for Truth," for "there you will find out more rapidly what it is. You hold it in your hand." And "Lenin's Truth" found in the factory "went over the whole world. ... And in October of the seventeenth year, the Truth announced itself, started to speak in a loud voice and ring over the entire world." "The workers and peasants went to war, 'And Lenin himself was leading them, together with his helper Stalin. ... And Lenin's Truth gained the upper hand' and from then on the people are not 'hunched over ... they do not water the earth with their tears—they are the owners of their factories, their earth, and their lives.'"

Stalin appears in the folklore as the direct successor of Lenin, as his helper during life, who derived his relations to the Truth directly from contact with Lenin. The folklore celebrates the occasion when Stalin is pictured as coming to join Lenin in exile, and Krupskaya, wife of Lenin, says: "Look out of the window, Il'ich, isn't that Stalin, glorious hero?" The story of Stalin's acceptance of Lenin's Testament is told: "The entire earth was wet with tears. Our hero —Stalin -light— took off his cap from his saddened head, and he spoke to the people, thus 'We are laying down an oath for eternity. ... We are laying down an oath that we shall carry out things as you wanted it. With your wisdom we shall live. ... Goodbye Il'ich, sleep quietly.'

A long saga asks the question: "Who is like Lenin, in mind and powerful force?" and answers "Stalin," who "held in his powerful hand" the "golden sun": "He is great and wise like Lenin. ... He is the same as Lenin, friendly and good." ... "Together with the Sun the Great Stalin brought to our tents the belief in our own strength. He is great and simple, like Lenin."

In the approved poetry of the new folklore, as in the continued repetition of the names of Lenin and Stalin and in the phrase Lenin-ism-Stalinism, the halo around the figure of Lenin is made to embrace Stalin also, and he, like Lenin, in obedience to Lenin, sharing Lenin's knowledge of the Truth, leads the people, will "give happiness to all the people." But at the same time the relationship of every Soviet cit-izen to the leader is stressed. "All have in their blood a drop of Lenin's blood," says a long poem, written sometime in the early thirties, and "We have become terrible for enemies as Lenin himself." This same theme appears in a postwar novel, *The Stozharovs*,[21] in which a young army officer, still in his teens, says: "... Stalin, he knows, and that is why he is so sure of the people, of our victory and of everything. ... It seems to me ... that in each Communist there is, a kind of particle of Stalin. In any true Communist, of course. And this helps him to be sure and calm, to know what to do, to what everything will lead if he acts as the Party commands ... a Communist ... he is a leader in every-thing and everywhere, a teacher of life for the people."

Throughout the folklore, as in the Party histories, the plot is the search for the Truth, for the power which in the folklore is repre-sented as the ring which, when grasped, will turn the whole world over. Lenin found it and Stalin carries on the tradition. In a recent Soviet poem[22] in the form of a lullaby, in which a father bids his baby daughter sleep safely now that atomic energy has been found, this fig-

21. Elena Katerli, *The Stozharovs*, 1948, pp. 147-49 and p. 169.
22. See Appendix G.

ure recurs—of a granite mountain, "which is barring our way. Long, long ago it should have been turned upside down, long, long ago it should have been forced to give up its ore, and now at the pre-arranged hour . the old mountain disappeared."

So we have an emphasis on the ideal leader's undeviating, absolute following of the Truth which Lenin found and from this Truth obtaining his power. Application of the Truth is expressed in foresight and long sight, and, in the folklore, this wide yet focused view is symbolized by placing in Stalin's hand a spyglass as he stands on the walls of the Kremlin, as he "looks and rules the country solicitously, he looks and looks without ever getting tired, His sensitive ear hears everything, his sharp glance sees everything; how the people live, how they work." This combination of wide perspective and power to direct is expressed of Lenin as follows: "Lifting his head higher than the stars, Lenin could see at once the entire world and he could direct the entire world at one time."

Again this same behavior is urged on the local leader, so a regional Party secretary moralizes in a recent novel, *In Some Populated Place*,[23] speaking of life in the country: "Our influence must express itself in all spheres. ... We know and understand that we must go deeper into the life of the Party organization. ... We will go forward only by seeing wider than one division, by seeing further than the present day. We must lead the whole life of the raion." And this same Party secretary is described as "the brains and soul of the raion ... walking idly among the crowd to listen to what the people are thinking."

These two aspects of leadership, the top leader who sees all without moving from his place on the Kremlin wall, the lower leader who combines his wider vision with a closer knowledge of the people, are summed up in the plot of a recent Soviet film, *The Train Goes East*, in which the heroine, a Communist girl, is delayed on a railway platform together with a great many other people. She first mingles with the people, learning all about them, and then, when the train dispatcher loses his voice, mounts to the traffic control tower and directs the people, about whom she now knows everything, absolutely correctly to their particular trains.

The Soviet critic is exhorted to "illuminate with a searchlight the road to tomorrow,"[24] and the criticism which surrounded the hero of a favorite juvenile war tale, Timur, first condemned the character of

---

23. Boris Galin, "In Some Populated Place" (*v odnom naselennom punkte*), *Novyi Mir*, November, 1947.

24. From the report of Andrei Zhdanov about the literary magazines *Zvezda* and *Leningrad*, published in *Literaturnaya Gazeta*, September 21, 1946.

Timur as having been just "thought up," but later the condemnation was retracted and it was recognized that the author, in a novel, "saw the boy of the future," "he discerned the tendency of development of the Soviet child such as he would be tomorrow,"[25] and a wife rebukes her husband, who questions a decision of local leaders: "You may argue how you like but 'they' are right, they see farther than we do."[26]

With this emphasis on all-seeingness, on a focused vision and a power of diagnosis which is wider and deeper than that of those who are led, goes a requirement to focus action, to go indeflectibly, though sometimes circuitously, toward the goal, and always to have perfect timing, being neither too early, which is Left, nor too late, which is Right. Stalin says: "It is the function of Leninist theory to diagnose the situation at the moment and thus determine the direction of the blow and to focus it on a proper line through the organization of revolutionary forces."[27] The Komsomol is described as organized and disciplined, firm, purposeful, and persistent in everything he undertakes. He should walk a narrow path to his goal without stopping, without swerving.

When we look at the history of the condemnation of the Right and Left deviations, as demonstrated in the late twenties and early thirties, we find the same emphasis on the need for steering a course between twin dangers. Stalin has given us graphic descriptions of both. In a 1930 statement about the Rights, he says:[28]

> They are suffering from the same disease as ... that ... hero of Chekhov, the man in the leather case. Do you remember Chekhov's story titled *The Man in the Leather Case?* That he always went about in galoshes and wadded coat, with an umbrella, both in hot and cold weather? ... "Why do you need galoshes and a wadded coat in July? ..." Belikov used to be asked.
>
> "You never know," Belikov replied, "what if something happens? There might be a sudden frost; what should I do then?" ... A new restaurant was opened, and Belikov was ... in alarm: "It might, of course, be a good thing to have a restaurant, but take care, see that nothing happens." ... Do you remember the affair of the technical colleges being transferred to the Economic People's Commissariats? We wanted to hand over only two

25. L. Kon, "The Educational Significance of the Works of Arkadii Gaidar," *Literature in School* (*Literatura v shkole*), April, 1948.

26. S. Babyevski, "The Cavalier of the Golden Star" (*Kavaler zolotoi svezdy*) published in *Oktybr'* April, 1947, p. 56.

27. J. Stalin, Political Report of the Central Committee of the 16th Congress of the Communist Party of the Soviet Union, in *Leninism*, Vol. 2, New York, 1933, pp. 414-15.

28. *Ibid.*

technical colleges to the Supreme Economic Council. A small matter it might seem. Yet we met with the most desperate resistance on the part of the Right deviators. "Hand over two technical colleges to the SEC? Why? Hadn't we better wait? Take care, see that nothing happens as a result of this scheme. ..." Or, for example, the question of the emergency measures against the kulaks. "Do you remember what hysterics the leaders of the Right opposition fell into on this occasion? ... Take care, see that nothing happens as a result of this scheme." Yet today we are applying the policy of liquidating the kulaks as a class, a policy in comparison with which the extraordinary measures against the kulaks are a mere fleabite.

In his political report of June 27, 1930, to the Central Committee of the 16th Congress,[29] Stalin discusses both the Left exaggeration (*peregib*) and the Right overestimation of the severity of the temporary setbacks to and arrests of the current offensive:

> ... (some) think that the socialist offensive is a headlong march forward ... without regrouping of forces in the course of the offensive, without consolidating the Positions occupied, without utilizing reserves to develop our successes, and, if symptoms have appeared of, say, an ebb of a part of the peasantry away from the collective farms, this means ... a check to the offensive. Is this true?

> Of course it is untrue. In the first place, not a single offensive ... takes place without some breaks and over-hastiness on individual sections of the front. ... Secondly, there never has been, and never can be, a *successful* offensive without a regrouping of forces in the course of the offensive itself, without consolidating the occupied positions, without utilizing reserve. ... In a headlong movement, i.e., one that does not observe these conditions, the offensive must inevitably work itself to a standstill and collapse. Rushing forward headlong is fatal in an offensive. Our rich experience in our civil war teaches us this.

The Left deviation represents uncontrolled, romantic, not properly calculated behavior; and the Right, spineless pessimism and a tendency to surrender easily before setbacks or obstacles.

But the Bolshevik leader must remain indeflectable, calm; he must be particularly wary against the seductions of the path of least resistance, of being seduced, without knowing it, into becoming a tool of the enemy forces. "Lenin said, 'The honest opportunities are the most dangerous,'" warns the new party secretary who is unmasking the old secretary.[30]

29.   J. Stalin, Political Report of the Central Committee to the 16th Congress of the communist Party of the Soviet Union, in *Leninism*, Vol. 2, New York, 1933.

30.   N. Virta, "Our Daily Bread" (*Khleb nash nasushchnyi*), *Zvezda*, June, 1947, p. 47.

In the same political report[31] in which Stalin satirized the Rights, he also said:

> In our party there are some who think that we ought not to have called a halt to the Left exaggerators. They think that we ought not to have offended our workers and counteracted their excitement, even if this excitement led to mistakes. ... Only those who want at all costs to swim with the stream can say that. They are the very same people who will never learn the Leninist policy of going against the stream when ... the interests of the Party demand it. They are tailists and not Leninists.

The young Komsomol is warned against being *respushchenyi*, *raskhlyabanyi*, and *razboltanyi*, words which together carry connotations of being lax, loose, relaxed and slovenly, untied, hanging loosely, and of talking too much.

But the virtues of proceeding firmly to overcome obstacles are of no use in themselves. They are only recognized when placed at the service of Party goals. A writer who apparently was taking the right course, i.e., "choosing historical themes,"[32] is condemned because his intent was corrupted by his choice of "the way of least resistance." Nor is it permissible for a Communist to choose a difficult task for the sheer enjoyment of struggle. The young hero of the Soviet film, *Secret Mission*, exclaims with delight when he is told by his Party superior about the dangerous German adversary with whom he is to match wits abroad. He is immediately rebuked for expressing any such preference; it would have been better for the cause "had he (the adversary) been weak." But of a favorably characterized Communist in a recent novel,[33] it is said, "He has become so familiar with the conception of the vanguard role of Communists that he cannot swim merely with the current of events," which he himself describes as "lagging behind."

The combined demands on perspective, puritanism, and refusal to swim with the current may all occur together, as in the comment by Stalin[34] that "this deficiency consists in the desire of a number of our comrades to swim with the current smoothly and peacefully, without pespective, without looking into the future, so that all around there is a festive and holiday feeling."

31. J. Stalin, Political Report of the Central Committee to the 16th Congress of the Communist Party of the Soviet Union, in *Leninism*. Vol. 2, New York, 1933.

32. Sofronov, criticizing the play of N. Pogodin, *The Bygone Years* (*Miluvshiye gody*), in *Oklyabtr'* February, 1949, p. 142.

33. Bubyonnov, "The White Birch," *Oktyabr,'* July, 1947, p. 24.

34. Excerpt from Stalin's report at 15th Party Congress, 1927.

Moving against the current is, of course, one way of maintaining the iron control which is also demanded of a Bolshevik. A heroine struggling with the moral problems facing Soviet youth is made to say of herself :[35] "Disgraceful! I have no character, no self-control, no real will. I fly down a slope and cannot check myself." In a much-discussed postwar novel, *Comrade Anna*,[36] the heroine, nearly going out of her mind from grief, considers shooting herself but is stopped by the thought of her child. This scene is omitted from later editions of the novel as being out of character for a positive Soviet heroine. (In this connection it is worth noting that women do not appear, except as the most casual mention includes men and women, in the official folklore as it refers to Stalin. Lenin is represented with his wife, but Stalin holds the sun in one hand and the moon—a feminine symbol in the old folklore—in the other and is credited with a long list of fructifying deeds: "Where he stepped, a trace remained, each step a new town, a bridge, a railroad … towns, houses, like cliffs; over the entire earth he sowed things that are stronger than granite." However, in the novels and plays, women appear in the lower ranks of the Party, faced with the same moral struggles as men in addition to the particular complications incident to their sex, so that material on female Party members at this level seems as valid as material on male Party members.)

With this requirement, that all behavior be controlled and directed toward Party goals, goes the requirement that the Party member treat himself as a tool to carry out the wishes of the Party, but that he be at all times a conscious tool, voluntarily submitting himself to the discipline of the Party. And the discipline must be minute and detailed, over himself and over his every movement. So an informant reports an encounter with a Soviet professor in Berlin, who told her that he smoked a pipe, "because while smoking a pipe the face does not reveal so much." Then he added:

> See, this we learned during the Soviet period. Before the revolution we used to say: "The eyes are the mirror of the soul." The eyes can lie—and how. You can express with your eyes a devoted attention which in reality you are not feeling. You can express serenity or surprise. It is much more difficult to govern the expression of your mouth. I often watch my face in the mirror before going to meetings and demonstrations and I saw. … I was suddenly aware that even with a memory of a disappointment my lips became closed. That is why by smoking a heavy pipe you are more

35. Elena Il'ina, *Fourth Height* (*Chetvertaya vysota*), Detgiz, 1948.

36. Antonina Koptyayeva, "Comrade Anna" (*Tovarishch Anna*), in *Otyabr'*, May, 1946, P. 97.

sure of yourself. Through the heaviness of the pipe the lips are deformed and cannot react spontaneously.

This quotation is a virtual diagram of the shift from the old pre-Soviet type of interpersonal relationship to the new: In the old, dissimulation is a pretense of positive feeling; in the new, it is a hiding of negative feeling. Contrasts such as this occur frequently in the course of the Bolshevik attempt to impose rigid controlled focus on a people whose habitual behavior had been diffuse, expressive, and less controlled. Echoes of the way in which the standard Bolshevik behavior is reflected among those who are opposed to the regime are found in the words of a recent emigre:[37] "We (the opposed) recognize each other at once by looking at the eyes, at the scarcely noticeable smiles, by the way such a man greets a Party member. He says: Hello, friendly. We recognize none the less, that he belongs to us. We recognize such a man by the way he sits at a general meeting, and also by the way he listens. But we consider it good manners to avoid personal acquaintance."

Both of these quotations throw some light on why the Party likes to have meetings, which often appear like mere mechanical rubber stamping of official policy; among other things, they provide an opportunity for watching for these tell-tale signs.

The Party member must never relax, never look for rest or for the good things of this world. "Our generation is not born to have a rest."[38]

Immediately after the war, there was added, to this demand for unrelaxed alertness, a positive stress on restlessness (bespokoistvo) which was illustrated in fiction by stories of the good Communists who returned from the front to find their own communities apathetic and self-satisfied. The restless veteran then became a leader who turned the local community upside down. Approval of restlessness was used as a prod to those who thought "after the victory will come a respite, that one would be able to work now with less than full strength," but this was castigated; people must work now "with active Bolshevik restlessness."[39] In late 1949 this stress on restlessness has disappeared; whether this is because there is too much real restlessness to be directed into useful channels or because the veteran has become such a commonplace that he no longer provides a useful model it is

37. N. Osipov, "Immigration Inside the USSR, *Grani*, Issue 5, Hanau, Germany, July-August, 1949.

38. K. Simonov, "Under the Chestnut Trees of Prague," *Znamya*, February-March, 1946.

39. S. Babayevski, "The Cavalier of the Golden Star" (*Kavaler zolotoi svezdi*), *Oktyabr'*, April, 1947.

impossible to tell. This ephemeral choice of a virtue for Party members, in terms of a special situation, and its later neglect is an example of the extreme contemporaneousness which, in the Soviet Union, accompanies the attempt to politicize every act and every mood.

Another extremely important characteristic of the Party leader, at all levels, is watchfulness *(bditel'noslt')*, which entails being continuously alert toward the self and toward others for the slightest signs of doubt or of slackening of effort, with the expected sequels: treachery and penetration by the enemy. "The enemies are not asleep," says an editorial in *Molodoi Bol'shevik*, "They use any sliver in order to create inside the country points of support for anti-Soviet propaganda."[40] But because this is so, watchfulness includes watchfulness over one's closest friends: "true friendship and comradely care do not. exclude but, on the contrary, presuppose the highest demands, the sharpest and most merciless criticism."[41] This demand, in an editorial in 1948, is a repetition, on a more routine scale, of the demand which accompanied the purge period in the thirties, that one's best friends be sacrificed to the Party. The leadership is surrounded by enemies, "walking as a small closed group on a steep and difficult road with solidly joined hands ... surrounded on all sides by enemies, they have to walk almost under their fire." [42] And always this enemy may be quite close to one. In contemporary novels, the upper Party man who proves to be dangerous to the well-being of the Party now is pictured as having many misleading good qualities. Today he is pictured as a large man, whereas fifteen years ago he was puny.[43] He is sympathetic, one of the group, not a stranger. His relationship with his family is good.[44] He is represented as strong and with strong convictions.[45] Under such circumstances the good Party leader has to be doubly watchful. "It is not enough," warns Sofronov,[46] "to pay attention to what is said, which may be quite in accord with the Party program, but one must pay attention to the tone, to the love with which a school teacher may quote the poems which are criticized in the (official) school program. The same thing may be said about the critics and the pleasure with which they cite the

40. Editorial, "Education Soviet Patriotism-the Most Important Task of the Komsomol," *Molodoi Bol'shevik*, September, 1947.

41. Editorial, "Care for the friend-a Komsomol duty," *Komsomol'skaia Pravda*, August 6, 1948, p. 1.

42. Quotation from Lenin in V. Ozerov, "The Image of a Bolshevik," *Bol'-shevik*, Issue 10, May, 1949.

43. Y. Olesha, *Envy*, Moscow, 1927.

44. K. Simonov, "Smoke of the Fatherland," *Novyi Mir*, November, 1947.

45. *Ibid*.

46. Sofronov, "About Soviet Dramaturgy," *Oktyabr'*, February, 1949.

plays which they condemn." And suspicion of vague, unrecognizable, inimical atmospheres is maintained by such statements as that of the Soviet writer, Perventsev,[47] who told an audience that "soon after the war was over" the theatrical market in the Soviet Union was inundated with "inscrutable speed" by foreign plays. This watchfulness for the enemy which lurks behind the most friendly facade is summed up in the play *Under the Chestnut Trees of Prague*,[48] when Petrov says to Masha, who has seen Prague:

> So you rode through the city, you saw people walking in the streets; these people seem to be more or less the same and everybody wears more or less the same hats, more or less the same glasses and gloves. But behind which glasses are hidden the eyes of a Fascist? Under which hat is the head secretly thinking about how everything could be turned back? In which gloves are the hands which would like to strangle us all with pleasure? All this you have not seen ?

Every Party leader must reckon with the fact that "one of the most important results of oppositionist work … is that it is used by a third force, outside the walls of the Party, which says it is not important to me who you are, but you are the enemy of my enemy; therefore you are my friend."[49]

The need for eternal watchfulness is enhanced by the Bolshevik refusal to admit that anything is accidental. As Lominadze says in his new pledge of adherence at the 17th Party Congress:[50]

> I must begin with the fact that the mistakes which brought me to the opposition were not accidental, People do not start on the opportunist path accidentally. Accidental opposition cannot exist in the Party.

The appropriate behavior for the Party leadership faced with such grave dangers within and without is to watch over everything and control everything. This demand for total responsibility, total control is reiterated again and again and has been discussed above (see page 60) in the image of the all-seeingness, all-directingness of the leader.

47. A. Perventsev, speech at Plenum Session, Board of All-Soviet Writers, *Oktyabr'*, February, 1949.

48. K. Simonov, "Under the Chestnut Trees of Prague," *Znamya*, February-March, 1946.

49. M, P. Tomsky, 16th Congress of the All-Union Communist Party (B) (*XVI f'ezd Vsesoyuznoi Kommunisfiche,skoi Partii*), stenographic (account, Moscow, 1931, p. 145.

50. Lominadze, 17th Congress of the All-Union Communist Party (B) (*XVII f'ezd Vsesoyuznoi Kovimuniuicheskoi Partii*), stenographic account, Moscow, 1934, p, 118.

At the same time, however, that these demands for total control and rigid discipline are made on the leaders, the image of the leader is presented popularly as one who leads through closeness to the people, using inspiration and persuasion rather than physical force. We have noted the discrepancy in the Soviet theory of leadership, which enjoins each Party member to be a model for those beneath him but which, instead of enjoining those below to model themselves reciprocally on their immediate superiors, enjoins all Party members of whatever level to model themselves on the top leaders, Lenin and Stalin. A second discrepancy can be found in the theory which alerts every leader to the need to control everything, as the slightest error may lead to total disaster (which is a virtual injunction to lead by harsh controls and force), and a theory of leadership, presented to those who are to be led, which represents the leader as friendly, happiness-giving, and approachable. In the folklore Stalin is thus "the leader and friend of all the people." The picture of the leader who leads by a focused vision which directs his people rather than by force is presented in the folklore picture in which the leader holds his spyglass in his right hand and the reins of his horse in his left, while the Don Cossack holds, in his right hand, a sword.

The images which stress the leader's patience, understanding, humaneness, power to awaken and sustain enthusiasm, are a source of continual confusion in the admonitions and models presented to Party members. There is no room in this picture for any physical force used against one's own people. "Lenin will be remembered in a different way. He sowed light once more where Nikolai made darkness … alone, in eight years he built what they had destroyed in a thousand years." And when asked about Lenin, the people answered, "he is the son of his own people, immensely powerful … and the peoples Surrounded Lenin even closer, like a flock of swallows." And of Stalin the folklore says:

> Where Joseph light walks
> There a spring will come to the surface
> A spring will rise, grass will grow,
> Grass grows, flowers bloom,
> The working people loved Joseph light.

In the Soviet propaganda film *Alexander Nevsky*, celebrating the medieval Russian hero, the conqueror —leader rides bareheaded into the city, catching up children into his arms to ride with him, and his soldiers do the same. In the same film, the conqueror releases the vassals of the German attackers, who are pictured as fighting involuntarily, and holds the leaders for ransom, and it is only the Russian traitor who has helped the Germans who is destroyed—by the People, not by decree of the leaders. In a recent Soviet newsreel showing the 1949 May Day parade, Stalin assumes to an unusual degree, as he has repeatedly done in the past, a warm, intimate, jovial mien.

Recently also Molotov has appeared in the juvenile literature as meeting groups of children—warm, interested in the children and their affairs and able to Put everyone at his case.

In the upbringing of children, corporal punishment is strictly forbidden and steadily inveighed against. "Parents must remember that nothing furthers more the growth of malignancy and stubbornness on the one hand, and on the other, of cowardliness, timidity, shyness … a spanking, however light, is no less insulting than a beating … measures of forcing are extreme measures which show that parents have been unable by other means to impose their authority on their children."[51] Everywhere the use of physical force against one's own, as distinct from the enemy, is presented as a sign of weakness. (An interesting side light on this objection by the Bolshevik to the need to use force is found in the violent controversies as to whether torture was used in the great trials. The violence of the denials can be related to the belief that such a use of torture would suggest that the Party was weaker than its own erring members, who are represented as strong but crushed beneath the weight of evidence of their own guilt. This, of course, does not apply to the use of any method against those who are regarded as being outside and therefore to be crushed by any means and totally annihilated.)

Instead of using force, the true leader should evoke, inspire, guide, and probe into the very souls of his followers. He himself must be full of initiative, he must work with the flame (*s'ogon' kom*), which should so animate him from within that it will glow so that all can see it. "Lenin did not rule long and his rule was like a bonfire. Some received light and warmth from itothers, fire and flame."

The bad leader is described as having limited his evaluation of people to their outward symptoms … contented himself with an evaluation of people according to their apparent behavior without looking into the motives of that behavior.[52] In contrast, the ideal leader of a collective farm is pictured as follows in an article in Pravda, January, 1949:[53]

51. L. Raskin, "Discipline and Culture in the Conduct of School Children," *Young Guard*, 1941.

52. "Discussion of Fadeyev's "Young Guard," in *Molodoi Bol'shevik*, June, 1947.

53. G. Nikolaeva, "Features of the Future," *Pravda*, January 7, 1.949.

He sits in his spacious office. He is not a large man, but he is a well-built man. He is lively as mercury, he is cheerful and understands everything quickly, newspaper articles, scientific discoveries, songs and poetry. His head with its great protuberant brow and the small, regular features of a clean-shaven, round, clean Russian face is always somewhat inclined. He has a quick, soft Viatskii speech, with a manner of suddenly smiling and throwing his head back. There was united in him Bolshevik passion and *muzhik* calculatedness, bold directness and slyness, the capacity to organize masses and the capacity to look directly into the heart of an individual.

Chapter 5

SOVIET OFFICIAL EXPECTATIONS REGARDING MOTIVATION

Motivation for Leadership

We may now ask what are the official views on how the members of the leadership group are to be kept eternally on their toes, always straining toward higher goals, more culture, higher production, a fuller Soviet reality. There is, of course, an elaborate system of rewards, citations, decorations and orders, which, although they seem to an outsider to be enormously multiplied beyond the point of meaningfulness, nevertheless have definite positive value.

Bolshevik materialism admits of no idea of immortality such as is allowed for in most religious systems, but the promise of being enshrined in History probably fills the same function in giving a sense of self-continuation. A place on the Red Wall, after a funeral with Stalin as pallbearer, is possible for a highly placed Party member who dies in the odor of sanctity. This is sufficiently highly valued to provide the context for an informant to speculate about Dimitrov's death, whether he might not have consented to die when it would be most useful, since a place on the Red Wall was assured. Also, the sufferings and deprivations experienced by Party members in the exercise of their duty are believed to be alleviated by a full understanding of the part which they are playing in the Historical Process. A recent novel, *Unusual Summer*,[1] begins:

> Historical events are accompanied not only by a general excitement, "a rise or decay of the human spirit" but by extraordinary sufferings and pri-

1. K. Fedin, "Unusual Summer" (*neobyknovennoye leto*), *Novyi Mir*, January, 1947, p. 37.

vations which a man is unable to avert. For one who is conscious about these events, who understands that they constitute the course of history, or *who is himself one of the conscious motors*, these sufferings exist also. But such a man does not carry his sufferings as does one who is not thinking about the historical character of the events. [italics ours]

The Bolshevik ideal is one who is driven by his own internalized, deep involvement in the never-ending struggle, by his deep dissatisfaction with things as they are. This is one instance in which there has been a genuine and possibly successful attempt to build a revolution-derived pattern of behavior into tile everyday life of the people [it I society which no longer consider,,, Itself to be in I state of revolution so the Bolshevik must see himself as living in a world in which "the merciless ideological fight of two systems, two world conceptions, two viewpoints regarding the future of mankind has always existed, still goes on and will be there permanently."[2]

In an article in *Bol'shevik*[3] for March, 1948, this struggle is spelled out:

The principle of each development is the struggle between two contradictions the struggle between the new and the old, between the dying and tile born. The Marxist dialectic follows from the fact that the struggle between these two contradictions constitutes the internal content of the process of development Stalin teaches: "something is always dying in life, But what is dying is unwilling to die simply but struggles for existence. Also something is being born, but it isn't born in a simple way, but whines, yells, insisting on its right to existence. The struggle between the old in,! the new between what is dying and being born— is the basis of our development. This struggle is expressed in Soviet society in a totally new form, not through class struggles and cataclysms, but in the form of criticism and self criticism, the long range directing force of our development, a powerful Instrument in the hands of tile Party."

"The process of forming the new consciousness, the new morality, is very complicated. It is not a peaceful process, it is a difficult, tense struggle."[4]

This deep dissatisfaction, which is based on a recognition of the never-ending struggle, should be of such a character that each success, each new step forward should produce a desire to go even fur-

---

2. K. Simonov, "Dramaturgy, Theatre and Life," *Literaturnaya Gazeta*, November 23, 1946.

3. "Critiism and Self-Criticism, Principle of Development of Socialist Society," *Bol'shevik* March 15, 1948.

4. E. BobovskayaBobmkaya and N. Chetunova, "Problems of the Family and Morality," *Oktyabr'* January 1948.

ther. The young Bolshevik should learn to seek actively, eagerly, for that sense of having achieved, which, however, can never be repeated at the same level. To yield the same sense of satisfaction, the next achievement must be on a higher level.

This is stated explicitly as an educational goal, one should give to the little child, just learning to stand and walk, "tasks which he is up to but which are always more difficult, for example to walk independently an always greater distance from a definite place to a goal set beforehand,"[5] and, apart from training a child in specific qualities, parents must "awaken and support in each child the urge to do better than yesterday." At the same time, "it is important not to destroy but to strengthen his belief in himself, in his ability to become this better person, not to blunt but to sharpen in him the feeling of pride in that achievement which demands work, effort, self mastery, and emphasize always those large perspectives of social significance which are possible on the condition of such upward movement."[6] (It should be noted that, in the admonition to give the child something which he is capable of achieving and so to strengthen his belief in himself, the Soviet system is perpetuating what appears to be an important aspect of the pre-Soviet system of child rearing, in which each child was trained to be as strong as he could be rather than spurred on by competitive motives.)

The mechanics of this new Soviet conscience are stated in detail in an editorial, "Training in Purposefulness":[7]

> "Calm conscience" as a result of awareness of duty fulfilled gives man an immense joy. And the one who experiences "torments of conscience" from a bad action, a breach of social duty, feels terribly oppressed. ... The habit of fulfilling that which one should do not only brings joy and satisfaction—calm consciousness as it is usually called—but develops a special sensitivity, that is, a special anxiety about Whether all has been done and done properly.

We have at present no measure of how successful the Party has been in making this continuous, self-promoting anxiety a part of the personality of Party members or of future Party members. The demand for self-criticism—that is, the demand for criticism of Party members or of Komsomols by each other, coupled with a self -casti-

---

5. A. A. Liublinskaya, "On the Misdeeds of Children," *Family and School (Sem'ya i Shkola)*, January, 1948.

6. *Ibid.*

7. Training in Purposefulness, editorial in *Family and School (Sem'ya i Shkola)* March, 1948.

gation, statements of error and promises of reform demanded from the one who is criticized—is a demand for the external conditions which would promote this continuous, productive anxiety. Simonov says:[8] "We have not only to go over what has been done badly but we should reproach ourselves for what we have not done sufficiently well from the standpoint of an artist of a socialist society."

In industry and agriculture we find the practice of confronting each individual, each work unit, with specific norms and then demanding that the norms be overfulfilled, so that mere fulfillment of a norm is automatically made unsatisfactory.

Throughout there is an ideal of combination of group pressure, actively exercised, and the response to group pressure of an individual whose conscience has been sensitized by lifelong admonition and training. If the individual's demand on himself, his continuous vigilant probing of his own behavior (Could he have done more? Should he have done more?) are developed to a degree equalling the group's public demands (made in the cell, at meetings, by local leaders of erring parents being brought to book, etc.), then a kind of balance between internal and external censure can be reached. The individual becomes wholly repentant, is wholly absolved, and suddenly feels at one with the group. In the fictional materials from which the following illustrations are taken, one kind of pressure is emphasized more than the other. This is shown in a description of a collective farm meeting to expel a member who has systematically neglected her work and who is publicly rebuked by a feminine Hero of Socialist Labor:[9] "Citizen Kucherenko, are you not ashamed that the whole collective farm, the whole country, is working for you?"; and in the appeals of a father, reported approvingly in the educational literature, in which he says to his 14-year old daughter:[10]

> You are already fourteen; soon you will be grown-up. But if now you do not want to help your brother, how will you work in the collective, help comrades, lend support to those behind schedule? Remember, you will have a bad time in life. An egoist is not liked in any work collective. And your work will give you no satisfaction or joy if you will hold yourself aloof and think only about yourself!

8. K. Simonov, "Dramaturgy, Theatre and Life," *Literaturnaya Gazeta*, November 23, 1946.

9. A. Agronovsky, "Day of Labor" (*Trudyen'*), *Literaturnaya Gazeta*, July 21, 1948, p. 2.

10. A. Pechernikova, *Teaching the Schoolboy to Share in the Family Work*, Uchpedgiz, 1948.

In a postwar novel,[11] a husband who was a deserter, whose wife rejects him for his desertion, gives himself up in order to be allowed to enter a penal battalion to wash away the blemish from his life, When at the end of the war he returns, after having fought courageously, his wife still will not accept him nor will his former friends and neighbors. And the former deserter says to his wife:

> You know, before I had thought the most dreadful thing was to undergo the punishment of the government. But what happened was that Life punished much more strongly, through you, the children, the collective.

The reliance on well-inculcated internal standards is expressed in such statements as the following:[12]

> In the factory, in the plant, the *peredovoi* (advance guard) young person is that young man or young girl who works honestly, according to shock methods, who carries out and surpasses the standards, who fights for the high quality of the production, who treats the lathe, the machines and the tools carefully, who masters the techniques of work and increases his own qualifications.

This statement, which stresses an entirely internal motivation which should theoretically operate in the absence of supervision or group pressures, will be balanced by such a statement as the following:[13]

> The older children become, the more important for their moral countenance and therefore for their behavior becomes the Collective of their comrades, its attitudes, its evaluations. Rules of conduct adopted by the Collective become binding, for the one who feels himself a member of this Collective; the evaluation by the Collective of various traits of character becomes absolute for each of its members.

I shall quote at some length one fictional account of the way in which individual sinfulness, as defined by the Soviets, is acted upon by the collective of the Komsomol group so as to bring the individual back into the type of accord with the group which is usually associated with religious absolution and which actually, in this modern Soviet account, uses conventional religious terminology. This account

---

11. Y. Mal'tsev, "From the Whole of the Heart," *Oktyabr'*, Issue 10, 1948, p. 86.

12. Tenth Congress of the All-Union Leninist Communist League of Youth, April 11-21, 1936 (*X S'ezd Vsesoyuznovo Leninskovo Kommunisticheskovo Soiuza Molodezhi 11-21 aprelia 1936 g.*), stenographic account.

13. A. A. Liublinskaya, "On the Misdeeds of Children," *Family and School* (*Sem'ya i Shkola*), January, 1948.

is taken from the story of a group of apprentices, one of whom, Aleha, has had his character distorted into individualism by his remaining to care for his mother in an area occupied by the Germans. In the foundry where he goes to work, he attempts to do too much by himself and sends his partner away to show that he can manage a furnace without assistance. An explosion occurs. In the subsequent investigation he also lies. Here follows a condensed account of the Komsomol meeting:[14]

(The day comes when Aleha applies to join the Komsomol. He goes through many painful apprehensive moments as he asks the old master (ironmaker) to recommend him and confesses to his *Komsorg* (Komsomol organizer) that he lied.) But at the meeting Aleha again understood that not so easily and quickly could all his sins be forgotten. Having finished recounting his autobiography, Aleha fell silent, awaiting the further moves of the meeting. Igor B. took the floor. "Our bureau has decided to accept the comrade. But this does not yet mean anything. The main thing is you, fellows, the Komsomol mass. We await your decision. To accept the comrade or to abstain. Let us think. ..." Aleha listened to these words with terror, They resounded in his very heart. Igor continued: "Comrade Polovodov (Aleha) has placed himself beyond the collective. He wanted alone to make use of the success and joy of Komsomol work. And it is unknown, had everything gone smoothly, how far he would have risen in his pride. Let him today answer all of us what he now thinks about himself, about us, about the Komsomol, about life. This moment is such that a man's soul can be seen even without glasses. So, say everything that you think, Polovodov. ... Many noticed that Aleha was trembling. His agitation immediately transmitted itself to all the others sitting in the hall, quickly from one to another, as a wave in the sea is stirred by wind. Everyone felt simultaneous pain and joy. Pain, because they clearly saw a man suffering and understood precisely from what (he was suffering) and already wished that he might no longer suffer. And joy because he was with them and was not separated, withdrawn any more. This could be seen by his sparkling eyes, his quivering lips which were preparing themselves already to pronounce other words, finally by his hands, stretched out uncertainly, with the fingers spread apart, as if he wanted to encompass in one embrace all those sitting there in the hall. ... No one was indifferent any longer. The soul (of each) wished to express itself. But the rules of the meeting were rigid, the chairman sat severe, immovable. He gave the floor to no one except Aleha. The boys wished that Aleha would take courage. He was now their comrade. They recognized this. After such a sudden frank expression of mutual feeling, Aleha did not really have to continue. Everyone understood what further he wanted to say. But Aleha himself unexpectedly calmed down and firmly decided to express his intentions to the meeting. "I, fellows, am not going to lie to you. What is there, is there. I am here in front of you as at confession. I

14. V. Kurochkin, "Brigade of the Smart" (*Brigada smyshlenikh*), *Oktyabr'*, September, 1947.

cannot feel my hands and feet, I feel so good. Do you still think that I like it better alone than with you? It is not so. Alone, I suffer, that is all. I am not glad to be by myself. But now it will be a completely different matter. Now I'll begin to work even better. ... Forgive me if I said anything to affront you." On this his speech ended and the meeting prepared to vote. Aleha felt that he was experiencing in himself some yet incomprehensible grace which affected all his feelings, urges, wishes. He had never imagined that it could be so pleasant. It was as if all were changing in him, each little vein becoming stronger.

The preparation for such a scene is allowed for in such pedagogical instructions as these:[15]

> Give him time to think and torment himself over the solution, but in the end, if necessary, point out to the adolescent that there is but one way, that of duty (in this case, to confess before his teacher and schoolmates).

The likenesses and differences between the old type of Russian motivation and the new Soviet type are brought out very strikingly in these examples. Under the old system, a child was reared and admonished by a very large number of persons of different castes and was given different sets of standards, which were very loosely tied together by the teachings of the Orthodox Church and were reinforced, in the teachings of peasants and nurses, by a large number of miscellaneous supernatural fears. Fear of being cut off from one's own group, fear of supernatural punishments, confusion among the many standards of conduct which were illustrated and enjoined, a diffuse sense of guilt which was willing to take upon itself a variety of sins committed perhaps only in thought, these characterized this earlier type of character. During the development of the early intelligentsia, with their rigorous revolutionary ideals, there seems to have been some narrowing of these multiple authority figures in the life of the child and the emergence of the demand, which we now characterize as Bolshevik, for a more rigidly defined, focused, and unyielding character in which forgiveness played much less of a role and a man judged both himself and his fellows more harshly. At the same time, theories of what community and collective life meant, the substitution of the social group for a supernatural, priest-mediated authority seemed, in the early days of the Soviet Union, to be placing all the emphasis outside the individual and encouraging a type of education in which the feeling of shame, if one were discovered and rebuked, was the behavior type which was most likely to result. This was par-

15. "Training in a Sense of Duty," editorial, *Family and School* (*Sem'ya i Shkola*), June, 1948.

ticularly so during the period in which the family was regarded as unimportant, and the group alone, whether it was in kindergarten, of Komsomols, or of fellow workers, was supposed to hear confessions and to administer public rebukes.

Today the literature suggests that the Soviet Union is moving toward a type of education which resembles (but, as we shall see, also differs from) the older Russian form of many authority figures operating upon an individual sense of general guilt and unworthiness. The authority of the parents has been re-emphasized after the attempts to reduce it during the first fifteen years of the regime, and parents are now recognized as the principal figures in the early life of the child, which means the reintroduction of persons of greater age and status as authority figures, and this is conducive to the formation of internalized standards of conduct. Furthermore, parents are seen as only one part of a completely harmonized attempt to bring up the young in the way they should go. "What does it mean," asks Likhacheva,[16] "to bring up a fighter for communism? It means that the school and the family and the society must bring up the young man." This bringing to bear of all available forces upon the target is a familiar Bolshevik theory of tactics, here applied to education. Instead of the old inconsistencies between standards and sanctions presented by many individuals in the environment, one set of standards is to be presented. When the parents fail, the Komsomol steps in, or the school may even apply to a trade-union to persuade an erring father to take an interest in his son's report card. "Aiding the strengthening of family relations and ties, socialist society thereby makes fast in the people many of those high qualities which characterize the moral countenance of the Soviet citizen."[17] And, in comparing the old and the new, a Soviet student of education puts his finger on the greater concentration on a unified effort today:[18]

> Belinsky wrote (about the pre-revolutionary school) that the family must make a man out of the child; the school, an educated citizen ready to struggle for the best ideals. ... Now the school and the family are joined in one wish: to nurture in us the traits of a real Soviet man, make us educated persons devoted to Our people, to our mother country.

Each of the agencies which impinge on the child are to put all their effort, all their thought into doing the same thing. This should

16. N. Likhacheva, "Mother-Tutoress," *Family and School* (*Sem'ya i Shkola*), March, 1948.

17. G. M. Sverdlov, *Marriage and Family,* (*Brak i sem'ya*) (pamphlet), Uchpedgiz 1946.

18. *Stories by Graduates of Moscow Schools*, Detgiz, 1947, P. 8.

produce a type of motivation and will power which does not occur in Western democracies, where there are a variety of different courses presented to a child in whom, ideally, the will to choose among them has been cultivated. Nor was such a character structure cultivated in pre-Soviet Russia. Instead, educational experiences tended to develop a diffuse sense of guilt and of responsibility, not for acts of will, but for the merest thought or intention.

Under this new Soviet character structure, the will should be developed without, however, any sense of the possibility of choice. If the child looks into itself, it should find only the same standards as those expressed all around it and which, when his parent errs, he is—in Soviet fiction—also ready to express. All authority figures converge upon him, and he, like Aleha, is to feel completely at one with and submissive to this standard, which is both inside him and outside him. "Soviet man feels himself an indivisible part of the industrial or social collective to which he is bound, with which he labors. Soviet man experiences achievements or lack of them in communal matters as his own personal successes or failures. He feels his moral responsibility for communal matters and thus he develops a sense of duty."[19] "The personal interests of Soviet man must combine harmoniously with communal interests; the personal must always be subordinated to the social."

It must be recognized that in such an ideal there should be no need for force, for physical coercion. The conception of character is one in which the individual, himself, is able to receive grace from a group whose standards he shares and so, with the past forgotten—the secular Soviet version of forgiveness—go on to a higher moral level. We shall see in later sections how incompatible this ideal, which would need no reinforcement by coercion or by political police, is with the Soviet demand for total control over every detail of the life of children. A character structure such as that described here is congruent with a complete respect for all human beings in a society, with a lack of hierarchy, and with a lack of any sense of gulf between a group ruling and a group ruled. But the leadership of the Soviet Union seems to have inherited and developed, from sources of its own, a deep contempt for the mass of the people and an attitude toward children, as individuals to be subordinated and ignored until they attain years of discretion, which do not provide the necessary conditions for the development of the kind of ideal character structure described here.

19. "Training in a Sense of Duty," editorial, *Family and School* (*Sem'ya i Shkola*), June, 1948.

Nevertheless, the political implications of the ideal character (which is always spurred on to new achievement because each achievement serves to define the necessary next step) are worth considering, especially in the choice of propaganda themes. Any propaganda which suggests present failure to the Soviet Union may merely provoke angry denial, but it may also act as a spur to greater activity. This type of personality is essentially puritanical, feeding upon a sense of its own deficiencies while presenting to the outer world a fyde of smugness and self-satisfaction. To the extent that the Soviet Union has succeeded in producing such a personality in its leadership group, it will have to be reckoned with.

We shall turn presently to the way in which these ideals of behavior are modified by the practical need to run a state, to produce manufactured goods, to equip an army, to produce food for a vast population, etc., and to what extent the actual administration of the Soviet Union has taken its models not from this Bolshevik theory of leadership by a self-propelled, self-critical, completely dedicated group, but from the traditional methods of control of the Tsarist state supplemented by observation of other modern autocratically organized nations.

Expectations Concerning the Masses and Children

We may now set this picture of the ideal leadership pattern, the type of char acter, and relationship to the led against the picture of what the led, the masses and the children, are expected to contribute to the whole. We have seen in the earlier discussion of relationships between different levels that each person who is in any sort of leadership role is expected to partake, in his relationship to those below him, of some of the behavior of the top leader upon whom he models his conduct. The Komsomol is to be in the vanguard everywhere— in industry, in society, in the family—giving the smallest and the greatest task his full attention. The parent, any parent, is seen as totally responsible for his or her children as is the Party secretary for the cell, the chairman for the collective.

Much of the literature suggests a single line from leader to smallest child, with those on the lowest levels of age or skill or knowledge of Bolshevism looking up, aspiring toward higher levels from which they in turn will serve as models for those below them. But this picture is confused by another in which the Party is a distillate from the whole group, fed by children, by youth, by workers and farmers, but is essentially a narrow group to which most of the population neither aspires nor is expected to aspire. The view of both children and

masses is quite different, depending on whether they are all seen as
future Party members (when they have advanced enough in wisdom
or stature), or whether they are seen as a great mass from which only
a very few, with the appropriate spiritual ambition and moral
strength, are to be drawn. When the non-Party masses are viewed as
many who will never join the Party, not even in the persons of their
unborn grandchildren, they present considerable confusion and difficulty to Bolshevik theories of authority. We have, in the works of
Lenin and in the early congresses, discussions about the relationship
between Party and non-Party: "In order to realize the leadership of
the Party it is indispensable that the Party be encompassed by hundreds of non-Party mass *apparati* (staff) which constitute tentacles in
the hands of the Party with the aid of which it transmits its will to the
working class, and the working class from [being] dispersed masses,
becomes the army of the Party."[20]

The dictatorship (of the proletariat) cannot be achieved without
some transmission belts from the vanguard of the masses to the leading class and from it to the mass of the laboring class. "The dictatorship of the proletariat consists in the leading directives of the Party
plus the carrying out of these directives by the mass organizations of
the proletariat, plus the transformation of the life of the population."[21]

With the lack of clarity regarding the relationship of the Party to
the masses goes a fear that some other center will develop which will
compete for their allegiance, sometimes localized outside the Soviet
Union, using propaganda, and sometimes inside, existing as remnants
of the bourgeois past. Sometimes it is feared that different elements
within the Party as well as among the non-Party masses may be won
over to some counterrevolutionary position. Stalin, at the time of the
15th Congress, 1927,[22] described these indifferent elements as *boloto*,
a swamp, a word borrowed from the terminology of the French Con-
stituante which described the undecided and wavering middle which
was dominated in turn by the different extremes. Said Stalin, "Discussion is an appeal to the swamp. The Opposition appeals to it in order
to tear off a portion. And they actually tear off the worse part. The
Party appeals to it to tear off the better part and to attract it to active
Party life. As a result the swamp has to *determine for itself what it will
do*, despite all its inertness. As a result of all of these appeals it actually
does make this determination, one part going to the opposition and
one part going to the Party, thereby it ceases to exist as swamp." [ital-
ics ours] Here the Party is seen as contending, against strong counter-

20.   Lenin and Stalin, *Partiinoye stroitel'stvo,* Vol. 2, pp. 322-23.
21.   Lenin, *Polnoye sobraniye.* Vol. 25, p. 96.

forces, for those over whom there should be no contention. In 1928, Stalin, quoting Lenin, said:[23] "*petit bourgeois* elements surround the proletariat from every side with a *petit bourgeois* atmosphere which permeates it and acts as a corrupting influence on the proletariat, debases it, makes it lose morality." [italics ours] This fear of the corruption which may spring up in that which is lifeless and inert has not diminished with the disappearance of those *petit bourgeois* elements who were once identified as a source of danger. The Bolsheviks seem to have difficulty in believing that the enemy is ever completely destroyed: "We have defeated the enemies of the Party, the opportunists of all shades, national deviations of all types but the remnants of their ideologies are still living in the heads of individual members of the Party and make themselves heard," said Stalin, in 1934.[24]

This danger is now more 'explicitly attributed to forces outside the Soviet Union, but this does not change the essential attitudes of the leadership toward the dangers lurking in the undifferentiated swamp. In a 1947 postwar story,[25] a youth is described who

> kept apart from the collective. He feared his personal success would be stolen. It is because there still operates in him as with some other peasant adolescents a yeast *(zakvaska)* foreign to us. ... Capitalists still today are attempting to build their final defense line in the hearts of men. They would be *glad to tear away from us* those who are weak, impatient; who believe little in the future, who, finally, have not yet learned to believe. Would not the enemy indeed wish that the little heart of a peasant adolescent should become the bastion of their ideals ?" [italics ours]

This theme is reiterated in the recent attacks on the West and on influences brought back to the Soviet Union by those returning from the West. "There still exist people who, after the victory, brought us the most thin and light fluids, alien to our psychology. The fluids have to be examined, named and perhaps through this, rendered harmless. The admiration of bourgeois culture is one of those fluids. It seems to be innocent in itself. ... The delicate scent of repose comes from these little things—these bits of foreign ideas—a cadaverous

22. J. Stalin, in a Report of the 15th All-Union Congress of the Communist Party (B) (*XV S'ezd Vsesoyuznoi Kommunisticheskoi Partii (B)*), stenographic account, Moscow, 1928, p. 173.

23. J. Stalin, "Of the Right Danger in the CPSU,- addressed to the Plenum of Moscow Committee and Moscow Control Commission of CPSU, October, 1928.

24. J. Stalin, Report of 17th Congress of CPSU, 1934.

25. Kurochkin, *op. cit.*

odor of prosperity."[26] From 1928 to 1949 the essential theme has not changed, the fear that there is an indifferent, apathetic mass of people who are dangerous because responsive to alien influences, whose indifference can be activated—unless they are completely protected— into a lethal corruption of the whole society. That which is almost dead may live again—in the wrong way.

This ambiguous attitude toward the undifferentiated masses whose relationship to the Party is so badly defined is complicated by the theory of purges. Yaroslavski[27] said:

> That is why we have to expel from the Party from time to time not only people originating from non-proletarian classes who are more susceptible to disintegration than proletarians, but also proletarians who have fallen under the petty bourgeois elemental forces of the past.

There is also the insistence upon keeping the Party itself clean and strong by constantly purging its ranks. As a 1933 directive stated: "The purging will raise to a high degree the feeling entertained by every Party member of responsibility for his organization.[28] But what happens to those who are purged? Unless they are physically liquidated, which was only true for larger numbers in the late thirties, they remain in the population, either to be actively rehabilitated and reinstated or to contribute significantly to the dangerous, unreliable quality of the swamp, the wavering, undecided mass of the people. This is a view of the population which is apt to support a belief in the necessity for rigid authoritarian controls rather than for education in moral autonomy, and it is reflected in the attempts to protect the Soviet population against foreign propaganda of all sorts, in admonitions to parents to watch carefully the companions with whom their children associate and by whom they can be corrupted. A belief that the children of one's neighbors, for whom under another part of Soviet.theory one is also responsible, are sources of corruption obviously tends to breed suspicion and a desire for more rigid control.

A second attitude toward the masses, and to some extent toward children, is a reliance upon them to provide the energy through which the Party is able to carry out its will. The masses of today provide the present energy; the children, "the Soviet citizens of tomorrow who are

26.   P. Antokol'skii, "About Poetry, Education of the Youth and Culture," *Znamya.* January, 1947.

27.   E. Yaroslavski, *Verification and Purging of the Party Ranks*, Moscow, 1933, p. I].

28.   Directive of January, 1933, Plenum of Central Control Commission of CPSU.

the children of today," provide the future sources of energy. Taking this view of the masses, Stalin said, in 1937:[29] "Like Antaeus, the Bolsheviks are strong in that they maintain their contact with their mother, the masses, which gave them birth, fed them and brought them up." On the other hand, Maksimovskii could say, at the 10th Party Congress in 1921, that the Party should "put ourselves in the position of a pedagogue, not a nurse,"[30] and Stalin,[31] "The distinction between the vanguard of the proletariat and the main body of the working class, between Party members and non-Party members will continue so long as classes exist, so long as the proletariat continues replenishing its ranks with newcomers from other classes, as long as the working class as a whole is deprived of the opportunity of raising itself to the level of the vanguard. But the Party would cease to be a Party if this distinction were widened into a rupture; if it were to isolate itself and break from the non-Party masses." This was said in 1928, and in an article in May, 1949, in *Bol'shevik*,[32] it is said: "the consciousness of their nearness with the people, the skill in leading the masses, define the main features of an active purposeful Bolshevik." In *Komsomol' skaia Pravda*, in 1949, an editorial insists: "Any Komsomol organization will wither, will perish, if it breaks this most important Party principle and separates itself from the young." This location of the source of energy in the masses appears in the impassioned speech of the chairman of a collective farm, reported in *Pravda*.[33] The chairman has been listening to the comments of the man in charge of accounts, who claims that there is no "secret" for the success of the collective except accuracy, consistency, and high agricultural technique.

> "It's not true" interrupted Pyotr Alekseyevich (the chairman). … We have a secret. Our secret is something that many chairmen underestimate and which our Party always puts at the head of everything. It's ideological education of the people." His words sounded strong and passionate. "The organization of labor, agricultural technique, connections with science, all these are very important matters, but at the first difficulty they become empty ciphers if there is no Party soul in the collective farm … ideological education for us is just like wings for an airplane."

29. J. Stalin, *Mastering Bolshevism*, Report to the 1937 Plenum of the Central Committee of the CPSU, printed in *Bol'shevik*, April 1, 1937.

30. Maksimovskii, loth Congress of the Russian Communist Party (B) (*X s'ezd Rossiiskoi Kommunisticheskoi Partii (B)*), stenographic account, Moscow, 1928.

31. J. Stalin, "Foundations of Leninism" (*Osnovi Leninizma*) as in Stalin, *Leninism*, New York, 1928.

32. N. Ozerov, "The Image of the Bolshevik," *Bol'shevik*, May, 1949.

33. G. Nikolaeva, "Features of Future," *Pravda*, January 7-8, 1949.

This "Party soul," this source of energy which lies in the people and is to be used to bring success to Party enterprises, was dramatized in the Soviet film *The Peasants*, in which the Party secretary, faced with a recalcitrant, rebellious collective farm committee who wished to distribute all the collectively grown pigs, called on the spontaneous devotion of the mass of the collective farm members to stage a demonstration of extra, voluntary work and turned the tide at the meeting.

The masses are thus seen as a source of strength and energy, and just as the leaders are credited with special foresight, so the masses are credited with a kind of insight.

Stalin expressed formal adherence to this point of view in 1937:[34]

> We leaders see things, events and people from one side only, I would say from above. Our field of vision, consequently, is more or less limited. The masses, on the contrary, see things, events, and people from another side, I would say, from below. Their field of vision, consequently, is also, in a certain degree, limited. To receive a correct solution to the question, these two experiences must be united (*obedinit*). Only in such a case will the leadership be correct.

Where the leader is to be, above all things, controlled, reserved, unimpassioned, the people are to have a "passionate Bolshevik desire" (*strastnoye zhelaniye*); "if a thing is passionately desired, everything can be achieved, everything can be overcome." In "Lamp of Il'ich" the electrification of collective farms is promised for the whole country, and the question is asked: "But where to find such a force capable of accomplishing such a difficult undertaking?"[35] The authors of the electrification plan answer: "We have such a force. The force is the people. If the people wish, nothing is impossible for them." And as soon as the plan was born, people in far-off and deaf villages began to compose a song about light, "Wires are humming, laughing, electricity now burns. All victories are possible, if the Party orders so."

This statement is an example of the combination of two omnipotence fantasies, the old Social Revolutionary fantasy of the overpowering energy of the masses combined with the Bolshevik fantasy of omnipotence by conscious control. This same zestful energy which is attributed to the people is also attributed to youth. A young Komsomol girl is represented as saying:[36] "I want to be a mechanic and I

---

34. J. Stalin, *Mastering Bolshevism,* Report to the 1937 Plenum of the Central Committee of the CPSU, printed in *Bol'shevik*, April 1, 1937.

35. E. Kriger, "Lamp of ll'ich," *Friendly Youngsters* (*Druzhnyie Rebyata*), December, 1947.

36. *Komsomol'skaia Pravda*, March 31, 1949, p. 4.

believe that I shall become one. ... Indeed, for us, for Soviet youth, the situation is this. What one plans one can achieve, if only one has the desire, the persistence, and the will."

In the educational system there is great emphasis upon developing these desirable mass qualities of strength and endurance, of zest and enthusiasm in the citizen of tomorrow. So the official pedagogy[37] insists: "Precisely in the first days of an infant's existence, training in this importance quality (endurance) should begin; naturally at this age one can talk only of training in physical endurance."

From the earliest days of the Soviet Union there has been an emphasis on physical care of children and an expressed interest in the child as a future citizen, necessary to society, who should "enter life properly prepared, communistically reared, and strong muscled."[38]

Throughout the educational system, a double emphasis is seen which can be taken as a reflection, in much more open form, of the attitude which the leadership group holds toward the masses. Throughout the discussion of child care and training, although there is frequent reference to the importance of maintaining a child's self-confidence, zest, and sensitivity, there is also great emphasis upon control, upon the establishment of habits of obedience, punctuality, neatness, thrift. Children must be firmly accustomed to "daily, regular, perhaps small but sensible efforts without waiting for an occasion for some heroic deed."[39] This admonition can be contrasted with the Komsomol statement that "the entire pathos of the Komsomol work must be carried into studying."[40] The Komsomols are bade: "take possession of the entire treasure house of human knowledge and culture."[41] For pupils whose wills are to be educated, "it is not enough to inspire them with great aims and ideals. ... The best training is in the accurate scrupulous fulfillment of daily modest ordinary cluties."[42] "Children must know exactly their bedtime, time of play and preparation of lessons. ... Children must have a capacity to repress, to control themselves." "Sexual education must consist in the development of that intimate respect for

37. "Training in Endurance," *Family and School* (*Sem'ya i Shkola*), January, 1948.

38. Perel and Lyubimova, *The Legal Position of the Child in the Family* (*Pravovoye polozheniye rebyonka v sem'ye*), Uchpedgiz, 1932.

39. Extract from Chap. 14, *Pedagogy*, Moscow, 1948, pp. 315-17.

40. Tenth Congress of the All-Union Leninist Communist League of Youth, April 11-21, 1936.

41. P. Razmyslov, "A. S. Makarenko's Views on Family Upbringing," *Family and School* (*Sem'ya i Shkola*), March, 1949.

42. A. S. Makarenko, *Book for Parents* (*Kniga dlya roditelei*, Gospolitizdat, 1937.

sexual questions which is called chastity. An ability to control one's feelings, imagination, rising desires, is an important ability." Girls who successfully subordinate their romantic interests to the demands of group activities are glorified in the model-setting literature.

The familiar emphasis upon the crucial importance of the smallest possible detail reappears here also. "Each action, each conversation, each word, either helps the blossoming of a child's spiritual forces, or on the contrary breaks and maims his spirit, accustoming him to rudeness, lying, and other bad qualities in upbringing, in this many-sided, deep process of personality formation, there is nothing that may be considered a trifle."[43] And with this importance of every trifle goes a demand for the continuance of parental responsibility which is hardly compatible with the development of independence and individual will. "The older a child becomes the more heightened becomes the parents' responsibility for his upbringing as well as for their own behavior."[44]

Another dichotomy is found in the attitude toward the imagination of children, which, again, may be regarded as a clue to the attitudes toward spontaneous inventiveness in the masses. On the one hand, Soviet pedagogy insists on the importance of play: "Our children must know how to dream and to realize their dreams in reality. ... The development of fantasy is an important task of the educator. For example, children prepare to fly to the moon. They represent in play that which has not taken place in reality. But such play arose as a result of stories of the remarkable flights accomplished by our fliers. These stories have created the conviction in our children that the heroes will accomplish ever new exploits, that they will continue the conquest of cosmic space. ... Obviously such make-believe is to be permitted and encouraged by the educator."[45] But, on the other hand: "The educator does not permit inventions which may create in children incorrect representations, incorrect attitudes to life. If children represent Soviet soldiers, fliers, workers, it is very important that their actions and words correspond to the role they adopt." In the recent critical survey of a nineteenth-century writer, Schneerman[46] distin-

---

43. N. Y. Yudina, "Parental Authority," *Family and School* (*Sem'ya i Shkola*), April, May, 1946.

44. *Ibid.*

45. D. Mendzherritskii, "Children's Play," *Play of Children*, Uchpedgiz, 1948. (Collection of articles from the magazine *Pre-School Education*.)

46. A. L. Shneerman, "Problems of the Psychology of Upbringing in the Course of General Pedagogy," *Soviet Pedagogy* (*Sovetskaya Pedagogika*), Vol, 4, 1949, p. 61.

guishes between two kinds of imagination *(mechta)*, the creative imagination and the narcotic imagination, and adds: "The ability of the young Soviet generation to guide their imagination, to develop it in the necessary direction, to utilize creative force in the interest of the communistic transformation of our Motherland—those are the concrete problems of the psychology of upbringing." And "In the process of play, parents should give the child as much freedom of action as possible, but only as long as the play proceeds properly."[47]

In this insistence on an imagination which can fly to the moon but must still be so rigidly channeled that no mistake is made in the play-acting of the role of a Soviet fireman, we find the familiar Bolshevik conviction of being able to harness all the forces in nature and in human nature and to use them for their own purposes. It is more difficult to get material which demonstrates attitudes toward the masses and the need for controlling them. This material, while it may be phrased in a manner protective and educational for children, contains contempt that denotes a lower level of expectation for adults. In official literature the masses must be spoken of with respect, but informal evidence suggests this same attitude of exercising rigid control and at the same time wishing to call forth the maximum zest obtainable.

The demand for zest is open and continuous. "All work in the representations of Soviet children is joyful work. .."[48]

> The clarity of the perspectives of our magnificent future, unshakable confidence in the triumph of Communism, awareness of moral superiority over those hostile to Communism, give rise to those feelings of cheerfulness and joy-in-life, which are imprescriptible traits of Soviet people. ... Communistic ideas are the most life-asserting, most light and bright, most optimistic ideas of mankind, a counterbalance to all ideas of "world sorrow," man-hatred, slavery and oppression.

"Of course, in the workaday life of the family unavoidable difficulties occur, deprivations and losses which bring sadness and cause suffering. Only real courage allows one to bear up steadfastly and to reestablish soon the temporarily disturbed, basically cheerful and joyful tone of family life."[49] Optimism and cheerfulness are seen as

47. A. S. Makarenko, "Lectures on the Upbringing of Children," *Book for Parents* (Kniga dlya roditelei), 1937.

48. "Influence of an Educator on Content of Children's Play," *Pre-School Education* (Doshkol'noe Vospitanie), August, 1948.

49. "On Cheerfulness and *Joie-de-vivre*," *Family and School* (Sem'ya i Shkola), May, 1948.

essential traits of Soviet people. Children should be prevented from ever feeling lonely, and all exclusive concentration on their own feelings, all withdrawal and misanthropy should be actively watched for. Critics excoriate novelists whose work is permeated with "a feeling of tiredness," who use "weak and anesthetic words," or who permit their characters pages of "weeping, sobbing, groaning." Feelings of "contemplation and passivity" are equally disapproved of.

These expressed fears of what may happen if children are left alone, if workers are not continuously subjected to inspiration and pressure, if people are allowed to read about characters who are melancholy and introspective provide information not about the children, workers, or readers, but about the members of the regime who, through their exhortations to joyousness and optimism and their attempts to control those they exhort, indicate apprehension that the fear and depression which has been officially outlawed will break through in others and in their own highly controlled personalities.

While it is loudly proclaimed that "we will permit no one to poison our youth with the venom of disbelief, pessimism and decadence,"[50] the tale is told of the aviator who almost lost his life because of an intrusive feeling of pity,[51] of the boy who pretends to be tubercular in order to stay with his mother, in whom something "did not grow together inside."[52] It is officially stated that "the socialistic regime liquidated the tragedy of loneliness from which men of the capitalist world suffer,"[53] but the juvenile literature is filled with lonely children and with incomplete families, and it is probably significant that the critics—following the official line—are able to find so many instances of characters in plays who are "lonely, injured, suffering from disassociation of personality." One postwar novel[54] describes vividly the feeling of Soviet men sent abroad after the war: "the idea that we might remain alone at the foot of this indifferent cliff, somewhere between Europe and Asia, among all those castanets, black-eyed Spanish girls, placid policemen with knuckle-dusters in their pockets; this idea that we might be left without mercy in a place where we were not necessary to anybody (and we for our part felt: 'why the devil do we need all that?)—this very idea made us shudder."

50. *Komsomol'skaia Pravda*, March 31, 1949, p. 2.

51. R. Fraerman, *Far Voyage (Dal'neye plavaniye)*, 1946.

52. Kurochkin, *op. cit.*

53. Editorial, "Education in Comradeship and Friendship," *Family and School (Sem'ya i Shkola)*, April, 1.948.

54. L. Kasil, and S. Mikhalkov, "Europe At Left," *Zvezda*, September, 1946.

A recent novel[55] covertly satirized vividly the fear which lies behind the whole Bolshevik attitude in the character of the Communist Izvekov, who in the novel is represented as being completely indifferent to the regret which the writer, Pastukhov, expresses, that in pursuit of such noble aims as those of the Revolution, "in the struggle for good, man is obliged to do so much that is evil." During an offensive of the Red army, the military unit to which Izvekov is attached is allowed to hunt a wolf in the forest. Someone succeeds in hitting the wolf, and Izvekov suspects that it is he himself who has done so. Suddenly he sees the wounded wolf not far from where he is and fires a second shot. After the wolf is dead, Izvekov analyzes his reason for firing that unnecessary second shot. Suddenly he realizes that, beyond all reason, he was pushed by unconscious fear of the mortally wounded and no longer dangerous beast. In the same instant that he confessed this fear to himself, he became ashamed and felt that all his body was bathed in a hot sweat.

This political fable may be analyzed at several levels: as a satire on the Bolshevik who is supposed (a) never to feel fear; (b) who is supposed, if he feels fear, never to express it; and (c) who is supposed to have such foresight and judgment that he would not commit such an unnecessary act as shooting an animal which was not dangerous. At a deeper level, this fable also expresses the Bolshevik belief that the least fear may lead to panic, to a completely false judgment of the potential dangerousness of the enemy. Such an animal might then appear able to destroy first oneself and then a whole village. Against such avalanche fears, very rigid defenses are necessary.

In summary, we find that Bolshevik ideas of leadership and the character appropriate to leadership provide for an alert, all-responsible, never-satisfied conscience, constantly stimulated by one achievement to attempt a higher one, which ideas are complemented by a picture of those who are led that is confused as to whether they are to be seen as future leaders, future members of the Party, or as permanent members of a mass and subject to appeals which may lure them away from the Party. These ideas are complicated further by the need for rigid control and continuous watchfulness enjoined upon the leadership, which makes them, while officially relying upon the strength, enthusiasm, and energy provided by the masses, fearful that unless the most rigid, minute, continuous, protective, and directive control is maintained, catastrophe will result.

55. K. Fedin, "Unusual Summer," *Novyi Mir*, 1945 (4,5,6,7,8,9); 1947 (1,5,9,12); 1948 (4,10).

Chapter 6

THE PLACE OF THE POLITICAL POLICE
IN THE SOVIET AUTHORITY SYSTEM

*W*e have now traced in some detail the Soviet ideal of the relationship between the Party and the masses and between the leader and
the people and also the way in which the leadership group is supposed both to draw upon the energy and strength of the people and
yet to remain above the people, guiding and directing them because
of a closer contact with the Truth. We have discussed some of the discrepancies within this ideal; for example, the way in which members
of each leadership level are expected to be models for those beneath
them, while those beneath them, although owing them legal allegiance as officials of superior rank who speak in the name of the Party,
owe them no personal allegiance, but instead are expected to give
their personal devotion to the top leadership of the Party only. Motivation is expected to result from such a close awareness of the never-
ending struggle in the world and from such an urge to reach ever
higher levels of achievement that each new activity must, to be
equally satisfying, be better than the last. The people themselves, the
masses and the children, are supposed to contribute a spontaneous
energy which nevertheless must always be manipulated, directed, and
kept within bounds. Every area of life is brought within the political,
and the whole of each individual's personality is conceived as being
involved in anything which he does).

This whole theory is conspicuously lacking in any theory of organization, and Lenin could, as late as 1917-18, define the ideal society
as one in which there would be no differentiation in function, no difference between leaders and led, no officialdom, and no hierarchy,
when the state should have "withered away." Meanwhile there was
an enormous chaotic society, ravaged by war and revolution, which
had to be not only reconstructed, but also transformed economically

and politically. The Bolshevik leadership, while advancing the ideal of a society in which the conscience of each fully devoted citizen would be the only necessary control over his behavior, was committed to a view of absolute truth which made it impatient of any delay in the realization of the ideal. Finally, the leadership came from a society in which bureaucratic controls had always been strong, and, while they had rebelled against Tsarist controls, they had nevertheless had little actual experience of any other way of administering a national state).

Within this varied set of conditions and amid the impatience and fear which seem to accompany dictatorships whose authority is new and unsupported by tradition, a system of state controls based on models inherited from Tsarist days has become tighter through the years. In the late twenties and early thirties, the Party membership was charged with the multiple roles of leadership, inspiration, checking accomplishment, and ferreting out slackness, failure, or treason. (The task of the political police which was stressed was the liquidation of the remnants of the old regime, the members of the condemned classes who could not be absorbed into the new society and so had to be excised from it Already dissenting socialists, anarchists, and peasants were included as targets. It was as if two societies lived side by side, the new, good, young Soviet Union, whose members were to be controlled not by physical force but by faith and discipline, and the remnants of the old, bad Tsarist society which had to be dealt with by the old political police methods. With a comrade, one reasoned, argued, or pled, but against one whose ancestry defined him as unredeemable the state used the old methods of arrest without trial followed by banishment or execution. The political police were themselves something foreign, headed by the Polish zealot, Dzerzhinski, whose motto was that it was better that one hundred innocent men die than one guilty one escape. Meanwhile, the struggle for dominance within the Party went on, and control of the political police became part of the struggle. The classification of "enemies of the people," once reserved for remnants of the old regime and for anti-Bolshevik parties, was extended to cover dissent within the Party, even while the legend grew that Lenin had warned that the Party must never pass a death sentence on one of its own members. The history of Stalin's rise to power, accurately mirrored in his accusations against Tito, is the history of a growing dependence on a form of administration within which the political police played a significant role. Today, the political police are an integral part of the ordinary governmental apparatus, with their own Party cells, responsible to the Central Committee and the Politburo to guard against their becoming independent of the Party, What the ordinary Party membership was earlier supposed to be—a single-mindedly devoted, incorruptible, ever-watchful, ruthless executive of the will of the Party—is now attributed to the political police (MVD-MGB). The political police now have a membership placed at somewhere over a million and a half, which includes frontier police and the administration of labor camps. They are placed strategically in every branch of Soviet life and are responsible for the security of the system and for defending it against sabotage and treason.

Informants' accounts show that, while the single-mindedness attributed to the political police is related to the demands made on Party members, they (the political police) are also felt to be predatory and alien. A DP informant reports on this attitude during the war:

> Every worker of the political police is like a monk in a monastery because he is surrounded by his (svoi) people and has almost nothing in common with the surrounding society They are like it wolf in the forest where there is always famine and seek food for themselves. farm ... The political police do not go to balls or other public diversions but if there is a political meeting some place in the city or in the collective farm they appear there and look for something for themselves at this meeting. The political police always do their work at night and sleep in the daytime. ... Here it should be emphasized that the political police worker is a very good family man and only does this because he sees an enemy of the people in every person and believes that every person carries in himself something or other hostile to the regime. His ideas are always imbued with this and therefore lie lives with his wife and children distinctly better than all other citizens in the USSR.

Here we have the whole picture, the wolf who preys on the rest of society, but impersonally, because it is his task, and who receives rewards from the state which he protects.

A strong contrast is drawn between the venality in ordinary civilian affairs and the behavior of the political police:

> As is known, everything in the Soviet Union can be bought for money- passports (travel authorizations), liberation from jail for stealing, speculation and similar crimes, but if one is taken into the hands of the political police then such things won't go for no one can buy them off. It might be said that this is because their business is known to many other political police and if one political police worker has to arrest someone, then the chiefs know about it, and one fears the other, therefore it is absolutely impossible to buy off the political police and liberate a political offender in these cases. [Reported by an informant who left the Soviet Union during the war.]

The fear that they inspire in all others is thus suggested as the sanction which keeps them incorruptible. Those who are fear-inspiring are also the most afraid. In the distinction which the informant draws between ordinary civil difficulties which can be settled and "cases which fall into the hands of the political police" can be seen a suggestion of a breakdown in the Soviet attempt to make every area of life equally political and sacred and every error of any sort into treason. Treason is here defined not by the act, but by which agency is called upon to punish the act. This is a further shift toward the dis-association of the criminal and the crime discussed earlier. The political police, charged with the arrest of a certain number of subversive people, prowl about among the populace (who are all considered in some degree to be guilty) and arbitrarily select particular victims. These thereupon, by definition, are no longer regarded as engaged in the minor law-breaking that is believed to be universally practiced and is ordinarily accepted as inevitable, but become "enemies of the people," traitors, saboteurs, wreckers, etc. The imputed impersonality of the whole procedure is illustrated by the belief that within the prison camps it was only necessary to have a given number of prisoners, so that a man could take another man's identity, answer to his name, and later escape without anyone being the wiser.

It is important to note, also, that while the Party member is expected to be stricter with himself and his fellow Party members than is a non-Party member, he is exhorted to maintain contact with his non-Party associates in factory and collective farm and by such contact to maintain his nearness to the masses and also his intimate knowledge of what is going on and so increase his power of manipulation. He is a part of a society which is meshed together. But the political police are meshed into the society only at the very top. Where the Party member draws at least part of his strength from the people, the political police draw their power from their *lack of association* with the rest of the population.

Where their foreignness was once emphasized by the number of non-Russians among them, today it is represented by the belief, expressed both by former members of the NKVD and by outsiders, that the ideal recruit for the political police is an orphan who has been reared in one of the institutions for homeless children. These children, utterly desolate and alone, are pictured as going out at night to steal from the local populace—all men are their enemies, but they are completely loyal to each other. With this ideal background—for we have no information on what proportion of the police are so recruited—they then become, both in the view of informants from inside and from outside, a group apart, specially privileged and immune to temptation and corruption.

Sometimes the political police, in making arrests, follow the particular occupational categories specified by the labor needs of the

Soviet Union, as allowed for in the section called "banishment" *(asylka)* in the Penal Code of the Soviet Union. To Western eyes, an order to a division of political police that twenty carpenters must be included among those arrested during the next few months expresses a degree of cynicism which makes it seem impossible that anyone involved in the system could be left with a shadow of faith in the *bona fides* of the state. These practices are related to older Russian practices— to the varieties of services for which it was customary to draft men in the Moscow state, to the practice of moving the whole population of a village, and to the practice, during the reign of Peter the Great, of assigning whole villages to work in factories. They are also related to old attitudes toward police arrests, well expressed in the report of an informant: "The police just have to arrest somebody. If this one escapes they will arrest two more. So why do they have to have this [particular] one?" The belief held by the police, that everyone in the population is to some degree guilty, is supported by the actual fact that everyone is involved in some order of illegality, if not of active hostility toward the regime. These antecedents make the combination of labor recruiting and punishment for political crimes less unintelligible. Within many Christian communities it would not seem inappropriate to select at random someone to play Judas, for all are believed to have, to some degree, betrayed their Savior in their hearts. The fortunate will be chosen for the role of Saints, of which they are unworthy, and the unfortunate will be chosen for the role of Judas Iscariot, which to a degree unfairly emphasizes their unworthiness.

An unpublished manuscript,[1] based on detailed investigation of attitudes of Soviet people imprisoned during the purges, describes an even more extreme type of explanation:

> Why was the prophet Jonah thrown into the sea? In order to find expiation and save all the rest. He was no more guilty than the rest, but it fell to his lot. The Soviet system cost the Russian people dear. Who paid for the famine of 1932 and 1933? Who should answer for all the sacrifices aroused by the imperfection of the system, errors in the plan, faults in the apparatus, inability of executives, etc. Those to whose lot it falls ... [must answer]. in order to save the system as a whole, in order to divert the wrath of the people from its leaders, it is necessary to sacrifice millions of innocent persons. Furthermore they are only relatively innocent for every Soviet person bears greater or lesser accountability for Bolshevism as a whole and in its parts.

The existence of such attitudes, combined with the expectation of total mobilization of the general population at all times, which West-

---

1. See footnote 38, p. 46.

ern societies expect only during wartime, and the confusion between labor for the state and punishment taken together, makes it possible for a political police to become an integral part of the system, one which people can accept with resignation, as they might the sufferings from rain and snow which fall unequally upon a people all of whom are guilty. And the number of arrests which the political police make each month, each year, serves as confirmation to those higher up that a great deal of counterrevolutionary activity, espionage, and sabotage does exist, which confirmation is well supported by fulsome written confessions. That the confessions are fabrications does not matter.

In discussing the hypothesis that all of the population are to some degree guilty of acts and thoughts hostile to the regime, it is necessary to bear in mind the Bolshevik doctrine that every act is a political act, that the whole personality is involved in all acts so that one cannot be a good father and a bad cell secretary, and that nothing is a trifle—any act however small may lead to disaster.

In addition to these ideas of universal guilt, it is of course important to realize that agriculture and industry, the arts and sciences, as well as the army, the navy, and the ordinary Civil services are all matters of state. Add further that Bolshevik theory connects organization so closely with the Truth that, if the true Line is followed, the true organization is expected to be available to be applied, so that bureaucratic inefficiencies, faulty distribution of labor, untrained supervision, and even failure of a crop due to weather conditions can all be easily regarded or presented as being due to someone's political failure to follow accurately enough the right Line. Experience with rapid industrialization in which there is a shortage of almost every sort of skill has demonstrated, in other countries, that this is a difficult operation which in any case involves a great deal of waste of men and materials. Experience with the state operation Of large enterprises, in which the coercive power of government is combined with the particular attempts of an employer of labor to run a railroad or to build a ship, again has demonstrated how many administrative pitfalls exist. Both of these conditions, rapid industrialization which outstripped the capacity to produce trained personnel and governmental operation of large-scale enterprises over very wide areas, existed in the Soviet Union. And, in addition, organization and efficiency are treated as ideological as well as technical problems. The discussion of the working out of Bolshevik ideology in the administration of agriculture and industry will be limited to the way in which the theories of organization and accountability overstrain the whole system, producing conditions in which almost everyone is accountable for things outside his control, to the results of this diffusion of accountability in inefficiency and illegality, and to the punitive measures with which the state attempts to correct it. To illustrate the effects of this politicizing of technical activities, it will be useful to examine in some detail an informant's account of the way technical failure is handled politically:

> A collective farm had a contract with a Machine Tractor Station that the Machine Tractor Station would work 600 hectares of land, in the course of 36 days beginning on the 15th of June, and that if this contract was not fulfilled, the MTS would be held responsible and would have to pay the collective farm a forfeit for the loss. At the contracted time the MTS sent tractors which were only in nominal repair, so that they were out of commission most of the time. When they were repaired they were taken off the work and sent other places (in the same sort of nominal fulfillment). At the due date they had not worked the land, nor did they work it later, and the land of the collective farm remained unworked. The collective farm turned to the secretary of the district Party committee and stated that as the MTS had not completed its work, the collective farm could not fulfill its contract with the state.

Now up to this point the story might occur anywhere where there are division of labor, machines which may be inadequately repaired, and contracts with forfeiture clauses in them. But from now on the account assumes a distinctively Soviet character:

> The first act of the district committee was to call the collective farm to accountability for interrupting the state plan and the NITS was called to accountability for sabotage. in the court, the collective farm attempted to stand on its contract, but this was not recognized. The court simply established that the collective farm had not completed its supply of grain to the state, and for interrupting the state plan, the chairman of the collective farm and 3 brigadiers were given eight-year jail sentences, and the case of the MTS was turned over to the political police as sabotage and the director of the MTS and two of his brigadiers were sent to a labor camp, without further trial, with ten year sentences.

Here the original trouble was technical—unrepaired tractors— which was not necessarily even within the control of the MTS but may have been a failure of some central agency to supply parts or even to manufacture them.

Punctuality has been exceedingly difficult to instill into a population unused to regular hours, and heavy fines and jail sentences have been introduced on a drastic scale—for example, lateness of twenty—one minutes might mean a loss of a third of the salary or a three-month jail sentence. Arguments about broken-down transports are not accepted, for it is held that every worker should have left his home in time to walk to the factory in case every other means of transportation failed. This provision illustrates neatly the high level of moral devotion expected of each Soviet citizen, the absence of which can in itself constitute a punishable offense, and the stress on the control of individual behavior (lateness) by punishment where the real need is for an improvement of the transportation system.

Examination of the functioning of any large ministry, agriculture or industry, shows that there is a continuous conflict between the diffusion of accountability, which exceeds the power to control, and the consequent uncertainty as to which agencies are actually responsible for anything, combined with interference from one accountable agency in the affairs of other agencies, in an effort to prevent the failures or exposures which are likely to be so severely and so indiscriminately punished. There also seems to be little distinction between mandatory and permissive interference and verification by one agency in the affairs of another.

One sharp editorial points out[2] that "some shortsighted people think that the execution of the threshing of the harvest is the affair of the collective farm," and adds that the NITS director should remember that he bears personal accountability for carrying out the grain threshing. A second[3] declares that "the capacity of the village Party organization to conduct mass political work among the masses is verified by the harvest and grain deliveries." This means that a secretary of a collective farm Party organization would supplement the work of a collective farm chairman by making personal observations of the threshing activities, investigating how much time was wasted for lunch, and raising these questions at general meetings, thus changing "the atmosphere" and introducing "a spirit of anxiety and self-criticism."[4] When it was further discovered that a grain dryer was needed, "the Party organization took this objective under its control, the Communists of the construction brigade were commissioned to prepare materials and particular Communists were commissioned to find equipment." The editorial then adds: "Having received concrete tasks people felt responsible."

On a collective farm, however, there is not only a management commission under the leadership of the chairman, but also a revision commission, which must conduct an "unrelenting struggle with mis-

2. "Grain to the Government on Time," from *Sotsialisticheskoe Zemledelie* (*Socialist Agriculture*), August 17, 1948.

3. S. Bardin, "The Kolkhoz Party Organization in the Harvest Days," from *Sotsialisticheskoe Zemledelie*, August 15, 1949.

4. "The Secretary of the Kolkhoz Party Organization," from *Sotsialisticheskoe Zemledelie*, August 10, 1948.

management in the collective," but "without interfering in the work of the management and without becoming a substitute for it.[5]

Furthermore, the Party is involved in what is taking place in the collective farms at every level. For example, a decree about sowing was issued jointly by the Council of Ministers of the USSR and the chief Party Secretary of the All Union Communist Party. On the county level, we find such interference as the refusal of a county Party committee to permit the chairman of a collective farm to remove or replace a link leader without its permission. But this involvement of the Party organizations in the details of administration in particular collective farms is explicable, as the Party committee officials may be held accountable for anything that goes wrong. In one case, upper-level Party organizations put the blame for backwardness and poor production of a group of collective farms on the lower-level Party organizations and dissolved one hundred and fifty of them. if skilled operators of agricultural combines are working in the wrong place, it is because the Party has not concerned itself with the "political and cultural growth of the combine operators."

Not only is the Party, at all levels, involved, but the ordinary executive organs of government are also involved and accountable if the collective farms do not make correct use of their capital funds or fail to contribute their seeds to the special seed reserves.

It must be stressed again that these multiplications of functions and agencies are not distinctive of the Soviet Union. It is possible to find instances in United States agriculture where ten or fifteen agencies are attempting to improve the functioning of a set of farmers in one community. The significant difference lies in the degree of accountability and in the way in which the officials of each agency, at each level, may be held totally accountable for events over which they have little or no control. We only need to add the belief that punishment in some degree implies some kind of guilt to picture a situation in which the alternatives are apathetic lack of initiative—for which one may be punished, for this is sabotage—and officious attempts to control the situation, which may also be stigmatized as misplaced interference and punished with demotion or worse.

If the management of a plant or the chairman of a collective farm and the Party Secretary do not get along together, there is possibility of endless friction with each jockeying for control and calling on associations higher up in his respective political hierarchy, a jockeying which is time-consuming and which lowers efficiency. If it ends

5. "Public Control in the Kolkhoz," from *Sotsialisticheskoe Zemledelie*, June 25, 1948.

in a victory for one or the other, this only inaugurates another struggle after the loser is replaced. The usual solution in American life
would be to try to work out an understanding between the two men,
both of whom must bear accountability for what goes on. But this
again is reprehensible and makes them guilty of the political sin of
"family relations."

Stalin in 1937 said:[6]

> To select workers correctly means to select workers according to objective
> criteria of business and suitability, not according to accidental, subjective,
> narrow and personal criteria. Most frequently so-called acquaintances are
> chosen, personal friends, fellow townsmen, people who have shown per-
> sonal devotion, masters of eulogies to their patrons, irrespective of
> whether they are suitable from a political and practical standpoint. ... In
> such family conditions there is no place for self-criticism of work by the
> leaders. Naturally, such family conditions create a favorable environment
> for the nurture of reptiles, not Bolsheviks.

In the struggles between the two, the director or chairman—who in a
great many cases today is also a Party member—and the Party Secretary, each is forced into the struggle, not necessarily by personal ambition but because each is accountable.

In the postwar fiction, there is an interesting reaction to the Party
doctrine that failure to achieve in production or agriculture is politically sinful. This is the development of the character of the very successful engineer-manager who during the war learned how to get
things done, using a variety of dubious methods, and who bases his
self-respect on his positive value to the state. If it is sinful not to
achieve, to fail for whatever reason, then, flows the logic which
underlies these characters such as Kondrashev[7] and Listopad,[8] it is
Virtuous to succeed by whatever means. The fictional stories of these
characters, as well as interviews with recent emigres and earlier experiences of Soviet industry and agriculture, support the contention
that the system is such that the most conscientious, the most enterprising and genuinely devoted executive is forced into a great number
of evasions of the law, into dodges and devices and illegal mutual
agreements in order to keep his enterprise running and to fulfill his
contract with the state, for the nonfulfillment of which he and many
others in far parts of the Soviet Union may suffer severe penalties.

6. J. Stalin, *Mastering Bolshevism*, Report to the 1937 Plenum of the
Central Committee of the CPSU, printed in *Bol'shevik*, April 1, 1937.

7. K. Simonov, "The Smoke of the Fatherland" (*Dym otechestva*), *Novyi
Mir*, November, 1947.

8. V. Panova, "Kruzhilikha," *Znamya*. November-December, 1947.

Whether it be the device by which a village store with clothes for sale refuses to sell for anything except eggs because the county was short on its egg delivery to the government, or the more complicated operations in which managers of big plants exchange supplies extralegally in order to keep their plants running, a great deal of wangling, scrounging, and arranging is needed to keep any Soviet enterprise functioning. It is even possible to publish a novel[9] representing collective farm life in idyllic terms, in which the heroine, chairman of the collective farm, succeeds in getting tractors for her fields at the expense of another collective farm because the director of the MTS is in love with her.

Within such a system—in which exist pull, bribery, mutual condonement of illegal actions, back-scratching, and wire pulling, all of which may be branded at any moment as "family relations," sabotage, or treason—there is obviously room for a great deal of petty theft, graft, and corruption, in which the conscientious and enterprising are joined with the venal and dishonest in a sort of strange collaboration which must increase, in the most devoted and hard working, the sense of being involved in political sinfulness. This type of alliance is represented in fiction in the similarities attributed to the successful, upper-level people, who are hard-headedly able to pursue success, and to the "lower depths," the completely extralegal people who flourish in the forbidden channels of illegal trade.[10]

The press periodically nags, scolds, and reports cases of heavy sentence passed on individual peasants for particular thefts, but the atmosphere seems to be one, if not of condonement, of at least a resigned acceptance of the fact that there is nothing to be done about the general conditions. Informants' accounts suggest a considerable development of elaborate accommodation devices, of which only one example will be given—from an informant who had been a doctor in a hospital in Vladivostok. When the informant went to this post,

> his first patient came in and asked for a statement of illness. When the doctor wished to examine him he was greatly surprised. "Don't you know our custom?" he said. "We pay a fixed price for a statement. I have to earn some money. When you give me a statement, I shall go to the market place and try to earn some money buying and selling." Since the doctor refused to issue a false report, the worker went to the chief of the hospital, complaining. After work the young doctor was called in to the chief and was told that if he behaved this way there was no place for him in the

9. A. Subbotin, *The Rank and File* (*Prostye Liudi*), Moscow, 1948.

10. Analyzed in detail as background for this report by Vera Schwarz (Alexandrova).

> hospital and besides the workers would beat him up. The reprimand was made in very general terms. The doctor was told he was preventing people from making a living.

This last statement, used as justification for the illegality, harks back to a deep rooted Russian attitude, found in the old *mir*, that every human being has a right to a living, a right which carries a kind of sanction of its own.

If full accommodation is to be reached between a governmental system which depends on terror and on mass or indiscriminate arrest and punishment rather than on techniques of administration which make it possible to limit and fix responsibility and the populace who are subjected to this terror, then what is required is an attitude toward the political police which reflects the general acceptance of illegality—something comparable to the American attitude toward traffic regulations about parking in a large city in which almost everyone breaks the rules and does not report his neighbor for breaking them. No systematic attempt is made by the police to stop the practice completely, but periodically there will be a great outburst of activity—a mass of tickets, fines, and summonses, which do not arouse undue resentment in those who get the summonses, they were just unlucky, that's all; and it's not the fault of the police—the streets were getting unbearably crowded, and obviously the police had to put on a show. In such a situation no one can feel unjustly treated, even though only a few hundred offenders may be singled out while guilty thousands go untouched. All are guilty and periodically some must be punished.

For such an attitude to develop in the Soviet Union, it would be necessary for the police to be regarded as impersonally as they were in the case described by an informant on page 91 (who saw them merely as wolves who must eat someone) and for the harshness of the punishments to be considerably mitigated. An account of an ex-White army officer and professor, who had worked faithfully for the Party for many years and was then accused of being a spy as his past seemed to lend color to the charge and make it difficult to refute, describes how he was kept in jail for a long time while an attempt was made to get a confession from him:

> The old professor said that if he had had some enemies he would have named them, but he had none. They would have let the professor go, but they had already held him too long and could not explain why they had held him so long if nothing was wrong.

In this account there is the underlying assumption that "it's just the system and no one is to blame."

But any assumption that the system rather than the individual is to blame runs completely contrary to Bolshevik moral doctrine, which, although insisting on an inescapable connection between an economic system and the over-all behavior of individuals within it, nevertheless holds the individual Party member or citizen to be completely accountable and does not allow any trifling slip to be overlooked. By holding everyone accountable for every slightest act, by holding all persons in responsible positions accountable for much that is due to the poor organization or administration for which they are not really responsible, the Bolsheviks create a system within which not responsible moral behavior, rigid correctness, nor meticulous honesty form the behavior which enables a man to survive, but in which a premium is placed upon the individual who can keep his head above water by devious means. The very extremity and exaggeration of their political moral demands are self-defeating by creating a political form which fails to reward those who take the demands seriously.

It is necessary to take the age of individual Soviet citizens carefully into account in making any judgment on trends in the Soviet Union. To the extent that the condoning and collaborative behavior occurs among the middle-aged and older, it may be regarded possibly as a residue of old-experienced attitudes of evasion and sabotage current in Tsarist Russia. This would still mean, however, that Soviet youth are exposed in the schools and youth organizations to one kind of official indoctrination and meet quite a different kind of behavior at every turn in their daily lives. The degree of contrast felt by the young between Bolshevik moral indoctrination and the real world of political dishonesty and evasion would then be one factor in the selection, from youth groups, of those who are most able to make the necessary moral compromises.

This study has concerned itself with attitudes toward authority, with the conduct models which are officially presented in the Soviet Union, and with informal and indirect evidence of the way in which actual practice diverges from these models. With such a framework, very little mention has been made of a subject which is, however, crucial to an understanding of the Soviet Union, that is, promises made by the regime of tangible material improvement and the extent to which these promises have been fulfilled. The major goal which Bolshevism has offered has been that of the good society in which, within an institutional framework where there would be neither exploitation of man by man nor domination of man over man, there would be abundance in which all would share. The realization of such a society is dependent on the actual existence of food, clothing, housing, and medical and educational facilities adequate for and available to the entire population. The inducements offered during the first Five-Year Plan to postpone the enjoyment of these material blessings for a few years in order to bring the good society nearer resulted in disappointment when the promises were not fulfilled.

Such experiences as that of Britain during World War II suggest that it is easier to induce a people to endure physical hardships in the name of values such as freedom and justice, sharing equally the burdens of abstinence and deprivation, than it is to induce one generation to go without butter so that the next generation can have it. In addition to failure to produce enough consumer goods to meet the expectations it had aroused, the Soviet regime, in order to strengthen its power, resorted to the device of giving differential access to the scarce consumer goods (1) by direct premium and prize giving, (2) by discriminatory rationing, and (3) by wage scales combined with special access to scarce or specially priced consumer goods. Higher officials have long been given special privileges. The expectation of loyalty of the political police today is calculated—in addition to a reliance upon the solidarity which comes from the risks and rewards of their being a group set apart from the population and with great power—on their being given economic privileges so great as to place them beyond ordinary temptation. From a Western point of view, the regime has been trapped in an abuse of its own value system by an attempt to approach the ideal of an equalization of material wealth by the creation of gross inequalities. From the Bolshevik point of view, however, which does not recognize this kind of connection between ends and means and regards any means as possibly appropriate to any end, this is merely a necessary detour in the approach to the perfect society.

One effort which the regime has made through the years to deal with the discrepancies between ideal and actuality, between promise and fulfillment, has been official insistence upon the superiority of material and of health and welfare service for the majority of people inside the Soviet Union as compared with the conditions of the majority of people in Western countries. Coercive measures since the war have been directed toward the danger that any large proportion of the population might discover, as a result of the experience abroad of Soviet troops or from Western propaganda, that the material conditions of the majority of the peoples of the Western countries are not, as the regime has pictured them, inferior to those in the Soviet Union but are actually better. This fear has been expressed in the rigid censorship on news, in suspicion of all those who have been abroad, and in the campaign against cringing before the West. It suggests that statements about relative conditions in the East and West have been such conscious falsifications that loyalty of the citizen is expected to flag and fail when confronted by evidence of workers' houses id Germany or by food conditions in Rumania. The harshness of the measures with which the regime combats any diffusion of knowledge about conditions in the West suggests that this fear can only be reduced if material conditions in the Soviet Union can be steadily and appreciably improved. But this possibility is rendered unlikely because the Bolshevik dogma that they are encircled by hostile enemies all crouching to attack makes it expedient to divert such a large part of Soviet manpower and resources into military operations that there is not the margin available for improvement. Yet without this improvement, the present fear of the top leadership, that knowledge of the real contrasts between East and West will reach and subvert the people, increases the severity of the measures which must be taken against a potentially treasonable population filled with potential wreckers and saboteurs and so diminishes the possibility of any relaxing of the controls exercised by the political police. There is, of course, evidence of considerable relaxation after the excesses of the late thirties but not sufficient to make it likely that the present level of police supervision will decrease.

Chapter 7

POSSIBLE DEVELOPMENTS IN THE SOVIET UNION

*L*et us assume that conditions in the Soviet Union remain somewhat as they are with (1) a steady belief in military threat from the West keeping up expenditures on armaments and so preventing the standard of living from rising, with (2) a continuing fear of the impact of news of the higher standard of living in the West producing disloyalty, keeping the feeling of need of tight police controls high, with (3) the tightness, harshness, and indiscriminateness of the police controls producing a general situation in which almost everyone, except the political police themselves, is involved in political crime of some sort, and with (4) a continuance of the system of moral-political education in the schools and youth organizations which is designed to build a strong individual conscience, strongly motivated by an exacting standard of devoted political behavior incompatible with an atmosphere of condonement, evasion, and general political corruption. We may then consider certain weaknesses or points of conflict in the system which are suggested by the particular material which has been analyzed in this report.

Two areas of weakness, related to the contrasts between the officially expressed ideals of the Bolsheviks and the actual coercive terroristic police state with its accompaniment of accommodation and corruption, may be identified.

1. Weakness in the area of leadership. The recruitment of youth for positions of responsibility and leadership may be most adversely affected by the inability of those who develop the desired strong individual conscience and high idealism to survive within the system of political dishonesty. Those who survive in a system in which there is such a strong contrast between the ideal and the actual practice are likely to be lacking in the very qualities of moral devotion and initiative which are necessary for the future development of Soviet society. To the extent that particular areas of Soviet life are relatively freer from the type of political pressure which interferes with any disinterested attempt to do a job well—as has been the case in the Soviet army at some periods—they may become relatively better staffed and more efficient than other areas. Such discrepancies may in turn put strains upon the system or provoke reprisals from other more politicized areas.

2. **Weaknesses in the masses of the people.** A diminution in the enthusiasm and available energy of the population may be the consequence of the methods used to preserve the security of the regime by the political police, whose incorruptibility is partly based, not on a moral-political faith, however fanatical, but on fear and the prestige derived from the disproportionate share of material goods and services which are placed at their disposal. In practice, this means that the group to whom the security of the system is entrusted are seen by the populace as being motivated by fear rather than by faith and as being treated by the state as if they were so lacking in innate devotion that, unless the rewards given by the state outdistance their possible underground methods of "self-supply" *(samosnabzhenia),* their loyalty cannot be relied upon. Popular feeling about these contradictions may accentuate the harshness and indiscriminateness of the police measures, since the police seek to counteract the fears of the regime concerning their reliability. But increased terroristic practices should weaken the feeling of the populace that where there is punishment there must be some guilt. In addition, Soviet methods of child rearing and education may reduce the tendency of the individual to feel guilty of the crime which he has committed only in imagination, now an important condition making for some acceptance of the terroristic methods of the political police.

A populace disillusioned regarding the hope of tangible rewards, subjected to terroristic pressure, living within a situation in which all are treated as suspect —and most of all those who must also be the most incorruptible—may become steadily less responsive to positive motivation, more apathetic, and less able to participate with any enthusiasm in Soviet life. The Soviet Union, however, has relied heavily on compensating for organizational inefficiency and for the gaps between plan and fulfillment by tapping the energies of the people and by such devices as correcting for a faulty budget for a given enterprise by whipping up the workers to the voluntary contribution of extra hours. A reduction in the availability of such energy in the population as the people react to loss of hope and increasing sharp controls administered by those who are seen as living on the fat of the land should lower the productivity of the system and its capacity to meet new strains and difficulties.

An examination of the great discrepancies between ideal and actuality, between Bolshevik Party ideal and Soviet State practice, discrepancies which are accentuated by the system of education under which everyone under forty-five has now been educated, therefore suggests that a loss of leadership personnel and an increase in apathy in the general population are two strong possible weaknesses of the Soviet authority system as it is currently inculcated and administered.

An increasing *strength* and *stability* within the Soviet Union would involve the following conditions: (1) a lessening of the fear of the top leadership of the imminence of capitalist attack, which lessening did not involve too much accompanying open struggle for power at the top; (2) a relaxation of the political police controls which reflect the fear of a population whose standard of living is kept low by armaments; (3) the development, in the political police themselves and throughout the entire bureaucracy, of sharper theories of function and responsibility accompanied by methods of detecting actual criminals; (4) the setting up of workable channels of authority within organizations; and (5) a growing closeness of fit between punishment and real guilt on the one hand and reward and real virtue, as virtues are outlined in the schools, on the other. Such a development is dependent (1) in part on world conditions, (2) in part on accidents of leadership within the Soviet Union, and (3) in part on the extent to which engineering and scientific training is likely to be reflected in increasing capacity for realistic organization. If, however, all of these conditions should come about, one might then predict that there might be a strong puritanical tone to the society.[1] In the light of our contemporary knowledge of the relationship between moral training and character, this would produce a population which, while better disciplined than the present Soviet population, might also be lacking in the reserves of zest and energy which the present population displays.

These alternatives are hot, of course, exclusive of other possibilities, but they are strongly suggested by this body of material and should be taken seriously into account in planning research and in contemporary propaganda plans as well as in longer-term estimates of the strength of the Soviet Union.

1.   A full description of the basis for this statement is beyond the scope of the present report.

Appendix A

Abstract of Research on Leadership in Soviet Agriculture and the Communist Party

A separate, full-length RAND report will soon be issued on problems of *Leadership in Soviet Agriculture and the Communist Party*, This study, by H. S. Dinerstein, was conducted as part of Studies in Soviet Culture. It is a comprehensive analysis of the morale-producing and morale-destroying features of Soviet agricultural organization.

Based on printed Soviet written materials and on interviews and private documents obtained from ex-Soviet citizens, the study presents a detailed analysis of the organization of the kolkhoz, its systems of incentives, the relations of the Machine Tractor Stations to the kolkhoz, and the role of county and province agriculture authorities in planning on local levels.

The difficulties of meeting unrealistically planned quotas and the techniques of evading responsibility for nonfulfillment are presented in considerable detail. The economic consequences of unrealistic planning, falsification of records, bribery, and personal profiteering are described. The responsibility of Party and government officials and the attempted control, enforcement, and punishment procedures are related to the effects on farm-worker morale, described in a setting which takes account of the historical development of collective farming, the psychology of the Russian peasant, and the political institutions of the Soviet system.

Appendix B

SUMMARY OF CONCLUSIONS OF RESEARCH ON SOVIET CHILD TRAINING IDEALS AND THEIR POLITICAL SIGNIFICANCE

(Conducted as part of Studies in Soviet Culture)

BY E. CALAS

*F*rom the earlier official attitude, which reflected the belief that socialist society would take upon itself in full the upbringing of children, the Soviet Government has shifted to an emphasis on the significant role of the family and family upbringing of children. Recent laws, decrees, and public announcements of leaders encourage the growth of a closely knit family and of parental authority. From the strengthened and united family the state expects full cooperation in the matter of molding "the moral countenance" of future Soviet citizens. Parents are held totally responsible for mental attitudes which they wittingly or unwittingly transfer to their children; they are called on to examine their own attitudes and behavior and to struggle against possible carry-overs *(perezhitkii)* from the capitalist past. Parents must serve as models of political and social activity, industriousness, unselfishness, and optimism. This will guarantee them the love and respect of their children. Children become emotionally alienated from parents who do not act in accordance with the precepts and ideals which the children learn in school and in the Pioneer or Komsomol organization.

In relation to children, parents must be unremittingly vigilant, exacting, and consistent in disciplinary demands and in the imposition of duties; no relaxation of effort on the parents' part is permissible for fear that the child may fall under bad influence and be controlled by antisocial elements. While parents should show warmth, affection, and understanding, they should not permit excessive intimacy, which might undermine their authority. Parents must not be all-forgiving, for conduct deviations in children cannot be tolerated. Parental indulgence interferes with proper upbringing and turns a child into a despot at home and into a difficult child in the school collective. The ideal parents are little differentiated as to their function in relation to the child, the father being encouraged to assume equal responsibility with the mother in the matter of upbringing.

Upbringing must develop in children the qualities of personality which, combined, form the moral countenance of a future fighter for communism: ideological purposefulness, strong convictions, patriotism, sense of duty, courage, endurance, tenacity, self-control, humanism, vigor, industriousness, optimism, generosity combined with the care of property, modesty, neatness, politeness, and sensitivity to the needs of others. Obedience is seen as the first step toward developing a disciplined will. Anxiety related to performance of duty is viewed as a virtue. Qualities are regarded as virtues if they are socially oriented; they are undeserving of approval when used to further purely personal interests. Training from early infancy is recommended; constancy of effort on a child's part and the carrying through of any undertaking to the end receive heavy stress. The will to overcome obstacles must replace the intolerable tendency to follow the line of least resistance. Most related "noncompulsive" behavior is ascribed to the influence of the past through the medium of faulty family relations and attitudes. The planned transformation of man is rationalized by the concept of the moral betterment of man: "The process of remaking man which is taking place under the influence of socialistic conditions, as well as the creation of a new man, must attract the exclusive attention of Soviet pedagogy." It is admitted that the process of forming the new morality involves a difficult and tense struggle.

In all circumstances, personal interests must be subordinated to collective ones. The desirability of a large family is stressed because it affords the child his first experience of collective life, accustoming him to respect older siblings and to give succor to the younger. From an early age a child should be trained in a feeling of responsibility to the collective and in upholding the honor of the group (his class, or Pioneer brigade). The child should be trained to value highly the approval of the collective and to fear its disapproval. "The rules of conduct adopted by the collective become binding on the member, and finally one's sense of responsibility to the collective becomes the basis of self-evaluation." While it is one's duty to confess errors and misdeeds, to accept criticism with respect and without offense, and to subordinate oneself to the demands of the collective, the moral gain for the culprit is placed in the foreground: "Courage is developed by the need always to say the truth, not to commit dishonorable, amoral deeds, and, if such are committed, courageously to recognize one's guilt before the collective and its leader, to submit to the condemnation of the misdeed and to become imbued with the determination to mend it." The emphasis is not on the cathartic release of guilt feelings but on moral growth. Adults may enlist the disapproval of a child's peers or may delegate authority so that corrective action comes from the child's collective. Organized collective (such as the Pioneer organization) may instigate corrective action independently by resorting to group accusation. While the role of comradeship and friendship is extolled, solidarity with the collective is placed above personal feelings of friendship. While interpersonal relations are generally approved, there is always the conditional factor: personal relations must fit into the required pattern, that is, they must serve the ultimate strengthening of the state.

Correct discipline should lead gradually to self-discipline. Every influence of the adult on the child, be it of encouragement or punishment, has as its aim the molding of the child's behavior, interests, views, and impulses, and the development of the convictions which will determine his future conduct. There is consistent emphasis on punishment as correction rather than as retribution. The nature of a misdeed dictates the handling of it, and when punishment is indicated it must fit the concrete circumstances of each case. Parents and teachers must be aware of the "point of application" of their educational influence *(vozdeistvie)*, which requires an understanding of a child's motivations in committing a deed. There are frequent warnings against an abuse of punishment and scolding as well as of praise and reward, because through repetition they lose their effectiveness. An "eye to eye" talk is a recommended corrective measure which must be carried out when both the adult and the child are calm, because an adult's raised, irritated voice throws the child into either a state of sharp excitation or of inhibition. All forms of verbal reaction must be controlled, and in no event may they be used as catharses for adult feelings. Corporal punishment is outlawed, and other forms are warned against. Irony and humbling of arrogance are resorted to in cases of inadequate performance or bragging. A recommended punishment is the withholding of a treat, but this may not involve food. Repeated misdeeds which reveal bad traits of character and distorted concepts call for starting anew all the work with the child, and it is recommended that in the first place the parent place himself "under the microscope" to see in what way he himself has been inadequate to his task.

Sources used by E. Calas in research on Soviet Child Training Ideals and Their Political Significance.

An editorial, "Education in Comradeship and Friendship," *Family and School* (*Sem'ya i Shkola*), No, 4, 1948.

An editorial, "Training in Sense of Duty," *Family and School*, No. 6, 1948. "From the Notes of a Teacher," Family and School, Nos. 7-8, 1946.

"Report on a Conference on Moral Education," *Family and School*, Nos. 4-5, 1946. An editorial, "Training in Purposefulness," Family and School, No. 3, 1948.

An editorial, "Training in Courage," *Family and School*, No. 2, 1948.

An editorial, "On Cheerfulness and *Joie-de-vivre*," *Family and School*, No. 5, 1948. An editorial, "Training in Endurance," Family and School, No. 1, 1948.

Alekseyev, A., and M. Andreyeva, "Report of a Working Mother," *Family and School*, No. 4, 1948.

Arkin, E. A., *Letters on the Upbringing of Children*, Uchpedgiz, 1940.

Bershanskaya, E. D., "After the War," *Family and School*, Nos. 4-5, 1946.

Bobovskaya, E., and N. Chetunova, "Problems of the Family and Morality," *Oktyabr*" No. 1, 1948.

Dogvalevskaya, A. I., "A Congenial Family," *Family and School*, No. 3, 1947.

Glazounova, E. I., "Experience in Pioneer Work," *Soviet Pedagogy* (*Sovetskaia Pedagogika*), No. 5, 1948.

Golosnitskaya, N., *My Work in Upbringing of Children*, Uchpedgiz, 1948.

Goncharov, N. K., *Foundations of Pedagogy* (Chap. VIII, "Foundations of Moral Education"), Uchpedgiz, 1947.

Katina, L. P., "Laying the Foundations of Cultural Behavior in Kindergarten," *Pre-School Education* (*Doshkol'noe Vospitanie*), No. 6, 1948.

Kolbanovsky, V. N., Prof., "Ideological -Political Education in the Family," *Family and School*, No. 10, 1947.

_____,For the Further Strengthening of the Soviet Family," *Family and School*, No. 11, 1947.

Kononenko, Elena, "The Rope," *Family and School*, No. 6, 1948.

Kornilov, K. N., "Role of the Family in the Rearing of Pre-School Children," *Pre-School Education*, No. 7, 1948.

Likhacheva, N. F., "Mother-Tutoress," *Family and School*, No. 3, 1948.

Liublinskaya, A. A., "On the Misdeeds of Children," *Family and School*, No. 1, 1948.

Mahova, K. V., *Notebook of a Mother*, Academy of Pedagogical Sciences, 1948.

Makarenko, A. S., *Book For Parents*, Gospolitizdat, 1937 (out of print), Academy of Pedagogical Sciences, 1949.

_____, Lecture on the *Book For Parents*, given in 1938, published in Family and School, No. 11, 1948.

Pechernikova, 1. A., *Teaching the Schoolboy to Share in the Family Work*, Uchpedgiz, 1948.

Perel and Lyubimova, *The Legal Position of the Child in the Family*, Introduction, Uchpedgiz, 1932.

Perel] (ed.), *Property Rights of Children*, Uchpedgiz, 1932.

Pisareva, L. V., "The Word in Upbringing," *Family and School*, Nos. 4-5, 1946.

Prozorov, G. C., Prof., "A. S. Makarenko on Pedagogical Tact in Family Upbringing," *Family and School*, No. 8, 1948.

Raskin, L. E., "Discipline and Culture in the Conduct of School Children," *Young Guard*, 1941.

High-School Students in the Family," *Family and School,* No. 6, 1948.

Sapirstein, L., "School Director E. V. Mart'ianova," *Family and School*, No. 3, 1947.

Sergeyeva, A. D., -Lbve and Obligation to a Mother," *Family and School*, No. 11, .1947.

Simson, T. P., Dr., *Nervousness in Children and Measures for Preventing It*, Izd. Mosoblispolkoma, Zdravotdel, 1932.

Smirnov, V. E., "Absent-Mindedness and the Struggle Against It," *Family and School*, Nos. 4-5, 1946.

Speransky, G. N., *The Young Child*, Zdravotdel, 1941.

Svadkovsky, 1. F., Prof., "Training in Obedience, Politeness and Modesty," *Family and School*, No. 3, 1947.

Sverdlov, G. M., *Marriage and the Family*, Uchpedgiz, 1946.

Syrkina, V. E., "Dreams and Ideals of Children," *Family and School*, No. 9, 1947.

Tadevosian, V. S., "Rights and Obligations of Parents in the Soviet State," stenograrn of a lecture read in Moscow, May 29, 1947.

Usova, A. P., "On Ideology in Educational Work of Kindergartens," *Pre-School Education*, No. 5, 1948.

Yudina, N. V., "Parental Authority," *Family and School*, Nos. 4-5, 1946.

Zhdanov, A., "Report on the Magazines *Zvezda* and *Leningrad*," Gospolitizdat, 1946, P. 36.

Periodicals

The 1947-1949 issues of the following magazines were read (but not including every issue, nor every item in any issue):

Novyi Mir (New World)
Oktyabr', (October)
Zvezda (Star)
Znamya (Banner)
Krokodil (Crocodile)
Zhurnal Moskovskovo Patriarkhata (Journal of the Moscow Patriarchate)
Sovetskaya Pedagogika (Soviet Pedagogy)
Murzilka
Vozhdi (Leaders)
Pioner (Pioneer)
Doshkol'noe Vospilanie (Pre-School Education)
Soviet Woman Literatura v Shkole (Literature in Schools)
Pediatria (Pedialry)
Nevropatologiia i Psykhiatriia (Neuropathology and Psychiatry)

Newspapers

Komsomot'skaia Pravada
Pionerskaya Pravda
Uchitel'skaya Gazeta (The Teachers' Gazette)
Morskoi Flot (The Navy)

Books

Of the thirty-five juvenile books read, the following were intensively studied:

Gaidar, A., *Timur and his Band (Timur y yevo komanda)*, Detgiz, 1940.
_____,*Timur's Oath (Klyatva Timura)*, Detgiz, 1941.
_____,*Snow Fortress (Komandant snezhnoy kreposti)*, Detgiz, 1945.
Kassil, L., *Chernysh, Brother of a Hero (Chernysh brat geroya)*, Detgiz, 1938.
Kalma, N., *Copy Book of Andrei Sazonov (Tetrad' Andreya Sazonova)*, Detgiz, 1948.
Voronkova, L., *Little Girl from the City (Devochka iz goroda)*, Detgiz, 1943.

Teplitskaya, L., *In Our Yard (U nas vo dvore)*, 1940 Handbook for Pioneer Leaders (Vozhatyi) in *Young Guard (Molodaya Gvardia)*.

Fraerman, R., *The Far-Voyage (Dal'nee plavanie)*, Detgiz, 1946.

Ilina, Elena, *Fourth Height (Chatvertaya vysota)*, Detgiz, 1948.

Paustovskii, K., *Summer Days (Letnie dni)*, Detizdat, 1937.

Likstanov, I., *Nalyshok*, Detgiz, 1948.

OSeyCva, V., *Vasek Truhachev*, Detgiz, 1947.

Kurochkin, V., *Brigade of the Smart (Brigada smyshlennykh)*, *Oktyabr' (October)*, No. 9, 1947.

Kaverin, V., *Two Captains (Dva kapitana)*, *Young Guard (Molodaya Gvardia)*, 1947.

Dekhtereva, B. (ed.), *We Studied in Moscow (My uchilis' v Moskve)*, Detgiz, 1947.

Nevskii, V., *The Bright Road (Svetlaya doroga)*, *Young Guard (Molodaya Gvardia)*, 1948.

From about thirty recently published adult novels, the following were examined closely:

Lifshitz, V., *Petrogradskaya Storona*, *New World (Novyi Mir)*, Nos. 10-11, 1946.

Fedin, K., *First joys (Pervye Radosti)*, *New World (Novyi Mir)*, Nos. 4-9, 1945.

Koptyayeva, A., *Comrade Anna (Tovarishch Anna)*, *Oktyabr'*, May, 1946.

Denison, L, *Pure Love (Chistaya liubov)*, *Oklyabr'*, No. 6, 1946.

Katerli, E., *The Stozharovs (Stozharovi)*, *Sovietski Pisatel' (Soviet Writer)*, 1948.

Bessonov, Y., Maria (Maria) in collection *Sudden Turn (Neozhidannyi povorot)*, *Sovietski Pisatel' (Soviet Writer)*, 1948.

Gausner, J., *We are Home Again (Vot my i doma)*, *Sovietski Pisatel' (Soviet Writer)*, 1948

Voronin, S., *On Their Land (Na svoyey zemle)*, *Sovietski Pisatel' (Soviet Writer)*, 1948.

Karaveyeva, A., *Running Start (Razbeg)*, *Sovietski Pisatel' (Soviet Writer)*, 1948.

Platonov, A., *Ivanov's Family (Sem'ya Ivanova)*, *Novyi Mir (New World)*, Nos. 10-1, 1946.

Perventsev, A., Honor from the Days of Youth (Chest' S molodu), Sovietski Pisatel' (Soviet Writer), 1949.

Panova, V., Kruzhilikha, *Sovietski Pisatel' (Soviet Writer)*, 1948.

Gerasimova, V., *Age Mates (Sverstnitsy)*, *Sovietski Pisatel' (Soviet Writer)*, 1948.

Appendix C

SUMMARY OF CONCLUSIONS OF RESEARCH ON PARTY AND NON-PARTY ORGANIZATIONS IN SOVIET INDUSTRY

BY L. H. HAIMSON

*T*he summary conclusions presented here stem from a study of the structure and functioning of Soviet industrial organization, largely as viewed by members of the Soviet elite. Attention is focused, in this analysis, on the rationale which underlies the coexistence of Party and non-Party organs at various hierarchical levels of the industrial apparatus and on the changing interaction among these organs during the list decade.

Two levels of abstraction were observed in our examination of Soviet writings on industrial organization and were consequently adhered to in the analysis. We distinguished a body of pure theory, from which was derived a set of general politico-psychological assumptions concerning the relation of human personality to leadership and administrative supervision, and a level of applied theory as exemplified by the structure of the industrial apparatus and its expected functioning. Our examination of the practical difficulties which arise out of conflicts and contradictions inherent within the industrial system constituted a third level of analysis.

For the three facets of the study a wide variety of sources was used: In our examination of the theory of leadership and administration we drew upon authoritative texts of political theory and administrative law, keynote speeches and resolutions at the Party Congress of 1939 and at the Party Conference of 1941, editorials and articles in *Pravda* and *Bol'shevik* since 1939, and various 'authoritative pamphlets on this topic. For information concerning the structure and expected functioning of Party and non-Party planning, administrative and control organs in industry, we also drew on studies by Soviet economists such as *Arakelian's Upravlenie sotsialisticheskoi promyshlennosti* (*Management of Socialist Industry*) and on Party periodicals such as *Partiinaya Zhizn* (*Party Life*).

Available printed discussions were not found adequate for a survey of the difficulties produced in practice by the contradiction within the system of organization and for an examination of the methods used in resolving these difficulties. Much relevant information on this topic, as on the topic of the preceding section (see Appendix 13, page 107) was found in the pages dedicated to "Party Life" in *Pravda*, However, to round out our knowledge we found it necessary to study some of the postwar Soviet novels based on industrial themes and to interview a number of DP engineers and technicians.

A full analysis of the organization and operation of industry in any society must include a number of analytically distinguishable factors. Purely economic and technological considerations, geographical and demographical factors are undoubtedly of foremost importance. That in this study the emphasis has been placed on psychocultural factors is owing in part to our own professional orientation and also to the very character of the premises upon which Soviet industrial organization is based.

Two basic differences between these premises and those which underly American theories and plans of industrial organization must be pointed out.

While American organizational blueprints are based on a consideration of the particular industrial complex to be erected, Soviet blueprints, as previously stated, are explicitly derived from a number of universal premises about the organization of human activity. While Americans tend to operate on the belief that the individual is only partially affected by the exercising of any particular role, Soviet theory emphasizes that the whole of human personality is involved in the successful performance of a job. Also, in American blueprints, considerations of morale or efficiency are usually relegated to the background. It is taken for granted that there exists a large labor force composed of individuals whose performance will not be greatly affected by the forms of organization in which they are placed. Changes in line or staff relationships are not expected to make a Dr. Jekyll out of a Mr. Hyde.

Grounds which are just as realistic can be found for the emphasis on morale in Soviet industrial organization. Soviet leaders and industry experts have attempted to harness to herculean industrial tasks a new and undisciplined labor force, relatively untrained in matters of timing and precision; the individuals who compose this labor

force are believed to respond powerfully to the form of the organization in which they are placed. Psychological states are assumed to
lend themselves to a high degree of manipulation, and performance
is believed to be greatly and immediately affected by them.

The psychological premises underlying Soviet administrative theory and the structure of Soviet industrial organization have oscillated
in the last decade or so between what can be considered as a complex
of Great Russian attitudes regarding leadership and authority and a
slowly emerging Soviet ideal of personality and social organization.
While these traditional attitudes become increasingly predominant as
one reaches down to the more concrete aspects of Soviet industrial
reality, to the actual behavior—to the actual interaction among members of the industrial apparatus (particularly in spots geographically
removed from centers of political authority, such as the Trans-Cauca-
sus region)—they still permeate the most abstract theoretical discussions, resulting in insoluble contradictions even at this level.

The traditional Great Russian attitudes to which we have referred,
attitudes tied to a long historical experience with arbitrary bureaucracy, are expressed in the concepts of *rukovodstvo* and *upravlenie*. The
term *upravlenie*, which can be translated as "administration," or
"direction," or "regulation," refers to those aspects of authority which
are felt by Russians to be restrictive, all-embracing, impersonal, inanimate, and, consequently, arbitrary. While a careful examination of
the nuances which differentiate the Russian concept from the American term *administration* is impossible in the present summary, we
must point out the degree to which the Russian term is more encom-
passing than its American counterpart, a difference which reflects the
Great Russian belief that it is upravlenle which in a sense gives the
personality its form, and that without it the individual would act in
explosive spurts of volatile energy.

The opposite pole of this Great Russian set of attitudes regarding
leadership and authority emerges in the term *rukovodstvo* (literally,
the act of leading by the hand), a concept which evokes a direct, positive, live relationship among individuals or among highly personal-
ized collective concepts such as the Party and the masses, a
relationship characterized by guidance and teaching and by the
absence of compulsion. To this category of leadership are assigned the
functions of planning and control. Only organs of *rukovodstvo* can
issue the directives upon which planning for the future and organization of the present are based, since only they possess the insight
and foresight necessary for the task. These organs alone, according to
these traditional attitudes, can—by virtue of the psychological immediacy of their relationship to the masses—control and redress the

abuses of bureaucracy, arouse in the masses the energy and enthusiasm required to break through bureaucracy's impersonal and arbitrary restrictions, and spur them on to the tasks ahead, whether a holy war against the foreign invader or the building of socialism.

The aged principles which we have outlined are still expected today to govern, to a large degree, the interaction of Party and non-Party organs of industrial leadership and administration and also partially to delineate within the intra-Party structure the relationship between the Party summit, its middle echelons—*oblast* (regional), city, and *raion* (district) committees—and the Party masses (primary Party organizations).

The adherence of Soviet leaders to this dogma, their assignment of *rukopodsvo* to Party organs and of the onus of *upravlenie* to non-Party organs in industry, of *rukovodstvo* to the summit and *upravlenie* to the middle echelons of the intra-Party structure, need not be explained purely by their belief in this body of doctrine. This division of functions provides a highly effective channel for diverting popular dissatisfaction from the Party leadership and an apparent remedy for the feared dissociation of the leadership from the masses which seems endemic in the Soviet elite. While the attitudes expressed in the concepts of *rukovodstvo* and *upravlenie* constitute today an important, if not always explicitly stressed, aspect of theory and practice in Soviet industrial organization, they have been slowly receding under the pressure of a new operative ideal of personality and social organization which has been emerging during the last two decades. For a highly articulated picture of the application of these still surviving attitudes, it is useful to turn to the structure of organization of Soviet industry before 1934.

The onset of rapid industrialization in the Soviet Union was accompanied by a sharp increase in the need for specificity of timing and purpose in the efforts of the untrained labor force and administrative personnel upon whose shoulders this huge task lay. The administrative-regulative organs, the organs of *upravlenie* which were to supervise the fulfillment of the planned assignments and to provide the pressure needed for making individuals conform to the specific and delicate needs of highly geared and complex industrial giants, were organized at first in a characteristic fashion. Since the problem was conceived as one of molding individuals within the confines of organizational restraint, it was felt that the more precisely an organization defined and distinguished an individual's task, the more likely he was to fulfill his planned assignment. In accordance with this logic, the functional principle of organization was universally applied in all branches and at all levels of the operative organs of the

Soviet industrial apparatus. This principle of organization was followed not only in regional Party committees and industrial trusts, but also in the smallest factory shops and in the Party cells of those shops. The universal application of this principle resulted in such absurdities as the division of a small shop administration of fewer than ten people into sectors of current production plans, cost norms, quality norms, supplies, labor organizations, and so on.

The structure of the administrative hierarchy also conformed in this period to the principle of *upravlenie*. Industrial ministries did not as yet exist, and the various branches of Soviet industry operated under the all-embracing supervision of the Supreme Economic Council. This tendency to set up catch-all administrative-regulative organs also appeared at lower levels of the administrative hierarchy in the predilection expressed for the *kombinat* forms of organization-large, unwieldy administrative structures which incorporated, sometimes with little logic, industrial units considered to be somehow related.

The organizational observance of the distinction between *rukovodstvo* and *upravlenie* was reflected by the rather rigid segregation, even within the non-Party structure, of planning and control functions from the function of administration. The political directives upon which planning is based were issued then, as they are today, by the Central Committee of the Party, and the spelling out and execution of those directives concerned purely with labor organizations were, then as now, a basic responsibility of Party organizations at various levels of the apparatus. A distinctive feature of this phase of the history of Soviet industrial organization, however, was the overwhelming concentration, the high degree of centralization, and the economic elaboration of these directives in the hands of the *Gosplan*, the State Planning Commission.

Control was organized in a similar fashion. Within the non-Party administrative structure this function was delegated to the Labor Peasant Inspection (RKI), a body which was expected continuously to control and check operations in every niche and nook of the Soviet economic apparatus and to correct the malfunctions discovered in this process of roving inspection. The control function of Party organizations over the administrative hierarchy and over the enterprises themselves was just as elastically defined.

The system of industrial organization which we have just outlined had evidenced, by the middle thirties, its complete unwieldiness and inefficiency. The functional organization of the administrative structure itself provided an ideal setting for what is called depersonalization in Soviet language, that is, escape from responsibility—passing the buck for failure. Further, excessive centralization and segregation of planning made frequent revisions of the plans, according to changes in the economic picture, almost impossible to achieve. Finally, the elastic definition of control and its concentration in the hands of external organs confronted these outside organs with the dilemma of either permitting the system to jam or of themselves taking over the current administration of the industrial apparatus. The pressure on the control organs, both Party and non-Party, to take over the current administation of the enterprises under their supervision was reinforced by a practice still current in Soviet administration: since the successful fulfillment of tasks was asserted to be dependent only on good organizational planning and efficient control (today, *verification* in Soviet language), the organs concerned with organizational planning and control were assigned complete responsibility for the successful fulfillment of tasks by the organizations under their supervision.

In the middle thirties, coincident with the maturation of a new generation of *Soviet Man*, a generation assumed to be endowed with more self-discipline, with a better sense of purpose and timing than its forebears, a new ideal of leadership and authority and a new definition of the organization of action were stressed by Soviet leaders. Within this new approach they began to remold the structure of industrial organization and, to a lesser extent, Soviet industrial practice.

The new ideal of leadership and authority, expressed in the concept of *edinonachalie* (literally, one-man leadership), stressed the necessity for a "full" concentration of both authority and responsibility for an organization in a single leader; it demanded "the incontrovertible subordination of the collective of workers to the single will of the leader." A measure of authority in both planning and control was entrusted to the heads of the administrative organs.

In line with these changes in the ideal of leadership, the definition of the organization of action underwent drastic verbal revision at the 1934 Party Congress. A closer union of planning, execution, and control was to be achieved, "a unity of word and action, of decision and fulfillment." Accordingly, the task of continuous roving inspection was Assigned to the staff of the administrative structure and to the leaders of their subordinate enterprises, and the activities of external organs of control were to be limited to the verification of fulfillment of specific directives.

The new attitudes toward leadership and the organization of activity were to be reflected in the *productive territorial* organization of the industrial pyramid, and, indeed, they were observed in the overhauling of the structure of the *operational administrative organs*. According to the productive territorial principle, as we have seen, every production division, whether brigade, division, shop, enterprise, trust, chief administration, or ministry was to be headed by a leader with full authority and responsibility for the work of the division, The leader of the production division was to receive his assignments only from the leader of the production division at the next higher echelon and to be subordinate only to him. Functional organs, according to this ideal system of organization, were to be fully subordinated to the production leaders and were forbidden to give orders to lower echelons.

The reorganization of the administrative machinery according to the *productive territorial* principle and *edinonachalie* was calculated, in the eyes of Soviet leaders, to eliminate irresponsibility and to encourage individual initiative among the members of the administrative personnel. By the setting up of a direct and shortened line of responsibility down to the production level—a chain of authority, each link of which was entrusted to a single person—it was also designed to provide satisfactory contact between the top and the bottom of the pyramid, to realize in a more efficient manner the desired psychological immediacy between the leaders and the masses.

The new principles of organization were, on the whole, observed, if we consider the overhauled administrative structure alone. The Supreme Economic Council was subdivided into a number of production ministries. Most *kombinats* were dissolved and replaced by smaller, less unwieldy industrial units. Serious attempts were made to subordinate functional divisions to production organizations on the same hierarchical level from the ministries (commisariats) and their chief administrations *(upravlenlie)* down to the plants and the shops. The function of current planning was to a large degree decentralized by placing a measure of responsibility for it in the hands of the planning divisions of the various hierarchical levels of the production ministries. The whole responsibility for inspection was turned over, on paper, to the heads of the enterprises themselves and to their direct superiors, and the Labor Peasant Inspection was accordingly replaced by Committees of Party and Soviet Control with much narrower functions. (In 1940 the Commission of Soviet Control became the Ministry of State Control, under the narrow jurisdiction of which comes the correction of criminal financial abuses.)

If one includes, as one must, the organs of Party leadership and control in this outline of Soviet industrial organization, the picture is drastically altered, even on a purely structural level. The 18th Party Congress of 1939, to be sure, abolished the industrial sections of the Party in order to strengthen the *edinonachalie*, the one-man leadership and control of management, and it severely forbade any usurpation by Party organizations of managerial functions. But the very same Congress reaffirmed the necessity for supervision by the Party organizations over the enterprises, both in organizational planning and control.

The formalistic character of the formulas by which the mutual relations of Party organs and industrial management are usually defined in newspaper editorial and conference resolutions allows easily for the many shifts on this question to which the Party Line has been subjected in the last decade. The type of injunction which encompassed all these shifts and gyrations would substantially state (in Soviet language) that "Party organizations should be the leaders of production, encourage technical initiative, be fully and continuously familiar with the work of the enterprises, and yet not get immersed in details, not take over managerial functions, not subject management to a petty tutelage." It is easy to see how any change of emphasis in this double-edged formula might constitute a major shift in the Party Line.

A review of the last decade of Soviet industrial administration gives some credence to the hypothesis that Soviet leaders have tended to regress most from the new *edinonachalle* ideal to the old formula of *rukovodstvo* and *upravlenie* in periods of acute political and economic stress.

In accordance with this hypothesis, the Party Line veered in 1941 to an emphasis on the active leadership of enterprises by Party organs, a shift which was reflected in the structure of organization by the effective restoration of the industrial divisions of the Party at the *oblast* (regional) and city levels, through the creation of industrial and transport secretariats. The outbreak of the war was accompanied by a frank concentration of power in Party organs, and, insofar as the supervision over factories was concerned, in the hands of the secretaries of the Party city and regional committees. The newspaper editorials during the war period were completely one-sided in their repeated calls for more vigorous leadership of industry by Party organizations.

With the end of the war emergency, the Party Line, as expressed in the Press, veered back, on the whole, to demands that Party organizations refrain from taking over managerial functions, but it shifted again at the end of 1947 and since then has been calling on Party members to take their economic responsibilities more seriously. (Our survey of the Soviet Press ends at the beginning of 1949.)

While the Party industrial organs provided a most glaring illustration of the way in which the principles of *edinonachalie* and of unity in current planning, execution, and verification of fulfillment are breached in the very structuring of Soviet industrial organization, they do by no means constitute the only instance of usurpation of managerial functions in administrative practice. Even administrative

aides such as chief engineers or representatives of functional divisions, such as chief bookkeepers or *Gosplan* delegates engage in such
interference throughout the administrative apparatus.

The causes for these violations of the rules are already to be found
in the rules themselves, in the very legal statements which are supposed to uphold the new principles of organization. We find, for example, that the legal definition of the full authority *(polnoe vlast)* of the
head of the enterprise is a relative concept, that it merely signifies that,
of all the staff of the enterprise, he is given the most *(naibolshyi)* rights,
We find that the administrative aides and the representatives of functional divisions who interfere with management are driven to do so
because they are fully responsible legally for the state of the enterprise.

This wide assignment of responsibility, extending beyond the
area of the individual's control, is partially responsible for another
kind of breach of the territorial-productive principle of organization
and of *edinonachalie*. The middle echelons of both the Party and the
non-Party hierarchies, which are assigned total responsibility for the
successful operation of subordinate administrative organs and enterprises, cannot afford to rely on unwieldy hierarchical channels. They
are driven to act directly upon the administration of the enterprises,
to reorganize their work and to check upon results achieved through
the intermediary of their own plenipotentiaries. Yet, according to the
accounts of DP's, the visits of commissions from Party and non-Party
centers, from Party regional or city committees, or from chief industrial administrations usually result either in further jamming of the
administrative system or in drastic changes in personnel which do
not change very much the chaotic state of affairs. And if this interference results in serious disruption of output, Party regional or city
committees, while they cannot now be asserted to be indifferent to
their economic tasks, can always be accused of excessive interference
with plant management or with the violation of the autonomy of Primary Party Organizations.

The managers, administrators, and Party representatives who are
confronted with this degree of industrial disorganization and division
of authority, and yet are expected to meet very high production quotas, tend to respond in either of two fashions: They may, particularly
if their enterprises are located near political power centers, play the
rules of the game and submit one another to inhuman pressures.
Under this order of things, the chief administration makes the life of
the manager miserable, the Party City Committee presses on the Party
factory secretary, and the latter in turn threatens the factory manager.
Alternatively, especially if the enterprises concerned are located in
outlying regions, the people in authority may engage in "family rela-

tions." They may stand by one another in falsifying production figures, in attributing fictitious reasons to accidents and breakdowns, and for a certain period of time, as retribution is never far off, the Party secretary and the plant manager may be able to go horseback riding together every morning.

The structure of the Soviet apparatus provides an alternative channel by which officials may be able to reduce the intolerable pressures to which they are subjected. This system of organization is characterized by a high degree of duplication of and interference with authority up to the very top of the power hierarchy. We have already alluded to the overlapping of authority and to the violation of hierarchical lines which characterize the functioning of the Party pyramid and the apparatus of industrial ministries. We have also referred to the overlapping of authority and to the duplications of functions in the relations between these structures. The interference of yet a third organization, the MVD (Ministry of Internal Affairs), confuses areas of authority even further. To the MVD is assigned the general responsibility of safeguarding industry from enemies of the regime. In view of the very elastic and wide definition given to sabotage in Soviet culture, a phenomenon undoubtedly related to the general emphasis on will and control in the personality, the officials of the MVD, like members of other hierarchies, are in fact assigned responsibilities which extend far beyond the formal definition of their roles.

The response to this situation made by higher officials is a struggle for power, for possession of power signifies less vulnerability and greater control over situations for which responsibility is unlimited. This power is found through personal alignments, informal cliques, which gratify both higher officials' need for greater informal authority and subordinates' desire for protection from pressure by superiors.

In the preceding discussion we have attempted to show that the present system of Soviet industrial organization is an amalgam of old and new patterns of organization, which themselves reflect traditional Great Russian and new Soviet attitudes about leadership, authority, and the organization of action. We have pointed out how the combination of internal and external controls, which has resulted from this mixture, tends to contribute to the continuous jamming of the industrial system. Since this is the case, one may well ask for the reasons why the system functions as well as it does.

The positive and compensatory feature of the system of organization we have described resides, we believe, in the mobilization by Party organizations of the workers' energies and initiative through such devices as production conferences, collective agreements, and socialist competition. We can only briefly summarize here some of the major characteristics of these organized forms of collective action and of the discussions, led by Party agitators and propagandists, which usually precede them.[1]

In factory meetings, Party propagandists and agitators may encourage criticism of the management by the workers and attempt to foster the feeling that the Party is a benevolent authority which sides with them against the frequently treacherous *intelligenstia* (the managerial staff) of the factory. The workers are expected to draw the conclusion that, through their own efforts and under the guidance *(rukovodstvo)* of the Party, they can overcome the passivity or resistance of organs of *upravlenie* and break through lines of administrative restraint. The organization of collective agreements and of socialist competition is similarly calculated to arouse in the workers a belief in their own importance and in the close affective bond which ties them to the Party.

Party activities are conducted in this connection according to extremely fluid organizational lines. The meetings which lay the groundwork for the socialist competition include participants from various levels of the administrative hierarchy of the plant, and in this way lines of organizational restraint are again effectively bridged.

Party leadership of workers' collectives in factories undoubtedly contributes to the disorganization of factory administrations. Its encouragement of distrust of the managerial staff by the workers undoubtedly encourages conflicts and breaches of discipline by the labor force. But these negative features are more than counterbalanced by the mobilization of initiative and enthusiasm achieved by these Party activities.

Sources used by L. H. Haimson in
Summary of Conclusions of Research on Party and Non-Party Organizations in Soviet Industry.

For studies of problems of Party organization:

Abranov, A., and Aleksandrov, *The Party in the Period of Reconstruction (Partiya v rekonstruktsionnyi period),* Moscow, 1934.

Bakhshiyev, *Organizational Foundations of the Bolshevik Party (Organizatsionnye osnovy bolshevistskoi partii),* Moscow, 1943.

Bubnov, Andrei, *All-Union Communist Party (of Bolsheviks) (VKP(b)),* Moscow, 1938.

---

1. See Appendix F.

Stalin, *Collected Works (Sochinenia)*.

_____, *Leninism*, London, 1932.

_____, "Mastering Bolshevism," *Bol'shevik*, April 1, 1937.

Yaroslavskii, E., *History of the CPSU (b)*. (*Istoriya VKP(b)*), Moscow, 1926.

_____, *How Lenin Dealt with the Party Purge* (*Kak Lenin otnosilsya k chistke partii*), Moscow, 1929.

_____, *Verification and Purging of the Party Ranks*, Moscow, 1933.

17th Congress of the All-Union Communist Party (*XVII s'ezd Vsesoyuznoi Kommunisticheskoi Partii*), stenographic account, Moscow, 1934.

18th Congress of the All-Union Communist Party (*XVIII s'ezd Vsesoyuznoi Kommunisticheskoi Partii*), stenographic account, Moscow, 1939.

1938 Plenum of the Central Committee of the All-Union Communist Party, Resolution, *Partiinoye Stroitelsivo* (*Party Construction*), February, 1938.

For studies of Soviet industrial organization and Party leadership in industry:

Periodicals

Partiinoye Stroitelstvo (Party Construction), 1939-40.

Partiinaya Zhizn (Party Life), 1945-49.

Bol'shevik, 1940-49.

Novyi Mir (New World), 1944-49.

Oktyabr' (October), 1944.

Znamya (Banner), 1944-47.

Sovetskoye Gosudarstvo i Pravo (Soviet Government and Law) (scattered issues).

Promyshlennost' (Industry) (scattered issues).

Newsapers

Pravda, 1944-49.

Books

Arakelian, E., *Management of Socialist Industry (Upravlenie sotsialisticheskoi promyshlennosti)*, Moscow, 1947.

Baykov, A., *The Development of the Soviet Economic System*, Cambridge University Press, London, 1946.

Bienstock, G, S. Schwarz, and A. Yugow, *Management in Russian Industry and Agriculture*, Oxford University Press, New York, 1944.

Chernyak, N., *Party Organization and Socialist Competition* (*Partiinaya organizatsiya i sotsialisticheskoe sorevnovanie*), Moscow, 1947.

Dewar, M., *The Organization of Soviet Industry*, mimeographed study, Royal Institute of International Affairs, London, 1945.

Evtikhiev, I. I., and V. A. Vlasov, *Administrative Law* (*Administrativnoe pravo*), Moscow, 1946.

Littlepage, J., and D. Best, *In Search of Soviet Gold*, Harcourt, Brace and Company, Inc., New York, 1938.

Panova, V., *Kruzhilikha*, Moscow, 1945.

Scott, J., *Behind the Urals*, Houghton Mifflin Company, New York, 1942.

Towster, J., *Political Power in the U.S.S.R.*, Oxford University Press, 1948.

18th Conference of the All-Union Communist Party (*XVIII Konferentsia Vsesoyuznoi Kommunisticheskoi Pariii*), Moscow, February, 1941.

Appendix D

Source Materials Used by Other Members of the Research Group

Sources used by Nathan Leites

The Crime of the Zinoviev Opposition, The Assassination of Sergei Mironovich Kirov, Cooperative Publishing Society of Foreign Workers in the USSR, Moscow, 1935.

Report of Court Proceedings in the Case of the Trotskyite-Zinovievite Terrorist Centre, heard before the Military Collegium of the Supreme Court of the USSR, Moscow, August 19-24, 1936, published by the People's Commissariat of justice of the USSR, Moscow, 1936.

Report of Court Proceedings in the Case of the Anti-Trotskyite Centre, Moscow, January 23-30,1937.

Report of Court Proceedings in the Case of the Anti-Soviet "Bloc of Rights and Trotskyites," Moscow, March 2-13, 1938.

The Case of Leon Trotsky, report of hearings on the charges made against him in the Moscow trials by the Preliminary Commission of Inquiry, Harper & Brothers, New York, 1937.

Ciliga, Anton, *The Russian Enigma*, The Labour Book Service, London, no year.

Fischer, Ruth, *Stalin and German Communism*, Harvard University Press, Cambridge; Mass., 1948.

Gorer, Geoffrey, and John Rickman, *The People of Great Russia: A Psychological Study*, Cresset Press, London, 1949.

Koestler, Arthur, *Darkness at Noon*, The Modern Library, New York, no year.

Krivitsky, W. G., *In Stalin's Secret Service*, Harper & Brothers, New York, 1939.

Letter of an Old Bolshevik, Rand School Press, New York, 1937.

Life of the Archpriest Avvakum by Himself, in *A Treasury of Russian Spirituality*, G. P. Fedotov (comp. and ed.), Sheed & Ward, Inc., New York, 1948.

Not Guilty, report of the Commission of Inquiry into the charges made against Leon Trotsky in the Moscow trials, Harper & Brothers, New York, 1938.

Plisnier, Charles, *Faux passeports*, Editions R. A. Correa, Paris, 1937 (trans. by Nathan Leites and Elsa Bernaut).

Schachtman, Max, *Behind the Moscow Trial*, Pioneer Publishers, New York, 1936.

Slater, Humphrey, *Conspirator*, Harcourt, Brace and Company, Inc., New York, 1948.

Souvarine, Boris, *Stalin*, Longmans, Green & Co., Inc., New York, 1939.

The Soviet-Yugoslav Dispute, Royal Institute of International Affairs, London, 1948.

Ypsilon, *Pattern for World Revolution*, Ziff-Davis Publishing Company, New York, 1947.

Sources used by Elsa Bernaut

Bubnov, A., *Basic Moments in the Development of the Communist Party (Osnovnye momenty razvitiya kommunisticheskoi partii)*, Moscow, 1923.

Bukharin, N., *The Economics of the Transition Period (Ekonomika perekhodnovo Perioda)*, Moscow, 1920 (also various articles in periodicals and papers quoted below).

Lenin, V. L, *Collected Works (Polnoye sobraniye)*.

Preobrazhenski, E., *From the NEP to Socialism (Ot nepa k sotsialisma)*, Moscow, 1922.

Stalin, J., *Leninism or Trotskyism (Leninism ili Trolskyism)*, Moscow, 1924.

_____, *On the Right Deviation of the CPSU (0 pravom uklone v VKP)*, 1929.

Trotsky, L., *History of the Russian Revolution (Istoria Russkoi Revolyutsii)*, Berlin, 1931-33.

_____, *My Life (Moya Zhizn)*, Berlin, 1930.

_____, *Bulletin of the Opposition (Byulleten' Oppozitsij)*, Paris.

Zorin, V., *On the Right Danger to the Communist Party (0 pravoi opasnosti VKP(B))*.

The Communist Internationale in Documents (Kommunsjticheskii Internatsional v dokumentakh).

Record of the Party Congresses.
Record of the Party Plenums.
Kommunist (periodical).
Partiinoye Stroitelsivo (*Party Construction*) (periodical).
Bol'shevik (periodical).
Partiinaya Zhizn (*Party Life*) (periodical).
Pravda (daily).
Izvestia (daily).

German

Rote Fahne, Berlin (daily).
Imprecor (periodical).
Fahne des Kommunismus (periodical).

Russian (additional)

Report of the Court Proceedings in the Case of the Trotskyite-
    Zinovievite Terrorist Centre, Moscow, 1936.
Report of the Court Proceedings in the Case of the Anti-Soviet
    Trotskyite Centre, Moscow, 1937.
Report of the Court Proceedings in the Case of the Anti-Soviet
    "Rights and Trotskyites," Moscow, 1938.

French

Souvarine, B., *Staline*, Paris, 1935.
Ciliga, A., *Au Pays du Grand Mensonge*, Paris, 1938.
Rossi, A., *Physiologie du Parti Communiste Francais*, Paris, 1948.
Yaroslawski, E., *Histoire du Parti Communisme de PURSS*, Paris, 1931.
L'Humanite (daily).

English

Not Guilty, Report of the Commission of Inquiry into the Charges
    against Leon Trotsky, Harper & Brothers, New York, 1938.
Krivitsky, W. G., *In Stalin's Secret Service*, Harper & Brothers, New
    York, 1939.
Mosely, P., "The Moscow Trials," *Yale Review*, 1938.
Shachtman, M., *Behind the Moscow Trials*, New York, 1936. *Report of
    the Royal Commission*, Appointed under Order in Council P.C.
    411 of February 5, 1946, to investigate the facts relating to and
    the circumstances surrounding the communication, by public
    officials and other persons in positions of trust, of secret and
    confidential information to agents of a foreign power, Ottawa,
    June 27, 1946.

Sources used by Nelly S. Hoyt

For Studies of Komsomol:

Komsomol'skaya Pravda, 1945-48.
Molodoi Bol'shevik, all issues for 1947.
Shokhin, A., *Short Sketch of the History of the Komsomol (Kratkii ocherk islorii Komsomola),* Molodaia Gvardia, Moscow, 1926.
Andreyev, A., *Communist Education of Youth and the Tasks of the Komsomol (0 Kommunisticheskom vospitanii molodezhi),* Molodaia Gvardia, Moscow, 1938.
What Was Decided at the Tenth All-Union Congress of the VLKSM (Chto ryeshili desiatovo vsesoyuznovo s'ezda), Molodaia Gvardia, Moscow, 1936.
The New Constitution of the VLKSM (Ustav Vsesoiuznovo Leninskovo Kommunisticheskogo Soiuza Molodezhi), Molodaia Gvardia, Moscow, 1940.
Victorov, R., *Ilyitch and the Komsomol (Ilich i Komsomol),* Molodaia Gvardia, Moscow, 1928.
Stalin, J., *About the Komsomol (0 Komsomole),* Molodaia Gvardia, Moscow, 1936.
Mishakova, 0., *Stalin's Constitution and Soviet Youth (Stalinskaia Konstitutsia i Sovetskaia molodezh),* Molodaia Gvardia, Moscow, 1945.

For Studies of the Satire:

Zosbchenko, M., collected works.

For Studies of the Folklore:

Andreyev, N., *Russian Folklore (Russkii Folklor),* Anthology for Higher Pedagogical Institutions, 1938.
*Bylin*y introduction by E. A. Latsko, St. Petersburg, 1911.
Bylini of the North (Byliny severa), Vol. 1, Mekhen and Pechora, introduction and commentaries by A. Astakhova, Leningrad, 1938. Kriukovoi, M. S., *Bylini,* Vols. 1 and 2, Moscow, 1941.
Chuvash Tales (Chuvashskiye skazki), Moscow, 1937.
Tales of the Altai Masters (Legendy bylini), 1938.
Lenin, Stalin, *Creations of the Peoples of the USSR,* Moscow, 1938.
Lenin and Stalin in the Poetry of the Peoples of the USSR (Lenin i Stalin v poezii narodov SSSR), Moscow, 1938.
Kriukova, M. S., *Legends about Lenin (Skazanie o Lenine),* Moscow, 1938.

Klimovich, L. I. (ed.), *Anthology of the Literature of the Peoples of the USSR (Khrestomatiya po literature narodov SSSR)*, Moscow, 1947.

Miller, Orest, *Ilya Muromets and the Kievan Heroes (Ilya Muromets i boga tyrsivo Kievskoye)*, St. Petersburg, 1870.

Russian Popular Epos (Russkii narodnyi epos), Comparative Texts, Moscow, 1947.

Azadovskii (ed.), *Russian Folklore (Russkii folklor)* (volume on epic poetry), 1935.

Shelly, G. K., *Folktales of the Peoples of the Soviet Union*, London, 1945.

Soviet Folklore (Sovetskii folklor), collection of articles, Leningrad, 1939.

Sovietskii Folklor (periodical).

Jakobson, R., Commentary to A. N. Afanasev, *Russian Fairy Tales*, New York, 1945.

Azadovskii, M., *New Folklore (Novyi Folklor)*.

Byalik, B., *Gorky and the Science of Folklore (Gorkii i nauka o folklore)*.

Dymshits, A., *Lenin and Stalin in the Folklore of the Peoples of the USSR (Lenin i Stalin v folklore narodov SSSR)*.

Astakhova, A., *The Russian Hero Epos and Contemporary Bylini (Russkii geroicheskii epos i sovremenniye byliny)*.

Vladmirskii, G., *The Singers of the Stalin Epoch (Pevtsy Stalinskoi epokhy)*.

Abramkin, V., *The Folklore of the Civil War (Folklor grazhdanskoi voiny)*.

Kaletskii, P., *The New Tale (Novaya skazka)*.

Eventov, I., *The Soviet Song (Sovetskaya pesnya)*.

Sources used by Vera Schwarz

Literaturnaya Entsiklopediya (Literary Encyclopedia), published in Moscow (11 volumes).

Bol' shaya Sovetskaya Entsiklopediya (The Great Soviet Encyclopedia).

Malaya Sovetskaya Entsiklopediya (The Little Soviet Encyclopedia).

History of Russian Children's Literature (Istoriya Russkoi detskoi literatury), published by the Scientific Pedagogical Publishing House of the Ministry of Education, Moscow, 1948.

Yarmolinsky, Avram (ed.), *A Treasury of Russian Verse*, The Macmillan Company, New York, 1949,

Novyi Mir (The New World), organ of the Union of Soviet Writers, a monthly published in Moscow by the publishing house Izvestia,

Oktyabr' (October), organ of the Union of Soviet Writers, a monthly published in Moscow by the publishing house Pravda.

Krasnaya Nov' (The Red Virgin Soil), organ of the Union of Soviet
Writers, published in Moscow, suspended in 1941.

Znamya (The Standard), organ of the Union of Soviet Writers,
a monthly published in Moscow since the beginning of
the thirties by the publishing house *Sovietskii Pisatel' (The
Soviet Writer)*.

Zvezda (The Star), organ of the Union of Soviet Writers, a monthly
published in Leningrad by the Unified State Publishing House.

Ogonyok (The Light), published by the publishing house Pravda.

Leningrad Almanac, published in Leningrad by the Newspaper,
Magazine and Book Publishing House.

Almanac Sever (The North), published in Arkhangelsk by the Unified
State Publishing House.

Sibirskiye Ogni (Siberian Lights), published in Novosibirsk.

Literaturnyi Kritic (The Literary Critic), suspended in December, 1940.

Literaturnaya Gazeta (The Literary Newspaper), organ of the Board
of the Union of Soviet Writers published since 1947 twice a
week, Moscow.

Sovetskoye Iskusstvo (Soviet Art), organ of the Department of Movie
Art of the Committee dealing with Arts of the Council of the
Ministers of the USSR and of the Committee of the Council
dealing with the Architecture of the USSR, a weekly, Moscow.

Kultura i Zhizn' (Culture and Life), newspaper of the propaganda
division of the Central Committee of the Communist Party,
published weekly in Moscow since 1946.

Bol'shevik (Bolshevik), theoretical and political magazine of the
Central Committee of the Communist Party, Moscow.

Pravda, organ of the Central Committee of the Communist Party, a
daily newspaper,

Izvestia, a daily newspaper published in Moscow.

Sotsialisticheskoye Zemledeliye (Socialist Agriculture), a daily, Moscow.

Trud (Labor), organ of the All-Union Central Council of Trade
Unions, published in Moscow.

Voprosy Istorii (Problems of History), issued by the publishing house
Pravda, Moscow.

Pedagogika (Pedagogy), Moscow, 1948.

Sources used by Ralph T. Fisher, Jr.

Aleksandrov, G., *et al.* (ed.), *Political Dictionary (Politicheskii Slovar')*,
1940, pp. 90-92.

Eleventh Congress of the Young Communist League of the Soviet Union," *Current Digest of the Soviet Press*, 1:13 (April 26, 1949), pp. 13-22; and 1:14 (May 3, 1949), pp. 8-22.

Fischer, Louis, *Thirteen Who Fled*, Harper & Brothers, New York, 1949.

Kaftanov, S., "The Komsomol in the Struggle to Master Advanced Science and Technique" ("Komsomol v bor'be za ovladeniye peredovoi naukoi i tekhnikoi"), *Izvestia*, March 29, 1949. *Komsomol' skaya Pravda*, March 29-31 and April 1-20, 1949.

Krivtsov, A. A., "Report of the Central Auditing Commission" ("Otchet tsentral'noi revizionnoi komissii"), *Komsomol'skaya Pravda*, March 31, 1949, pp. 3-4.

Mikhailov, N. A., "Report of the Central Committee of the VLKSM at the 11th Congress" ("Otchet TsK VLKSM XI s'ezdu"), *Komsomo'l sjkaya Pravda*, March 30, 1949, pp. 2-3; March 31, 1949, pp. 2-3.

Shelepin, A. N., "Report of the Mandate Commission of the I Ith Congress of the VLKSM" ("Doklad mandatnoi kornissii XI s'ezda VLKSM"), *Komsomol'skaya Pravda*, April 1, 1949, p. 2.

Tyurin, N., "All-Union Leninist Communist League of Youth" in the *Great Soviet Encyclopedia (Bol'shaya Sovetskaia Entsiklopediya)*, supplementary volume entitled *Soyuz Sovetskikh Sotsialisticheskikh Respublik* (USSR), 1948, pp. 1712-40.

Appendix E

EXCERPT CONCERNING THE COMMUNIST "ELECTION OF MAY, 1948, IN CZECHOSLOVAKIA"– TAKEN FROM CHAPTER XVI OF UNPUBLISHED MANUSCRIPT "CZECHS, SLOVAKS, AND COMMUNISM"

BY DAVID RODNICK

*T*he Czech Communists worked on the assumption that "talking makes things so." in order to build up the "legality" of a one-party election, a campaign was begun on April 7, 1948, to make it appear that it was the "people" who wanted a unified election list; that the Communists preferred to take their chances in competition with the other "paper" political parties but it was up to the "people" to decide whether the government should have a one-party slate or separate party lists. The Communist leadership knew that in any free and open election, the Communist vote would have been an extremely small one. No one thing that the Communists had done since their assumption of complete power in February antagonized the non-Communist Czechs and even many within the Party as much as the hypocritical building-up of an artificial public opinion that was created for the Party to manipulate as puppets. Nothing showed the megalomania of the Communist Party leadership more than this tendency to project its desires onto paper organizations and a synthetic public opinion-a move which assumed a lack of critical intelligence on the part of the non-Communists. It was a striking example of the amorality of the Communists who cynically assumed that by throwing words to the people, the latter would accept them as realities. The level of rationalization which this political campaign employed was one that could have appealed only to psychotic individuals. The only possible motivation was that the Communists had the power, expected to keep it, but wanted to cloak their intention with a synthetic "legality" which they assumed would satisfy the Czechs. Only the Nazis could have equalled the contempt for the dignity and commonsense of the human being that the Communists displayed in their crude maneuvering. At the same time, they assumed a naivete on the part of the outside world which would be willing to accept such an obvious hoax. Actually the Communists had gone the Nazis one better in preparing their unity list.

The maneuver started on April 7th when Antonin Zapotocky, who at that time was Deputy Prime Minister and Chairman of the Trades Union Council, addressed a meeting of this Council on how it should work in the coming election. In the course of his remarks, he said, "There is one more matter facing us in this question of the elections. This question must be discussed. It is a political question, for the results will determine the structure of the future Parliament. If the political parties of the regenerated National Front go independently into the election, what should our attitude be. Should we recommend separate lists of candidates of all individual parties, or *should we use the weight of our influence to see that the results of the election would be such as to give us a guarantee that future progress will be on the lines we want? ...* [italics ours]

"I make this question a subject of discussion. We should frankly put the question to ourselves whether it is necessary for each party in our re-born National Front to present its own list of candidates or whether the time has already come to consider a joint election list."

Immediately according to plan, Evuzen Erban, the Minister of Social Welfare, General Secretary of the Trades Union Council and a prominent Social Democratic leader, rose to give his approval of Zapotocky's proposal to have a single election list. He said, "I am convinced that this proposal will meet with a great reception among the working class of our country, and that also all of our political leaders if they feel any responsibility to the nation and to the working class will wholeheartedly agree with this proposal. We shall thus succeed in creating the same harmony in both our economic and political life." Mr. Erban went on to make remarks which would seem to indicate that he felt guilty and on the defensive. In them, he appeared to work on the assumption that the single list, though it had been suggested for the first time only a few minutes before, was an accomplished fact. He went on to say, "In the West, they will of course lament that the disintegration of our democracy is continuing. Yes, the disintegration of our bourgeois democracy is continuing. We have no need to wage any political class warfare because we have won our battle. ... The

Western democracies and the capitalists of the West will naturally fail to understand us, and we won't even attempt to make them understand. We have our truth and they have theirs."[1]

After "deliberation," the Trades Union Council the next day passed unanimously a resolution calling upon "all political parties as well as the Central Action Committee of the National Front to negotiate the safe-guarding of the splendid victory over reaction by a joint election action."

On the same day, a spokesman for the Action Committee of the Communist controlled Czech Socialist Party (before February, the National Socialist Party) announced his "full support for a joint list." He declared he considered it his duty to convince all members of the Action Committee of his Party to support this "patriotic proposal." Then, on the same day, the Social Democratic Parliamentary group met and agreed to "recommend that the Presidium of the Party accept this proposal."[2] On the following day, the People's Party decided that "after considering all circumstances, we have decided to take a positive attitude toward the simplification of the election and to express our approval of the joint election list of the National Front.

"A joint list of candidates will prevent the traditional discord and strife of election campaigns. Now that there will be no election battle, the people can devote themselves calmly to their work. Many hours wasted at meetings will be saved, as well as much paper wasted on election posters."[3]

On the same day, the Press Section of the Central Action Committee of Czechoslovakia (completely composed of Communists, such as Gustav Barevs, one of the leading spokesmen for the Cominforin in Czechoslovakia; J. Sila, the editor of the trade-union and Communist newspaper *Prace*; Vaclav Dolejsi, chairman of the Union of Czech journalists, a Communist organization; Jiri Hronek, chief editor of the Czechoslovakian radio which has been in Communist hands since 1945 and Secretary-General of the International Organization of Journalists; along with the chiefs of divisions in the Ministry of Information, and the editors of the official Communist publication *Rude Pravo*) issued a statement in support of the joint election list. "Acceptance of this proposal," the statement said, "will prevent forever the *partisan misuse of the Press* and will enable the Press to devote itself *fully to creative criticism*."[4] [italics ours]

1. *Daily Review*, Prague, April 8, 1948.
2. *Ibid.*, April 9, 1948.
3. *Ibid.*, April 10, 1948 (taken from *Lidova Demokracie*, same date).
4. *Ibid.*

The confusion even in propaganda tended to "let the cat out of the bag" when an editor in *Pravo Lidu*, the Communist-controlled Social Democratic paper, wrote on April l0th in support of this proposal, "The Social Democratic Party has no reason to oppose the joint election list proposal which is to express clearly and uncompromisingly the will of the Czechoslovak people to put an end to the bourgeois democratic political game and to enter a new path of unity of all people of good will. The Social Democratic Party agrees with Mr. Zapotocky's proposal without any ulterior motive. ... It was the left-wing Social Democrats who helped to fight for the victory of the working class. It was the Social Democratic Party which foiled the plan of reaction to break up the majority of the government in Parliament. We shall never fear sincere cooperation with Communists and we therefore need not regard the joint election list with them as a way of *escaping* the wrath of the electorate."[5][italics ours]

As a result of this "persuasion" on the part of the "people," the Central Executive Committee of the Czechoslovakian Communist Party very reluctantly on April l0th decided to bow to the will of the synthetic public opinion which it had created and had tried to cloak with reality, and by an "unanimous vote" decided to go along with the other "people's representatives" to accept and approve the proposal for a joint election list. When we remarked to a fanatic Communist on April 11th how rapidly the proposal was made and then accepted by "public opinion," he enthusiastically replied, "Communism builds unity among the people and is therefore more efficient than the capitalistic bourgeois democracies."

Two days later, non-Communist Czechs were rather amused when the date of the coming "election" was changed from May 23rd to May 30th. The reason for this shift was given by the Communist press as being due to the fact that the earlier date would conflict with the opening of the All-Slav Agricultural Exhibition to be held in Prague on May 23rd. The election was considered "in the bag."

We have given this background to the election in some detail because we think it an excellent example of how the Communists even when in power still behave as conspirators. They make no attempts to be honest in their intentions with the people whom they are governing. They apparently feel it necessary to cloak their secret intentions with words which have no relationship to what they expect to do and which they utilize as substitutes for reality. The Communist leadership does not trust its own membership, and words are used only as a sop to build up some kind of a link with those they

5. *Ibid.*

do not trust. Words to the Communists have no meaning except as a bridge to the non-Communist population in order to divert it from the intentions which the Communists think they are keeping secret. A good Communist pays little attention to these words. He is imbued with a faith that whatever the Party does is right and is done in order to build up Party power.

The use of words to translate unsavory intentions into socially-acceptable ones was well exemplified in the following article which appeared in the official Communist newspaper Rude Pravo on April 11th. "The Communist Party had been seriously preparing for an election campaign in competition with the other political parties. The Communists were looking for-ward to the election day when they could have shown the greatness of their Party in its full glory, and the fact that there is to be a joint election list does not mean that the Communist Party will play a less prominent role. The unanimous decision of the Party Executive Committee clearly reflects the responsible manner in which the Communists solve their statesmanlike tasks and the way in which they understand their leading position in the nation."[6]

An "opposition" was also permitted to put out its own list of candidates. But then came the veiled threat which was expressed in *Rude Pravo* on April 11th by a Communist spokesman who said, "If anyone opposes the People's Democracy, let him do so openly." If any group in the population wanted to present an opposition list of candidates at the election, it had to gather 1000 signatures on a petition which was to be turned over to the election committee of the People's Democracy (Communist Party) in order to make certain that none of these individuals were "enemies and saboteurs who were against the progress of the working class."

Some weeks before the so-called "election," every storekeeper was required to put in his front window a poster urging support for the unity list. In all public offices and railroad stations there were banners or placards with the words, "He who loves the Republic will vote for the Republic," or "White ticket—black thoughts," and so on. It took courage for an individual to use the white voting slip in the "election" on May 30th. In almost all polling stations, the box for the white ballots was out in the open and surrounded by watchers from the local Communist Party. Each voter had been given two ballots

---

6.   This sacrifice which the Communist Party was making was accepted because the other "paper" political parties which they controlled "insisted" upon cooperating with the Communists for the general welfare of the Communist Party.

beforehand; a red ballot which had the government list inside and a white one which was blank. Each ballot was in an envelope and could be marked at home, sealed, and brought back to the voting station. There a voter's name was checked off the list and he was permitted to go to the back of the room where the ballot boxes were theoretically supposed to be behind screens. No screens were in any of the polling stations we heard of; both boxes were out in the open. The voter was supposed to drop a ballot in either the government box or the white-ballot box and to discard the ballot he did not use in either the waste-basket for the red ballots or the one for the white ballots. As many "paper" Communist watchers told us later on, it was very difficult to get by them. They were supposed to mark down the names of all individuals who voted the white ballot and to try to intimidate them by asking them if they weren't going in the wrong direction when they approached the white-ballot box. It was impossible to cast a ballot without everyone's knowing how one voted. Many individuals who wished to cast a white ballot, but were afraid of the consequences, used their red envelope, but instead of putting in the red ballot they inserted pictures of Thomas G. Masaryk, President Benes, Jan Masaryk, Franklin D. Roosevelt, Winston Churchill, caricatures of Josef Stalin, Gottwald, Hitler, toilet paper, or nothing. Many also wrote notes attacking the Communists. Official counters from various parts of Czechoslovakia told us later on that the Ministry of Interior in Prague confiscated ballot boxes without permitting them to be counted, or if they had already been counted, gave out abnormally low figures. One counter in a city of 35,000 told us that in his district alone he counted 860 white ballots, and friends of his who had also served as counters in other parts of the city told him afterward that they counted as much and sometimes more than in his district. The official count for white ballots in the whole city was 216! In other parts of Czechoslovakia we were told of similar instances, where the total white ballots for a whole town or city would be given out as much smaller than had been counted in only one district.

On the basis of the official figures put out by the Communists themselves on June 6th, 6.5 per cent of the voters abstained from voting, 3 per cent cast invalid votes, while 10.8 per cent cast white ballots. According to these statistics, a little over 20 per cent did not vote for the unity list. On the other hand, the Communists counted only what they considered the valid votes and to their great surprise discovered that they had 89.2 per cent of them! It was rather interesting that the largest numbers of white ballots counted by the government were in the industrial cities such as Zlin, Pardubice, MoravskaOstrava, and Plzen where the official count showed between 16 and 20 per cent of white ballots. In the Catholic areas of Slovakia and Moravia, few white ballots were cast and the government received almost 100 per cent of the vote. In the Hana area of Moravia, however, the white ballots went up to 30 per cent. It was no fault of the Communists that they did not get 100 per cent throughout Czechoslovakia. Their failure to do so was mainly due to the large number of "Communist" watchers and counters who had no enthusiasm for interfering with the voters and who tried to make an accurate count of whatever white ballots were cast before they went to the Ministry of Interior. The latter put them through their special Communist tabulating machine which was geared to make certain that the final figure would be within certain limits. In later conversations with convinced Communists, we were told, "Well, maybe we didn't get 89 per cent, but we got at least 60 per cent." Most Czechs were quite surprised at the election result, because they had expected the Communists to get at least 99 per cent of the vote.

"To Aid the Agitator," From Pravda, May 27, 1948

*W*hat follows is a translated quotation from a fairly complete report of an agitation meeting, conducted by one of the best agitators of the Stalingrad region, in a shop of the "Red October" metallurgical factory, an account published fully in *Pravda* for the benefit of other party agitators. To prepare for his discussion, the editor's preamble to this account states, the agitator, Andrei Koliada, studied a number of specified works by Lenin and Stalin and also used materials from newspapers. The foreman of the shop presented the agitator with facts about production, examples in particular brigades. Wall newspapers and diagrams about the growth of production in the shop and about the role of each brigade in the struggle for plan fulfillment were prepared in advance.

At the beginning of his talk, Comrade Koliada described the tasks laid by Stalin of overfulfilling prewar production in the first postwar Five-Year Plan. ... He presents figures which illustrate the prewar industrial growth. ... You remember Comrades, what our factory was like in 1928. Here are sitting a number of older workers, they remember this very well. Maybe one of them will describe what the factory was like before the Five-Year plans. Let the young workers listen.

Kazenkov (a welder): I can tell. [He then described the technical backwardness of the factory in 1928.] Only after the reconstruction of the basic shops and the construction of new Martin furnaces did "Red October" become transformed into a first class metallurgical plant.

Koliada: Correctly said, Ivan Ivanovich.

[Koliada then describes the war destruction of the factory, which for anyone but Bolsheviks would have made the task of restoration appear impossible. He then tells of the postwar reconstruction.]

In the last thirty years, even Soviet people have changed. As Zhdanov said, "We are not today what we were yesterday, and will not be tomorrow what we are today...." Some people may ask, "Why hasten the tempo and fulfill the Five-Year Plan in four years?" Maybe someone still thinks:

Why hurry; it is better to fulfill the indicated plan and not realize its overfulfillment? Is that so?

Kurtin (another worker): No. To fulfill the plan in four years means to speed up the strengthening of our country, the beautifying of our lives.

Ivanov (another worker): Right, Comrade Kurtin, every one of us wants to improve his life, to have a good apartment, good food, good clothes, that our children grow healthy and happy, that they study. Everyone of us wants that not only our children, but that we ourselves live in a Communist society. We fully deserve this because who if not we carried on our shoulders all the difficulties of this gigantic struggle ... that we must work, work hard, to realize these goals.

Koliada: I fully agree with your words. The Party and Government are doing everything to improve the life of the workers, the peasants, and the intelligentsia. [As proof of this he cites the abolition of rationing, and the monetary reform.] Where in the capitalist world, could you find a state which has reconstructed its economy as rapidly after a severe war. [He speaks of inflation, unemployment in the United States.] And American workers have still worse days ahead. A crisis of terrific impact. A Five-Year Plan in four years is needed further because of the surviving agitation for war in foreign countries.

[Koliada now turns to the need for reducing costs. He criticizes a number of members of the managerial staff for their lack of concern over machinery. He then turns to his audience to ask whether they have any additional remarks to make.]

[Kravchenko (a brigadier) criticizes the foreman of another shop and a number of other workers. Some other workers criticize their foremen.]

Koliada: These people are working without a soul, without a soul, without fire. [He emphasizes the importance of the struggle for economy in the use of metal, fuel, instruments; criticizes the way in which chisels and pincers are thrown about. He then turns to a worker.] How many pincers did you throw out, Comrade Gusenkov?

Gusenkov (*master* of the pneumatic sledge hammer division): Many.

—And where are they?

—Everywhere.

—They have been thrown about everywhere.

—Let us take the chisels? How much does a chisel cost, Comrade Gusenkov?

Gusenkov: I didn't count.

Koliada: But for example, two, four, six rubles?

Gusenkov: No, more, ten rubles.

Koliada: Here, you see, ten rubles. And just imagine that while going around the shop you find ten-ruble notes thrown on

the floor. Each one of you would undoubtedly lean down to pick them up. Why, then, are the chisels which are worth ten rubles lying around and nobody picks them up? Is it possible to have such an uneconomical attitude towards work? ...

Savenkov: Will the administration of the shop and the administration [*upravlenie*] of the plant support the plan of repair or not?

Koliada: It is difficult for me to answer that question. I don't know what the administration plans to do. But I do know that the Ministry of Ferrous Metallurgy issued a directive to the effect that planned … preventive repairs be carried out firmly in correspondence with the ability of plant and shop.

Fedorov (another worker): [Starts out by saying that each worker will ponder about the significance of the example of the chisel.] Along with this, I want to say something about the disorders in our shop. … We still have a *master* who only realizes the production program quantitatively and not qualitatively, who doesn't think of economizing metals and materials. Machinery is neglected. Cranes will become worn soon, if things go on this way.

The prewar order must be restored, Until the war, the *master* was felt more in the shop as the boss of his division, and we, the workers, were consulted. I will ask as a worker: More discussions, more meetings must be held with us. Before the war, there were more meetings, more criticisms of one another and things went along more happily, inadequacies were repaired more quickly. …

Koliada: Comrade Federov, I agree that the role and accountability of the *rukovoditel* on his assigned division must be raised, but a single *master* and brigadier cannot do anything if he is not supported, if the workers do not aid him.

[A number of other people discuss ways to raise production.]

Koliada: Your remarks are correct. I have taken them down to give them to the foreman of the shop to take measures. There is no doubt that with the aid of the party organization of our shop which will study all these remarks, your proposals will be brought to life.

A Voice: These remarks should be shown to the director of a factory, Comrade Matevosian.

Koliada: Yes, I will do this. Secondly, as to instruments, pincers, chisels, etc., here much can be done without the intervention of the director of the factory, or of the foreman of the shop. And it must be done right away, without waiting for directives from above. Third, from all your remarks one thing is clear. The Five-Year Plan can be realized in the factory and in particular in our shop not only in four years, but even sooner. We will fight persistently for this. Fourthly, I will ask you to discuss what we have said here with all the members of your brigade, with all absent comrades, so as to mobilize them for the fulfillment of the Five-Year Plan in four years. … You must tell them in such a way as to speak from your heart how indispensable, how important for the people and the State is the fulfillment of the Five-Year Plan in four years. I am convinced that our glorious collective with new work advances will answer the appeal of those from Leningrad to fulfill the Five-Year Plan in four years.

Appendix G

"YOUR STRENGTH"[1]
(Poem about Atomic Energy)

You shuddered. The distant hollow rumble
Of your carriage
Sounded like a wind.
Sleep, my baby,
Your doll, your teddy bear and your little black devil are sleeping
    peacefully like children.
Where did that sudden jolt come from?
What does that signify?
In the Taiga, far away from here
In quite another end of the country,
Where the color of the yellow leaves
Does not glow away until spring.

There stands a granite mountain
Which is barring our way.
Long, long ago it should have been turned
Upside down
Long, long ago it should have been forced to give up its ore.
Sleep, my daughter,
The night is dark,
Sleep, my baby.
At that place there lived a group of geologists
In frost and heat.
Twelve months long

---

1. Y. Dolmatovsky, "Tvoya Sila" ("Your Strength"), *Novyi Mir*, July, 1949, p. 170; translation in *The New York Times*, September 25, 1949, used here with slight alteration.

They were groveling around on the mountain.
Then there came an airplane full of professors to that place and
    then a platoon of army engineers,
First class lads,
And their young commander,

And he was ordered to lay down an explosive shell.
It was not gunpowder, nor dynamite.

There is far more powerful stuff
Now in your country.
I will not tell its name.
Sleep, my baby.

At the pre-arranged hour, the explosion occurred.
The granite was blown asunder to dust.
The Taiga around the mountain was illuminated
By golden radiance.
The old mountain disappeared and the roar of the explosion
    interrupted at five in the morning
The sleep of children
As a breath of wind
From far, far away.

Sleep, little girl,
Your hand lies in my hand.
May the sound wave reach the foreign coasts
And warn our enemies Who hear it there.
The mountain moldered away like flame and gave away its ore,
Not long ago only a fairy tale,
This has now occurred.
Sleep, my baby.

INDEX